Statistics with Confidence

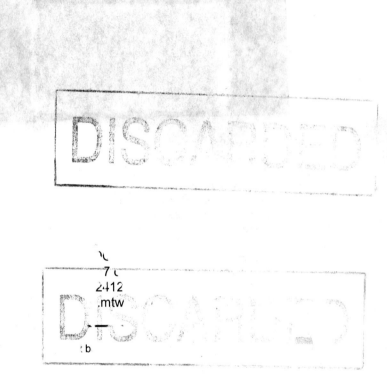

Department of Statistics,
University of Glasgow,
Mathematics Building,
University Gardens,
Glasgow G12 8QW

Statistics with Confidence

Michael Smithson

 SAGE Publications   London • Thousand Oaks • New Delhi

SAGE Publications Ltd
6 Bonhill Street
London EC2A 4PU

SAGE Publications Inc
2455 Teller Road
Thousand Oaks, California 91320

SAGE Publications India Pvt Ltd
32, M-Block Market
Greater Kailash - I
New Delhi 110 048

British Library Cataloguing in Publication data

A catalogue record for this book is available from
the British Library

ISBN 0 7619 6030 9
ISBN 0 7619 6031 7 (pbk)

Library of Congress catalog card number 97-061783

Typeset by Keyword Publishing Services Ltd
Printed in Great Britain by The Alden Press, Oxford

To my daughter, Kia

'The touchstone of knowledge is the ability to teach' (Auctoritates Aristotelis)

Contents

Preface

This book is intended for students in the behavioral and social sciences who are undertaking their first course in statistics. It covers descriptive and inferential statistics, for one and two variables (with some material on multivariate techniques), and treats all statistical concepts at an introductory level. I have oriented the book to students with no more background than high-school algebra. This is not a mathematical book. The emphasis here is on understanding fundamental concepts and being able to use data-analytic techniques to enhance and extend our mental powers. There are no proofs or derivations, and the formulas or computations that have been included are intended to enhance conceptual understanding.

Additionally, unlike many statistics textbooks for psychology students, this book uses psychology and related disciplines extensively for examples and to inform the discussions of statistical concepts and techniques. In my view, psychology and the social sciences have a great deal to contribute to our understanding of how we make sense of data, construct scientific accounts, and debate those accounts throughout the course of our research and teaching. The perspectives offered by these fields also keep instructors and students alike mindful of the fallibility and tentativeness of any research method (statistical or otherwise), or controversies and changes in methods, and the realization that no method is set in stone.

Chapter 1 introduces statistics as a way of managing statistical uncertainties, which is only one kind of uncertainty in research. This chapter also poses the idea that gaining or imposing certainty in one area may require various kinds of tradeoffs. One of the most common tradeoffs is a repeated motif throughout this book – whereas greater precision makes it more likely that we will be wrong, more vagueness renders our statements less informative, diagnostic, or predictive.

Chapters 2 and 3 emphasize exploratory data analysis (EDA), in the sense of graphical and tabular techniques for displaying data, and 'packages' of summary statistics such as the five-number summary. Students are advised that EDA comes in two flavors: data reduction (summarizing, truncating, or combining data) and data enhancement (elaborating, explicating, or dissecting data). Chapter 2 addresses the basic concepts involved in measurement and the construction of variables, providing students with a framework in which to understand various kinds of data and measurement issues. Chapter 3 then presents techniques for EDA, including descriptive statistics and data displays.

Chapter 4 introduces statistical inference, staying with the concepts of random sampling and randomized assignment, the fundamentals of probability, and building up probability distributions from there. This chapter also informs students about different sampling designs, and the fundamentals of designing experiments.

Chapters 5 and 6 present confidence intervals as a way of displaying the range of plausible values for a population parameter, given the data at hand. These two chapters set this book apart from most other introductory statistics textbooks, because they present a confidence interval framework in lieu of the traditional significance-testing approach. They also set the standard for the treatment of most of the inferential techniques dealt with in subsequent chapters.

The main goal of this book is to enable students to understand and make clear, sensible statements about data and to know what degree of confidence can be ascribed to those statements.

In addition to the confidence interval framework, I emphasize two related themes through this book:

- Measuring the size of an effect and establishing benchmarks for effect sizes, rather than focusing on Type I error rates. I find that concepts such as statistical power can be conveyed clearly and simply by using confidence intervals and effect sizes.
- Model-comparison as a way of assessing the relative merits of competing models or hypotheses. Hypothesis-testing (as in significance tests) is presented as a special case, starting with Chapter 6.

Chapters 7, 8, and 9 introduce bivariate statistical techniques, starting with the between-subjects t-test and ANOVA (Chapter 7), then proceeding to correlation and regression (Chapter 8), and thence to chi-square and odds-ratio techniques for categorical data (Chapter 9). Chapter 10 provides a glimpse into multivariate analysis, with an emphasis on two-way analysis of variance. Chapter 11 concludes the book with an overview and guides for choosing appropriate statistical techniques.

At this point, I feel compelled to offer a few remarks concerning my reasons for adopting a confidence interval framework. Quite simply, on all counts it seems clearly superior to the traditional significance-testing approach. Persuasive arguments to this effect have been offered for many years in psychology. Early examples include Rozeboom (1960) and Meehl (1967). The groundswell of authoritative opinion against significance testing and in favor of confidence intervals mounted to a tidal wave by the 1980s and early 1990s (e.g., Oakes, 1986; Hunter & Schmidt, 1990).

And still, instructional and editorial policies largely clung to significance testing. Frustrated commentators such as Oakes (1986: 68) asked why it hadn't been abandoned long ago, and yet a large-scale survey of American graduate psychology programs around that time (Aiken *et al.*, 1990) found little evidence of change. Recently, calls for banning significance testing altogether have appeared in high-profile journals (e.g., Hunter, 1997; Schmidt, 1996).

A task-force on this topic in the American Psychological Association (APA) published its report on the APA website in 1996, recommending substantial reforms in statistical analysis, but stopping short of stipulating a ban on significance tests. Their chief recommendations have been taken up in this book:

- More extensive descriptions of data (i.e., means, standard deviations, sample sizes, five-point summaries, box-and-whisker plots, other graphics, and descriptions related to missing data as appropriate);
- Routine reporting of both direction and size of effects as well as their confidence intervals.

Rather than banning significance tests, I think a healthier approach involves teaching confidence intervals and model comparisons, while presenting significance testing as a special case so that students can read the older literature. Even from a hypothesis-testing viewpoint, there are advantages to a confidence-interval-based approach. Confidence intervals alert us to all the null hypotheses we can and cannot reject. Power is much more easily taught with confidence intervals. That said, there is also clearly a need for statistical methods instruction to move away from significance testing so that the next generation will not repeat and perpetuate our errors. This book is my response to that need.

Finally this book was written to be used with computers, but it is free of computer-specific material. There are three reasons for this. First, even the most user-friendly software still requires getting used to, and examples based on computer statistics packages tend to be opaque to students who haven't become acquainted with the packages concerned. Second, software and operating systems are changing much more rapidly than the 'half-life' of a book, and it is far easier (and less expensive) to update computer-based material on electronic media than in a new edition of a book.

Third, one of the real advantages of computer-based educational materials is their interactivity, which lends itself to both exploratory intuition-enhancing materials as well as an endless supply of practice problems. Rather than having the book bear the entire burden of instruction, I have elected to 'export' many exercises and instructional enhancements to electronic media.

For this reason, the book contains only a small set of exercises at the end of each chapter, with more problems and exploratory modules available on the electronic media accompanying it.

As far as possible I have endeavored to make the computer-based extras platform-independent. For the most part, that entails Windows and Macintosh versions of files and executables. These materials include the following:

- Data-files referred to in the book, in ASCII, Excel, and SPSS formats;
- Answers to exercises and problems in HTML so they may be viewed by most web browsers;
- StatPatch, a suite of tutorial and exploratory modules;
- Demos, a suite of Excel wordbooks also for tutorial and/or exploratory purposes.

I also maintain a website associated with this book. It may be found at http://psy.anu.edu.au.staff/mike/Statbook/TOC.html. It contains more supplementary material, corrections to any errors found in the book, and links to other helpful sites and resources.

Acknowledgements

This book benefited enormously from input and assistance generously provided by many colleagues, and I am indebted to them. Valuable suggestions and advice for the book and statistics teaching have come my way from Natalie Albon, Neil Black, Michael Cook, Geoff Cumming, Suzy Dormer, Margaret Foddy, Wolfgang Grichting, JoAnn Lukins, Elinor McKone, James Neill, Peter Raggatt, Paul Reser, Judy Slee, Susan Smithson, Neil Thomason, Ross Wilkinson, and several cohorts of second-year Psychology students at The Australian National University and James Cook University. I would also like to thank Cobie Brinkman, Michael Cook, Bernd Heubeck, Jeff Ward, and the Australian Consortium for Social and Political Research for their generosity in providing me with data-sets, examples, and key illustrative materials.

My greatest thanks are owed to those who read drafts of the entire manuscript: John Beale, Alex Haslam, Craig McGarty, and Michelle Ryan. Michelle read two or three drafts of every chapter, and John shouldered the burden of indexing. The impact from these four colleagues went far beyond mere proofreading and error-spotting. Any parts of this book that read clearly and communicate effectively probably do so because I took their advice. On the other hand, any errors, lapses, or omissions remain my responsibility.

Michael Smithson, Canberra, December 1998

Uncertainty and Psychological Research

1

What are we doing here and why?

Not many students enter into psychology with a burning desire to study statistics. Most of us are really interested in the subject matter of psychology: people. We want to find out about the secrets of human behavior and mental life. So, it is quite reasonable for us to wonder why we have to study statistics. After all, it has a world-wide reputation for being both boring and difficult.

A traditional short-term answer is that we need some understanding of statistics in order to read psychological research of the sorts that we encounter in other courses. Those of us who end up doing any psychological research need to understand statistics fairly well. This answer seldom satisfies everyone, and some of us go on to ask why psychology, of all disciplines, should seem so preoccupied with statistics. This, too, is a fair question, whose answer I hope will become clear long before you have reached the end of this book. For now, it will have to suffice to say that statistical methods are ways of coping with some of the uncertainties in psychological research and theory.

Another traditional answer is that learning about statistics and data analysis will provide you with very marketable, portable skills that not only equip you well to go on in psychology but in many other areas as well. I regularly receive letters, emails, or phone-calls from students who are kind enough to let me know that they got their present job or promotion partly because they were the only applicant who could handle data. Even those who claim they had forgotten everything say that having done statistics before gave them the confidence that they could do what was required of them. It is certainly the case that in recent times many types of employment have come to require data-analytic skills, familiarity with information technology, and a capacity to conduct research on people – and a course in statistics contributes directly to all of these.

The best, most long-term reason for studying statistics, however, is the same as for studying psychology or anything else at a university. It hands us one of the keys to improving how we live. We all must live amidst risks, for instance, and these days we are compelled to take account of more risks than at any time in the past. Assessing risks without any understanding of statistics is akin to flying blind. Probability and statistics comprise the best frameworks invented for dealing with uncertainty and assessing risks. They enable us to think about uncertainty and risk in ways that are totally unavailable to anyone who knows nothing of probability or statistics. Statistical knowledge also equips us with a special critical acumen that can help us to see through scams and falsehoods generated by those who juggle numbers and graphs. In fact, one of the first things you will learn in this book is some techniques for lying with statistics, so that you may know a statistical falsehood when you see one.

The approach and structure of this book

The main goal of this book is to enable you to make clear, sensible statements about data and to know what degree of confidence can be ascribed to those statements. Accordingly, in the first few chapters we will be focusing on ways of thinking about, describing, and presenting data; and from Chapter 4 onwards we will deal with techniques for making inferences and estimates from data and assessing how much confidence we can have in them.

This is not a mathematical book, although it does contain some formulas. There are no proofs or derivations, and what computations there are have been included to enhance your conceptual understanding. The emphasis throughout is on concepts, along with practical knowledge of how and when to use statistical techniques and what they can and cannot tell us. New terms and concepts are set out in **bold**. They are recapitulated at the end of each section. Likewise, questions and problems are included at the end of each major section, with answers to questions with **bold** numbers provided in the Answers section at the end of this book.

As much as possible, the examples in each chapter have been based on real research from a variety of psychological topics. Although that sometimes entails digressions by way of explaining what the examples are about, it should more than make up for that in the extra understanding of how statistics is used in genuine psychological studies. Likewise, the exercises and problems have been made as realistic as possible.

This first chapter begins with an overview of scientific research and how it is related to other ways of knowing, learning and discovering. We then move on to sections dealing with uncertainties in research and issues that arise when we count or quantify things. The themes that run throughout this material are the place statistics has in psychological research, what it is designed to do, and some important considerations about when and how to use statistics.

Chapter 2 concerns measurement and variables. It starts with strategies for observing and measuring aspects of human behavior and mental life. Concepts of validity, reliability, and error in measurement are introduced, with the understanding that people are reactive and intelligent and therefore cannot be studied in quite the same ways as we would study inanimate things. The 'technical' portions of this chapter introduce you to the different kinds of data and ways of working with them, as well as issues raised by missing or incomplete data.

Chapter 3 builds on the material in Chapter 2 by elucidating basic principles of data description, exploration, and summarization. It also leads you through alternative ways of displaying data, including ones that can mislead or misrepresent. This is the chapter that deals with descriptive statistics, which are quantities for summarizing and characterizing larger collections of data.

Chapter 4 is where we begin to work with inferences, or plausible statements about numbers. It is not enough to just describe a particular research finding; we wish to be able to generalize from it and also infer possible explanations of the phenomena being studied. This chapter thereby introduces the idea of inferring a characteristic of a population from a random sample of data, and the related concept of randomized assignment in experimentation as a basis for inferring an experimental effect. The basis for these inferences is probability, so the second half of Chapter 4 explains the basic aspects of probability theory and how it can be applied to statistical inference.

From here on, it becomes difficult to describe chapter contents in much detail because they involve increasingly many terms that have not been introduced yet. Chapters 5 and 6 are in many ways the backbone of this book. Chapter 5 introduces the idea of a *confidence interval*, which is an interval around an estimate that is associated with a certain level of confidence. You have probably encountered intervals around estimates before (e.g., 'The latest prediction is that the unemployment rate will be somewhere between 8% and 10% next year'). The same general idea applies to estimating a numerical characteristic of a population when we have only a representative sample from that population. For instance, if we take a random sample of a thousand people from the city of London and measure their heart-rates, the average heart-rate of the thousand will not necessarily be exactly the true average of the entire London population. How far away might it be, and with what probability? Chapter 5 enables us to answer that kind of question.

Chapter 6 applies these concepts to *hypothesis testing* and *comparisons between alternative models* of underlying reality. These extensions provide the keys to understanding a great deal of experimental psychological research. Chapters 7, 8, and 9 bring those concepts into the realm of predicting one variable from another, which is one of the Holy Grails of scientific research. Chapter 10 briefly introduces some additional concepts needed for psychological research that involves more than one predictor at a time. Finally, Chapter 11 provides a review and retrospection on the material covered in this book.

Some advice and support materials

Students encountering statistics for the first time often worry about whether they will be able to understand the material or keep up with the pace of instruction. They fear that their lack of training in mathematics will jeopardize their chances of doing well. If you feel you don't have a strong mathematics background, do not worry: that will not stand between you and understanding the material in this book. For one thing, most of your fellow students and your instructors are not mathematically inclined either. For another, this is most certainly not a course in *mathematical* statistics, although it introduces and uses some concepts from that field. Instead, it is aimed at a practical and conceptual understanding of what statistics is for, how to use it wisely, and how to interpret what others have done with it. There are *some* arithmetical concepts and techniques that you need to be reasonably familiar with, but they involve nothing more than basic arithmetic and secondary school algebra. With a bit of patience and effort, you will find that things will come more easily as time goes on.

Perhaps the most important thing is if you don't understand something in the book, *please ask someone*. Don't worry about sounding stupid; there is no such thing as a 'stupid question' in statistics. In picking up a foreign language you have to ask people what this means or how to say that, and the same is true of statistics and research. Study the material with a friend as much as possible. Often two heads really are better than one, and even when you are the person doing the explaining you'll find that you learn more from having to articulate your knowledge.

The second thing you need to bear in mind is that studying a research methods book is a lot like reading in a foreign language for the first time. Take things slowly and make sure you understand the meaning of each symbol, new term, or formula before going on to the next bit. Try to do small amounts of study regularly rather than cramming just before an exam or assignment is due. If you find yourself getting lost, make a note of where you got lost and why before going to someone for help.

Something else that you can do to aid your learning is to make use of available support and resources. The electronic media accompanying this book provide helpful materials in addition to the questions and problems at the end of major sections and chapters. First, there are data-files corresponding to the appropriate problems and most of the main examples. These are in SPSS, Excel, and ASCII formats, so they should be readable by most statistics packages.

Second, there is a suite of tutorial modules collectively called *StatPatch* and *Demos*, and you will see references to them throughout this book. StatPatch is a mix of exploratory and problem-generating modules designed to build understanding and intuition in statistics. Demos is a collection of Excel workbooks, serving much the same purposes. One advantage that they have over textbook problems is that these modules generate infinitely many problems as well as providing immediate feedback, so you can learn at your own pace and have as much practice or exploration as you wish.

Finally, I maintain a website associated with this book. It may be found at http://psy.anu.edu.au/staff/mike/Statbook/TOC.html. It has links to other sites and helpful resources for psychology students studying statistics and research methods. While I would have liked to include web addresses in the book, I decided not to, mainly because many addresses change fairly often and new resources appear all the time. You are more likely to obtain the latest sites and correct addresses if I maintain them on the web.

Paths to knowledge or belief

Researchers are sometimes called 'knowledge workers.' This phrase suggests that their main contributive goals are adding to what we know or believe about the world, and correcting erroneous beliefs. Since many psychologists and other kinds of researchers claim to be using 'scientific methods' in their pursuit of knowledge, it is worthwhile briefly considering what they mean by this claim and how scientific methods are related to and distinguished from other ways of acquiring knowledge.

The following list is not exhaustive, nor is it the only possible list of different methods of knowledge acquisition. It is partly based on debates in the philosophy and sociology of science over whether science is an institution that is truly distinguishable from other institutions, and whether it has a defensible claim to superiority over those other institutions in getting us closer to truth or even reducing untruth. Fascinating as those debates are, we will not go into them here. Instead, the intention is to provide a rough guide to various paths to knowledge and belief, including scientific research:

- Personal (first-hand) experience
- Authority and/or consensus
- Intuition
- Common sense and tradition
- Rationalism and reasoning
- Scientific methods

DEFINITION   **Personal experience** encompasses events that we describe with phrases such as 'I saw it with my own eyes' or 'hands-on.' For many people, first-hand personal experience is synonymous with reality-testing. It is virtually impossible for us to see ourselves holding false beliefs here and now; the best we can do is to realize retrospectively that we once held a belief that we now consider false. This 'blind-spot' points towards one of the main drawbacks to reliance on personal experience, namely that without adequate precautions and comparisons with others' experiences, we may easily be led astray.

For one thing, personal experiences are necessarily very circumscribed and may not even comprise a representative sampling of the totality of experiences. Our experiences of blind people, avalanches, dugongs, and snowflakes encompass only a tiny and unrepresentative fraction of the blind people, avalanches, dugongs, and snowflakes to be found anywhere and for all time. Nevertheless, we sometimes overgeneralize on the basis of our experiences, as in making inferences to the entire population of dugongs from the only one we ever saw.

Worse still, we may be deluded or fall prey to illusions in our own experiences. You undoubtedly already know that your senses (sight, for instance) can be fooled by a magician or an optical illusion. We suffer from cognitive illusions as well, some of which we will become acquainted with in this book.

Personal experience is nevertheless a crucial component of any scientific
DEFINITION   method, because scientific methods are grounded in empiricism. **Empirical methods** are those based on first-hand experiences of the world, so personal experience is a necessary component of those methods. **Empiricism** is a doctrine that ascribes superior truth-status to things that have been directly observed or manipulated over things that cannot be observed or manipulated. Most scientists are empiricists of one kind or another.

There are prescriptions in the scientific versions of personal experience that distinguish them from the usual versions. Most importantly, a scientist is supposed to adopt a stance of **impartiality** (or **disinterestedness**) towards all competing opinions or theories, including their own. That does not mean they cannot have values or pet ideas, although many writers confuse impartiality with the notion of being value-free (whereupon they rightly contend that no one is value-free and then wrongly conclude that scientists cannot adopt an impartial stance). It does mean that a scientist should take precautions in their research so that someone with different values and opinions could repeat their investigations and arrive at the same conclusions. An experiment set up so that the experimenter is 'blinded' with regard to which subjects have been assigned to which treatment condition is an example of such a precaution. Another example is designing a study expressly for investigating conditions under which the scientist's theory should fail if it is incorrect.

In direct contrast with personal experience, using **authority or consensus** as a path to knowledge entails relying on second- or third-hand accounts of others' experiences. Authorities are sources with high status in our eyes. Parents, teachers, scientific experts, and religious leaders are examples of authorities. So are encyclopedias, scientific journals, television news programs, and computer programs. When every relevant authority agrees on a proposition (e.g., 'the world is round, not flat'), we have a consensus that makes that proposition appear indubitable. It is not difficult to see that the vast majority of what we think we know is based on appeals to authority and/or consensus. DEFINITION

Authorities can, of course, be wrong. A Dean of the Harvard Medical School was renowned for declaring to incoming first-year students that before they graduated they would have to commit some 40,000 'facts' to memory. Within 10 years of their graduation, about half of those 'facts' would be shown to be wrong. Unfortunately, he was fond of concluding, we never know which half. We have no way of knowing which of today's authoritatively established truths will become tomorrow's laughingstock. Moreover, the greater the authoritative consensus behind a belief, the less likely anyone will buck the tide to find out whether it is wrong after all.

Scientific methods rely on appeals to authority, and agreement among relevant authorities is a legitimate goal in scientific work. All scientists are members of one or more scientific communities and none of them remain uninfluenced by those communities. Scientific communities have norms and institutions that many have argued make them less likely than other communities to fall prey to a misleading authoritative consensus. A **norm** means a usual or expected practice, rather like a custom. One of the most popular and also widely criticized lists of scientific norms is Robert K. Merton's (1973). I have added one more to his original four (Honesty). DEFINITION

- **Universalism**: Research and theory are to be judged on their own merits, regardless of the scientist's gender, ethnicity, creed, political affiliation, or any other characteristic. Blind peer review of research papers is an example of this norm in action, since the authors of the paper and the reviewers are unknown to each other.
- **Organized skepticism**: All ideas and evidence should be carefully scrutinized and subjected to skeptical inquiry. No results or conclusions should

be accepted other than provisionally, and even then subject to replication by other independent researchers.

- **Communalism**: Scientific knowledge should be shared freely with everyone. Proprietary secrecy is contrary to this norm. Where ethically possible, research practices, processes, data, and other 'raw' instruments or products should be publicly available for scrutiny.
- **Disinterestedness**: Alternative ideas are to be considered and tested on an equal footing with one's own, in such a way that someone with other views could repeat the tests or investigations and arrive at the same conclusion.
- **Honesty**: Cheating or dissembling is an especially strong taboo in scientific communities, so much so that an instance of it may result in banishment or ostracism.

This list of norms has provoked heated debate, both about whether scientists really adhere to them and whether they should. While there are plenty of counterexamples against each of these norms (e.g., instances of prejudice, discrimination, credulity, secrecy, or fraud among scientists), defenders of the scientific community point to the institutional practices that embody them and observe that to the extent that anyone adheres to those norms they are adopting a scientific outlook and attitude (cf. Grinnell, 1987).

Now let us turn to **intuition**. In one sense, having an intuitive understanding of or belief about something entails not being able to ascribe that understanding or belief to a legitimate basis. Another sense of this term refers to the sudden, blinding insight that seems to arrive from nowhere. Both of these meanings amount to tacit knowledge, knowing something without knowing how we know it. It is here, perhaps, that scientists most closely resemble everyone else. While some famous scientists have written popular accounts of having flashes of intuition and while many scientists prize good intuition as highly as the rest of us, they also happily confess that they don't know how it happens either! There is a widely held view among scientists that intuition alone is not sufficient to justify an idea, but that is not news to most people.

There is one respect in which scientists may diverge somewhat from popular views about intuition and common sense. They tend to be fascinated with research outcomes that fly in the face of intuition or common sense. It is possible that the fascination with counter-intuitive findings simply reflects a shrewd judgment that such findings are unlikely to have been discovered before and quite likely to advance one's scientific career, but there seems to be more to it than that.

Common sense and traditional truths are repositories of second- and third-hand knowledge loosely organized into theories and explanations of how the world works. Common sense is certainly a good place to begin but may be a bad place to end for scientific research. Moreover, psychology probably has one of the most difficult relationships of any discipline with common sense. The main reason for this is that most of us are pretty good common-sense psychologists, at least within our own cultures. Otherwise, we could not make our way through everyday life. In contrast, most of us are rather poor common-sense chemists and very poor common-sense subatomic particle physicists. Fortunately, we have little need to depend on our common sense in those areas. We can leave them to experts.

Psychological research often is accused of not going any farther than common sense while taking much longer to get there. There are two lines of defense against such accusations. One is that common sense contains mutually contradictory propositions that are not recognized as contradictory because people use them at different times. It is not difficult to think of opposing proverbs that demonstrate this, for instance:

- Look before you leap, vs. He who hesitates is lost.
- Opposites attract, vs. Birds of a feather flock together.
- Absence makes the heart grow fonder, vs. Out of sight, out of mind.
- Many hands make light the work, vs. Too many cooks spoil the broth.
- It's never too late to learn, vs. You can't teach an old dog new tricks.
- No one is an island, vs. We die alone.

Haslam & McGarty (1998) make amusing and instructive use of the third pair of proverbs to demonstrate how one might build up a research program to investigate which one is correct under various conditions. The other line of defense refers back to scientific norms of organized skepticism and disinterestedness. No matter how many people have endorsed a common-sensical assertion and no matter how long it has been believed, if it has not been properly tested then it is not scientific knowledge.

Finally, we turn to rationality and reasoning. **Rationality** involves adherence to a system of reasoning (usually standard logic). A popular view of science and, to a greater extent, mathematics, is that it relies heavily on logical reasoning and thereby rationality. While scientific research does make use of logic, logic is by no means sufficient on its own. Traditionally, rationality (along with rationalism) has been linked with knowledge and certainty. While ancient canons of rationality comprised substantive contents and told people what to believe, those versions were gradually supplanted by procedural and algorithmic prescriptions. Instead of directing people to specific conclusions, modern versions of rationality tell them how to reach conclusions. That is why most widely accepted versions of rationality boil down to some kind of logical consistency and coherency.   DEFINITION

What is **rationalism**? It amounts to faith that rationality is the 'best' guide   DEFINITION
to decision making. Anything else (i.e., the nonrational, irrational, or anti-

rational) is considered to be worse. Rationalists are anti-Heraclitans, which means they think there is sufficient regularity and stability in the universe for us to learn generalizable lawlike properties of it. They share this view with many empirical scientists (and much common-sense reasoning as well!). If we do not have a learnable world in some minimal sense, then rationality has no use. The usefulness of logical consistency assumes predictable, stationary relations among things in the real world. So does much scientific research. Some of the debates about whether psychology can or should be a science hinge on just this issue.

Where does statistics fit into all of this? Statistics is the offspring of a liaison between empiricism and rationalism. Statistical techniques are derived from general frameworks for understanding empirical data, so statistics and empirical research go hand-in-hand. Statistical models are based on theories of probability that, in turn, have some rationalistic and mathematical foundations. The marriage of empiricism and rationalism has not always been a peaceful one, and there are competing theories of statistics and probability. The versions we will use in this book are the most popular in psychology and work quite well under a wide range of conditions, but it is always wise to bear in mind that they are not the only approaches that could be used.

SUMMARY

The alternative **paths to knowledge** and belief reviewed in this section include:

- Personal (first-hand) experience
- Authority and/or consensus
- Intuition
- Common sense and tradition
- Rationalism and reasoning

Science makes use of all of these, albeit in ways that differ from their uses in everyday life.

Scientific communities have **norms** that many have argued make them less likely than other communities to fall prey to a misleading authoritative consensus:

- Universalism
- Organized skepticism
- Communalism
- Disinterestedness (or impartiality)
- Honesty

Scientific methods are grounded in **empirical methods**, based on first-hand experiences of the world.

Empiricism is a doctrine that ascribes superior truth-status to things that have been directly observed or manipulated over things that cannot be observed or manipulated.
Rationality involves adherence to a system of reasoning (usually standard logic).
Rationalism is a faith that rationality is the best guide to decision making.

Statistics and probability are a combination of empiricist and rationalist ideas.

Uncertainties in research

The phrase 'psychological research' claims a large and diverse terrain, perhaps larger and more diverse than at any time in the history of the discipline. Pick 500 psychologists at random, ask them to describe how they do their research, and the answers will probably include experiments, surveys, case studies, in-depth interviews, ethnographies, test construction, discourse analysis, and computer simulations. You might encounter some who are doing historical or archival investigations, or even archeological studies.

It may seem as if there are no concepts or methods shared by all of these approaches to studying human beings. There are certainly practitioners of specific approaches who say that their approach has absolutely nothing in common with others. Nevertheless, there are good reasons to be suspicious of this sort of territorial statement and to think that researchers may share a few common bonds after all.

First, all researchers engage with the unknown in one sense or another. They begin by claiming that there really is something new under the sun and they are going to return from their voyaging to tell us something about it. Accordingly, they grapple with uncertainties, trade in novelties, map uncharted seas, and make discoveries. For all researchers, ignorance and uncertainty are both friend and foe, sometimes simultaneously. Without ignorance or uncertainty, there is nothing new to discover and the research game is over. In the grip of ignorance or uncertainty, however, the researcher is seldom in a position to demonstrate or prove anything conclusively. The physicist Richard Feynman captured this essential characteristic of scientific work in his 1955 address to the American National Academy of Science:

> The scientist has a lot of experience with ignorance and doubt and uncertainty, and this experience is of very great importance, I think. When a scientist doesn't know the answer to a problem, he is ignorant. When he has a hunch as to what the result is, he is uncertain. And when he is pretty

darned sure of what the result is going to be, he is in some doubt. We have found it of paramount importance that in order to progress we must recognize the ignorance and leave room for doubt. Scientific knowledge is a body of statements of varying degrees of certainty – some most unsure, some nearly sure, none absolutely certain. (Feynman, 1988: 245)

Second, all researchers are members of one or more research communities. These are collections of people who agree sufficiently with one another to be able to share a conceptual framework, but whose discourse within that framework is characterized by vigorous argument, disputation, and conflict. Like ignorance, disagreement is both friend and foe to the researcher. Researchers crave consensus, but only up to a point. Complete agreement is a disaster for research, because no one is able to move outside the accepted way of thinking and there is nothing genuinely creative going on. Disagreement, while essential for motivating research, is often also agonizing for the researcher. Given the stylistic conventions of the time, a medical researcher turned philosopher of science, Ludwik Fleck, expressed this very well in 1935: 'At the moment of scientific genesis [discovery], the research worker personifies the totality of his physical and intellectual ancestors and of all his friends and enemies. They both promote and inhibit his search.' (Fleck, 1935/1979: 95.)

Third, all researchers make mistakes, both in their own eyes and the eyes of others. Here again, error is friend and foe. Anyone who gets it right the very first time really has learned nothing new. Making an error and realizing that it is an error are necessary components of any learning process, and therefore any process of discovery or creation as well. Again, Fleck is right on the mark: 'Discovery is thus inextricably interwoven with what is known as error. To recognize a certain relation, many another relation must be misunderstood, denied, or overlooked.' (Fleck, 1935/1979: 30.)

This does not mean, of course, that making any kind of mistake leads to discovery or learning. It *does* mean that reluctance to take a step for fear of making a misstep will surely impede discovery and learning. All researchers strive against indoctrinated fears of failure, error, and ridicule, much of it traceable to years of formal education that has rewarded them only for correct answers to problems whose solutions already are known. We can always dream of a system of education that does not penalize students for making mistakes! On a slightly more sober note, we can reward ourselves and others for risking productive and interesting mistakes, along with careful descriptions of them and our current states of ignorance. The University of Arizona's Medical Curriculum on Ignorance (Kerwin, 1993) is a salutary (and, alas, nearly solitary) example of a curriculum that invites students to describe and study not only knowledge but also what they don't know, and sustains ignorance as an object of study throughout their entire degree program.

This book is about uncertainty in psychological research and some widely shared methods for understanding and coping with it. It is also about how to make productive mistakes by taking strategic risks in designing and conducting research. That said, this book does not cover anything like the full gamut of research styles and techniques, the varieties of uncertainty, or their sources. That would require many books. None the less, there are some reasons behind the choices of research styles and uncertainties that inform this book's core.

To start with, we can place this book's focus in the context of various kinds of ignorance and uncertainty. The following list is adapted from Smithson (1989) and divides ignorance into two major chunks:

Types of ignorance and uncertainty

1. Distortion
   - Qualitative: Confusing one thing for another.
   - Quantitative: Systematic inaccuracy.
2. Incompleteness
   - Absence: Missing information.
   - Uncertainty: Indeterminate information.
     - Probability and statistical uncertainty: Likelihood of an event.
     - Ambiguity or vagueness: Multiple possible meanings or a range of values.

The first chunk, **distortion**, is usually taken to be some kind of systematic descriptive error. Its qualitative version consists of **confusion**, mistaking one DEFINITIONS thing for something else (as in a misdiagnosis), and its quantitative version consists of **inaccuracy** (as in a miscalibrated weighing scale).

The second chunk, **incompleteness**, refers to information that is **absent** (missing) or **uncertain** (indeterminate). Indeterminacy of information is then subdivided into two categories: probabilistic and ambiguous or vague. **Ambiguity** and **vagueness** refer to ways in which information can be blurry, have multiple interpretations, or have shades and degrees of meaning. **Probability**, on the other hand, refers to the likelihood that something will happen.

Psychological research (indeed, perhaps all research) necessarily traffics in all of these kinds of ignorance and uncertainty. In psychology, problems of distortion are usually the province of measurement and ascribing meaning to our observations. We will introduce some of the basic concepts of measurement in Chapter 2, and discuss some issues concerning distortion in measurement there. Entire textbooks are devoted to measurement, however, and that is not the primary focus of this book (see Kaplan & Saccuzzo, 1989, on psychological testing and measurement, for example, or Foddy, 1993, on designing questions for surveys and experiments).

Incompleteness, on the other hand, is mainly the province of data-analytic techniques, particularly statistical techniques. Most of this book focuses on incompleteness, especially probabilistic or statistical uncertainty. Uncertainty is generally held to be more difficult to deal with than distortion, and less likely to be eliminated even from the best research. However, uncertainty can be described, sometimes quantified and estimated, and even manipulated in the service of the researcher. In this book we will encounter these three strategies for managing uncertainty many times.

Another viewpoint on uncertainty in research emerges once we distinguish among the sources of uncertainty that become salient during the research process. One way to understand this is to begin with a schematic guide to that process. Like almost any schematic, the one in Figure 1.1 is oversimplified. It begins with the researcher defining a topic and research goals, developing questions and/or hypotheses, and then going on to design the study, collect and analyze data, and finally interpreting the findings and revising what is known about the topic on the basis of those findings.

The feedback loops indicated in this figure are not the only possible feedback effects, and to some extent the revisability of the earlier stages depends on the kind of research being conducted and the norms of the research community involved. A rigorous experiment, for example, designed to test very specific hypotheses, leaves little room for the researcher to revamp those hypotheses in midstream. None the less, the feedback loops represent the fact that the research process may not be a one-way sequence but can involve successive iterations, whereby the researcher oscillates between stages until satisfied enough to move on.

DEFINITION   The six stages in this schematic also provide convenient labels for sources of uncertainty. **Topical uncertainty**, to begin with, concerns how the researcher is to describe the object of their investigations. Consider psychological research on affect or emotions. Are we studying emotional traits such as temperament, or more temporary states like moods, or even briefer episodes?

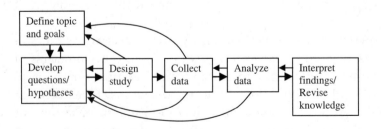

FIGURE 1.1 Research process

Are emotions best thought of as physiological, somatic, or socially based? What does the topic of emotions include and what does it exclude? Until we have at least tentative answers to questions such as these we cannot be sure about our topic.

Investigative uncertainty concerns research questions and hypotheses. The kinds of questions that are sensible to ask about a topic are influenced to some extent by prior views and assumptions about the topic. For instance, if we assume that emotions are primarily products of physiological processes, then the most obvious starting-point would include aiming at an accurate description of the physiological concomitants of each distinct emotion. If, on the other hand, we assume that emotions are mainly interpretive constructs that arise from social interactions, then inquiring about physiological states and arousal would seem less relevant.

Methodological uncertainty refers to the design of the study and whether it will suit our purposes, answer our questions, or test our hypotheses. This term is taken from Haslam & McGarty (1998, Ch. 11) but used somewhat more broadly here. They distinguish between two kinds of methodological uncertainty, whereas I will use three:

- Design uncertainty
- Internal uncertainty
- External uncertainty

Design uncertainty concerns the overall method to be used in the study. Should we set up an experiment? A survey? What about a qualitative field study? **Internal uncertainty** refers to whether the researcher can interpret the outcomes of the study correctly, and **external uncertainty** refers to whether the study's results can be generalized to other populations or settings. These concepts may seem quite abstract now, but they will become clearer in the chapters to follow. For the present time, let's consider a few examples of research that has involved methodological uncertainty.

One of the chief concerns for anyone using more than one method to study something is that the methods might produce conflicting findings. Researchers must then sift through the studies and findings for possible explanations of the differences among them. For example, self-report or 'subjective' measures may differ from 'objective' indicators, as is often the case on topics such as risk or quality of life. A researcher faced with this situation will attempt to weave an explanation for it into a general account of risk perception, or health consequences of perceived versus objective quality of life. This explanation might refer to how people's perceptions and attitudes differ from so-called 'objective' measures, or to differences between the phenomena being studied, or even effects of studying the same phenomenon in different ways.

DEFINITION

DEFINITION

DEFINITIONS

As an example of the latter case, in a study in which I was involved (Smithson *et al.*, 1991) we found that survivors of suicide attempts were much more likely to admit to consuming alcohol at the time of their attempt if we asked them directly about it than if we left them to tell about the event in their own words. Any reasonable attempt to explain this contrast would require a theory of how people reconstruct such memories and then edit them into narratives about themselves.

A much earlier example is Hovland's (1959) review of the experimental versus survey research evidence on attitude change subsequent to exposure to a change-inducing message. He found that surveys were less likely to find evidence of attitude change than experiments. He ascribed this divergence to a tendency of the surveys to attract people who already favored the view advocated by the message, the shorter time-intervals used in experimental studies, and differences in the kinds of attitudinal issues used.

Sometimes the issues involved in comparing different methods may simply be too complex or researchers may be too biased in their views for a resolution to be achieved. Consider, for instance, the contrast between one group of primarily quantitative studies of mental patients and another group of mainly qualitative studies reviewed by Weinstein (1979) whose review is discussed at length in Bryman's (1988) textbook. The first group used structured survey questionnaires with rating scales, multiple-choice questions, sentence-completion tests, and the like. For the most part, these studies reported that mental patients had favorable attitudes towards their institutions, benefited from and even enjoyed hospitalization. The qualitative studies, on the other hand, used unstructured interviews with patients who in turn answered questions in their own words, observation by researchers masquerading as patients, and observations on hospital wards. These studies consistently found evidence of debasement and oppression by hospital authorities; and patients' feelings of anxiety, boredom, powerlessness, and betrayal.

Weinstein's review provoked controversy over how best to account for these different findings. He found fault with the methodologies of the qualitative studies. Critics of his review responded that Weinstein had tried to force a comparison between two relatively noncomparable sets of studies. They pointed to differences between the two groups on the admission status of the patients, and whether patient experiences or patient attitudes and outcomes were the object of investigation.

As Cook & Campbell (1979: 66) observe, relying on just one method to study a phenomenon when we know little about it lays the researcher open to accusations of 'mono-method bias.' The challenge in using more than one method is to do so in a strategic and even-handed fashion so that contrasting findings suggest new avenues for research and ways of integrating the findings. That way lies progress in any field.

The major portion of this book is devoted to **statistical uncertainty**, which is uncertainty related to the analysis and, to some extent, interpretation of data. **Descriptive statistics** characterize the data themselves, and so **descriptive uncertainty** concerns those characterizations. Suppose you have taken an exam in a cognitive psychology class, and the instructor is about to distribute the exam results. Before doing so, she mentions that the class average score was 64%. How well would this describe each student's score, including your own? The less variability in the scores, the closer the average would be to describing individual students' scores.

DEFINITIONS

Inferential statistics, on the other hand, are used for drawing conclusions about populations or underlying processes from the sample of data at hand. **Inferential uncertainty**, therefore, arises when we are not sure what kinds of statistical inferences we can make from our data. For example, the instructor might wonder whether your class has scored higher than last year's class, whose average was only 59%. She would realize that the difference between class averages of 59% and 64% might occur simply by chance, and she would use inferential statistics to address that possibility.

DEFINITION

Finally, **interpretive uncertainty** arises when, despite having good data and sound statistics, we are still unable to decide between competing interpretations for what we have found. Suppose the instructor finds out that your class probably did perform better on the exam than last year's class. Is your class more intelligent? Did they work harder? Did she do a better job of teaching? Were the exams equivalent, or was this year's exam easier? These are plausible alternative explanations for her findings, and she would want to eliminate all but one of them if possible.

DEFINITION

Given all of these different sources of uncertainty, research might appear to be a very daunting enterprise. Most research, however, does not deal with all of them simultaneously. In fact, researchers routinely distinguish one kind of research undertaking from another in terms of which of these uncertainties are being dealt with. The labels we will work with here are 'exploratory,' 'descriptive,' and 'explanatory' research (Neuman, 1997, also uses these).

Exploratory studies deal primarily with topical and investigative uncertainties. If we do not know anything about a topic, if little or nothing has been written about it, then we need to refine our comprehension of it and develop questions that may be used to guide future research. Until topical uncertainty has been reduced to some extent, little progress on the other sources of uncertainty can be made. This is not to say that topical uncertainty must or can be completely eliminated. Some of the most interesting topics in psychology, creativity and consciousness being two examples, still are quite vague and sharply disputed even though they are the objects of long-running mature research programs.

DEFINITION

  Descriptive studies focus mainly on investigative uncertainty, although the research may also end up dealing with methodological and descriptive statistical uncertainties. The goal of description is to provide an accurate portrayal of the phenomena that leads to further questions, hypotheses, and eventually explanations and theories. Developing a better way of measuring anxiety would be a good example of a descriptive study. Descriptions may be in either qualitative or quantitative form, and quite often the researcher will use this research to organize understanding of the phenomena.

  As you might already have imagined, some studies can be both exploratory and descriptive. In the mid-1980s I worked with a former stomatherapist nurse, Therese Turner, who wanted to do her Honours research project on how colostomy patients managed their stigmatized condition in everyday life after their operations. Since a colostomy entails rerouting the colon so that it empties involuntarily into an external plastic bag instead of via the rectum, people who have had a colostomy are often at risk of public embarrassment. A search of the literature at the time revealed almost no relevant studies, so she elected to conduct a descriptive study based on in-depth interviews of former colostomy patients. She began by asking them what they thought were the major problems they faced and how they dealt with them. The matters raised by these people in the interviews generated further questions, and she returned to her informants for additional information. In the end, their accounts provided many fruitful suggestions for future research as well as advice that could be provided to such patients before and after the operation.

  Given a topic about which something is known and some descriptions of it, we tend to wonder why it is so. In **explanatory** research, the principal objects are reasons, causes, and interpretations. Explanatory studies therefore concentrate on statistical and interpretive uncertainties. They often test hypotheses or theories. We conduct such studies when we already have a good idea of the nature of our topic and what methods to use in studying it. Experiments are perhaps the best examples of explanatory research, because they require enough prior knowledge about a phenomenon to be able to manipulate some aspects of it in order to observe the effects that follow.

  A number of concepts and terms have been introduced in this section, some of which may seem abstract and unfamiliar. If you can bear with it, these ideas will become clearer and form the basis for a genuine overview of psychological research that will stand you in good stead, not just for learning the material in this book but for understanding the diverse kinds of research throughout psychology.

Research of any kind has three things in common that are both friend and foe:
1. Dealing with ignorance and uncertainty,
2. Disputation and conflict within a framework shared by other researchers, and
3. Learning and discovery through errors.

The kinds of uncertainty dealt with in research include the following:
1. **Distortion**: systematic error.
   - **Confusion**: Mistaking one thing for another.
   - **Inaccuracy**: Systematic miscalibration.
2. **Incompleteness**: Missing or indeterminate information.
   - **Absence**: Missing information.
   - **Uncertainty**: Indeterminate information.
   - **Probability** and statistical uncertainty: Likelihood of an event.
   - **Ambiguity or vagueness**: Multiple possible meanings or a range of values.

Sources of uncertainty in research arise at each of its six stages:
Topical uncertainty concerns how the researcher is to describe the object under investigation.
Investigative uncertainty concerns the nature of research questions and hypotheses.
Methodological uncertainty refers to the design of the study and whether it will answer our questions or test our hypotheses.

- **Design uncertainty** concerns the overall method to be used in the study.
- **Internal uncertainty** refers to whether the researcher can interpret the outcomes of the study correctly.
- **External uncertainty** refers to whether the study's results can be generalized to other populations or settings.

Statistical uncertainty concerns the analysis and, to some extent, interpretation of data.

- **Descriptive statistics** characterize the data themselves, and so **descriptive uncertainty** concerns those characterizations.
- **Inferential statistics** are used for drawing conclusions about populations or underlying processes from the sample of data. **Inferential uncertainty** concerns what kinds of statistical inferences we can make.

Interpretive uncertainty arises when the researcher is unable to decide between competing interpretations of the research findings.

Quantifying and counting

Since statistics are closely allied to quantification and counting, we should examine both of those practices before sailing off into areas where we take them for granted. We will start with counting, since that is the more venerable of the two and easier to conceptualize.

Counting assumes that the things being counted all belong to the same category. Its main advantage over using words is obvious once we grant that assumption. Saying that 'many' people in the class are right-handed is a nearly useless description compared to saying that 72 out of 83 are. Moreover, we can perform arithmetic operations with counts that are impossible with linguistic terms. Numbers and mathematics are not arbitrary social conventions. They have been successful because they help us think more clearly about certain things. To get a quick appreciation of this assertion, try multiplying 'three hundred and twenty-five by one hundred and twelve' versus 325 by 112, or try doing division with Roman numerals (if you are curious about other counting systems, take a look at Barrow, 1992).

Before counting behaviors, manifestations of cognitive processes, or the like, we need to be sure that they really do belong to the same category. For instance, consider the act of choosing the correct alternative on a true–false question in an exam. If we count the number of people who chose that alternative, we are lumping together those who knew the answer and those who happened to guess it. There may be no harm in counting how many got the question right, but we would be mistaken if we went on to say that was the number of people who knew the answer.

Quantification involves assigning numbers to distinguishable observations. While some concepts such as speed, duration, or length seem 'naturally' quantifiable, many psychological concepts provoke debates over whether they are quantifiable and if so, how best to quantify them. We will explore concepts in this book that inform those debates. When it is successful, quantification has much the same advantages as counting. It enables us to say not just that change or differentiation has taken place, but *how much* of it has occurred.

There are some popular arguments against quantification and counting, and we should examine them before moving on. One of the most pervasive is that 'reducing people to numbers' is anti-humanistic. It degrades people by ignoring their uniqueness as individuals. It is true that quantifying and counting require that we lump people together in some respects, thereby ignoring unique features. All general descriptions and theories do this. However, careful description and measurement never degrades anyone or anything. Also, words can just as easily and far more tellingly debase people by distorting or glossing over important characteristics.

Another related argument is that many important, observable things cannot be quantified. Characteristics that are not quantifiable tend to be ignored or discounted in favor of those that are quantified. There is some truth to this argument too, but the fault does not lie with quantification itself. After all, even qualitative characteristics ultimately must be codified, summarized, and counted once sufficiently many instances of them have been collected. Problems about quantification arise mainly when numbers become separated from their contexts. Good researchers know that every numerical datum has a context that needs to be considered before combining it with other numerical data, such as realizing when an EEG is showing 'artifact', that a rat went to sleep in the middle of a maze-running trial, or when a child is not paying attention in a reaction-time task.

A more general overview of the tradeoffs involved here might refer to 'data reduction' versus 'data enhancement.' Ragin (1994: 92) provides slightly different terms, and aptly observes that data reduction enables a researcher to see the big picture at the expense of attending to details, while data enhancement provides surrounding contextual information about the data that enables the researcher to better understand a particular case. **Data reduction** entails *combining* or *truncating* data. In order to perform either operation, we must treat the data as if they are combinable or comparable, or as if their qualitative differences are irrelevant. **Data enhancement** entails elaborating a set of data by *dissecting* it into components, or *supplementing* it with related data. Data enhancement involves an assumption that each datum is unique or distinctive in some relevant way that needs further explication.

DEFINITIONS

For instance, suppose we take weekly measurements of 100 people's levels of self-esteem using a well-established self-esteem index that consists of 15 questions, for a period of 11 weeks. An example of data reduction via combination would be averaging each person's self-esteem scores over the 11-week period. An example of reduction by truncation would be to rank their scores from lowest to highest, and use the middle (6th-ranked) score as their 'typical' score, ignoring all the other scores above and below it.

Likewise, an example of data enhancement via dissection would be breaking each score into the responses people gave on every one of the 15 questions in the self-esteem index. Data enhancement via supplementation, on the other hand, might consist of having people keep a diary of self-esteem-influencing events that would then be listed along with their score for the week (e.g., being reprimanded at work, or winning a ribbon in a local fun-run). Another kind of supplementation would be asking people to record their thoughts, feelings, and reasons for responding to the self-esteem questions, so that we have an elaboration of their accounts of the meanings behind their responses.

Many of the statistical techniques covered in this book have been designed to effectively condense or reduce data in various ways. In Chapter 3, for example, we will explore various kinds of summary statistics (such as the average, or arithmetic mean) that reduce a collection of scores to a few pieces of information about the properties of those scores. Other techniques, mainly those concerned with various ways of displaying data in graphs or tables, involve data enhancement as well as reduction. Although Ragin (1994) is oversimplifying somewhat, there is some truth in his claim that quantitative research techniques are mostly data condensers.

The tradeoff between these two ways of treating data is fairly obvious. Reducing large volumes of data to a few pieces of information is grist for any scientist's mill because it is compatible with the scientific goal of general-izable explanations and theories. A general theory effectively tells us that we may treat numerous specific cases as if they are essentially identical. When appropriately and intelligently applied, data reduction can reveal hidden order, regularity, or relationships among data in a powerful and even elegant fashion.

On the other hand, reducing means combining or truncating information and therefore ignoring it. The researcher who condenses data thereby risks ignoring important details or distinctions among particular cases. If taken to extremes, data reduction techniques can 'reduce people to numbers' by omitting crucial information about where the numbers come from or what they mean. In a somewhat different sense of the word, Dennett (1994) coined the term 'greedy reductionism' to refer to excessive reductionistic ambitions. Researchers can sometimes get carried away by the power of their data-reducing techniques, especially since the advent of computers. So can consumers of research. A friend who is an analyst in a large govern-ment department concerned with health and safety has repeatedly told me that she is always under pressure from her superiors to 'boil it down to *one* number.'

Data enhancement provides ways of grounding information in context. Even quantitative data may require data enhancement in order to be properly understood. For example, consider the effect of an income increase of $100 per week on someone with a $150 per week income versus someone whose income is $10,000 per week. Or compare the student who has scored 70 on an exam with 70 on both the 'technical' and 'conceptual' components, with another student whose score of 70 is the average of 95 on the technical and 55 on the conceptual components.

The disadvantages and pitfalls of data enhancement are twofold. First, the researcher may become overwhelmed by elaboration and thereby unable to see the forest for the trees. This is simply the opposite side of the reductionism coin as outlined earlier.

Second, inappropriate or irrelevant contextual distinctions can mislead us into separating data that should be combined. This is a somewhat subtler point that the first one, but a simple example can illustrate it. Shoe-sizes are numbered according to different conventions in the U.S. than they are in Australia. I wear a size 11 shoe if I purchase it in the U.S. but only a size 9 if I buy it in Australia. A survey of shoe-sizes with samples from both Australia and the U.S. would therefore require that we record where the respondent's shoes were purchased. However, if the survey were restricted to Australia, then separating shoe-sizes by the state in which they were purchased would be irrelevant.

When should we choose data reduction or data enhancement? There is no simple answer. It depends on the researcher's goals and what is already known about the area. One strategy that is frequently used is to begin at one extreme (either reduction or enhancement) and then work back towards the other as far as is needed. To conclude this section, here is an example of a debate that is frequently found in psychology, namely whether a psychological concept should have more than one dimension or not. The concept in question is risk.

The editorial in a recent issue of the *Royal Statistical Society News* (October 1998) bemoaned the fact that people choose their risks in an 'irrational' way. According to the editor, people 'refuse to engage in activities which have known, but quite negligible, risks yet fearlessly participate in those whose dangers are orders of magnitude greater' (p. 1). He recounted the solution put forward by the past president of the RSS, which was that a 'Richter-type' scale of risk be constructed whereby people could compare known risks in a systematic way. A very similar proposal was made by the mathematician John Allen Paulos in his book, *Innumeracy* (1988). Such a scale would be an example of data reduction, since it would collapse all risk evaluation down to one dimension.

Eating a peanut-butter sandwich every day for one month, working in a coalmine for a few hours, and living next to a nuclear power plant for five years all involve an increase in risk of death of about one in a million, so if we were weighing risks on just that basis, we should equally value these three. But most of us do not. A large empirical research literature demonstrates that people perceive and evaluate risk along several dimensions. The list below contains the influences on risk preference identified in studies of risk perception (Otway & von Winterfeldt, 1982):

1. Involuntariness of exposure to the risk.
2. Lack of personal control over outcomes.
3. Uncertainty about probabilities or consequences of exposure.
4. Lack of experience or familiarity with the risk.

5. Difficulty in imagining consequences.
6. Delayed effects.
7. Genetic effects.
8. Catastrophic size of consequences (either geographically or numbers of people affected).
9. Benefits are not visible.
10. Benefits go to others but not oneself.
11. Human-caused rather than naturally caused.

The Richter-type risk scale does not provide a valid way of characterizing people's valuations of risk. It does, however, provide a worthwhile benchmark against which to compare how people do evaluate risks, because it orders risks along the continuum that we would use if probability of injury or death were our only concern in risk assessment. Given a person who has accurate information about such probabilities, we may use the Richter-type scale as a way of determining whether they are evaluating risks solely on the basis of probabilities. If we find that their preferences for risks disagree with the rank-ordering of those risks on the scale, then we know that we need to take more than just probabilities into account when attempting to describe people's risk preferences.

The moral to this example is that data reduction and enhancement can work together in getting a start in an unknown area. The field of risk assessment began with attempts to 'reduce' risk perception to a one-dimensional scale and the failure of that simple model stimulated the search for additional dimensions. This is an example of a pattern commonly encountered in scientific research, namely beginning with a simple, reduced model and then complicating it as necessary to fit the phenomena. The reverse process also can be found in some areas, whereby researchers begin with elaborate data enhancement and then systematically eliminate unnecessary features until they arrive at a more parsimonious model.

SUMMARY

Quantifying or even counting should not be undertaken without first considering whether these are sensible given possible arguments to the contrary.

Counting assumes that the things being counted all belong to the same category. *Quantification* involves assigning numbers to distinguishable states.

- **Data reduction** entails *combining* or *truncating* data.
- **Data enhancement** entails elaborating a set of data by *dissecting* it, or *supplementing* it with related data.

Two common strategies in research are to begin with data reduction and then enhance as much as necessary; or to start with data enhancement and then reduce as much as possible.

Questions and exercises

Q.1.1. Which are examples of scientific, rationalistic, intuitive, and authoritative methods of gaining or creating knowledge?

(a) Using a voltmeter to see whether your torch battery is flat.

(b) Your doctor says you have dermatitis, and you decide that you have dermatitis.

(c) Figuring that because only dogs make barking sounds in your neighborhood, the source of the barking sound outside your front door is a dog.

(d) Even though you haven't got a formal definition of creativity, you know it when you see it.

(e) Looking up the meaning of an English word in the *Oxford English Dictionary*.

(f) The curried chicken was too hot last week, so you try using one half-teaspoon less Madras powder this time.

Q.1.2. Give two examples of statistical descriptions.

Q.1.3. Give two examples of statistical inferences.

Q.1.4. Suppose a psychological researcher points out that everyone sees the same distinct bands in the rainbow regardless of how they classify or name colors, and uses this observation as an example of categorization that is independent of culture. Another psychologist argues that this phenomenon is not categorization at all. What kind of uncertainty is involved here?

Q.1.5. Give an argument for why happiness should be measured on a single scale, and an argument for why it should be measured on two separate scales (one 'positive' and the other 'negative').

Variables and Measurement

2

CONTENTS

Observational and measurement strategies

Why should we concoct systematic strategies for observing or measuring anything? There are at least four compelling reasons. First, all of us have only very limited first-hand knowledge of anything about the world, including human existence. The vast majority of what we think we know or believe is based solely on second- and third-hand accounts by authorities such as parents, teachers, and the media. Often, that is the best we can do. Nevertheless, without first-hand experience, second- and third-hand accounts require us to make assumptions about their truth-status. Even our own experiences are sometimes of doubtful pedigree – all of us are potentially fallible observers and recorders, to say nothing of memorizers. Moreover, our first-hand experiences are not just haphazardly constrained, but systematically truncated by social conventions, matters of interpersonal attraction, and political and other instrumental agendas. To gain a wider experience of what a representative sample of people thinks, feels, or does is no small undertaking and requires far more time, strategic work, and resources than most of us can bring to bear.

A second reason is that systematic measurement strategies and instruments are ways of extending our senses. We cannot directly see electrical activity in the brain when someone is listening to music, but we can measure that activity at least indirectly by using sensing and imaging techniques beyond our own capacities. Likewise, we cannot hang around a temple for 500 years and count the number of worshippers, but we can arrive at the scene 500 years after the temple was built and measure the wear on the steps at its entrance. Finally, while we do not have immediate access to any animal's preferences for one food over another, we may infer those preferences by watching which foods the animal selects when it is given a choice.

A third reason for strategic measurement refers to the demands on our time and attention. We cannot pay attention to everything, and we do not have much time. Nevertheless, we may make some careful choices about what to pay attention to, how to set about it, and how much time to devote to it. Depending on the researcher's goals and theoretical orientations, some kinds of observation and measurement are more relevant, important, or probative than others.

Suppose you are investigating the mental processes involved in reading, and you are debating with your colleagues about whether the capacity to recognize the meaning of a word operates independently of the capacity to recognize how it should sound. Then you should be very interested in finding people who have suffered head traumas that have left one capability intact but not the other, since that would unambiguously support the separate capacity theory. Unfortunately for opponents of that theory, head-trauma victims who have lost both capabilities do not provide unarguable support for their position. Likewise, you should be more interested in native readers of languages such as Chinese or Japanese, where the symbols representing meaning are sometimes separate from those representing sound, than readers of languages such as English, where the same symbols do both kinds of work.

A fourth reason for strategic observation and measurement is overcoming or guarding against biases and hidden assumptions. At one time some people claimed that scientific measurement could be freed of bias and uninfluenced by values. These days, some people have gyrated to the opposite extreme of claiming that all measurement is inherently biased and driven by researchers' values, ideological orientations, and preconceptions. Neither of these positions is true, and both invite intellectual laziness born of complacency in the first case and nihilistic relativism in the second. A more viable position that also gives us something to work with is that at least some biases can be identified and many of those can be overcome, even though we must bear in mind that there probably is no infallible method for doing so. Two kinds of perennial biases are those that direct our attention toward certain phenomena and away from others, and those that compel us to explain certain events but not others. One thing that makes these biases important is that they can entrap nearly everyone regardless of their ideological orientation or even their motives for doing their research.

We shall turn first to attentional biases. In 1986, the American space-shuttle 'Challenger' exploded shortly after take-off, killing all on board. A key cause of this tragedy was the failure of 'O-rings' that held the booster's fuel tank to the rest of the rocket. A *post-hoc* investigation revealed that these O-rings tended to fail when the temperature outside the rocket fell below a certain level. Why didn't the highly trained engineers who designed and tested the rocket figure this out beforehand? It turned out that they had considered the possibility that the O-rings might be sensitive to temperature. They had even examined the relationship between the number of O-ring failures and temperature for all previous space-shuttle flights when one or more O-rings had failed. What they had omitted to do was check the temperatures involved with flights where *no* O-rings failed. Had they done so, they would have seen that all those flights had temperatures above a critical level.

This is an example of our predilection for being much better at detecting the presence of something than its absence. We are greatly inclined to see objects and not the spaces around them – indeed, a famous basic exercise for beginning artists is to learn to see and draw those spaces – and we, along with other animals, learn much better from a cue linked to the presence of something than a cue linked to an absence. Thus, a common mistake in early medical and clinical psychological research was to focus exclusively on the clinical cases instead of also studying people who did not have the clinical condition.

Let us also consider a related bias that befalls even trained researchers. Suppose each of the cards in Figure 2.1 has a number on one side and a letter on the other, and someone tells you 'If a card has a vowel on one side then it has an even number on the other side.' Which of the cards *must* you turn over in order to decide whether the person is right? Try deciding which cards these would be before reading on.

Now imagine that you are a forensic criminal psychologist specializing in serial murderers, and your experiences in the field have inspired a hypothesis: 'All serial murderers kill domestic pets before turning to killing people.' If you were going to investigate whether this hypothesis is true, which of the following kinds of people would be most important to incorporate in your study? Try rank-ordering them from first to fourth most important, before reading on.

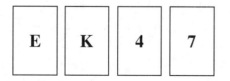

FIGURE 2.1 Card Task

- Serial murderers
- People who are not serial murderers
- People who have killed pets
- People who have not killed pets

If you are like most people, your response in the card task was to choose to turn over E and 4. Relatively few people give the logically correct answer, which is E and 7. The reason this answer is correct is that turning over the E card will disconfirm the rule if you find an odd number on its other side, and turning over the 7 will disconfirm the rule if you find a vowel on its other side. The other two cards are not relevant, since the rule states 'if vowel then even number' (and not, for instance, 'if even number then vowel'). The card task was first studied by Wason & Johnson-Laird in 1972 and is a classic example of the **confirmation bias**, namely the tendency for people to attend to instances   DEFINITION that confirm their hypotheses or beliefs and ignore instances that might disconfirm them. Likewise, to rank pet-killers as more important to study than people who have not killed pets would be to fall prey to this bias.

Now let's briefly consider explanatory biases. Perhaps the most widespread is what might be called the **expectancy bias**, whereby we feel compelled to   DEFINITION explain the unexpected but not the expected. Events that follow what we believe is the 'natural' or 'typical' order do not seem to require explanation, but 'unnatural' or 'atypical' ones do. Thus, we have seen many more studies of the causes of homosexuality than of heterosexuality, and one of the reasons is that a large and influential sector of Western societies perceives homosexuality to be 'unnatural'. Furthermore, we tend to think that atypical phenomena require special explanations over and above those for typical phenomena. Thus, from time to time people have proposed special theories of criminal behavior or of psychological disorders that are largely separate from theories of ordinary behavior or nonpathological psychology. The seductive nature of explanatory biases owes a great deal to the fact that if any phenomenon is merely what we expected it to be or what seems natural to us, then that is because we already have a theory about that phenomenon. However comfortable with our theory we might be, we should be prepared to subject it to as much rigorous testing as any other, and so we should be willing to investigate the ordinary, mundane, or expected along with their extraordinary counterparts.

Basic concepts of measurement

Whenever we measure anything, it is reasonable to distinguish between the record we make of this activity and the thing we are measuring. The record incorporates our measurements and any other relevant information; the thing

DEFINITION

we are measuring often is called a 'construct.' A **construct** may be an abstract concept such as verbal latency, information search strategy, anxiety, or appetite; but it may also be something that is quite tangible, such as reaction time, the trajectory of eye movement, galvanic skin response, or the amount of food consumed in a day. Some constructs, moreover, may serve as **indicators** of other constructs so that by knowing about one construct we obtain information about another. Thus, we might use reaction time as an indicator of latency, eye movement to indicate something about information search strategy, galvanic skin response to indicate nervousness, or daily food consumption to indicate appetite. Indicators that involve recording something about the real world are often called **operationalizations** of their respective constructs, and if we are convinced that one or more indicators truly represent everything

DEFINITION

about a construct, then we claim that they **measure** that construct. These two terms are important because they involve strong claims on the part of a researcher. Anyone who says they have *operationalized* a construct is claiming that they have a way of observing that construct's real-world manifestations, and if they further say they can *measure* the construct then they are claiming access to the totality of its real-world manifestations.

DEFINITION

A **variable** is an operationalization of a construct that can take on different values or states for different people (or even for the same person on different occasions). What is or is not a variable depends on the population being studied. If we are studying a group of 10-year-olds' reading ability, age is not a variable in that study. But if we are studying reading ability in children from an entire primary school, then age is a variable. Moreover, we must specify the conditions under which the construct can vary. Some constructs may change over time, or differ across people, or across situations for the same person.

As with most other aspects of research, deciding what will be treated as a variable is a matter of judgment and may be controversial. Gender, for example, is not a variable for most people during their lives, but it can be (transsexuals are those whose gender has varied at least once). In most, but not all, research on people it is sensible to treat gender as varying across people but not over time for the same person. However, a current issue in the psychology of the self is the extent to which an individual's personality or self-concept can vary throughout one's lifetime or even fleetingly from one situation to another.

All measurement strategies require the researcher to take at least some theoretical stances and risks, because in the absence of any theory the researcher has no idea what can or should be measured, let alone how to set about it. If we think that personality is fully formed and constant throughout adulthood, then the idea of measuring personality traits makes good sense. On the other hand, if we think that personality changes from one situation to another, the most we can hope for is to measure personality states at various points in time.

Even constructs themselves may be altered or redefined as theoretical frameworks develop. For instance, definitions of 'mental disorder' changed sufficiently throughout the 1970s that homosexuality was eliminated from the list of disorders in the more recent editions of the *Diagnostic and Statistical Manual* of the American Psychiatric Association.

It should not be surprising, then, that psychologists can differ dramatically on what is possible or appropriate to measure, and what the same measurements signify. Radical behaviorists, for instance, claim that we have no access to anyone's internal mental states or processes, so it is impossible to measure any such thing as a belief, attitude, or emotion. Their focus is exclusively on behavior and its causes, and unlike cognitive psychologists they do not infer cognitive states from behaviors. Likewise, where cognitively oriented researchers argue over whether various paper-and-pencil tests reveal people's underlying beliefs or attitudes.

The main point here is not simply that there is no such thing as theory-free measurement, although that is a popular view among psychologists and social scientists. Almost any measurement can be interpreted via many theories regardless of its origins, so that the same measurement may be given different meanings or evidential status by researchers using different theoretical perspectives. In fact, many controversies in psychology really are propelled by disputes over what certain data or measurements mean and imply. When conducting research or reading others', it is important not only to understand the researcher's theoretical standpoint on what is being measured, how, and why; but also how other theoretical perspectives would answer those questions and what uses they would make of the same measurements.

SUMMARY

The **confirmation bias** is a tendency to attend to instances that confirm prior hypotheses or beliefs and ignore instances that might disconfirm them. The **expectancy bias** is the inclination to explain the unexpected but not the expected, or the unnatural but not the natural.

A **construct** is a concept, usually a characteristic or property, that underlies measurement.
A construct is an **indicator** of another construct if knowing about one provides information about the other.
Indicators are **operationalizations** of their respective constructs if they give us access to some aspect of their real-world manifestation.
If an operationalization captures the totality of a construct's real-world manifestation, then we claim that it **measures** that construct.
A **variable** is an operationalization of a construct that can change.

Measurement validity and error

DEFINITIONS
Nearly every psychological perspective or theory incorporates stipulations of what are valid ways of measuring psychological phenomena and what constitutes measurement error. **Measurement error** occurs whenever measurements are influenced by something other than what the researcher intends to measure. **Validity**, on the other hand, is a general term denoting the extent to which measurement is not contaminated by error. Researchers who use randomized assignment in experimental studies or random sampling from populations distinguish between two kinds of measurement error. The first kind, **systematic error**, refers to influences on measurement that contain regularities and therefore bias the measurement outcomes. The second kind, **random error**, is not regular and therefore does not bias measurement outcomes, but nevertheless renders them less precise.

DEFINITIONS

As an example of systematic error, suppose we have a test of verbal intelligence that is written in Russian. For those of us who do not read and write Russian fluently, this test will systematically underestimate our verbal intelligence. An example of random error would be a test of verbal intelligence in the test-taker's native language, comprising 25 questions randomly chosen from a large bank of such questions. By luck of the draw, some of the 25 questions will be easier than average and some will be more difficult, but the error in this case is distributed randomly throughout the test.

DEFINITION
A related term that is often used in psychological research is **reliability**, the extent to which measurement is free of random error. That is, a measure is reliable if it produces the same result every time under identical conditions. Although reliability and validity might seem similar at first, they are not synonymous at all. Our verbal intelligence test consisting of randomly chosen questions may be valid but it will not be perfectly reliable because of random error. On the other hand, we can have perfectly reliable measures that are nevertheless invalid. A verbal intelligence test in Russian administered to people who know no Russian at all will be very reliable, since each person will get a low score no matter how many times they take the test without learning more Russian in the meantime. No reasonable assessor would claim such a test is a valid measure of verbal intelligence for those people.

There is a large variety of systematic errors that psychologists have to contend with, and because validity is such a huge topic, they often subdivide it into several specific kinds of validity to be dealt with more or less separately. We will discuss errors first, and then return to the different kinds of validity. In their influential textbook, Rosenthal & Rosnow (1991) divide systematic errors into those arising in such a way as to not affect the respondent's responses (which they call 'noninteractional') and those that do ('interactional'). **Noninteractional errors** usually are caused by the researcher or
DEFINITIONS

measuring instrument, whereas **interactional errors** may be caused either by the researcher, measuring instrument, or the respondent. The distinction is important because for noninteractional errors, the responses of the people being studied may be valid and so only the researcher needs correcting; whereas interactional errors contaminate the responses themselves and are usually more difficult to disentangle or correct.

Perhaps the most common kind of error arises from the researcher's expectations about how the findings ought to turn out. These **expectancy effects**, although pointed out as early as 1933 (by Rosenzweig), were not seriously examined until Rosenthal and his students took up the topic in the 1960s. An example of a noninteractional expectancy effect is researchers who, when hand-timing rats' progress through a maze, consistently click their stopwatches just before rats in one experimental condition reach the maze exit, but click their watches just after rats in another condition reach the exit. The result will be erroneously fast times for the former rats and slow times for the latter. An example of an interactional expectancy effect is a medical researcher who is friendlier, more optimistic, and more positive when administering a new experimental drug to patients than when administering a placebo to the control group patients. The patients in each condition might respond accordingly, and the resulting better outcomes for the experimental group will then reflect the researcher's behavior toward them rather than just the effects of the drug or placebo.

Another widespread kind of effect stems mainly from the respondent, and is sometimes called the **good subject effect** (Orne, 1962). People who participate in experiments or surveys usually are aware of the fact that they are being studied, and often they try to anticipate what the researcher is trying to study, or what the hypotheses are. Many (but not all) respondents are obedient or altruistic, and may attempt to provide researchers what they are looking for. These are adopting what Orne referred to as the 'good subject' role. A more general notion along these lines is the concept of **demand characteristics**, DEFINITIONS which refer to aspects of the tasks in a study that motivate respondents toward certain behaviors and away from others in ways that are extraneous to what is being measured. One important example of a demand characteristic is social desirability, which usually arises when people are asked to make choices in a setting where some choices clearly will make them seem nicer or better than others. Another demand characteristic that frequently occurs in survey research is a bias toward positive (or negative) responses induced by presenting the respondent with a list of questions whose response formats all point in the same direction.

A number of strategies have been proposed for eliminating systematic errors that arise from researchers and/or respondents, and the interested reader will want to consult Rosenthal & Rosnow's (1991) text and the works cited therein. Several of the most effective strategies boil down to unobtrusiveness and blindness. **Unobtrusive measures** are those that do not alert people to the fact that they are being studied or measured, thereby minimizing the likelihood that any respondent-driven errors will arise. **Blindness** means keeping the people who run the experiment and/or the respondents participating in it ignorant of the object of inquiry, of what experimental conditions respondents are assigned to (e.g., which one is the drug and which the placebo), and of the hypotheses – thereby minimizing expectancy effects.

Let us return to validity. There are two key motives for identifying different kinds of validity. First, measurements may be valid in some respects but not others, so it is incumbent on researchers to specify the way(s) in which their measures are valid. Second, many important psychological constructs are so indirectly observable or measurable that researchers can claim only quasi-validity or something approximating validity. Much of the literature on measurement validity distinguishes among three types: content validity, criterion validity, and construct validity.

Content validity (sometimes also called 'face validity') is attained when measurements refer exclusively and exhaustively to the things that the researcher intends to measure. Clearly this is a subjective claim, requiring judgments by appropriate experts or informants. Researchers could claim to have evidence for content validity in their battery of tests of artistic creativity, for instance, if a panel of artists agreed that its contents referred to artistic creativity as they understood it. The researchers' claim would be stronger yet if the panel of experts concurred that *all* aspects of artistic creativity were captured by the test battery.

Criterion validity is the degree to which a measure is corroborated by a criterion that is known to be valid already. At first glance, this might seem silly – why bother to invent a new measure if we already have a valid one? The most common reason is that an established valid measure may not be widely usable for practical or ethical reasons. Nevertheless, it may serve as a criterion against which to validate another measure that can be used widely.

In clinical psychology, diagnoses of psychological disorders by qualified clinicians are often time-consuming, expensive, and even intrusive. A paper-and-pencil test, on the other hand, is quick, inexpensive, and more private. A game that incorporates the test tasks and elements may not only be quicker and more pleasant, but even therapeutic! If the test yields the same diagnoses for clients whose disorders have already been ascertained by clinicians, then the test has shown criterion validity. Likewise, any aptitude or ability test may be said to have criterion validity if it retrospectively distinguishes between people who are known to perform well on tasks requiring the ability and those who perform poorly.

Construct validity refers to whether one measurement relates to other DEFINITIONS measurements in the ways that mirror the relationships among their respective underlying constructs. If two measures are supposedly alternative ways of measuring the same construct, then they should correspond to one another (this is called **convergent validity**). Suppose, for example, that we have two tests of eye–hand coordination: throwing a ball at a target, and tracing a figure on paper while looking at it in a mirror. If both of these tasks are indicators of the same construct, then someone who gets close to the target in the ball-throwing task should take only a short time to complete the mirror-tracing task; and likewise someone who throws wide of the target should also take a long time to trace the figure in the mirror. On the other hand, if two measures pertain to distinct constructs, then they should not covary (this is called **discriminant validity**). If musical ability is distinct from mathematical ability, for instance, then not everyone who scores high on a music test of one should score high on a mathematical test. So a test of musical ability would be said to demonstrate discriminant validity if people's scores on it did not mimic their scores on a well-established test of mathematical ability.

Now, let us return at last to random error in measurement. This is the kind of error that statistics handles, and we will deal with it at some length in this book. Because random error is *not* systematic, we may still get reasonable estimates of 'true' measurements in the presence of random errors because they tend to cancel each other out in the long run. One way to put random error in perspective with everything else we have discussed so far is to imagine taking an examination on your knowledge of quantitative methods in psychology after reading this book. No test is perfect, so this hypothetical exam might very well suffer from systematic error (such as being too difficult or too easy). However, even if there were no systematic errors, your score on the test could be influenced by a host of randomly occurring factors – be they illness, lapses in concentration, or lucky guessing on some questions. So, if we were to construct a miniature theory or model to account for your score on the exam, we would have to hypothesize that there is the score you should have obtained given your knowledge and preparatory efforts, plus the influence of random error. That is,

Your Score = True Score + Random Error.

If this model were accurate, then in a science-fiction universe where we could erase your memory of having read this book and get you to start again, if we did that over and over, your scores on the same exam should average out to your True Score. We would be assessing what is called **test–retest reliability**, which is the extent to which a measurement gives the same result when DEFINITION repeated under identical conditions. As you may have surmised, test–retest reliability may be ascertained only when tests or tasks are repeatable under identical conditions. This requires that the respondent be able to forget the previous occasion sufficiently that memory does not affect their current performance, and that there be no effect from practice.

Of course, no one can erase a person's memory that selectively, but psychological testers can present people with a batch of approximately equivalent items in a test, and obtain their average score on all of them. In a test of ability, for instance, classical test theory assumes this model of a person's score on each item:

$$\text{Item Score} = \text{True Score} + \text{Random Error.}$$

By collecting a person's scores on a large number of approximately equivalent items, the tester obtains estimates of two things: the person's true score, and the items' average departure from the estimated true score. The latter indicates the test's reliability, insofar as the smaller the average deviation away from the true score the more reliable the test is as a whole. Methods for assessing the reliability of an entire test-bank of items by analyzing the extent DEFINITION   to which people score similarly on those items are said to be assessing **internal consistency reliability**.

SUMMARY   Measurement error occurs whenever measurements are influenced by something other than what the researcher intends to measure, in other words extraneous influences.
Validity denotes the extent to which measurement is not contaminated by error.
Systematic error refers to extraneous influences on measurement that contain regularities and therefore bias the measurement outcomes.
Systematic errors that do not affect the respondent's responses are **noninteractional**, whereas those that do are **interactional**.
Demand characteristics are aspects of the tasks in a study that motivate respondents toward certain behaviors and away from others in ways that are extraneous to what is being measured.

Unobtrusive measures are those that do not alert people to the fact that they are being studied or measured.
Blindness means keeping people involved in a study ignorant of certain characteristics of it, such as the object of inquiry, the experimental conditions respondents are assigned to (e.g., which one is the drug and which the placebo), and the hypotheses.

Random error is not regular and therefore does not bias measurement outcomes, but nevertheless renders them less precise.

Reliability is the extent to which measurement is free of random error.

Test-retest reliability is the extent to which a measurement gives the same result when repeated under identical conditions.

Internal consistency reliability is the extent to which items that are supposed to measure the same construct yield similar results under identical conditions (see also construct validity).

Content validity (sometimes also called 'face validity') is attained when measurements refer exclusively and exhaustively to the things that the researcher intends to measure.

Criterion validity is the degree to which a measure is corroborated by a criterion that is known to be valid already.

Construct validity refers to whether one measurement relates to other measurements in the ways that mirror the relationships among their respective underlying constructs.

Types of measurement and varieties of data

We have already seen that in most psychological perspectives, measurements and observations are not the same as the construct being measured or observed. Theories of measurement, therefore, are accounts of the imperfect correspondence between measurements or observations and the construct itself. So far, we have concentrated mainly on the psychological aspects of measurement. Now we will borrow some useful concepts from the mathematical side.

Most of the mathematical aspects of measurement boil down to what Funtowicz & Ravetz (1990) call 'craft skills with numbers.' Measurement amounts to using symbols such as numbers to represent states or values of the construct being measured, so these skills include knowing how to use those symbols and numbers appropriately and meaningfully. For instance, those people wearing digital watches who read out the time right down to the second are displaying craft ignorance about numbers if their watches are not accurate to within one second (and they usually are nowhere nearly that accurate).

One crucial, though risky, judgment that each of us as researchers must make is what we may presume about the relationships between our measurements and the constructs to which they pertain. Suppose we try to measure people's knowledge about HIV by setting them a test with 100 multiple-choice questions designed by appropriately qualified experts on HIV. The test scores have a range from 0 to 100 correct. At first glance, it might seem that we could assume a perfect correspondence between their score and the amount of knowledge they have about HIV. Were that the case, a statement such as 'a person who scores 80 is twice as knowledgeable as someone who scores 40' would be true. After all, 80 is twice 40.

A bit of thought, however, should convince us otherwise. Even a 100-question test would be unlikely to include all relevant questions about HIV. So someone who got a score of 0 might not be totally ignorant about this topic – they just were not asked the 'right questions.' If 0 does not correspond to total ignorance, then 80 does not necessarily indicate twice as much knowledge as 40. Likewise, someone who scores 100 does not necessarily know everything about HIV.

What about a statement such as 'an increase in score from 80 to 100 indicates the same increase in knowledge as an increase from 0 to 20?' Both are 20-point gains in test score. Nevertheless, it might be more difficult to attain the knowledge required to move from a score of 80 to 100 than that required to move from 0 to 20. The statement would be plausible only if we were convinced that the 100 questions were equally difficult. This example demonstrates that it is quite possible to reduce an apparently fully quantified scale, in the harsh light of honest examination, to a scale that merely indicates whether someone knows more than someone else. It also underscores the necessity of carefully investigating the measurement properties of any scale before coming to conclusions about how it may be used.

Discrete and continuous variables

One of the most fundamental properties of any variable is whether its domain consists of distinct possible states or values, or a range of possible values.

DEFINITION   **Discrete** variables can only take particular states or values and no others. Gender is usually treated as a discrete variable with two states. An employee's rank in her or his organization's hierarchy is a discrete variable with ordered states, each corresponding to a particular rank. Many numerical variables are discrete as well. Any counted variable is a discrete variable because it can only have integer values such as 1, 5, or 23 (e.g., a family cannot have 2.3 children). The same is true of rank-order, as in the finishing order in a race – even taking ties into account.

DEFINITION   **Continuous** variables are those which (theoretically) could take any value within their range. Weight, strength, agreement with an attitude, happiness, and task motivation all are examples of continuous variables, because they are not only matters of degree but in principle infinitely fine-grained. Some confusion can arise from the fact that many variables are *made* discrete even though their underlying constructs are continuous. A widespread example is the Likert scale of agreement or disagreement, as shown in Figure 2.2. The underlying construct is degree of agreement or disagreement, even though there are only five possible values associated with the variable itself. Whereas discrete variables are accurately measurable in principle, continuous variables can only ever be measured approximately (i.e., with limited precision). In practice, therefore, *all* variables are rendered discrete because of limits to precision. So why is this distinction important?

First, how we think of a construct in terms of variables influences how we treat it statistically and what can be meaningfully said about it (hence the gibe about 2.3 children). A continuous variable can take any value in its range, so reporting fractional values (such as saying someone is 42.5 years old) may be meaningful. Second, in some areas of psychology the issue of whether a construct is inherently discrete or continuous constitutes a worthwhile topic in itself. Early work in psychophysics, for example, addressed the issue of whether the sensation of intensity (as in loudness, brightness, or heaviness) was best regarded as continuous or having discrete thresholds (see Luce, 1997, for a thoughtful reminiscence concerning that research). Recent investigations of how people categorize things or think about categories have drawn psychologists to realize that people do so using both discrete and continuous (or 'fuzzy') heuristics (for an entertaining, brief, but informative exegesis on human category heuristics, see Pinker, 1997: 308–311). Discrete categories are characterized by hard-and-fast rules about what is or is not a member of that category, whereas fuzzy categories have blurry boundaries and are described in terms of prototypical members, key features, and family-like resemblances.

Likewise, some variables that once were assumed to be discrete have been found to be continuous. Handedness is a good example. I write, draw, throw, thread a needle, and use a hammer with my left hand, but I wield a racquet, bat, computer mouse, and use chopsticks with my right hand. Am I left-handed or right-handed? I am not simply ambidextrous since in each of those activities I have a definite preference for one hand over the other. These days most researchers use measures of handedness that permit degrees of preference for the left or right.

Finally, some of our most important social issues hinge on decisions about whether a variable should be thought of in discrete or continuous terms. Racial or ethnic identity, employment status, gender, and sexual preference

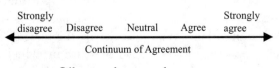

FIGURE 2.2 Likert scale example

are good examples of constructs that often are treated as if they are discrete for certain political purposes and continuous for others. Political agendas may be ubiquitous, but researchers must take responsibility, especially where politicians and bureaucrats will not, for critically assessing the status of the variables they use in their investigations. In clinical psychology, many 'pathologies' are treated as if they are discrete for diagnostic purposes (e.g., either you are clinically depressed or you are not), even when the tests or scales used to measure them use continuous variables. Educational institutions often do the same – students either fail or they do not, regardless of whether they fail by four points or 40.

In summary, the issue of whether a construct is best thought of as discrete or continuous is fundamental and often not easily settled. Luce's (1997) retrospection on unresolved matters in mathematical psychology includes the discreteness–continuity question, along with the issue of how to handle uncertainty and vagueness, in his list of thorny problems. In the next section, on levels of measurement, we will revisit this issue in the form of constructs that seem to be both categories and continuous scales at the same time.

Levels and types of measurement

Not only do we need to decide whether a variable is best thought of as discrete or continuous, but also what **level of measurement** is involved. The main reason for this is so that we may ascertain what constitutes meaningful or appropriate uses of our data, and what kinds of questions may be answered with those data.

The conventional wisdom in psychological research is that there are four
DEFINITIONS   levels of measurement:

- **Nominal**, in which a variable has categories or states that differ in kind but not in order or degree;
- **Ordinal**, in which a variable has states or ranks that are ordered but whose differences are not quantifiable;
- **Interval**, in which a variable has values on a scale whose differences are quantifiable but which lacks a true zero-point;
- **Ratio**, in which the differences are quantifiable and the scale has a true zero-point.

Nominal variables are by definition discrete. The simplest kind is a binary variable that has two categories: presence and absence. More complicated nominal variables have more categories, and they may also have nested categories, i.e., where one category contains others. We could classify the teachers at a university according to which department or division they are in, which would give us a nominal variable with departments as the categories. Suppose that every department also is assigned to one faculty. Then departments are nested inside faculties, so the entire framework has two levels. We now have two nominal variables, faculty and department, with the former containing the latter.

Constructing nominal variables is often more difficult than it seems. The most important criteria to bear in mind are these:

- *Exhaustiveness*: Do the categories cover all conceivable cases?
- *Exclusiveness*: Are the categories unambiguously distinct, or do they overlap?
- *Appropriate specificity*: Are the categories as fine-grained as they need to be, without being hair-splitting?

In many research situations, it seems tempting or even practical to sacrifice exhaustiveness, especially when we do not know all of the possible categories in advance or when there are a great many of them. The most common method of truncating an undetermined or lengthy list of categories is to stick a **catch-all** category at the end, labeled 'Other' or 'Miscellaneous.' However, we take two risks in doing this. One is that the catch-all category will obscure important differences among cases that it includes. The second risk arises when the catch-all category is used as one of the alternatives that may be chosen by the respondent in answering a question, and stems from what is called the 'catch-all underestimation bias,' or CAUB (Fischhoff, Slovic & Lichtenstein, 1978). This is a tendency for people to recall fewer instances or to underestimate the likelihood of the catch-all option in comparison with explicitly listed options.

The issue of appropriate specificity is related to the CAUB problem. People are more likely to recall events that are explicitly represented in a list of alternatives than those that are not (Tversky & Koehler, 1994). Likewise, unpacking a category into specific subcategories may remind people of possibilities they have overlooked. Consequently, our ability to recall instances of some category may be boosted by unpacking that category into subcategories. For example, if people are asked how many times they have been dishonest in the past month, they will generally remember fewer instances than if you ask them how many times in the past month they have lied, stolen anything, concealed anything from someone, led someone to believe something that was not true, and so forth. However, the solution is not always to provide exhaustive lists of specific alternatives. Instead, we need to take specificity into account when drawing inferences about people's recollections of events, especially if we are comparing events or different studies.

Since many of the categories that humans use in natural language are 'fuzzy' in the sense that they have blurry boundaries and overlap with one another, constructing exclusive categories is not always easy and may seem contrived. Consider the difficulties involved in deciding whether a person's death from a self-inflicted gunshot wound while under the influence of alcohol is a suicide, a self-injury without an intention to die, or an accident. Even if we had a great deal of information about the person's emotional state, thoughts, and actions at the time, it is quite possible that we would still be undecided about how to classify this event.

The problems of category exclusiveness and ensuring that there is one category per case are related, but not identical. Exclusive categories are necessary but not sufficient to ensure that there is one category per case. For instance, in Huston *et al.*'s (1981) study of who was likely to intervene in a violent crime incident, the investigators classified respondents according to whether they had received emergency training or not. The classification scheme they used included first aid, life-saving, self-defense, police, and medical. The potential problem here is not that these categories overlap but that one person may have received more than one of these kinds of training.

Now let us turn to **ordinal** variables. Although it makes almost no difference in how we analyze ordinal data, there are two rather distinct ways of thinking about these variables. One is in terms of ordinal categories, which are ordered from lowest to highest. For example, the widely-used Likert-style format indicating degree of agreement or disagreement with a statement is a categorical ordinal scale because it places respondents in one of five ordered categories: strongly agree, agree, undecided, disagree, or strongly disagree. The other, more general way is in terms of rank-ordering cases from lowest to highest, as in the finishing order of a race. The main reason for mentioning this distinction now is to avoid confusion later on, since some statistical techniques refer to values on an ordinal scale and others to 'ranks.'

Ordinal variables (and their more quantifiable cousins) may be further divided into **bipolar** and **monopolar** variables. The agree–disagree format is an example of a bipolar variable, because it has two opposite ends with a 'neutral' midpoint. The so-called 'bipolar personality disorder' of manic depression is an example of a bipolar construct, ranging from extreme mania to extreme depression. Monopolar variables, on the other hand, range from low to high on attributes that are unidirectional. A variable measuring degree of anxiety that ranges from 'low' to 'very high' is an example of a monopolar variable.

Bipolar variables are very popular, but they are also more easily misused than monopolar ones. First, the researcher must be sure that the opposite poles really should be located on the one dimension and not separate dimensions. There have been extensive debates in psychology over such issues as whether happiness and unhappiness require separate monopolar rating scales, or whether masculine–feminine is a bipolar or two-dimensional construct. Second, the researcher should ensure that the midpoint on these scales has only one meaning for respondents. It is possible for someone to place themselves at the midpoint of an agree–disagree scale because they have no opinion on the issue concerned, or because they are in great conflict and therefore ambivalent about it, or because they are genuinely balanced between agreement and disagreement. If we anticipate getting two or more of these responses from people, then we should provide separate response categories for them or filter those responses out with a prior question.

All ordinal variables, whether monopolar or bipolar, must have an unambiguous and agreed-upon ordering of their response categories. For instance, in a variable designed to measure level of satisfaction with a service, respondents might not agree on the order among options that are too similar, such as 'so-so' versus 'adequate' versus 'satisfactory.' Options with similar meanings should therefore be avoided when constructing these scales.

Likewise, specificity and vagueness may need to be taken into account. Experimental studies of the meanings people attach to probability phrases such as 'very likely' or 'low probability' (e.g., Wallsten *et al.* 1986) have found that these phrases usually refer to a range of probabilities, and the ranges may overlap and differ in width. A term such as 'possible' is so vague for many people that it encompasses probabilities from nearly 0 to nearly 1, so it is useless as a response option. The lesson to be learned here is to try to ensure that response categories not only have distinct meanings but are similar in their specificity.

Finally, the meanings of response categories may vary considerably with context. 'Very often' could mean more than twice in one year when referring to earthquakes on the Australian East Coast but not in New Zealand, and certainly not when referring to how frequently citizens of either country brush their teeth. One way around this problem is to standardize and specify the context by providing a **reference frame** and **anchors**.

Suppose we want to evaluate the performance of public transport bus drivers, and we are designing a question to elicit customers' perceptions of their driving performance. If we simply ask them 'How skillful is X as a driver on this route?' and request them to choose a response on an ordinal scale ranging from 'very unskillful' to 'very skillful,' we will be unable to tell what *reference frame* the passengers have used in answering this question. Skill, after all, may be judged with reference to:

- what they expect,
- the average bus driver,
- the average automobile driver,
- their ideal driver,
- their beliefs about what is adequate driving skill,
- other bus drivers they have known, etc.

A better version of this question would include the references of our choice in the question and appropriate *anchors* within the scale. For instance, we could ask 'Compared to other bus drivers you have known, how skillful is X as a driver on this route?', and then incorporate anchors in the scale, such as 'About average in skill' or 'Less skillful than any of them.'

The ordered categories in an ordinal scale usually denote differences in magnitude or intensity, as in the illustrations thus far. Another kind of ordering is *cumulative* or inclusive, so that someone who is described by one category is also described by the categories that lie below it. For instance, someone who has completed secondary schooling also has completed primary schooling, but not vice versa. This kind of scale is called a **Guttman scale**, although examples of them had been used before Guttman described their properties in the 1940s. An example that commonly occurs in educational psychology and testing generally is a scale composed of several questions that differ in difficulty. People who answer a particular question correctly should answer all the less difficult questions correctly too. This kind of scaling in educational testing was further elaborated by Rasch in the 1960s and others since then.

DEFINITION

By analyzing the response patterns to a set of items, a research may determine whether they form a cumulative scale. We won't plumb the details of that analysis here, but instead will settle for an appreciation of what is involved through a simple example. Imagine investigating people's attitudes about capital punishment, and asking them whether they would prefer that the death penalty be legally available for various criminal offenses. If all of our respondents believe that the death penalty should be available only for the most serious crimes and if they also agree on which crimes in our list are more serious than others, then we should be able to find a cumulative scaling pattern in their responses. For illustration, consider this very short list: multiple homicides, one homicide, multiple rapes. If our respondents agree that this list is ordered from the most grave offense downward, then each should provide one of response patterns 1–4 in Table 2.1. All of the other possible patterns would disconfirm the cumulative scaling hypothesis.

TABLE 2.1 Response patterns

Pattern	> 1 homicide	1 homocide	> 1 rape	
1	No	No	No	
2	Yes	No	No	Confirm
3	Yes	Yes	No	scaling
4	Yes	Yes	Yes	
5	No	Yes	Yes	
6	Yes	No	Yes	Disconfirm
7	No	No	Yes	scaling
8	No	Yes	No	

Sometimes we would like to treat a construct as if it was both a scale and a category at the same time. Many clinical diagnostic constructs have this property because they are matters of degree and therefore measurable by using scales. Depression is an example, because even though people may be depressed to a greater or lesser degree, certain cutoff points on indicators of depression must be exceeded before someone is diagnosed as 'clinically' depressed. Under these conditions, it is worthwhile to think of ordinary scales in a cumulative way, by considering the set of people who score at least as high as each of the points on the scale. The further up the scale we go, the smaller (and therefore more exclusive) the set of people we will find. As we move down the scale, we include more and more people. To distinguish this viewpoint from the Guttman scale, we may refer to it as the **cumulative scale** view- DEFINITION
point. By way of illustration, suppose we ask 150 people to indicate their level of subjective fear of snakes on the five-point scale shown in the next table, and then we ask them to do the same for their fear of dogs. The number of responses in each category is displayed in the leftmost two columns.

The right-hand columns with the boldfaced numbers redisplay the same information from a cumulative scale point of view. Each level is associated with a set of people who have scored at least as high as that level. For instance, 60 people have indicated that they fear dogs at least at a Moderate level. If a specialist in phobias were to say that anyone who expressed at least a 'severe' fear level was phobic, then we could immediately see that there are three times as many snake phobics in this sample as dog phobics (75 vs. 25). In fact, at any level we care to choose, snake fear is a *more inclusive phenomenon* than dog fear, since the number of people whose snake fear is a certain level or higher is greater than the number of people whose dog fear is the same level or higher. So an advantage of the cumulative scale view is that we are able to treat fear as if it is both a category and a scale, thereby enabling us to address questions such as whether more people fear snakes than dogs.

Finally, let us consider **interval** and **ratio** levels of measurement. We have already seen that an interval level of measurement requires that we have

TABLE 2.2 Snake and dog fears

Fear level	Number at each level		**Cumulative viewpoint**		
	snakes	dogs	snakes	dogs	
Profound	25	5	**25**	**5**	**at least Profound**
Severe	50	20	**75**	**25**	**at least Severe**
Moderate	45	35	**120**	**60**	**at least Moderate**
Slight	20	40	**140**	**100**	**at least Slight**
Not at all	10	50	**150**	**150**	

intervals between scale values that are quantifiable and therefore comparable. Conventionally, the intervals are equal, which entails that they have a *linear relationship* with their underlying construct. The percentage of questions a student answers correctly on an exam, for instance, has this property if we agree that the underlying construct is quantity of knowledge about the subject matter of the exam and all of the questions are equally weighted.

The issue of whether we can ascertain when we have interval-level measurement has provoked debates in many areas in psychology. A brief review of the more common pitfalls in these debates may help you in your own research and in critically assessing others' efforts. First, it is not always clear that we can establish whether there is a simple linear relationship between our constructs and our measures. Revisiting our example of the percentage of correct exam answers, someone could take a cumulative scale viewpoint and point out that whereas 30 members of the class got at least 60% of the questions correct, 20 got 70% correct and only seven got 80% correct. If instead of mere quantity of correct answers, we consider difficulty as well, we might conclude that percentage of correct questions is not linearly related to knowledge of (more difficult) subject material after all. Likewise, as in the earlier HIV exam example, we might want to investigate whether some questions are more difficult than others.

It is also easy to confuse the properties of the numbers on a scale with the scale's measurement properties. A famous suggestion that dates from 1738 illustrates this point quite well. The suggestion by Daniel Bernoulli hinges on the observation that increasing a poverty-stricken person's wealth by $100 is much more highly valued by that person than increasing a billionaire's wealth by $100. People's subjective valuation of money declines with increasing wealth. Even though the monetary scale has equal intervals, it is not linearly related to people's subjective valuation and therefore *as a measure of subjective utility*, money does not provide an equal-interval measure.

The HIV examination example discussed earlier also highlighted a frequently misunderstood distinction between having a zero on a scale and having that zero correspond to a true zero in the construct. While there is nothing wrong with saying that someone got no questions correct on an exam, we usually cannot infer from this that they know nothing about the subject. The same is true of many psychological scales, such as self-esteem or depression. Zero scores on such scales do not entitle us to conclude that someone has no self-esteem or zero depression.

That said, it is also worth bearing in mind that some scales may have an absolute zero and yet be ordinal. Psychological state and trait questionnaires have legions of items whose response formats are something like 'Never,' 'Rarely,' 'Sometimes,' 'Frequently.' Moreover, some counted data must be coded in unequal intervals for practical or ethical reasons. A typical case is a question about drug usage, in which a respondent is asked to indicate how many times they have used a particular drug: 'Never,' 'Once,' '2–4 times,' and 'more than 4 times.' Neither of these scales has equal intervals, but both have true zeroes.

How do researchers decide what level of measurement they can or should use? To some extent they tailor their variables to the hypotheses they want to test or the questions they want to answer. Many hypotheses and research questions contain implicit assumptions or requirements about measurement. A good researcher will figure out what these are before constructing a measurement instrument.

Some examples may help illustrate the issues involved. Suppose we are interested in whether women and men are differentially treated in the engineering profession. Here are some of the ways in which we might formulate hypotheses about this discrimination:

1. Women are underrepresented in engineering.
2. Female engineers tend to have lower status than male engineers.
3. Female engineers tend to earn less than male engineers.

What kind of variable do we need for the first hypothesis? One thing we could do would be to compare the percentage of women in the labor force who are engineers and compare that with the percentage of men in the labor force who are engineers. We could contrast that with similar comparisons in other professions. In either case, we just need a variable that measures whether an employed person is an engineer or not. That is a nominal variable, since it has two categories (Engineer, Not engineer) which are not ordered.

The second hypothesis has a key concept, 'status.' Since there are higher and lower-status positions, we know that we must measure status at least at the ordinal level. We would find that there are standard designations for engineers' occupational positions that distinguish between the lower and higher levels in the profession. Or we might want to construct a measure based on public perceptions of the status of engineers. That is all we need if we want only to determine whether females occupy lower-status positions than males.

If we wanted to go further and ask 'how much lower?' then we would need an interval- or ratio-level measure of status. Unfortunately, we would find that engineer grades form only an ordinal-level scale. We would have to conclude that 'how much lower?' cannot be meaningfully addressed with the measure of status available. The third hypothesis also requires only an ordinal scale for earnings. But in this case if we want to ask 'how much less?' perhaps we can get an answer if we are willing to use salary as a measure of status.

SUMMARY

Discrete variables can only take particular states or values and no others.
Continuous variables are those which (theoretically, at least) could take any value over their range.

The conventional four **levels of measurement** are:
- **Nominal**, in which a variable has categories or states that differ in kind but not in order or degree;
- **Ordinal**, in which a variable has states or ranks that are ordered but whose differences are not quantifiable;
- **Interval**, in which a variable has values on a scale whose differences are quantifiable but which lacks a true zero-point;
- **Ratio**, in which the differences are quantifiable and the scale has a true zero point.

In a **Guttman scale**, anyone who is described by one category also is described by the categories that lie below it.
In the **cumulative scale** viewpoint, each value on a scale is associated with the number of people who have scored as high as that level or higher.

Missing data, absent people, and the fallacy of false precision

When data are only partly known or imprecise, there is an understandable temptation to represent them as if they are nevertheless fully known and precise. In the psychology of judgment under uncertainty, several researchers have studied what they call 'ambiguity aversion' (Ellsberg, 1961; Einhorn & Hogarth, 1985), which is a tendency for people to prefer precise information over imprecise information, even when imprecision is more realistic. Ambiguity aversion has been found not only in hypothetical situations but also in gambles with real payoffs, and even after people are exposed to written arguments persuading them not to indulge in it.

Aversion to imprecision of any kind manifests itself at the institutional and organizational levels as well. Some organizational agendas also promote illusory precision because it makes the organization appear to be in control and more authoritative (Downs, 1966; Linnerooth, 1984). As the scientific policy analysts Funtowicz & Ravetz (1990: 11) point out, the 'simplest, and still most common response of both the decision-makers and the public is to demand at least the appearance of certainty. The scientific advisors are under severe pressure to provide a single number, regardless of their private reservations.'

Unfortunately, once data are recorded as if they were precise, any further analysis of them will treat them as if they actually are precise. Sloppy estimates will appear as if they are error-free. Forecasts or decisions based on them will be made with greater confidence than is warranted, and so on. I refer to this trap as the 'fallacy of false precision' (Smithson, 1990). Avoiding false precision entails recording both qualitative and quantitative information about uncertainty, including the likely causes of it, on a case-by-case basis.

Missing data may arise from a variety of causes, especially in the early stages of a research project when measures are still being refined and data collection methods are most error-prone. Many popular statistical packages designate missing data with only one symbol, but this is often inadequate. The following list contains the most common reasons why data end up missing. Recording the type and cause of missing data enables a researcher to ascertain whether there is any pattern or regularity in missing data that might invalidate their measurements or conclusions.

- Respondent refused to answer.
- Question is not applicable to respondent.
- Respondent did not understand the question or task.
- Respondent's answer does not fit any available categories.
- Respondent's answer varies among categories depending on circumstances.
- Respondent's answer is incomprehensible.
- The data were lost or misrepresented.

Not only can data go missing, so can people. Participants in experiments may drop out before the conclusion of the study, potential respondents may refuse to be interviewed for a survey, and former patients may be impossible to track down for follow-up studies. Rather than ignoring these issues, patterns in missing data and/or missing people should be studied and understood. There are at least two reasons for doing so. The most common reason is that missing data may bias the findings of a study, and any conscientious researcher will want to ascertain whether that is a possibility. A typical example is a longitudinal study of cognitive impairment in elderly Japanese (Liang *et al.*, 1996), in which the researchers found that although urban residents were more likely than rural residents to drop out of the study, the dropouts did not differ from the stayers in mental or physical health.

The second reason for analyzing missing data patterns is that sometimes they may constitute an important research finding in themselves. For instance, in a social psychological study of gender solidarity in organizations, Fajak & Haslam (1998) presented members of an organization with hypothetical organizational charts in which people were identified by gender and position, and asked who should be promoted if a position at a certain level became vacant. They analyzed the patterns of *refusals to nominate a candidate*, as part of the evidence of when a participant identified with or declined to identify with their own gender.

Questions and exercises

Q.2.1. In an educational psychological study, the amount of time each participant spent reading the material in preparation for a test was recorded to measure motivation. What is the *construct* in this study?

Q.2.2. Give an example of systematic error in measurement. Give an example of random error in measurement.

Q.2.3. What kind of effect is likely to contaminate people's responses to the following question:
'How much money did you donate to charities during that last financial year?'

Q.2.4. Why is having a rat run the same maze several times *not* a good assessment of test–retest reliability?

Q.2.5. A well-known statistics textbook author was criticized for using the 'number of hairs on a goat' as an example of a continuous variable. He corrected this mistake in a later edition. Why was the criticism correct?

Q.2.6. Which is true of the variable reaction-time, measured in milliseconds?

(a) It is continuous.
(b) It is discrete.
(c) It has ordinal-level measurement.
(d) It has nominal-level measurement.
(e) It has interval-level measurement.

Q.2.7. For what purpose(s) would your score on a statistics exam have interval-level measurement? For what purpose(s) would it have ratio-level measurement?

Q.2.8. Which is true about 'self-esteem as measured by how many out of 10 positively worded statements about the self a person agrees with?'

(a) It is continuous.
(b) It can never equal 0.
(c) It has interval-level measurement.
(d) It has ordinal-level measurement.
(e) It has nominal-level measurement.

Q.2.9. Which of the following variables are discrete and which continuous?

    (a) Religious denomination.
    (b) The temperature of a person's palm.
    (c) Response time in a test of reflexes.
    (d) Number of successes in a series of puzzles.
    (e) Subjectively judged distance from self to an object.

Q.2.10. From the standpoint of measurement error, what is problematic with this question?
'What was your income during the most recent financial year?'

Exploring, Describing, Displaying, and Summarizing

CONTENTS

Exploration, description, display, and integrity

Tables, charts, graphs, and statistical summaries are very popular ways of displaying and communicating data. They are also widely misused. In this chapter, we're going to start with simple statistical and graphical displays and progress to more sophisticated techniques, with examples of the good, bad, and ugly in graphical and statistical practice. Here, psychology gives you an advantage over most other fields, because knowing how perception works and how the mind interprets images is exactly what you need to understand why some ways of displaying information 'work' and others don't. You will also acquire some dangerous knowledge about how to deceive others with graphical gimmickry, but I'm sure that this knowledge is in safe hands.

It has been fashionable at various times to claim that statistics can be found and shaped for any rhetorical purpose whatsoever. A typically postmodernist position would have it that statistical arguments are just another form of rhetoric, whose main work is the legitimization of moral discourse. The essence of this position is nothing new. It goes back at least as far as Disraeli's frequently quoted admonition that there are 'lies, damned lies, and statistics,' and is motivated by a suspicion that statistics are more often used to bamboozle us than to help us see things clearly.

While this suspicion is not without foundation, we should not be lured by it into the simple cynical relativism implicit in such slogans as 'anything goes' nor cynical pragmatism as in 'all's fair in love and war.' In psychology, as in any other professional or scholarly discipline, we owe a duty of care to one another to speak and write clearly and truthfully, and to display data as clearly and truthfully as possible. Such practices are hallmarks of intellectual integrity, and they signal to other professionals and laypeople alike that we are trustworthy.

Good uses of statistics, tables and graphs include:

- Exploring and understanding patterns in data.
- Conveying such patterns accurately and honestly to others.
- Providing alternative ways of understanding the same data.

Less laudable or outright bad uses include:

- Impressing people with gee-whiz graphics or complex tables.
- Using graphs, tables, or statistics as a rhetorical device for solely purposes of persuasion.
- Deliberate deception.

Once we get more than a handful of cases or a few variables, almost all of us require mental assistance in seeing the forest for the trees. All of the tools and techniques we'll cover in this chapter are potential allies in our quest for discovering, interpreting, and communicating patterns in our data. We've already seen that for some purposes, numbers help us think more clearly than words. It should come as no surprise that in some instances pictures help us more than numbers, and summaries help more than a mountain of data.

We will start with discrete variables, and then move to continuous ones. We will introduce ways of displaying and describing data that make use of tables, graphs, and statistical summaries. We'll also find that, even though there are guidelines for appropriate and effective uses of these techniques, choosing the best one requires us to exercise judgment and understanding. What is best for exploring, discovering, and understanding aspects of data may not always be best for communicating about them to others, but most of the time these two purposes coincide. It is fairly likely that a table, graph, or other summary that enables you to really understand your own data will help other people understand it too.

Describing data from a nominal variable

DATA
FILENAME
HEART

Let's begin with the simplest kind of variable: a discrete variable with only two categories. Suppose we are conducting a study of 50 heart patients, and we want to report the number of females and males in our sample. We could simply state that there are 12 females and 38 males. If we wanted to convey information about the percentages of each, we could add that 24% of the sample are females and 76% are males.

That kind of description often is fine for variables that have only a few categories. For more than four or five categories, however, it becomes cumbersome and a frequency distribution table often works better. A **frequency distribution** presents the categories of a variable (or scores, for a quantitative variable) and the frequency with which each occurs. The frequency distribution table (Table 3.1) shows the number and percentages of males and females from our data set. Even though there are only two categories, this table sets out the information in a manner that is clearer and stands out more than simply burying it in the middle of a sentence.

DEFINITION

The question of whether to use frequencies or percentages is not as easily answered as it might seem. There are some reasonable guidelines, but they cannot be treated as hard-and-fast rules. First, we should not use percentages to refer to very small numbers of cases. An old journalist's trick is to blare a headline such as 'Murder Rate Up by 200%!' This sounds frightening enough until we realize that there was one murder last year and there were three this year. After all, if there was *no* murder last year then the headliner could claim that murders had increased infinitely many times. The antidote for this misleading practice is to insist that both frequencies and percentages are reported

TABLE 3.1 Frequency distribution of gender

Value	Frequency	Percentage
Female	12	24%
Male	38	76%
Total	50	100%

when it is appropriate to use percentages at all. How many cases are required before we can use percentages? Some authorities say at least 100 cases, but I have found that percentages may be usefully employed when there are as few as 20 or 30 cases, as long as frequencies are reported along with them.

Merely using frequencies without percentages can be misleading too, mainly when comparisons are being made. Suppose the Aardvark Company boasts that it employs twice as many female managers as Badger Pty. Ltd. does. This might sound impressive, until we find out that Aardvark happens to have three times as many managers as Badger. In reality, Badger employs a higher percentage of managers who are female than Aardvark! In making comparisons, percentages are essential.

Do we need a chart or graph for displaying the information in the frequency distribution table above? Perhaps not, but let's see. There are a little more than three times as many males as females in this sample. Did that fact leap out at you from the table or the earlier verbal description? If not, a bar chart may help. A **bar chart** is used for displaying the frequency distribution of a   DEFINITION nominal variable. The height of the bars represents the frequency of occurrence for each category. The bars should be separated by space between them to indicate that the variable's categories are not really 'adjacent' to one another or ordered in any particular way. If you examine the bar chart in Figure 3.1, you will see that you don't have to do any conscious mental arithmetic to see that the bar for the males is about three times longer than the one for the females; your visual acuity does it all for you.

Bar charts have their critics, among them some of the highest authorities on graphical techniques. Edward Tufte (1983: 96), for instance, points out that a labeled, shaded bar chart like the one shown above represents the same data in six different ways:

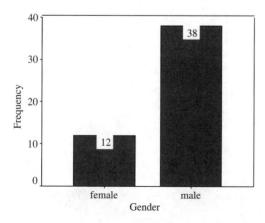

FIGURE 3.1 Bar chart of gender. This graph was done using SPSS

1. The height of the left line on each bar.
2. The height of the right line.
3. The altitude of the top horizontal line.
4. The height of the shading.
5. The position (not the content) of the number at the top of the bar.
6. The number itself.

He has a valid point – surely we don't need all six of these elements in every bar chart, and some of them really are mere conventions. On the other hand, it does seem reasonable to convey both position and number, since they trigger quite different kinds of mental processes. Figure 3.2 presents a less 'redundant' graph that is similar to the 'dot chart' invented by William Cleveland (1985), and it conveys the same information as the bar chart does without wasting nearly as much ink.

When a variable has only a few categories, bar charts may not be needed. A table or even just reporting frequencies in a sentence will do just as well for many purposes. Bar charts (or dot charts) become more useful when the variable has many categories, particularly when the categories are meaningfully grouped. For example, the next frequency distribution table (Table 3.2) shows how 484 people responded to the question 'Where would you go or who would you turn to for help in an emergency?' Their answers were sorted into 20 categories, so we have to search through the table before we can even identify where most of the respondents placed themselves.

DATA
FILENAME
SUICIDE

Compare that with the chart in Figure 3.3, which is a bar chart turned on its side. Several patterns are immediately evident in this chart. We can immediately see that the most popular response is 'Ambulance/hospital,' but it is also clear that a sizeable number of respondents would turn to family or friends.

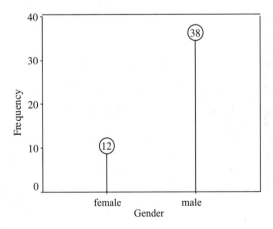

FIGURE 3.2 Dot chart of gender

TABLE 3.2 Where to go for help

Category	Frequency
Offspring	19
Spouse	49
Parent	44
Sibling	35
Grandparent	5
Aunt/uncle	10
Cousin	2
Other relative	10
Unspecified relative	24
Friend	56
No one	7
Solitary action	2
Minister of religion	18
Counsellor	2
Welfare agency	6
Ambulance/hospital	153
Police	22
DCS, ADC	7
Other	13

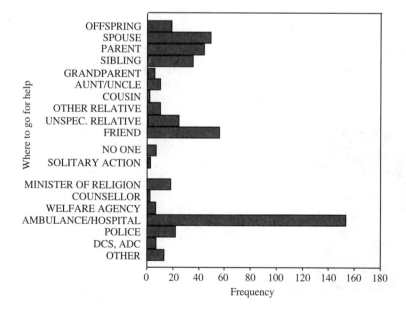

FIGURE 3.3 Bar chart of help. This graph was done using SPSS

SUMMARY

A **frequency distribution** presents the categories of a variable (or scores, for a quantitative variable) and the frequency with which each occurs.

A **bar chart** is used for displaying the frequency distribution of a nominal variable. The height of the bars represents the frequency of occurrence for each category. The bars should be separated by space between them to indicate that the variable's categories are not really 'adjacent' to one another or ordered in any particular way.

Bar charts versus alternatives

DEFINITION

There are several popular alternatives to and embellishments of the bar chart. The most widely used alternative is the pie chart. A **pie chart** conveys the same information as a bar chart, but the width of the pie wedges is used instead of bar heights to represent frequency. Generally, the bar chart is easier for people to judge accurately because people are better judges of lengths than angles. Pie charts, and especially tilted pie charts, are avoided by professional statisticians and researchers who wish to convey their data clearly. The next example (Figure 3.4) illustrates why.

DATA
FILENAME
STAFF

The chart is supposed to convey the numbers of staff in each of five departments at a small university. Even though there are only five categories in the variable on which this pie chart is based, it is difficult to ascertain which of them contains the largest number of staff, which the second largest, and so on. As the number of categories increases, pie charts become less likely than bar charts to adequately convey frequency information. Redisplayed in a bar chart, the differences between the number of staff in each department are readily apparent (Figure 3.5). It is easy to see that Sociology has the most staff, followed by Biology and Computer Science, then Psychology, and then Anthropology.

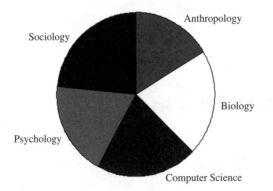

FIGURE 3.4 Pie chart of staff in departments. This graph was done using SPSS

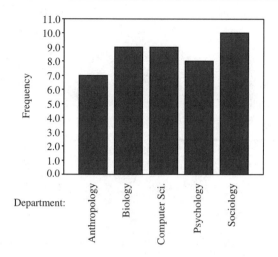

FIGURE 3.5 Bar chart of staff in departments. This graph was done using SPSS

Popular embellishments of bar charts include using different colors or different fill patterns for the bars and rendering the bars in three dimensions. The 3D effects contribute nothing, and may obscure the true relative heights of the bars. Different fill patterns may make identical bars appear to have different widths, as the two pairs in Figure 3.6 illustrate. Even different colors may produce this effect, so color-coding of bars should be done cautiously.

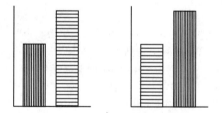

FIGURE 3.6 Effects of fill patterns on bars

The statistician William Cleveland has published two books (1985, 1993) on graphical methods for statistics. His empirical research on the accuracy with which people judge relative quantities as depicted graphically suggested the hierarchy of methods in the next list. A bar chart style of display is best, while area is worse, volume worse still, and color worst of all. By way of illustration in the figure below, one line is half the length of the other; one angle is half the other; one square has half the area of the other, and so on.

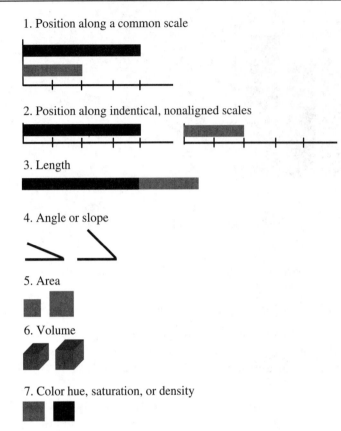

1. Position along a common scale

2. Position along indentical, nonaligned scales

3. Length

4. Angle or slope

5. Area

6. Volume

7. Color hue, saturation, or density

Cleveland's ranking of graphical comparisons

Cleveland's rankings notwithstanding, there are important uses for color and shading in graphs. Perhaps the best example of a situation where using different colors for bars is justified is when we want to superimpose frequency distributions for the same variable from two or more groups of people. We need a way of distinguishing the groups, and assigning each a particular color

DATA

FILENAME

SUICIDE

works well. The next bar chart (Figure 3.7) shows percentages of men and women from our survey falling into the various categories of 'employment status.'

This graph causes the main differences between the men and women to stand out:

- The percentage of permanently employed men is about twice that of women.
- The same is true of unemployed people.
- Nearly the reverse is true of casual employees.
- Only women identify themselves as housewives.

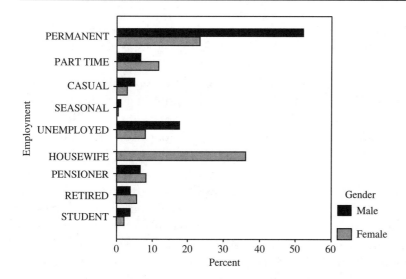

FIGURE 3.7 Male and female employment statuses

How to lie with graphs: Lesson 1

Perhaps because area, volume, and color can mislead the eye, they are often used to make deceptive charts. Sometimes this is done deliberately, but quite often deceptive charts are constructed out of ignorance rather than malice. Figure 3.8 shows one of the most common ploys, which is to use the height of two- or three-dimensional objects to represent magnitude. These perfume bottles have height-ratios of $3:2:1$, but their areas have ratios of $9:4:1$, and if we think of them as three-dimensional then their volumes have ratios

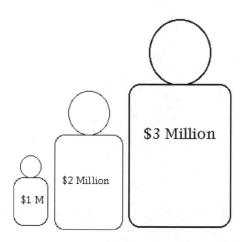

FIGURE 3.8 Three-dimensional perfume sales

of 81:16:1! Compare these misleading bottles with the honest bars in Figure 3.9. The 3:2:1 ratio is conveyed by their heights *and* areas, since they each have the same width.

Three-dimensional perspective lends itself to a great assortment of trickery. Most of these use slant, shape, and tilt cues that we utilize for making sense out of two-dimensional representations of perspective. Tufte's (1983) book includes a wonderful catalog of examples, but I'll adapt just one of them to illustrate the point. If we want to exaggerate or de-emphasize the 3:2:1 ratio in the 'perfume sales' graph, we may arrange the graph so that the bars march away from or toward us in ascending order, as Figure 3.10 shows. This graph lacks proper perspective because of the kind of projection used, one employed in many computer packages. That projection is called 'isometric,' which means that all of the elements are represented with their actual measurements instead of according to the rules of perspective. So the bars in both graphs are identical, but the tallest bar seems considerably taller and thicker in the right-hand graph. Likewise, the shortest bar seems shorter and thinner in the right-hand graph, so the net effect is to make the increase seem greater in that graph.

If we do incorporate perspective, we obtain graphs like those in Figure 3.11. It helps make the graphs more honest, but problems still arise because of biases in our judgments of slope and slant. Many people find, for instance, that the increase does not look linear in the right-hand graph.

The upshot is that we should avoid 'three-dimensional' graphs unless they are essential for conveying information, and even then we should use them very cautiously. Any three-dimensional graph should be tried from a variety of viewpoints to ensure that the viewer does not get invalidly different impressions about the data depending on viewpoint.

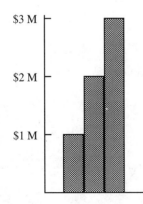

FIGURE 3.9 Two-dimensional perfume sales

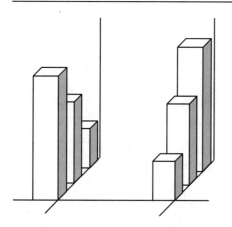

FIGURE 3.10 Bars with no perspective

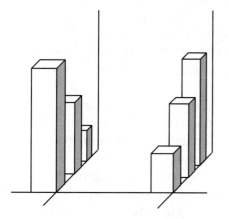

FIGURE 3.11 Bars with perspective

Describing an ordinal variable

Frequency distributions for ordinal variables give us one more matter to keep track of, which is the fact that they have an ordered scale. Frequency distribution tables for ordinal categorical variables usually start with the lowest value in the first row of the table and end with the highest value in the last row, although that is merely a convention. For example, Table 3.3 shows a frequency distribution for a ordinal categorical variable called 'Exercise.' The 50 heart patients in this study were classified according to the following levels of exercise:

DATA
FILENAME
HEART

　　0 = None　1 = Light　2 = Moderate　3 = Heavy

TABLE 3.3 Exercise levels

Level	Frequency	Percentage	Cumulative frequency	Cumulative percentage
0 = None	19	38%	19	38%
1 = Light	20	40%	39	78%
2 = Moderate	9	18%	48	96%
3 = Heavy	2	4%	50	100%
Total	50	100%		

DEFINITION

DEFINITION

DEFINITION

This table also contains two columns, 'cumulative frequency' and 'cumulative percentage,' that were not in the frequency tables for nominal variables. These quantities make up what is called a **cumulative frequency distribution**. The **cumulative frequency** associated with a particular score on a variable is the number of occurrences that are at or below that score. For instance, the cumulative frequency associated with Light exercise is 39 because 20 people were classified as Light exercisers and 19 as engaging in None. The **cumulative percentage** is the percentage of all occurrences that are at or below that score. Thus, the cumulative percentage for Light exercise is 78% (that is, 39 is 78% of 50).

What about graphing the distribution of an ordinal variable? The most popular choice for a graph under these circumstances is a histogram. A **histogram** is used for displaying the frequency distribution of an ordinal variable or a continuous one whose scale has been divided into intervals. It is similar to a bar chart, but the bars have no space between them, indicating that they are in a fixed order. The area of the bars is proportional to the number of cases they represent. In our example (Figure 3.12), the bars 0, 1, 2, and 3 are ordered from left to right.

Describing a quantifiable variable

Frequency distributions for quantifiable variables pose some more challenges but also more opportunities to exercise judgment. Since the cases do not fall into categories, how do we effectively display the data without tediously listing each case? Let's deal with frequency distributions first. The most popular way of displaying a frequency distribution for a quantifiable variable is very similar to the layout for an ordinal one. In those instances where the scale has relatively few values, in fact, the layout is identical.

When there are a lot of values on the scale, we may need to make two decisions. The first one is whether to truncate the scale. As an example, consider the problem of showing the frequency distribution of 465 responses to the question 'In the last month, how many days were you absent from work

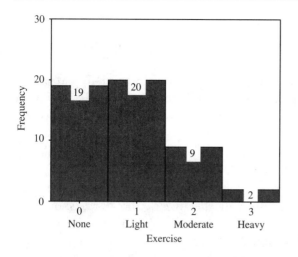

FIGURE 3.12 Histogram of exercise levels

because you were unwell?' As you might expect, most respondents in this
survey had no absences and a sizeable minority took a few days off (seven
or fewer), but a small group of them took quite a few days off. This group is
scattered from eight to 31 days with large gaps in between them. An effective
way of summarizing the frequency distribution is to truncate the upper end of
the scale, as shown in the Table 3.4. Here, we can see exactly how many days'
absence about 95% of the respondents took, and the remaining 23 cases have
been incorporated into an interval labeled '8+.'

The second decision is whether to group cases into intervals containing
several values from the scale. This problem can crop up in both frequency
distribution tables and histograms. Suppose we want to display the distribution of cholesterol levels at the outset of a study of 50 heart patients. The scale

DATA
FILENAME
SUICIDE

TABLE 3.4 Days absent

Value	Frequency	Percentage	Cumulative frequency	Cumulative percentage
0	313	67.3%	313	67.3%
1	31	6.7%	344	74.0%
2	39	8.4%	383	82.4%
3	18	3.9%	401	86.2%
4	17	3.7%	418	89.9%
5	8	1.7%	426	91.6%
6	3	0.6%	429	92.3%
7	13	2.8%	442	95.1%
8+	23	4.9%	465	100.0%
Total	465	100%		

DATA

FILENAME

HEART

for measuring cholesterol levels is quite fine-grained, but if we construct a histogram whose bars have a width of just 1, then we obtain the sparse graph shown in Figure 3.13.

Many of the bars have a height of only 1, and there are many gaps. This graph does not convey the shape of the distribution very effectively. In Figure 3.14, the bars have been made too wide, thereby obscuring too much information about the distribution.

A happy medium represents the overall shape of the distribution while still conveying information about isolated or unusual cases (called 'outliers'). Our third attempt at a histogram for the cholesterol data (Figure 3.15) uses bars with a width of 10, which seems reasonably effective. So, how wide should the bars be? There is no context-free answer. This is one of many decisions we will encounter in data analysis and display for which there is no hard-and-fast rule, but which instead is a matter of judgment.

When you construct your own tables and graphs, first investigate the distribution in order to ascertain whether you need to make either of the two decisions described thus far. Are there gaps, or long tails at either extreme? If so, it is wise to try several alternatives before settling on a final version.

Histograms versus alternatives

DEFINITION

Like bar charts, histograms have been criticized for presenting information redundantly, inaccurately, and ineffectually. Perhaps the most reasonable alternative to a histogram is a **stem-and-leaf plot**. The stem-and-leaf plot is like a histogram rotated 90 degrees clockwise (so it's easier to read the

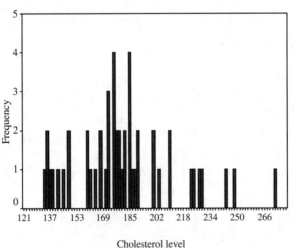

FIGURE 3.13 Narrow bandwidth histogram

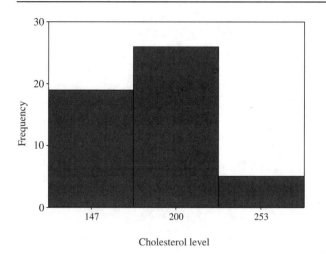

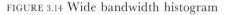

FIGURE 3.14 Wide bandwidth histogram

numbers). Table 3.5 shows a stem-and-leaf plot of the cholesterol data. The bars are the same length as the bars in a histogram, but they consist of stacks of numbers. Each number is the trailing digit in the value of the corresponding observation. The numbers in the 'Stem' column, on the other hand, consist of the leading digits. For instance, in Table 3.5 the first entry '13|4' corresponds to a person whose cholesterol level was 134. Thus, the five individuals represented in the top row have cholesterol levels of 134, 135, 136, 137, and 139. It is worth comparing this table with the 'happy medium' histogram below.

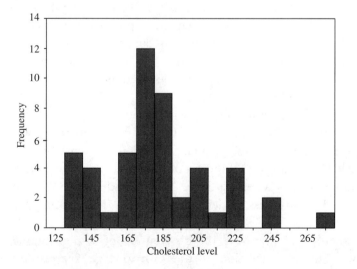

FIGURE 3.15 Appropriate bandwidth histogram

TABLE 3.5 Cholesterol stem-and-leaf plot

Frequency	Stem	Leaf
5	13	45679
4	14	2589
1	15	9
5	16	02577
12	17	122355667899
9	18	022555679
2	19	01
4	20	0039
1	21	0
4	22	3489
0	23	
2	24	49
0	25	
0	26	
1	27	3

This stem-and-leaf plot conveys more information than the histogram. For instance, you can tell exactly what the values of individual cases are and it is easier to ascertain the exact number of cases in each bar. However, the histogram may be easier to comprehend in a 'gestalt' manner. Moreover, stem-and-leaf plots still may require you to make some decisions about how wide the stems should be. In this plot we have used a width of 10, but we could have chosen 5, for instance. Finally, when the number of cases is more than around 150–200, stem-and-leaf plots may become too cumbersome because there are too many cases to list individually.

DEFINITION   A second popular alternative to the histogram is a **frequency polygon** (sometimes also called a **line chart**). The frequency polygon uses a line whose bends occur where the centers of histogram bars would be (Figure 3.16). The main advantage it has over a histogram is that it clutters the chart region less, and therefore enables more than one frequency distribution to be superimposed on one another.

An example of this capability is shown below, where frequency polygons for cholesterol levels in the first and second years of the heart patient study are displayed. Whether you use a histogram, frequency polygon, or stem-and-leaf plot depends on which you judge to be the more effective and informative display, and the familiarity that your audience has with different kind of graphs (stem-and-leaf plots are less widely known than histograms, for instance).

DEFINITION   Finally, one more method of graphing the distribution of a quantifiable variable that deserves our consideration is the **cumulative frequency plot**. This kind of plot shows the cumulative frequency on the vertical axis

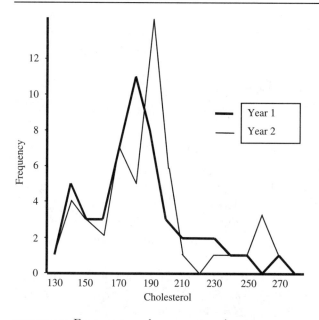

FIGURE 3.16 Frequency polygon comparing two years

and the variable's scale on the horizontal axis. As an example, compare the plot in Figure 3.17 with the frequency polygon plot of Figure 3.16. Both contain the same information for comparing the distribution of cholesterol levels in the first and second years, but communicate it in rather different ways.

The cumulative frequency plot is very effective for comparing two or more distributions, and should be preferred to the frequency polygon for that purpose. Actually, the most common version of this plot is a cumulative *percentage* plot (instead of cumulative frequencies). The reason for this is that when we

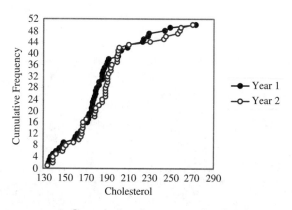

FIGURE 3.17 Cumulative frequency plot for the two years

are comparing distributions, we should use percentages rather than frequencies unless the total number of cases for each distribution is the same.

How to lie with graphs: Lesson 2

With quantifiable variables, there are several more tricks that we can perform to make a rhetorical point. In the heart patient study, cholesterol levels were measured on four occasions (one for each year of the study). First, Figure 3.18 shows an honest graph of the increasing average levels of cholesterol over the four years. It is honest because the scale on the vertical axis runs from the lowest value in the data (130) to the highest (290), which is an appropriate setting in which to view this increase. This graph suggests that although the increase is noticeable, it is not spectacular given the range of cholesterol levels among the patients.

However, we can exaggerate the trend by two well-known devices. First, we truncate the range of the cholesterol scale to 180–200 instead of 130–290. Second, we compress the horizontal axis. The result is Figure 3.19, which makes the increase look much steeper and scarier than it really is. Such tactics are very frequently employed to make rhetorical points instead of honestly representing patterns or trends in the data.

At this point, we should be ready to receive some words of wisdom from the graphics gurus to whom I have referred in this chapter. Edward Tufte has published two books on the graphical presentation of data, and takes a graphical designer's approach to the problem. Bill Cleveland also has published two books on the topic as mentioned earlier, and takes a statistician's approach. Their viewpoints overlap considerably, however, and they both have surprisingly similar perspectives on graphical best practice.

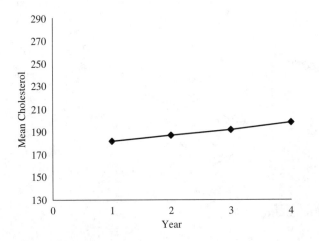

FIGURE 3.18 Honest graph of increase in cholesterol

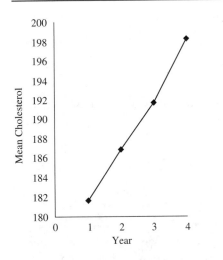

FIGURE 3.19 Dishonest graph of increase in cholesterol

Tufte's (1983) primary stance is that excellence in statistical graphics consists of complex ideas communicated with clarity, precision, and efficiency. *Graphical displays should*:

- show the data;
- induce the viewer to think about the substance rather than about methodology, graphic design, the technology of graphic production, or something else;
- avoid distorting what the data have to say;
- present many numbers in a small space without clutter;
- make large data sets coherent;
- encourage the eye to compare different pieces of data;
- reveal the data at several levels of detail, from a broad overview to the fine structure;
- serve a reasonably clear purpose: description, exploration, tabulation, or design;
- be closely integrated with the statistical and verbal descriptions of a data set.

Cleveland's (1985, 1993) approach may be summarized as follows:

Clear vision

- Make the data stand out. Avoid superfluity.
- Use visually prominent graphical elements to show the data.
- Do not clutter the data region.

- Superposed data sets must be readily visually discriminated.

General strategy

- A large amount of quantitative information can be packed into a small region.
- Graphing data should be an iterative, experimental process.
- Graph data two or more times when it is needed.
- Many useful graphs require careful, detailed study.

SUMMARY

The **cumulative frequency** associated with a particular score on a variable is the number of occurrences that are at or below that score. The **cumulative percentage** is the percentage of all occurrences that are at or below that score.

A **histogram** is used for displaying the frequency distribution of an ordinal variable or a continuous one whose scale has been divided into intervals. The bars have no space between them, indicating the fact that they are in a fixed order. The area of the bars is proportional to the number of cases represented by them.

A **stem-and-leaf** plot is used for displaying the same kind of information as a histogram, but uses numbers to represent the cases instead of bar-heights. The number associated with each case is the trailing digit in the value of that case's score. The numbers in the stem column consist of the leading digits.

A **frequency polygon** (or **line chart**) is used for displaying the same kind of information as a histogram, but uses a line whose bends occur where the centers of histogram bars would be.

A **cumulative frequency plot** is a line chart whose vertical axis represents cumulative frequency (alternatively, cumulative percentage) instead of frequency (or percentage).

Summarizing distributions: Central tendency

Thus far, we have introduced frequency distributions and cumulative frequency distributions, and explored several ways of representing them with tables and graphs. Sometimes distributions do not suit our purposes, but summaries of them do. Some examples of these occasions are listed below, using the cholesterol example.

- What cholesterol level does a typical heart patient have?
- How 'spread out' or 'clumped together' are the patients' cholesterol levels?

- Has the typical cholesterol level increased, decreased, or remained the same for four years?
- Have cholesterol levels become more heterogeneous or more homogeneous during that time?

A frequency distribution table or graph does not address any of these questions very well. The first two questions require that we summarize aspects of the distribution, such as what a typical cholesterol level is. The second two not only require summaries, but are also too complex to answer by displaying frequency distributions.

The summaries that we are after are statements or measurements that tell us what a 'typical' score is or how much spread there is in a distribution. Statistics are designed to provide such summaries in a compact, quantitative form. A **statistic** in this technical sense is a number based on data, that summarizes or quantifies a characteristic of those data. Here, we will investigate statistics constructed to quantify central tendency (the typical score) and dispersion (spread). **Measures of central tendency**, then, are statistics designed to describe typical scores. The three most commonly used measures of central tendency are the mean, median, and mode.

DEFINITION

DEFINITION

The **mode** is simply the most common score in the distribution. In a bar chart or histogram, you can find the mode by looking for the tallest bar. If there are two or more scores that tie for having the highest frequency, then all of them are modes and they should all be reported when you discuss modes. Since the mode just relies on frequency, it may be used for any kind of variable and any level of measurement. In fact, when we have a nominal variable, the mode is the only appropriate measure of central tendency. In the very first frequency distribution we examined in this chapter (the one for gender), the mode was 'Male' because 38 of the 50 cases were men.

DEFINITION

As with any summary statistic, you should always make a considered decision about whether the mode is adequate for your purposes. Modes are useful summary statistics when the distribution needs summarizing and when most of the cases are at or near the mode. The bar chart of 484 responses to the question of where people would turn to in an emergency (Figure 3.3) is a good example, because the distribution needs summarizing and the 'Ambulance/Hospital' category has about three times as many cases as any other category. On the other hand, the bar chart showing a distribution of staff in university departments (Figure 3.5) is not well-described by using the mode, not only because there are only five categories but also because all of the departments' staff numbers differ by only a few cases. To merely report that Sociology was the mode would ignore the fact that the other departments had nearly as many cases, so here the mode is not a useful summary.

DEFINITION   The **median** is the 'middle score' in the sense that 50% of the cases lie below it. Suppose we have N cases, we sort them in ascending order and label each with a numeral from 1 to N. If the number of cases is odd, then the median has the score associated with the case whose numeral is $(N + 1)/2$. For example, if we have 99 cases sorted in ascending order then the 50th case's score is the median. On the other hand, if N is an even number, then the median lies between the case whose numeral is $N/2$ and the one whose numeral is $1 + (N/2)$. For instance, if $N = 100$ then the median lies between the 50th and 51st cases.

This last rule causes no trouble if the two adjacent middle cases have the same score. The median is just the score of either the two cases. However, if those two cases have different scores then we need to decide what score the median should have. If our variable is quantitative and we are willing to think of its underlying scale as a continuous one, then it is reasonable to assign the median a score midway between the two middle cases. If the scale is not continuous but still quantitative (for example, counts such as the number of correct answers on an exam with 10 questions) then this assignment may produce a median score (such as 6.5 correct answers) that is not one of the possible scores. Many researchers would not be uncomfortable with this minor fiction, but what about a genuinely discrete ordinal variable? Suppose we have conducted a survey for a brewery, asking 100 customers to name their favorite beer, and the alternatives are Supalite, Lite, Draft, and Heavy. If 50 respondents nominate Supalite or Lite, and the 51st nominates Draft, what 'score' do we assign to the median: 'Extra-Strength Lite,' perhaps? In situations where this is a genuine concern, it is probably best to report that the median is on the border between the two categories.

There is one last complication with medians (and some other summary statistics too), and it arises when a continuous scale has been chopped into intervals so that we do not know each case's *exact* score, only which interval it belongs in. In surveys this is a common practice when eliciting somewhat sensitive information such as a person's income or their age. In those situations, a conventional practice is to *interpolate* the median score by *assuming that the cases in each interval are evenly distributed along that interval*. Here is an example of how this works. Suppose we have a sample of 99 children whose ages are given to the nearest year, and when we sort their ages in ascending order it turns out that the 46th through the 53rd scores all fall in the '9 years old' interval. If we were to interpolate the median in this interval, assuming that the children's ages were evenly distributed throughout that interval, we would have to imagine this interval to contain children whose exact ages ranged from 8.5 to 9.5 years. Then we would have to divide the interval into eight equal subintervals, each containing one of the 46th through 53rd cases, as shown in Figure 3.20. The 50th score is the median since it is in the

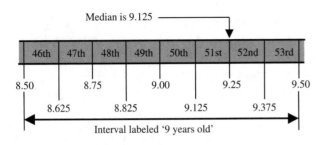

FIGURE 3.20 Median age of 99 children

middle of the 99 scores, and the interpolated score assigned to it is 9.125 years of age.

All of this may seem like hair-splitting. Nevertheless, there are at least two practical reasons why it is not. First, for some scales it makes good sense to say that the median really corresponds to a value on a scale rather than an interpolated value. If our sample of 99 children had given responses to the question 'How many times did you eat ice cream last month?' and the 46th through 53rd responses were '9 times' then we would be well-advised to report the median of this discrete variable as 9, not 9.125. Second, various statistical packages differ in how they estimate medians, and by being aware of these issues you will be able to choose the most appropriate method (or at least, detect when an inappropriate one is being used).

The **mean** is the most popular measure of central tendency, and it is the DEFINITION sum of all the scores divided by the number of scores. Unlike the median, the mean can often produce a value that is not one of the possible ones on the scale and we have no way of avoiding this other than rounding off the mean (hence all those jokes about the mythical average family with 2.3 children). Whether that is problematic depends to some extent on the researcher's purposes and taste. Some adopt a purist stance and refuse to calculate a mean for any ordinal or discrete variable. Others are quite content to report means whose values lie between categories on discrete ordinal scales. Perhaps the most frequent example of the latter practice is in the use of Likert scales for attitude surveys. A reasonable guideline is that if the underlying construct for a variable is considered to be continuous (even if the scale itself is not) and the researcher can argue or is willing to assume that the intervals on the scale are equally spaced, then a mean can be sensibly employed.

The mean also has an explicit formula that may be familiar to you. It is denoted by '*X*-bar', which is written $\bar{X}$, and its formula is

$$\bar{X} = \frac{\Sigma X}{N}$$

The Σ (a Greek letter pronounced 'sigma') stands for summing the scores, the X denotes the scores to be summed, and N denotes the number of scores being summed. If you want to find out more about the 'sigma notation' and how it is used, read the material on summation notation below.

SUMMARY

A **statistic** is a number based on data that summarizes or quantifies a characteristic of those data.

Measures of central tendency are statistics for describing typical scores in a distribution.

The **mode** is the most frequently occurring category or score.

The **median** is the score below which 50% of the cases lie.

The **mean** is the sum of all the scores divided by the number of scores.

Summation notation

Most of the time we can get away with simply writing ΣX if we want to represent the sum of all scores. Sometimes you'll see a more complex version of this notation, which we won't use in this book until it's required. Each score is indexed with a numeral from 1 to N. This index often is denoted by the letter i and attached as a subscript to X, so each score is written as X_i. Likewise, Σ is sometimes given a lower and upper value for i so that we know exactly what range of scores is being summed. Usually the lower number is 1 and the upper number is N. The whole shebang looks like this:

$$\sum_{i=1}^{N} X_i$$

It reads, 'sum the scores X_i from $i = 1$ to $i = N$.' You may be wondering why anyone would use this cumbersome bunch of symbols when they could just use ΣX instead. The main reason is that if we don't want to sum all of the scores but only, say, the first five of them, then we can say so using this notation. Instead of putting N on top of Σ, we would put 5 there. We will encounter some situations later on where we want to be that precise.

There are also some rules for using summation notation that are useful for understanding 'where the numbers go' in statistics. They are really simple algebraic rules in disguise. Here are two that will help us with the material in the next section.

1. Suppose we add some number, C, to all the scores. Then summing N scores with C added to each of them is equivalent to summing the N scores and then adding N times C to that sum. Expressed in a formula, this rule is

$\Sigma(X + C) = \Sigma X + NC$. The same is true if we subtract C from each score: $\Sigma(X - C) = \Sigma X - NC$.

2. Suppose now we multiply each score by C and sum them. That is equivalent to summing the scores and multiplying the sum by C, so $\Sigma CX = C\Sigma X$. The same is true if we divide each score by C: $\Sigma(X/C) = (\Sigma X)/C$.

Variability and dispersion

Distributions are usually not adequately summarized by reporting central tendency alone. Most researchers also report how spread-out the scores are around a typical value, and for this they use a measure of **dispersion**. Why is dispersion important? It is a special type of heterogeneity, and therefore important for the same reasons that heterogeneity is. Two distributions could have identical means but entirely different spreads around those means. Humans have difficulty taking dispersion or variation into account; we almost always underestimate it or neglect it outright unless it is made apparent. Policy-makers often base laws on 'average' cases as if there were no variations. Educators often 'teach to the middle' of the class, thereby ignoring the bright and the slow. And as a friend of mine used to remark, 'Stand barefoot in a bucket of ice and put your face on a hotplate. On average, you're comfortable.' We are truly reducing people to numbers if we ignore dispersion or variation and just pay attention to central tendency.

Because dispersion uses a typical score as a reference-point, most measures of dispersion are associated with measures of central tendency. That is, a measure of central tendency and a measure of dispersion usually are 'packaged' together. The main exception to this rule is measures of dispersion for nominal variables, which we will put aside for now because they involve some extra considerations that are beyond the scope of this book. A popular measure of dispersion about the median is called the 'interquartile range' (sometimes also called the 'inter- DEFINITIONS quartile deviation'). The median, you recall, divides the data into two halves. **Quartiles** divide the data into four quarters (each containing 25% of the cases). The first quartile is the score below which 25% of the cases lie, the second is just the median, and the third is the score below which 75% of the cases lie. The **interquartile range**, then, is the difference between the third and first quartiles. The interquartile range contains the *middle 50%* of the cases.

As you might imagine by now, we could go on splitting the distribution into smaller chunks. These chunks are called **percentiles** (sometimes alterna- DEFINITION tively, 'Quantiles'). The median is the 50th percentile for example, and likewise the first quartile is the 25th percentile. A popular five-number summary of a distribution includes the 10th, 25th, 50th, 75th, and 90th percentiles. This percentile package often is graphically displayed by a rather effective device known as a 'boxplot'. This term was coined by Tukey in 1977, but others had invented the graphical device before him (Spear's (1952) 'range bar' for example).

DEFINITION

Boxplots are shown in Figure 3.21. The one on the right-hand side of the graph has been labeled so that you can see which percentiles each part of the boxplot refers to. The four boxplots summarize the distributions of cholesterol levels in our heart patient study for each of the four years spanned by the study. As you can see, a great deal of information about those distributions is conveyed by the boxplots that would otherwise be difficult to extract from comparing four histograms or stem-and-leaf plots. This graph shows that the lower 50% of the cholesterol scores have not increased but the upper 50% have, and the strongest trend is in the upper 10% of the scores (represented by the 90th percentile).

In fact, the percentile package and boxplot enable us to comprehensively address the second pair of questions posed at the beginning of this section:

- Has the typical cholesterol level increased, decreased, or remained the same for four years?
- Have cholesterol levels become more heterogeneous or more homogeneous during that time?

If we use the median to represent the 'typical cholesterol level' then the answer to the first question is that it has remained much the same. The second question is answered by using the interquartile range, which has increased during the four years. In other words, the cholesterol scores have become more heterogeneous.

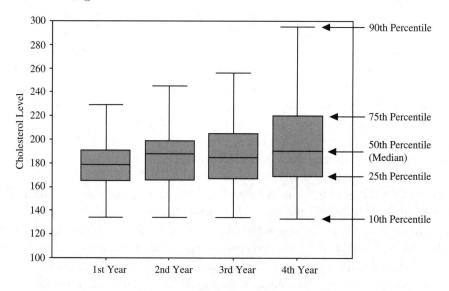

FIGURE 3.21 Boxplots of cholesterol levels for four years

Now let us consider a measure of dispersion about the mean. All candidates for such a measure are based on the difference between each score and the mean,

$$X - \bar{X}$$

However, the apparently logical approach of adding up the differences between the mean and each score and then taking their average will not work because the positive and negative differences cancel each other out. This outcome actually follows from our first rule about summation notation: $\Sigma(X - C) = \Sigma X - NC$. That is,

$$\Sigma(X - \bar{X}) = \Sigma X - N\bar{X} = 0,$$

since the sum of the scores is just N times the mean of the scores.

If this difficulty is caused by negative and positive deviations canceling out, why not ignore the sign and treat all deviations as positive? The **mean absolute deviation** (abbreviated m.a.d.) does exactly that by using what are called 'absolute values'. Absolute values treat any number as positive, and they are denoted by a pair of vertical bars surrounding a number (for instance, $|-8| = 8$). So the formula for the m.a.d. is   DEFINITION

$$\text{m.a.d.} = \frac{\Sigma|X - \bar{X}|}{N}$$

The m.a.d. solves the problem and is simple to use. Despite its appeal, however, it has not been used very much in statistics or in psychology for reasons that are beyond the scope of this book. In essence, it lacks certain mathematically attractive properties possessed by another candidate for a dispersion measure, namely the squared difference between each score and the mean.

Summing these squared differences and dividing by N to obtain the mean squared difference gives us the **variance**:   DEFINITION

$$\text{Var}(X) = \frac{\Sigma(X - \bar{X})^2}{N}$$

Its main drawback is that it tells us the average *squared* deviation, and we would like a measure of dispersion that is in the variable's own units, not those units squared. The remedy for this problem is to take the square root of the variance, thereby giving us the **standard deviation**:   DEFINITION

$$SD(X) = \sqrt{\frac{\Sigma(X - \bar{X})^2}{\mathcal{N}}}$$

In many research publications, the standard deviation of a sample is denoted by *s* or sometimes by s.d. The variance is usually denoted by s^2.

DEFINITION   Just as the percentile package has its boxplot, the mean and standard deviation package has the **error-bar** plot. Figure 3.22 shows the mean cholesterol level (represented by a dot) and the standard deviation (represented by the length of the bar extending above and below the dot) for each year in the heart patient study. The bars are often referred to as 'one-standard deviation bars' or sometimes simply 'error bars' and are a commonly used method of summarizing a distribution in a graph where several (or even many) distributions are to be compared.

It is evident from this graph that not only is the mean cholesterol level for this sample increasing each year, but so is the standard deviation. Another thing you can see here is that the cholesterol reading for people one standard deviation *below* the mean has not increased, but the cholesterol reading for people one standard deviation *above* the mean has increased, and at a greater rate than the mean. So this graph conveys the same impression imparted by the boxplots, which is that most of the change has occurred in the higher cholesterol levels. However, the answers to our two questions provided by the mean and standard deviation package differ in one respect: the median has not increased but the mean has.

So far, we have examined measures of dispersion for every kind of variable except nominal ones. Almost no research methods texts in psychology deal with this issue, and most of them do not even mention it. Pragmatically speak-

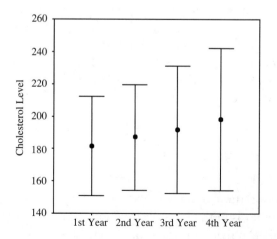

FIGURE 3.22 Error-bar plot for cholesterol levels for four years

ing, most of the time there is little need for such measures, in part because most nominal variables are easily summarized with frequency tables or bar charts. Nevertheless, if you were wondering whether they exist, be assured that they do (see Agresti, 1990: 24–25) and there are some situations where they are useful.

Choosing summary statistics

Now that we have various measures of central tendency and dispersion available to us, how do we choose among them? There are no hard-and-fast rules for doing so, but knowing the properties of each of these measures can help you to make an intelligent choice. We will compare three 'packages' of summary statistics: The mode; the percentile package that includes the median, quartiles, and 10th and 90th percentiles; and the mean and standard deviation package.

To begin with, the mode has the advantage of being applicable to any kind of variable, whereas the median and mean cannot be used on a nominal variable. For questions concerning where the greatest number of cases has ended up, the mode is, by definition, the best answer. The mode has its disadvantages, chief among them that it may not be sensitive to very many of the cases in the distribution. Suppose two teachers are being evaluated by the students in their respective classes on a scale from 1 (very poor) to 100 (excellent) and the mode for both of them turns out to be 1. In teacher A's class all 51 of the students gave a 1, whereas in teacher B's class six students gave a 1 and each of the other 45 gave unique ratings from 2 through 100. Clearly the mode fails to distinguish between these two very different distributions.

Now let's turn to the percentile package. The median and any other percentile may be used on ordinal categorical variables when the mean and standard deviation may not be meaningful, and in some areas of research this is a distinct advantage. Percentiles are somewhat more sensitive to the overall distribution than the mode is, but they are most sensitive to the cases that are in their immediate vicinity and relatively insensitive to cases further away. Depending on the researcher's preferences, this property may be good or bad.

The median, for instance, is most sensitive to cases that are near the middle of the distribution and unaffected by extremes. When there are a few extreme scores in a distribution (also known as 'outliers', as mentioned earlier), the median is much less influenced by them than the mean. If we are evaluating the central tendency of a small suburb in which 10 households have an income of $20,000, five have an income of $30,000, and one has an income of $40,000 then the median is $20,000 and the mean is $24,375. Now suppose the household with the $40,000 income sells up and the place is bought by a family whose income is $200,000. The median stays at $20,000 but the mean suddenly leaps to $34,375, higher than 15 out of the 16 households in the suburb. It is for this reason that some experimental psychologists prefer to work with medians when they are measuring a variable whose distribution is likely to include outliers, such as reaction times.

Finally, the percentile package can effectively represent the *shape* of a distribution under some conditions, 'skewness' in particular. A distribution is **skewed** if it is not **symmetric**, so that most of the cases are bunched closer to one end of the range of scores than the other. **Positive** skew means that the extreme scores lie to the right of the bunch, and **negative** skew means they lie to the left of the bunch. Figure 3.23 illustrates both kinds of skew.

DEFINITION

If you re-examine the four boxplots of the cholesterol data, you will find that the distributions become more skewed over time, because the lower half of the distribution remains almost unchanged while the upper half is increasingly stretched upward. This trend is indicated by the fact that the boxplots become more asymmetric, with the 90th and 75th percentiles reflecting the positive skew.

Given that the mean and standard deviation require us to assume an equal-interval scale, are more greatly influenced by outliers, and produce values that may not correspond to any of the scores in the data, they might seem to have little to recommend them. However, the mean and standard deviation package has several important redeeming features. Two of them are readily understandable now; the others will have to wait until we proceed further.

First, the mean may be interpreted as the 'balance point' of a distribution in the following sense. Suppose we have gathered a small data set with 10 cases by asking 10 adults how many magazines and newspapers they subscribed to during the past month. Their responses are {1, 1, 2, 2, 2, 3, 5, 6, 8, 10}. Imagine that each case is represented as a small cube, and we stack these cubes along a bar whose length is the range of the data, as shown in figure 3.24. The mean of these cases is 4, and if we placed a fulcrum there, the bar would be perfectly balanced.

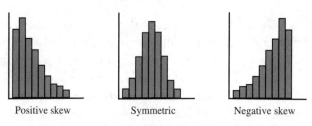

Positive skew   Symmetric   Negative skew

FIGURE 3.23 Skewed versus symmetric distributions

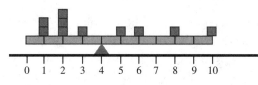

FIGURE 3.24 The mean balances the distribution

Second, the mean produces the smallest sum of squared differences between scores and any value. If you had to choose one value as your 'best guess' for each of the 10 cases as they were being pulled out of a hat, and if the error in your guesses were measured by the squared difference between each guess and each case's score, then your best strategy would be to guess the mean every time.

SUMMARY

A **percentile** is the score below which a specified percentage of cases fall.
A **percentile rank** of a score is the percentage of cases below that score.

Measures of dispersion are statistics designed to describe the spread of scores around a typical value, usually an associated measure of central tendency. Two of the most popular are the interquartile range and the standard deviation.

The **interquartile range** is the difference between the third and first quartiles, that is, between the 75th and 25th percentiles.
The **standard deviation** is the square root of the **variance**, which is the mean squared difference between each score and the mean of those scores.

A **boxplot** is a graphical representation of a five-number summary of a distribution, conventionally comprising the 10th, 25th, 50th, 75th, and 90th percentiles.
An **error-bar plot** is a graphical representation of the mean and standard deviation.

A distribution is **skewed** if it is not **symmetric**, so that most of the cases are bunched closer to one end of the range of scores than the other. **Positive** skew means that the extreme scores lie to the right of the bunch, and **negative** skew means that they lie to the left of the bunch.

StatPatch

YOU CAN EXPLORE SUMMARY STATISTICS FURTHER WITH HISTOPATCH

Questions and exercises

Q.3.1. What is wrong with the following statement? 'Sales volume in our Department increased by 350% over last year.'

Q.3.2. Here are some 1998 estimates of the percentages of households in several countries with PCs who use them to access the World Wide Web. Try graphing them so that the differences between the countries appear as large as possible. Then try graphing them in such a way as to make those differences appear as small as possible. How do you think an 'honest' graph would display these data?

Country	Percentage
France	6.5%
Germany	11.7%
Hong Kong	12.0%
Italy	5.8%
Japan	18.0%
U.K.	9.5%
U.S.	16.0%

Q.3.3. Suppose the mean score on a self-esteem scale is 20.

(a) What will the mean become if we add 5 to each score?
(b) What will the mean become if we divide each score by 5?
(c) What will the standard deviation become if we add 5 to each score?

Q.3.4. The data tabulated below are taken from the 1991 Census figures for a suburban population in an Australian town. Questions 3.4–3.7 refer to these data. Construct cumulative frequency and percentage tables for the males and females in the table (starting from the oldest and accumulating *downward* to the youngest).

Age group	Male frequencies	Female frequencies
80+	95	203
70–79	294	426
60–69	462	514
50–59	522	591
40–49	715	714
30–39	831	825
20–29	1110	1032
10–19	899	1073
0–9	799	810

Q.3.5. Without actually calculating the median for the male and female age distributions, which of them is likely to be the higher? On what do you base your view?

Q.3.6. Would you expect the mean age for the males to be higher or lower than their median age? Why?

Q.3.7. Construct a cumulative percentage plot for the male and female age distributions. How would you summarize the differences between these two age distributions?

Q.3.8. Consider the table below, which shows the ratio of people per Net server in 14 countries as of 1998.

Country	Ratio of people/server
Finland	25
U.S.	50
Australia	60
Singapore	125
U.K.	130
Hong Kong	310
Japan	470
Taiwan	850
South Korea	1,500
Brazil	8,000
Thailand	15,000
Indonesia	87,000
China	561,000
India	1,200,000

Is there an effective way of graphically displaying these data? Why or why not? If you'd like to try your hand at graphing these data, they are in the Excel and ASCII files called Ch3Q8.

Q.3.9. In Figure 3.21, as remarked earlier in this chapter, the boxplots there show that median cholesterol levels did not increase during the four-year heart patient study, but Figure 3.22 shows that the mean levels did increase. What might account for this apparent discrepancy?

Q.3.10 This question is based on the **StatPatch** module called **HistoPatch**, but you may be able to answer all three parts without the aid of HistoPatch. Suppose we have a scale that is numbered $1, 2, 3, \ldots, 10$. Imagine now that you can distribute scores on this scale any way you wish, as long as you do not assign any more than 110 observations to any one score (e.g., no more than 110 '3's'). This is the scenario that you will find in HistoPatch.

(a) What kind of distribution would produce a mean and median equal to 2?

(b) What distribution will produce the largest difference between the median and the mean?

(c) What distribution will produce the biggest possible standard deviation?

Q.3.11. Here are some additional issues to explore using HistoPatch.

StatPatch

(a) Can you construct a skewed distribution in which the boxplot is still symmetric? What does this tell you about using the boxplot as a way of detecting whether a distribution is skewed?

(b) Can you alter a distribution so that the boxplot stays the same but the mean and standard deviation both change? How, or why not?

(c) Can you alter a distribution so that the median changes but the mean stays the same? How, or why not?

(d) Can you construct a distribution such that the median, 25th, *and* 75th percentiles do not correspond to any of the scores in the distribution? How, or why not?

Research Design and Probability

4

CONTENTS

Validity in research design

In Chapter 2, you were introduced to measurement validity, the extent to which measurement is not contaminated by error. In this chapter, we begin by focusing on ways of ascertaining whether a researcher's inferences and conclusions have validity. The question of whether an apparent effect really is due to an experimental manipulation rather than some other cause is an example of an issue in research design validity. This chapter also introduces basic concepts in statistical inference that are used in designing both experimental and non-experimental studies and interpreting their findings. Since the foundation of statistical inference rests on probability, we will end the chapter with a section that introduces the basic ideas in probability.

In order to design a study, the researcher must have a set of criteria in mind for what constitutes a good strategic design. The primary purpose of design strategy is managing the uncertainties that arise in research, in such a way as to either reduce those uncertainties or at least describe and estimate them (see Chapter 11 in Haslam & McGarty, 1998). In two highly regarded classics in the literature on research methods, Campbell & Stanley (1963) and Cook & Campbell (1979) distinguished among several important kinds of validity issues and the uncertainties associated with them. We will use the three that are most frequently dealt with in research design.

DEFINITION   First, **statistical conclusion validity** concerns whether a researcher has correctly assessed the behavior of a variable, including its relationship with other variables. In psychology, assessing statistical conclusion validity normally involves understanding or making use of random processes. Most of the statistical techniques covered in this book have been designed to enhance

DEFINITION   statistical conclusion validity. A **random process** generates events or values that are independent of one another, so that the nature of the event generated now does not depend on what was generated previously. The random processes involved in psychological research practices usually consist of random selection from a population or random assignment to an experimental condition, or both. We will find out more about these processes later in this chapter. In Chapters 5 and 6 we will learn about specific threats to statistical conclusion validity and ways of anticipating and defending against those threats.

DEFINITION   The second kind of validity is **internal validity**, which refers to whether a researcher correctly identifies the possible influences on (or causes of) a variable. Experimenters in particular expend considerable effort in designing experiments that have high internal validity, and the experimental research literature uses several technical terms associated with aspects of internal validity.

DEFINITIONS   Researchers distinguish between independent and dependent variables when describing experimental causes and the effects they produce. An **independent variable** is considered to be a predictor or, in experiments, a cause of another variable. In experiments the independent variables under experimental control are sometimes referred to as the 'experimental variables.' In nonexperimental research, they are often called 'predictors.' A **dependent variable** is the variable predicted or caused by independent variable(s).

A researcher who thinks that low self-esteem causes obesity, for instance, is treating self-esteem as the independent variable and obesity as the dependent variable. Conversely, a researcher who thinks that obesity causes low self-esteem has switched the roles of these two variables, with obesity now in the role of the independent variable and self-esteem as the dependent variable. This example illustrates something about variables studied by psychologists: many of them may be thought of as either dependent or independent variables, depending on what the researcher is studying. A psychologist interested in influences on self-esteem, for instance, will design studies with self-esteem as a dependent variable; and a psychologist interested in eating disorders will design studies with obesity as a dependent variable. None of this prevents them from holding the view that self-esteem and obesity influence one another (i.e., low self-esteem leads to increased obesity, which in turn leads to lower self-esteem). Of course, not all independent and dependent variables may trade places at the pleasure of the researcher. Some variables have genuine causal priority over others. Gender, for instance, might very well be an influence on self-esteem but self-esteem usually does not determine a person's gender.

The 'holy grail' for many experimenters is the ability to establish valid conclusions about causes and effects. Following the writings of the 18th century Scottish philosopher David Hume (1739/1945), experimental researchers traditionally abide by *three rules for demonstrating that an independent variable causes a dependent variable*. First, the cause and effect must co-occur (**covariation rule**). Returning to our example, if it is true that obesity causes low self-esteem then whenever someone is obese then we should find they also tend to suffer low self-esteem. However, this criterion alone is not sufficient to establish that obesity is a cause of low self-esteem. One possibility is that they co-occur because low self-esteem in fact causes obesity.

To take care of this objection, a second criterion is that the cause should always precede the effect (**temporal precedence rule**). That is, the researcher must show that obesity occurs before a decline in self-esteem. Even with this second criterion, we still are not finished. A critic could justifiably object that some third factor could be causing both weight-gain and decline in self-esteem. For instance, depression might cause people to eat more, gain weight, and also lose self-regard.

This kind of objection may be dealt with by introducing a third (and very tough) criterion, namely that plausible rival causes must be ruled out or at least discounted (**rival cause discount rule**). Most of the strategic efforts in experimental designs are devoted to fulfilling this criterion. That is, they are attempts to defend against various threats to internal validity in the guise of plausible rival causes or 'confounds'. We will examine some of those threats and the experimental design techniques for defending against them later in this chapter.

Finally, the third type of validity we will deal with in this book is **external validity**, which refers to the generalizability of a study's findings and/or conclusions beyond the specific circumstances of the study and the cases observed. Without any capacity for generalizability, the findings of a study and any conclusions based on them are restricted to the study's place, time, and participants. The result is an extreme and impoverished particularism, whereby nothing that we can find out about anyone under any circumstances can apply to anyone else, nor even to the same person in another time or place. While both experimental and nonexperimental researchers desire external validity and therefore wide generality, this kind of validity tends to be emphasized more by nonexperimentalists. Sampling designs and several aspects of statistical inference are devoted to tackling certain parts of the external validity issue, and we will explore these in the next two sections.

DEFINITION

SUMMARY

Statistical conclusion validity is attained when a researcher correctly assesses the behavior of a variable, including its relationship with other variables, taking random processes into account.

A **random process** generates events or values that are independent of one another, so that the nature of the event generated now does not depend on what was generated previously.

Internal validity is achieved when a researcher correctly identifies possible influences on (or causes of) a dependent variable.

External validity refers to the generalizability of a study's findings and/or conclusions beyond the specific circumstances of the study and the cases observed.

An **independent variable** is a variable that is considered to be a predictor or sometimes a cause of another variable. In experiments the independent variables under experimental control are sometimes referred to as the 'experimental variables.' In nonexperimental research, they are often called 'predictors.'

A **dependent variable** is the variable predicted or caused by independent variable(s).

Three rules for establishing a causal relationship:
1. **Covariation rule**: The cause and effect co-occur.
2. **Temporal precedence rule**: The cause always precedes the effect.
3. **Rival cause discount rule**: Plausible rival causes must be ruled out.

Statistical inference

In Chapters 2 and 3 we explored many different ways to describe quantifiable information about people in statistical and graphical form. Descriptive statistics, as informative and even compelling as they may be, still leave many crucial questions unanswered. We have already seen that some of these questions concern statistical conclusion validity, internal validity, and external validity. All three types of questions are partly answerable through inferential statistics.

DEFINITION   The primary object of **statistical inference** is twofold:

- To infer some characteristic of a population or phenomenon on the basis of a sample of evidence.
- To describe and estimate the degree of confidence with which that inference may be made.

The 'characteristic' oftentimes is a statistic of some kind (e.g., the mean height of the population). The 'population' may be a real one or merely hypothetical. In a survey based on a sample of adults in a community, we might wish to make inferences about the mean height of the adult population in that community. This would be an example of inferring from a sample to a real population. In an experiment in which 25 rats choose between two food sources, we might want to infer that their choices come from a hypothetical population of rats who are equally likely to choose either source.

The two objectives are pursued through **parameter estimation**, in which the researcher attempts to obtain a reasonable estimate of the magnitude of a population characteristic. We will introduce techniques for parameter estimation in Chapter 5. If there are rival theories, models, claims or hypotheses about this characteristic, then the researcher may take one further step and use statistical inference to assess the extent to which the evidence favors one model or hypothesis over another. Traditionally, this kind of decision-making is called 'hypothesis testing' or 'model comparison,' and it will be discussed in more detail in Chapter 6.

To give these concepts some more substance, let us consider a few examples. Suppose you wanted to find out the percentage of people who are unemployed in Australia during the month of May. It is not feasible to find out the employment status of every eligible person in the country unless you happen to be doing a census (and perhaps even not then!), so you have to be satisfied with obtaining a sample of people. The percentage of people in your sample who are unemployed is the **sample estimate** of the value of the **population** DEFINITION **parameter** (the actual percentage of Australians who are unemployed during May).

What kind of sample should you get? How should you select such a sample, and can you avoid obtaining a biased sample? How big should the sample be? How close is your estimate likely to be to the true percentage? What degree of confidence should you have in this estimate? These are examples of questions having to do with parameter estimation that can be answered by inferential statistics.

These concepts are important because most studies in the human sciences involve generalizations and inferences beyond the people who have been studied. Among the kinds of generalization made are:

1. To the population from which the sample came;
2. Across time (i.e., to past and future populations);
3. To populations other than the one sampled.

Usually, statistical inference can deal with only the first kind of generalization. This does not necessarily mean that we cannot generalize over time or to other populations. Instead, it simply means that we can use inferential statistical techniques only in inferences from a sample to its parent population. So, statistical inference effectively handles only a specific type of external validity question.

One of the best ways of ensuring a basis for statistical inference is when we have a special kind of sample from the population, namely a random sample. DEFINITION **Random sampling** entails using a random process to determine who shall be selected from the population. It should become clear by the end of this chapter that statistical inference cannot be conducted without direct reference to random processes and probability theory.

The use of inferential statistical techniques to estimate the imprecision of a sample estimate also is important. In Chapter 2, you may recall that we encountered the 'fallacy of false precision.' In the real world, many rather imprecise sample estimates masquerade as population parameters. Many popular newspaper polls still do not indicate how much error there could be in their estimates, and it is rare to find any indication of how imprecise those disease-risk statistics are that medical practitioners use to frighten us.

Statistical inference is often used to decide between competing claims about population characteristics. Suppose the estimated percentage unemployed in May of the previous year was 8.7%, and your sample estimate for May this year is 7.5%. As a section head of the Bureau of Statistics, you are obliged to advise the appropriate Minister whether this is likely to reflect an actual decline in unemployment from last year. The sample estimates certainly differ, but can you infer that the true unemployment rates also differ? The Minister wants to be able to claim that unemployment has fallen; the Shadow Minister from the Opposition would like to claim that it has not. Can either claim be ruled out as implausible, on the basis of your sample estimate? This kind of decision-making quandary typifies what statistical hypothesis testing and model comparison are about.

Now let us consider the role played by statistical inference in settling issues pertaining to internal validity. The ability to make decisions between competing hypotheses is an important motivation for using inferential statistics which lies at the heart of experimental designs as well as sample surveys. In most psychology experiments, it is difficult to tell whether some result has arisen by chance or because there is a real effect. Since random effects may be mistaken for nonrandom ones, random processes are a genuine source of rival causes and therefore a threat to internal validity.

Here is an example from perception research. A fairly well-known perceptual phenomenon is called the 'size–weight illusion.' In a size–weight illusion experiment, participants are presented with two objects, one larger than the other. When asked to judge which of two objects is heavier, according to the size–weight illusion hypothesis, the majority will pick the larger object even though both objects weigh the same and have the same cross-section for their lifting surface. A skeptic might propose a rival hypothesis, namely that the size of the object makes no difference to participants and they are therefore equally likely to pick either object.

Suppose we ran an experiment with 20 participants randomly sampled from a population of adults, and found that 13 of them picked the larger object. Can we claim victory for the size–weight illusion hypothesis? Our sample estimate of the proportion of people who pick up the larger object is 13/20, but how far off might this be from the true proportion? The skeptic, after all, could argue that the experiment resulted in 13/20 simply by chance, much as an unbiased coin could be tossed 20 times and produce 13 heads.

Finally, consider a related example that occurs outside experimental laboratories. In university courses that are team-taught, sometimes the staff share out the task of grading exams or assignments. In Table 4.1 we have summaries of five staff-members' examination mark distributions, including the number of exams, means, and standard deviations. Colin's mean is only 60.5, which appears to be substantially lower than the means for the other four markers. Are Colin's marks really lower than everyone else's, or could the apparent difference between his mean and the others have arisen by chance alone?

As in the size–weight illusion experiment, we are considering two hypotheses to explain these different exam means:

- *Hypothesis 1*: The difference is due to chance and therefore is not real; versus
- *Hypothesis 2*: The difference is real, and therefore Colin's marks are lower.

Among the many possible explanations for the difference between Colin's marks and everyone else's, one of the most obvious candidates is that Colin was given an inferior set of exams. In experimental terminology, the assignment of exams to markers was biased. If we could rule out that possibility, then we would be in a much better position to assess whether the difference was real. A very effective way of doing this would be **randomized assignment**, whereby   DEFINITION participants are randomly allocated to experimental conditions. In this instance, the exams are cast in the role of 'participants' and they are randomly allocated to makers, who are in the role of 'conditions.' In this chapter, we will find that randomized assignment is as essential for the use of statistical inference in experiments as random sampling is for its use in surveys.

TABLE 4.1 Exam marks by staff

Staff	N	Mean	S.d.
Colin	22	60.5	22.1
Peter	24	69.3	18.3
Sandra	23	69.1	18.7
Jenny	20	68.1	23.5
Mike	23	70.0	17.7

SUMMARY

The primary object of **statistical inference** is twofold:
- To infer some characteristic of a population or phenomenon on the basis of a sample of evidence;
- To describe and estimate the degree of confidence with which that inference may be made.

The value of a statistic based on a sample from a population is the **sample estimate** of the value of the **population parameter**.
Random sampling requires determining by a random process who shall be selected from the population.
In **randomized assignment**, participants are randomly allocated to experimental conditions.

Sampling methods

This section has two purposes. One is to introduce the main types of sampling procedures, the rationales behind them, and their strengths and weaknesses. The second is to explain why random samples are essential for many kinds of statistical inference. By and large, researchers in psychology tend not to think about sampling. They should, and many know it. The population most thoroughly studied by psychologists is university undergraduates, and the sampling method used most often is sheer convenience. If you are equipped with the essential concepts behind sampling, then you will be in a much better position than most psychologists to design studies that take sampling into account. You will also know when someone else's study is problematic or deceptive because of inadequate sampling. We will start with some rather general concepts about sampling, and then move to nonrandom sampling methods. The last part of this section will be devoted to random sampling methods.

DEFINITION   One of the matters that must be decided before designing a sample (or even an experiment) is the unit of analysis. The **unit of analysis** constitutes the items to be sampled from a population. In a typical psychological experiment or social survey, the unit of analysis is the individual person. However, that is not always true and sometimes even seasoned researchers may be mistaken on this issue. Couples, families, organizations, institutions, or nations can be units of analysis. So can social situations, behavioral episodes, 10-second epochs, or spikes within a particular bandwidth of an EEG output.

The unit of analysis is determined primarily by the phenomenon we wish to investigate, in the sense that it should be at the level at which the phenomenon occurs. A clinical psychologist researching the effectiveness of family thera-peutic techniques, for instance, must decide whether his primary focus is on outcomes for individual family members or the family as a unit. If it is the former, then his unit of analysis is the individual; but if it is the latter then his unit of analysis is the family. Likewise, a neuropsychologist studying brain-wave patterns as a function of particular activities is unlikely to use the individual organism as her unit of analysis. Instead, her preferred unit of analysis is more likely to be at a micro-level, such as a time-period of a particular duration.

Sampling processes have three components that determine the nature of the sample:

1. A **sampling frame** which defines the population from which the sample is taken;   DEFINITION
2. A **selection procedure** by which the sample actually is taken, and
3. **Extraneous influences**, which denote unintended influences on sample selection (e.g., refusals to participate in research or volunteer effects).

In order to fully specify the relevant population, a sampling frame must identify every unit in the population eligible for selection. In most instances, the sampling frame is simply a list or a list-like definition. Each of the following is an example of a sampling frame.

- A White Pages telephone book lists all households that have a phone in its service area. The unit of analysis here is the household. The population of households defined by it does not include all households, of course, only those that are 'on the phone' and whose phone numbers are not unlisted. A selection procedure applied to this sampling frame would determine how households would be selected for a sample.
- An electoral roll defines a population of individuals from a polling region who have enrolled to vote. The unit of analysis is the individual. Again, that does not include all individuals who reside in the region, since not everyone there may be eligible to vote and some who are eligible may have failed to register. A selection procedure applied to this sampling frame would determine how individuals would be selected for a sample.
- A collection of 50 20-second epochs in the output of a rat's EEG defines a population of such epochs. The unit of analysis is the epoch. A selection procedure applied to this sampling frame would determine how epochs would be selected for a sample.
- Almost any text or speech recording may be used as a sampling frame. An obvious unit of analysis (but not the only possible unit) would be the word. A selection procedure applied to this sampling frame would determine how words would be selected for a sample.

Perhaps the most important general criterion for an effective sample frame is that it includes the relevant population. For instance an electoral roll may be an effective sampling frame for a political scientist studying influences on people's voting, but not if she is studying the determinants of who votes and who does not. For the latter, she needs a representative sample of the entire adult population in the area. A class-list of first-year university students may be a viable sampling frame for a cognitive psychologist who is studying steropsis, since he needs to sample adults with visual systems in good condition and university students include a high proportion of such people. On the other hand, first-year university students would not be an adequate population for a developmental psychologist who wishes to study certain changes in mental functioning over the entire life span, since this population has a restricted age range and a highly skewed age distribution.

DEFINITION Now we turn to selection procedures. Sampling may be done in one of two ways that determine whether a unit is eligible to be selected more than once:

- **With replacement**, which permits a unit to be reselected;
- **Without replacement**, which ensures that a unit will not be reselected.

Sampling without replacement is the most widely used procedure in psychological research, but some research purposes require sampling with replacement. An example is the 'capture–recapture' technique used in field studies in which the purpose is to try to estimate the size of a population by 'tagging' each unit that has been selected so that when it is reselected the researcher realizes that it has been encountered previously. This kind of sampling was initially popularized by field biologists, but has also been used to study transient human populations.

DEFINITION Another fundamental distinction is between random and nonrandom procedures. **Random selection procedures** make use of randomizing devices to DEFINITION determine the probability of a particular unit being selected for the sample. Any kind of random sample involves a random selection procedure. **Nonrandom selection procedures** make use of nonrandom systems or criteria for determining which units will be selected.

One of the most sought-after criteria in sampling is the absence of unintended selection bias. Biased samples may ruin otherwise well-designed studies because they distort sample estimates and discredit the researcher's claim to accurately characterizing the population from which the sample came. A biased sample has poor external validity. Perhaps the most frequently cited example of both an inappropriate sampling frame and selection bias is the 1936 American Presidential election poll conducted by the *Literary Digest*, which showed Alf Landon beating Franklin D. Roosevelt by a landslide (57% to 43%). Roosevelt won 62% of the vote, and the pollsters retrospectively realized that their biased sample had led them astray. The sampling frames used by the *Literary Digest* underrepresented the poor, a great majority of whom voted for Roosevelt.

Unfortunately, that example makes biased sampling sound as if it is a thing of the past. This is by no means true. Research based on biased samples not only continues to be done, it gets published and often has a huge impact on the credulous media and their publics. In the September 1992 issue of the American teenage girls' magazine *Seventeen*, readers were invited to complete a questionnaire on sexual harassment designed by a project director with the Wellsley College Center for Research on Women. Other methodological problems aside (for an account of them, see Sommers, 1994: 181–184), completed questionnaires were returned by only 4200 of the magazine's 1.9 million subscribers, a 0.2% response rate. It should come as no surprise that nearly all of the respondents indicated that they had been harassed (as defined by the questionnaire). A claim from this survey that 9 out of 10 respondents were harassed made news headlines.

When the final report arising from this survey appeared in 1993, American newspapers carried prominent articles about it, almost all of which uncritically treated the findings as if they reflected accurate estimates of the true rates of sexual harassment among teenage girls in schools. This is a case in which both a biased sampling frame and selection bias overwhelmingly rob the survey of any value whatsoever. Motivations for responding would have largely determined who ended up in the sample and who did not. *Nothing* can be concluded from the study about the harassment rates among the 99.8% of the readers who did not respond to the survey, to say nothing of the population of American teenage girls. This kind of self-selecting poll is referred to by competent pollsters as SLOPs (Self-selected Listener Opinion Polls, a term coined by researchers at the National Opinion Research Center at the University of Chicago).

There are conditions in which selection bias serves important research functions, but they require intentional and systematically controlled selection. It is not uncommon for researchers to deliberately include a predetermined percentage of their sample from a certain subpopulation. When sampling of this kind is not random, it is known as **quota sampling** (or sometimes, proportional sampling). While quota sampling may be pursued in the interest of avoiding over- or underrepresentation in the sample by sub-populations, it may also be used to 'oversample' small subpopulations that are of particular interest to the researcher. Oversampling usually is used to obtain sufficiently large numbers of units from the subpopulations concerned to guarantee reasonably precise sample estimates.

DEFINITION

A major drawback for quota sampling is that while it may ensure proportionate representation on those variables attended to by the researcher, it will not do so for all other variables. Quota samples may be strongly biased on some of those other variables. As Marsh (1988: 179) points out in her book on data analysis for social scientists, most opinion polls in Britain (including a lot of marketing surveys) are conducted on quota samples. The researchers specify the types of people they want in their survey and the percentages of each type, and the interviewers hired by the company conducting the poll are then left to find and interview appropriate quotas of those types of people. It is likely that the interviewers tend to choose cooperative, friendly, talkative and outgoing people more often than those who are not. In doing so, they unintentionally engage in biased selection procedures.

DEFINITION   Another frequently used procedure is **criterion-based selection**, which involves sampling and then either admitting or rejecting candidates for the sample on the basis of some criterion (e.g., sampling visitors to medical centers and then admitting them into the study sample if they are HIV-positive but rejecting them if they are not). This procedure is a substitute for having a sampling frame that defines a population by the desired criteria (for instance, there is no publicly available register of HIV-positive people). Researchers in clinical and health-related areas often use criterion-based samples.

DEFINITION   A third kind of selection procedure involves selecting people who are suggested by those already selected for the sample. This is often called **snowball sampling**, since the sample 'snowballs' outward from a small starting-group. Research on populations that have no sampling frame, such as drug-users, the homeless, or members of a secret organization, often must resort to snowball sampling.

DEFINITION   Two other nonrandom selection procedures are less defensible but nevertheless widely used. Perhaps the most frequently used kind of sample in psychological research is the convenience sample. **Convenience sampling** amounts to selecting from a sampling frame that is available to study at the time. The first-year class of psychology students is an example of a convenience sample, as is a clinical psychologist's current clientele or the inmates of a prison. There are research situations in which convenience sampling is the only practical option, and institution-based research is a prominent example. In most societies any researcher who wishes to study the psychological effects of institutionalization must confine their sample of inmates to those who have been officially incarcerated.

DEFINITION   Haphazard sampling, while not frequently used by scientific researchers, sometimes is mistaken for random sampling and therefore deserves a mention here. **Haphazard sampling** refers to the practice of including whatever units are encountered at the time in a sample. News reporters frequently employ this procedure when interviewing 'the person in the street.' It is closely related to convenience sampling but usually lacks even a well-defined sampling frame for a basis.

Now we turn to random selection procedures. The **simple random sample** uses a randomizing device to select units from a population in such a way that each unit has the same probability of being selected. Often the randomizing device is a table of random numbers or a pseudo-random number-generating computer program. Each unit in the sampling frame is given a unique identification number. If this number is randomly selected then that unit is included in the sample. The simple random selection procedure is unbiased on all conceivable variables, and this is one of its great strengths.

DEFINITION

Are random samples also representative of their parent populations? A brief answer is that *on average*, random selection produces a representative sample. This point is important, and often catches people unawares. Random selection does not guarantee exactly the same proportions of, say, men and women in a sample as there are in the population. By luck of the draw, we might end up with a greater proportion of men or of women. However, if we drew random samples over and over again, the average proportions of men and women would converge to their true population values, just as tossing a fair coin hundreds of times will give a proportion of heads that gets very close to 0.5. At first glance, this might seem to be a severe drawback to random selection. Yet, thanks to inferential statistical techniques and the probability theory underlying them, it is not a drawback. Some of the material in this chapter and Chapter 5 will equip you not only to understand why this is the case, but also to estimate how much variability you can expect in a random sample.

A closely related sampling procedure is the **systematic** sample, which entails simply choosing every kth unit in the list (e.g., every 100th name in a phonebook). It turns out that systematic samples give results that are very close to random samples, and so this more convenient procedure often is used instead of going to the trouble of random selection. The main caution to be observed in using a systematic procedure is to make sure there is no bias or pattern built into the order of the list. That is, systematic sampling is like random sampling only when the list is randomly ordered.

DEFINITION

Simple random samples require a complete enumeration of the population, and that is often a severe practical limitation. A viable alternative is **multistage cluster sampling**, whereby 'clusters' of units are randomly sampled and then units are sampled from within each of the selected clusters. Perhaps the most common example is a two-stage household-occupant sample. Households are randomly sampled from a list of addresses (e.g., taken from the phonebook), and then one person is randomly selected from each household that has been included in the sample. Educational psychologists sometimes use multistage cluster sampling for large-scale studies, selecting schools, then classrooms, and then students.

DEFINITION

Researchers with access to sampling frames that contain relevant information about each unit, on the other hand, may use that information to ensure that their samples contain exact proportions of the characteristics that have been identified. Institutions and organizations often have lists of members that identify characteristics such as gender or age. The procedure that they adopt under such conditions is called **stratified random sampling**, in which the researcher stratifies the population on one or more characteristics and then randomly samples units from within each of the strata. A developmental psychologist, for instance, might decide to stratify the children in a primary school into five age categories. From the student records, suppose he found that the categories divided the population into subgroups containing 21%, 15%, 23%, 19%, and 22% of the children. If he wanted to ensure that his sample contained exactly the same number of children from each age group, then he could take five random samples of the same size from each age category, or stratum.

DEFINITION

One reason it is important to know whether simple random sampling, cluster sampling, or stratified random sampling has been used is that *they have a different impact on the variance in any sample estimates of population parameters*. This impact on the variance is called a sample 'design effect'. We will not venture into the technicalities of design effects, but they merit a brief explanation of what they are and why they are important. Consider the rather fanciful population in the small town of Outcome. Outcome's residents live in three suburbs, each of which has the peculiar property that every residence in a given suburb has exactly the same income. The households' incomes are listed in Table 4.2.

TABLE 4.2 Income in outcome

Lodown	Middleton	Indulgencia
$2000	$20,000	$200,000
$2000	$20,000	$200,000
$2000	$20,000	$200,000
$2000	$20,000	$200,000
$2000	$20,000	... (50 times)
$2000	$20,000	
$2000	$20,000	
$2000	$20,000	
$2000	$20,000	
$2000	... (100 times)	
$2000		
$2000		
$2000		
$2000		
... (150 times)		

Suppose a survey researcher wants to obtain a sample of 30 households in Outcome for the purpose of estimating the mean income (this researcher does not have access to our information about household incomes in Outcome). If she performs a simple random sample, then every household will have an equal probability of being selected. Since the entire town consists of $50 + 100 + 150 = 300$ households, that probability is 30/300, or 1/10. Her sample mean will not always equal the true mean (which, by the way, is $41,000), but its value will tend to be somewhere nearby.

But suppose she reasons along the following lines: 'These three suburbs are far apart and I have only enough money and time to survey one of them. So I'll randomly pick one of them and then randomly sample households within that one. To make things unbiased, I'll set up my selection probabilities so that $P(\text{Lodown}) = 1/2$, $P(\text{Middleton}) = 1/3$, and $P(\text{Indulgencia}) = 1/6$.' What will happen to her sample mean? It will either be $2000, $20,000, or $200,000 but never $41,000. The point to be gleaned from this example, then, is that *cluster samples inflate sampling variation* in the relevant sample statistic insofar as they select homogeneous clusters from which to sample (such as families, schools, or suburbs).

Lastly, suppose she decides to stratify her sample on the basis of suburb. 'I know there are 150 households in Lodown, 100 in Middleton, and 50 in Indulgencia. So I'll sample proportionally from each of those suburbs. I'll randomly select 15 households from Lodown, 10 from Middleton, and 5 from Indulgencia.' Now her sample mean will equal exactly $41,000 every time. In this extreme case, since income corresponds perfectly with suburb, the sample mean's variance has been reduced to zero. In general, we can see that *stratification reduces the sampling variation* of the relevant sample statistic, since it eliminates variation from one or more of the characteristics that otherwise could contribute to variability.

An introduction to sampling methods would not be complete without acknowledging the fact that random selection procedures do have limitations. The most commonly problematic among them are these three:

1. Random selection procedures require a complete enumeration of the population. Stratified random sampling requires even more information than a mere list.
2. Refusal rates or dropouts from the sample can seriously compromise or destroy sample representability and may introduce bias.
3. Sometimes random selection may be ethically or politically unviable, for instance if inclusion in or exclusion from a sample changes the status of a person in the eyes of others.

SUMMARY   The **unit of analysis** constitutes the items to be sampled from a population. Sampling processes have three components that determine the nature of the sample:
1. A **sampling frame** which defines the population from which the sample is taken;
2. A **selection procedure** by which the sample actually is taken;
3. **Extraneous influences**, which denote unintended influences on sample selection (e.g., refusals to participate in research or volunteer effects).

Random selection procedures make use of randomizing devices to determine the probability of a particular unit being selected for the sample.
Nonrandom selection procedures make use of nonrandom systems or criteria for determining which units will be selected.
Sampling may be done in two ways that determine whether a unit is eligible to be selected more than once:
● **With replacement**, which permits a unit to be reselected;
● **Without replacement**, which ensures that a unit will not be reselected.

There are five commonly used types of **nonrandom selection procedures**:
1. **Quota sampling** (either unbiased or intentionally and proportionately biased) entails deliberately including a predetermined percentage of the sample from specific subpopulations;
2. **Criterion-based sampling** involves selecting and then either admitting or rejecting candidates for the sample on the basis of some criterion;
3. **Snowball sampling** entails selecting people who are suggested by those already selected for the sample;
4. **Convenience sampling** amounts to selecting from a sampling frame that is available to study at the time;
5. **Haphazard** (but not random!) **sampling** is the practice of including whatever units are encountered at the time in the sample.

There are three commonly used **random selection procedures**:
1. **Simple random sampling**, in which each unit has the same probability of being selected from the population;
2. **Multistage cluster sampling**, whereby 'clusters' of units are randomly sampled and then units are sampled from within each of the selected clusters; and
3. **Stratified random sampling** entails stratifying the population on one or more characteristics and then randomly sampling units from within each of the strata.

Experimental design, randomized assignment, and statistical inference

As mentioned earlier, the most popular uses for statistical inference are estimating population parameters from random samples and deciding between competing claims about those population parameters. In psychological research, experimenters tend to be most interested in the latter, while psychologists conducting nonexperimental studies tend to be more interested in the former. In fact, experimenters often do not have an actual population or random sample at all. Instead, they usually use statistical inference to help them judge whether an apparent effect from their experimental manipulations is 'real' or whether it might have arisen by chance, and they do so by making inferences from their data to imagined or hypothetical populations that correspond to rival models of the phenomena under study.

This is exactly the kind of inference required to settle the debate over the interpretation of the findings in our size–weight illusion experiment. As you will recall, in this example 13 out of 20 participants picked the larger object as being the heavier of two objects even though both objects have the same weight. Although that is a majority and therefore appears to support the size–weight illusion hypothesis, a skeptic could argue that the experiment resulted in 13/20 simply by chance variation. In doing so, the skeptic is casting doubt on the internal validity of the experiment by proposing a rival hypothesis, namely that the size of the object makes no difference to participants and they are therefore equally likely to pick either object. The experimenter may be able to deflect this criticism by using statistical inference to assess the plausibility of the claim that these 20 choices could have come from a hypothetical population in which either object is equally likely to be chosen.

Before discussing the role of statistical inference in experiments any further, we need to introduce the basic kinds of experimental designs and survey their strengths and weaknesses. Almost all experiments allocate the units of analysis (e.g., people) to distinct **experimental conditions**, which correspond to states or values of the independent variables. For instance, a study of the effects of alcohol consumption on reaction times might have two conditions: an 'alcohol present' condition in which the participant's blood-alcohol level is elevated to a specified value (say, 0.07), and an 'alcohol absent' condition in which there is no detectable alcohol in the participant's bloodstream. The independent variable in this experiment would be the amount of alcohol in the bloodstream, and the experimental conditions would correspond to just two values: 0.07 and 0.

Perhaps the most important distinction between experimental designs is whether the unit of analysis is exposed to all experimental conditions or only one. Designs that expose units to all conditions are called **repeated-**   DEFINITIONS

measures or **within-subjects** designs, and those that expose each unit to only one condition are known as **between-subjects** designs. Between-subjects designs require **randomized assignment** of each subject to an experimental condition. In our alcohol effect study, a within-subjects design would involve measuring participants' reaction times under both the alcohol-present and absent conditions. A between-subjects design would measure some participants under the alcohol-present condition and others under the alcohol-absent condition, with participants being randomly assigned to one condition or the other.

Each type of design has advantages and drawbacks. First, let us consider the effect that our choice of design has on our ability to make valid inferences about the effects of alcohol on reaction times. In the between-subjects design, the mean reaction time in the alcohol-present condition might be greater than in the alcohol-absent condition. This difference might be due to the effects of alcohol, but it could also be simply because some slower people might have been assigned by chance to the alcohol-present condition. A within-subjects design would not suffer as much from chance variation in reaction times, because the mean reaction times of a group of people under identical conditions will tend to be more similar than the mean reaction times of two different groups of people. Generally, within-subjects designs have less variation than between-subjects designs for much the same reason that a stratified random sample has less variation than a simple random sample.

That said, within-subjects designs nevertheless suffer some drawbacks that between-subjects designs do not. Most of these drawbacks involve threats to internal validity. Four of them are history effects, maturation effects, test–retest effects, and instrumentation changes.

DEFINITION   A **History effect** simply means anything that may change between one measurement occasion and another that is not under the experimenter's control. For instance, an earthquake in between the alcohol-absent and alcohol-present conditions could distract participants and affect their concentration, thereby altering their reaction times. Although experimenters may take special pains to screen participants from any extraneous events or changes (e.g., by confining them to a laboratory for the duration of the study), it is often very difficult to ensure that no such changes occur.

DEFINITION   **Maturation effects** refer to any age-related process that can affect the dependent variable, be it a 'positive' or 'negative' effect. An experimental study of the impact of a new sports coaching technique on primary school-children's coordination levels, for instance, would be confounded by the fact that children's coordination may be improving because of their natural physical development. Maturation processes typically cannot be brought under an experimenter's control.

Test–retest effects refer to the influence of earlier measurements of the dependent variable on later measurements. Learning experiments are among the best examples of this problem. Someone who has been taught touch-typing by one method, for instance, cannot be retaught to touch-type by another method later on because they have already learned. Nearly any performative task involves learnable skills so a person's performance may improve from one condition to the next by mere practice or familiarity. DEFINITION

Instrumentation changes are any alteration in the measurement properties of whatever instrument is being used to measure the dependent variable. Unlike test–retest effects, this usually is not a serious problem for within-subjects experiments unless the instrument is influenced by uncontrolled characteristics of the environment in which the experiment takes place. This problem can be particularly deleterious if the measurement properties are affected by changes in the independent variable itself. DEFINITION

In summary, within-subjects designs involve a tradeoff between reducing error and revealing bogus effects due to threats to internal validity. It is worth bearing in mind, however, that neither type of experimental design guards against threats to *external validity*. This fact underscores the importance of incorporating sampling as well as experimental design strategies and considerations into any research project.

Between-subjects and within-subjects designs are not the only alternatives available to experimenters, and in this section we have barely scratched the surface of the topic of experimental design. Psychological researchers routinely use designs that combine within- and between-subjects arrangements, and they also employ special kinds of within-subjects designs in which the order of the experimental conditions differs among participants so as to handle some of the problems faced by ordinary within-subjects experiments. In this book, none the less, we will restrict our attention to 'pure' between-subjects and within-subjects designs for the sake of clarity.

Experimental conditions correspond to states or values of the independent variables. SUMMARY
Repeated-measures or **within-subjects** designs expose units to all conditions.
Between-subjects designs expose each unit to only one condition.
Randomized assignment of units involves using a randomizing device to allocate units to conditions.

The following threats to **internal validity** are handled by between-subjects designs but not within-subjects designs:
1. **History effects**: Anything that may change between one measurement occasion and another that is not under the experimenter's control.

SUMMARY

2. **Maturation effects**: Any age-related process that can affect the dependent variable.
3. **Test–retest effects**: The influence of earlier measurements of the dependent variable on later measurements.
4. **Instrumentation changes**: Any alteration in the measurement properties of whatever instrument is being used to measure the dependent variable.

An introduction to probability

The modern concept of probability was invented and formalized in the mid-1650s (for an interesting account of its history, see Hacking, 1975), although the word itself is older. The oldest version of this concept is the 'a priori' or 'theoretical' version, in which probabilities may be deduced by reasoning

DEFINITION   about how many ways an event can occur. An **a priori probability** of an event is the number of distinct ways in which that event could occur divided by the total number of distinct occurrences.

For example, when we toss a fair coin, the probability of it landing on 'heads' is 1/2, since there is only one way that a 'heads' event can occur and there are two possible occurrences ('heads' or 'tails', if we ignore extraordinary possibilities such as the coin landing on its edge, or being snatched in mid-air by a bird). Likewise, with a fair die, the six faces are taken to be equally likely so the probability of rolling a '5' is 1/6.

Here is a slightly more complicated example. If we have a fire-fighting squad of two men and one woman, and we select a two-person team at random, what is the probability that the team will have one man and one woman on it? To figure this out, we need to know how many ways we could choose a team consisting of one man and one woman; and we need to know how many different two-person teams we could choose. One way to do this is to label each of the squad members (say, M1, M2, and F). There are two ways of forming a team of one man and one woman, namely {F, M1} and {F, M2}. There is only one other team that could be formed, which is {M1, M2}. Since there are two ways to form a team of one man and one woman out of a total of three possible teams, the probability of getting one man and one woman on the team is 2/3.

We usually do not know enough about real-world events to calculate a priori probabilities, although researchers often use them to construct idealized models of experiments with randomized assignment or studies using random samples. Such models must be constructed with due caution. For instance, it can be quite dangerous to assume that two events are equally probable simply because we do not know what their probabilities are.

A more modern version of probability is based on empirical observations of event frequencies, and therefore is often called the 'frequentist' or 'empirical' version. A priori probabilities may be deduced before anything has been observed, but frequentist probabilities are calculated after observations have been made. A **frequentist probability** of an event is the number of times DEFINITION that event has occurred divided by the total number of occurrences in the relevant sequence of events. If you want to find out whether a coin is unbiased or not, then throw it many times and record how often the heads and tails occur. The probability of a heads is then estimated by the number of times heads occurs divided by the total number of coin-tosses (or trials). This fraction is also known as a **relative frequency**. The greater the number of tosses, DEFINITION the more stable and therefore valid the result. Frequentist probability is the dominant version of probability in the psychology and the social sciences, and an influential school of statistical inference is founded on it.

Because probabilities are expressed as fractions of a total, they always take values between 0 and 1. They behave like proportions. Sometimes people express proportions as percentages by multiplying them by 100, and for some purposes that is an acceptable way of representing probabilities. A probability of $\frac{1}{2}$ may be expressed as $\frac{1}{2}$, 0.5, or 50% as long as the usage is logically consistent. If in doubt, however, use proportions.

Probabilities also sum to 1 if they are added up across all possible and nonoverlapping events. The reason for this is that ultimately *something* must happen. Notice that the probability of getting a 'heads or tails' on a coin-toss is $\frac{1}{2} + \frac{1}{2} = 1$, since we have covered all possible events.

Both a priori and frequentist probabilities are linked to the concepts of taking a random sample from a specified population and repeatable, independent trials. It is easy to confuse these concepts with statements about unique events. Suppose a nationwide census establishes that 10% of the people eligible for employment are unemployed. Does that mean you have a 0.10 chance of being unemployed right now? No, since either you are employed right now or you are not. The 10% figure refers only to the probability of selecting an unemployed person if we sampled randomly from the national population of people eligible for work at the time of the census.

There are kinds of uncertainty that admit neither to the a priori nor the frequentist approaches. What, for instance, is the probability of nuclear war? What is the probability that you will become a millionaire? Most of us have some notions of probabilities such as these. However, they are unique events with no a priori justification for logical probabilities, so they are subjective probabilities. **Subjective probabilities** may be thought of as 'coherent' DEFINITION degrees of uncertainty, in the sense that they obey the rules of probability theory. They form the basis for 'Bayesian' schools of statistical inference. Bayesian inference will not be covered in this book, but it is influential throughout statistics and is used in fields such as statistical decision theory, economics, artificial intelligence, and risk assessment.

Empirically based probabilities often do not accord with our subjective estimates, especially in matters where our own perceptions and beliefs are influenced by second-hand accounts from the media or authoritative sources. Pause for a moment and try answering these three questions.

1. Which kills more people: automobile accidents or diabetes?
2. Now ask yourself to estimate the number of endangered mammalian species and the number of endangered invertebrate species.
3. How many words of the form _ _ _ _ _ n _ exist in the English language? How many words of the form _ _ _ _ ing exist?

DEFINITION   If you are like most people, your answers to these questions will be guided by what is called the **availability heuristic**, judging the likelihood of an event by how readily previous instances of it come to mind, or how easy it is to imagine it (see Plous, 1993, for an accessible explanation of this and related heuristics). Most of us tend to think more people die on the road than from diabetes, but in fact the latter kills more people than auto accidents do. Auto accidents are more 'available' to us because we have absorbed so many news stories about them, but not many about diabetes. Most of us tend to over-estimate the proportion of endangered species that are mammalian and under-estimate the proportion of invertebrate ones for much the same reason. According to reasonable estimates, there are many more invertebrate species that are endangered, primarily because there are so many invertebrate species to start with. Likewise, we can recall seven-letter words ending in 'ing' much more easily than seven-letter words with 'n' in the sixth position, so many of us are led to think that there must be more _ _ _ _ ing words than _ _ _ _ _ n _ words. Of course, by definition the reverse must be true, since the collection of _ _ _ _ _ n _ words contains all those of the form _ _ _ _ ing.

Another important concept to bear in mind about probabilities is that they are expectations rather than exact predictions of what will happen in a finite number of trials or when we take a finite random sample from a population. Our intuitions usually lead us astray in this matter. If you find probability rather counter-intuitive, you are not alone. In fact, most people, including the intelligent and well-educated, do not find probability easy to understand and often make mistakes when dealing with it intuitively. From time to time in this and later chapters, we will compare human intuition with the prescriptions of probability theory.

DEFINITION   One of the most common intuitive blunders is called **gambler's fallacy**. It amounts to a belief that random events are 'self-correcting' and therefore a tendency for us to think that the proportion of an event's occurrences in a limited number of trials will be very close to that event's probability. Suppose you've observed five tosses of a coin that you know is fair, and the sequence has been: HHHHH. What is the chance of a tails coming up on the next toss? It might seem quite high because the coin, although fair, has just landed on heads five times consecutively. It still is 0.5 because the tosses are independent of one another (otherwise they would not be random, would they?). Here are two related things to try.

1. Imagine that you have tossed a fair coin twice, and it has come up heads both times. You are about to toss it eight more times. Out of the total of 10 tosses, how many heads should you expect to occur?
2. Which of the following sequences seems more like it was generated by a random process (e.g., flipping a coin)?
   (A) HTHHHTTTTHTHHTTTHHHTH
   (B) HTHTHTTTHHHTHTHTTHHHTH

For the first question, if you answered that you expected five Heads in 10 tosses, you fell for gambler's fallacy, the belief that luck 'balances out' even in the short-run. *Given that you already got two heads*, in tossing the coin eight more times you should expect four heads which would result in a total of six heads rather than five. The coin does not remember how it landed on the first two tosses. Whereas nonrandom processes may behave as if they have memory, random ones do not.

As for the second, if you chose sequence (B) as more random-looking than (A) then you are like most of us. Most people choose (B) because it alternates between H and T more often than the first one does (on 14 out of 20 occasions). That kind of switching seems to represent randomness for us. The first one, however, more closely resembles a genuinely random sequence in which H and T are equally probable because it switches from one to the other on only 10 out of 20 occasions. If we expect more fluctuation and variability in random sequences than is reasonable, then we will tend to see the clumps in truly random sequences as patterns that require explanation. During the WW II London Blitz, the fact that some suburbs were left untouched while others were devastated by bombs led many commentators to elaborate theories of why the Germans were targeting one suburb rather than another. But the distribution of the strikes turned out to fit a random distribution very well, and Londoners were finding 'patterns' that did not exist.

This example highlights a very important point. Before we start trying to explain any phenomenon, especially those involving apparent patterns or coincidences, we should ascertain whether there is anything to explain at all. In other words, we should check the possibility that random processes might have produced those phenomena. That is one of the main reasons for learning about statistics.

Let us set the stage for further considerations of this issue through another example. The secretarial pool in a small organization consists of Boris and Ingrid. Each day one of them is allocated to handle receptionist duties at the front desk. Instead of a systematic roster, the boss claims to be tossing a coin to decide which it will be. How do Ingrid and Boris know that the boss is not selecting them via some other biased method?

They decide to keep a tally of who is selected, to see whether there is any apparent bias or pattern. The first 10 days' sequence looks like this:

$$\{B, I, I, B, I, I, B, B, I, I\}.$$

Ingrid has been assigned six out of 10 times and feels cheated. However, she decides that she is willing to wait until they have a longer sequence before accusing the boss of discrimination. They wait until they have tallied 30 days' assignments:

$$\{B, I, I, B, I, I, B, B, I, I, B, B, B, B, I, B, I, B, B, I, B, B, I, I, I, B, B, B, B, I\}.$$

Now Boris feels discriminated against, because he has been assigned 17 out of 30 times. Should he confront the boss? Ingrid and Boris need to know how likely it is that if the boss really is tossing a fair coin, their shares of the receptionist duty assignments could fluctuate as much as they have. We will explore ways of addressing this kind of question in this chapter and the next.

SUMMARY

A **probability** takes a value from 0 to 1. An event that never can occur has a probability of 0, and an event that always occurs has a probability of 1. Probabilities sum to 1 if they are added up across all possible and nonoverlapping events.

An **a priori probability** of an event is the number of distinct ways in which that event could occur divided by the total number of distinct occurrences.

A **frequentist probability** of an event is the number of times that event has occurred divided by the total number of occurrences in the relevant sequence of events. This is also known as a **relative frequency**.

A **subjective probability** is a judgment about the likelihood of an event that is 'coherent' in the sense that it obeys the rules of probability theory.

The **availability heuristic** is judging the likelihood of an event by how readily previous instances of it come to mind, or how easy it is to imagine it.

Gambler's fallacy arises from a belief that random events are 'self-correcting' and therefore the proportion of an event's occurrences in a limited number of trials will be very close to that event's probability.

Compound events and conditional probabilities

Suppose a company employs 20 people, of whom seven are smokers and nine are under the age of 30. If we wanted to ascertain the probability of selecting someone at random from this company who is under 30 and a smoker, then we would be trying to assess the probability of a compound event, which we could describe as 'under 30 and a smoker.' **Compound events** are those that consist of more than one event, joined by conjunctive words such as 'and' and 'or.' In this section, we will find out how to determine probabilities of compound events, and that knowledge will turn out to have a large variety of uses.

DEFINITION

Now, suppose we already know that four people in the company are both smokers and under 30. Then we have everything we need for calculating the probability of randomly selecting someone from the company who is either a smoker, under 30, or both. In Figure 4.1, you may do this by simply counting these people, but let us also do this in a more generally useful way. If we simply added the smokers and under-30s together, we would get $7 + 9 = 16$. This would 'double-count' the four people who both smoke and are under 30, however, so we would need to subtract them from this sum to obtain the correct number of people who are either a smoker, under 30, or both: $16 - 4 = 12$.

Probabilities work in exactly the same way. Denoting smokers by 'S' and under-30s by 'U,' we may represent the probability of selecting a smoker by $P(S)$, which is 7/20, and the probability of selecting someone under 30 by $P(U)$, which is 9/20. If we were to add these two probabilities together, they would 'double-count' people who are both smokers and under 30. So we would subtract $P(S$ and $U)$, which is 4/20, from $P(S) + P(U)$ to get $P(S$ or $U)$:

$$P(S \text{ or } U) = P(S) + P(U) - P(S \text{ and } U) = 7/20 + 9/20 - 4/20 = 12/20.$$

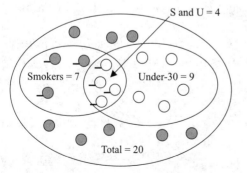

FIGURE 4.1 Population of 20 employees

StatPatch

YOU CAN PRACTICE WORKING WITH COMPOUND PROBABILITIES IN PROBPATCH

DEFINITION   This formula is known as the **addition rule**. In general, for any two events labeled A and B,

$$P(\text{A or B}) = P(\text{A}) + P(\text{B}) - P(\text{A and B}).$$

DEFINITION   If $P(\text{A and B}) = 0$, the events A and B are called **mutually exclusive** because they cannot co-occur. A person cannot be under 30 and over 50 at the same time, for instance. The probability of randomly selecting someone from the company who was under 30 (U) or over 50 (O) would be

$$P(\text{U or O}) = P(\text{U}) + P(\text{O}),$$

since $P(\text{U and O}) = 0$.

It may have already occurred to you that probabilities can differ depending on circumstances. Many health- or safety-promoting campaigns appeal to this idea, by arguing that your risk of suffering X will decrease if you follow the campaign's prescriptions. These days it is common for people to consider themselves to be in various 'risk categories' wherein their likelihood of suffering from X is greater or less than other risk categories. Probabilities that refer to

DEFINITION   specific subcategories in a population are called **conditional probabilities**.

Consider our small population of 20 employees. The probability of selecting a smoker at random from the entire population is $7/20 = 0.35$. However, if we sampled from only the under-30s, the probability of selecting a smoker would be $4/9 = 0.44$, which is higher than 0.35. We would say that the probability of getting a smoker conditional on the person being under 30 is 0.44. A shorthand way of expressing this conditional probability is

$$P(\text{S}|\text{U}) = 0.44,$$

where $P(\text{S}|\text{U})$ reads 'the probability of S given that U is true,' or simply 'the probability of S given U.' We can also have $P(\text{U}|\text{S})$, 'the probability of U given S.' This is the probability of selecting someone under 30 if we sample from the smokers, and it is $4/7 = 0.57$.

FORMULAS FOR   For any events A and B, a *general way of computing the conditional probabilities* if
CONDITIONAL   we know $P(\text{A})$, $P(\text{B})$, and $P(\text{A and B})$ uses these formulas:
PROBABILITIES

$$P(\text{A}|\text{B}) = P(\text{A and B})/P(\text{B})$$

and

$$P(\text{B}|\text{A}) = P(\text{A and B})/P(\text{A}).$$

So the probability of selecting a smoker given that the person is under 30 is

$$P(S|U) = P(S \text{ and } U)/P(U) = (4/20)/(9/20) = 4/9 = 0.44$$

and

$$P(U|S) = P(S \text{ and } U)/P(S) = (4/20)/(7/20) = 4/7 = 0.57.$$

It may seem arbitrary whether we are computing $P(A|B)$ or $P(B|A)$, but it actually is quite important to keep track of which of these conditional probabilities we are using, and what they mean. Suppose we have two overlapping populations:

- Australians: 18,000,000
- Native English-Speakers worldwide: 400,000,000.

Now suppose we also know how big that overlap is:

- Australian Native English-Speakers: 15,000,000.

Let us denote the Australians by A and the Native English-Speakers by E. If we randomly sample from the Australians, what is the probability of selecting a Native English-Speaker? In other words, what is $P(E|A)$? It is

$$P(E|A) = \frac{15,000,000}{18,000,000} = 0.8333$$

Now, what about the probability of getting an Australian if we sample from the Native English-Speakers of the world (i.e., what is $P(A|E)$)? It is

$$P(A|E) = \frac{15,000,000}{400,000,000} = 0.0375$$

$P(E|A)$ is huge compared to $P(A|E)$, because one of the subpopulations is so much larger than the other. Indeed, they are answers to two very different questions.

Nevertheless, in many real-world decisions conditional probabilities are routinely confused with one another. The DNA fingerprinting argument in criminal cases, for example, is based on experimental evidence that tells us the probability of getting a match between the DNA of someone other than the actual criminal and the DNA found at the scene of a crime. This conditional probability is, of course, very small. *But it is the wrong conditional probability,* namely $P(\text{Matching DNA}|\text{Not the criminal})$. What the jurors and magistrate require is $P(\text{Not the criminal}|\text{Matching DNA})$. Unfortunately there is no guarantee that P(Matching DNA|Not the criminal) and P(Not the criminal|Matching DNA) are not vastly different in magnitude.

When $P(A|B)$ and $P(A)$ differ, it indicates that events A and B are **dependent** on one another. On the other hand, if $P(A|B) = P(A)$ then A and B are **independent** events. Imagine that in another company of 20 employees, there were eight people under 30, four of whom smoked; and of the remaining 12 people, six smoked. That would make 10 smokers altogether, so $P(S)$ would be 10/20 or 0.5. Likewise, $P(S|U)$ would be $4/8 = 0.5$. The probability of randomly selecting a smoker from among the people under 30 would be the same as getting a smoker if we sampled from the entire company. The probability of selecting a smoker would not depend on whether we were sampling from the under-30 subpopulation or not, so we could say that smoking and being under 30 are independent of one another.

We will return to the issue of dependent and independent events later in this book, but before leaving it let's retrieve a couple more useful pieces of information. If events A and B are independent, then $P(A \text{ and } B) = P(A)P(B)$. This is known as the **multiplication rule** for the 'joint probability' of independent events. This rule arises from a line of reasoning that runs as follows. First, the definition of independent events entails that $P(A|B) = P(A)$. Our formula for conditional probabilities is

$$P(A|B) = P(A \text{ and } B)/P(B).$$

We may replace $P(A|B)$ with $P(A)$, which tells us

$$P(A) = P(A \text{ and } B)/P(B).$$

So $P(A \text{ and } B)$ must equal $P(A)P(B)$.

The multiplication rule is very useful for working out the probability of sequences of independent events. It could assist Ingrid and Boris in their quest to ascertain how likely it is that if the boss really is tossing a fair coin, their shares of the receptionist duty assignments could fluctuate as much as they have. They now know, for instance, that if the boss is using a fair coin so that the assignments are independent events and both $P(B)$ and $P(I)$ are $\frac{1}{2}$ for every assignment, then the probability of any particular sequence of N assignments is just $\frac{1}{2}$ multiplied by itself N times. The probability of Ingrid being assigned four times in a row, for instance, is $(\frac{1}{2})(\frac{1}{2})(\frac{1}{2})(\frac{1}{2}) = 1/16$.

Thus far, we have established that when events A and B are mutually exclusive, $P(A \text{ and } B) = 0$, and when they are independent, $P(A \text{ and } B) = P(A)P(B)$. How large can $P(A \text{ and } B)$ be? By way of comparing your intuition with the answer and also illustrating why this is important, take a short time to read the brief description below and complete the subjective rating exercise.

> At school Jim was generally withdrawn, studious, and unemotive. While excelling in mathematics, science, and business subjects, he performed indifferently in the humanities and the arts. The single exception was that he showed a flair for music.

On a scale from 0 to 1 rate how likely you think each of these outcomes is. As an adult, Jim:

(A) became a professional artist who solved crossword puzzles for a hobby.
(B) became an accountant.
(C) read novels for a hobby.
(D) played jazz for a hobby.
(E) became a forest ranger.
(F) became an accountant who played jazz for a hobby.

Given the description, most of us tend to think that Jim sounds like the kind of person likely to become an accountant. We may have no strong views about the likelihood that he plays jazz for a hobby, but the bit in the description about his talent for music makes us think it's even *more* likely that he is an accountant who plays jazz for a hobby. So we might think that $P(F)$ – became an accountant who played jazz for a hobby – is larger than $P(D)$.

If you rated $P(F)$ more highly than $P(D)$, then you may have fallen prey to a famous cognitive illusion (cf. Plous, 1993). Option F is a compound event, namely B and D, so $P(F)$ is the same as $P(B \text{ and } D)$. Can $P(B \text{ and } D)$ be larger than $P(D)$? Imagine sampling from a population containing some accountants and jazz players. There cannot possibly be more accountants who play jazz than accountants, so $P(B \text{ and } D)$ cannot be larger than $P(D)$. In fact, two events cannot be more probable than the *least probable* of either one. The famous cognitive illusion referred to at the beginning of this paragraph is the **conjunction fallacy**, in which intuitive probability judgments violate the rule that $P(A \text{ and } B)$ is always less than or equal to the smaller of $P(A)$ and $P(B)$.

Compound events are those that consist of more than one event, joined by conjunctive words such as 'and' and 'or.'
The **addition rule** is that for any two events labeled A and B,

$$P(A \text{ or } B) = P(A) + P(B) - P(A \text{ and } B).$$

SUMMARY

SUMMARY   Probabilities that refer to specific subcategories in a population are called **conditional probabilities**. $P(A|B)$ is the probability of A given that B is true, and $P(B|A)$ is the probability of B given that A is true. Conditional probabilities obey these rules:

$$P(A|B) = P(A \text{ and } B)/P(B),$$

and

$$P(B|A) = P(A \text{ and } B)/P(A).$$

If $P(A|B) \neq P(A)$ then events A and B are **dependent** on one another. On the other hand, if $P(A|B) = P(A)$ then A and B are **independent** events. *Rules concerning $P(A \text{ and } B)$:*
1. If the events A and B are **mutually exclusive**, then $P(A \text{ and } B) = 0$.
2. If A and B are independent events, $P(A \text{ and } B) = P(A)P(B)$ (the **multiplication rule**).
3. $P(A \text{ and } B)$ is always less than or equal to the smaller of $P(A)$ and $P(B)$. The **conjunction fallacy** occurs when intuitive probability judgments violate this rule.

Probability distributions

In Chapter 3, we examined frequency distributions and various ways of describing and summarizing them. Probability distributions are closely related to frequency distributions and indeed differ primarily in using probabilities rather than frequencies, so the definition of a probability distribution is very DEFINITIONS   similar to the definition of a frequency distribution. A **probability distribution** presents the categories of a variable (or scores, for a quantitative variable) and the probability with which each occurs.

In the first example of a frequency distribution in Chapter 3, we used a study of 50 heart patients that included 12 females and 38 males. The probability of selecting a female if we sampled randomly from these 50 people would be 12/50, or 0.24, and the probability of getting a male would be 38/50, or 0.76. Table 4.3 shows the resulting probability distribution along

TABLE 4.3 Probability distribution of gender

	Frequency	Probability
Female	12	0.24
Male	38	0.76
Total	50	1.00

with the frequency distribution. As you can see, for this kind of data the probability distribution conveys the same information as percentages do.

Given the similarities between percentage and probability distributions, it should probably not surprise you that cumulative percentages are very similar to cumulative probabilities. A **cumulative probability** associated with a   DEFINITION particular score on a variable is the probability of occurrences at or below that score. These probabilities are appropriate for any variable that has an ordinal, interval, or ratio level of measurement. Again, we may borrow the 50 heart patients from Chapter 3, this time sorted once again according to their level of exercise. Table 4.4 compares the probability and cumulative probability distributions for exercise level among these heart patients. All of the descriptive statistical and graphical techniques and concepts in Chapter 3 may be used to help understand probability distributions. Probability distributions may be symmetrical or skewed, for instance. They may be graphed using bar charts, histograms, or frequency polygons as appropriate.

Thus far, the probability distributions we have examined are **observed**   DEFINITIONS **distributions** based on a sample of data. Some very useful probability distributions are based on a priori probabilities. They are **theoretical distributions**, and can provide researchers with powerful models of phenomena in which random processes play a role. To conclude this chapter, we will investigate two such distributions: the binomial distribution and the normal distribution.

Suppose we have a series of N trials with only two possible events on each trial (as in tossing a coin, whether Boris or Ingrid is assigned receptionist duty, or a therapeutic intervention that either does or does not improve the client's wellbeing). The two events are mutually exclusive, so they cannot both occur on the same trial. Moreover, we will assume that the trials are independent of one another, so that what happens on one trial does not influence the outcomes in future trials. For the moment, let us assume that either event is equally likely to occur, so each event's probability of occurring on a trial is $\frac{1}{2}$. We are interested in the probability of getting 0, or 1, or 2, or ... N occurrences of one kind of event in N trials.

TABLE 4.4 Probability distribution of exercise

Level	Frequency	Probability	Cumulative frequency	Cumulative probability
0 = None	19	0.38	19	0.38
1 = Light	20	0.40	39	0.78
2 = Moderate	9	0.18	48	0.96
3 = Heavy	2	0.04	50	1.00
Total	50	1.00		

In other words, we would like to construct the probability distribution for
the number of occurrences out of N trials, which is called the **binomial
distribution** ('binomial' means two names, referring to two events).
Remember Boris, wondering whether his boss is using a fair coin because he
has been assigned reception duties 17 out of 30 times? If the boss is using a fair
coin and the probability of Boris being assigned, $P(B)$, really is $\frac{1}{2}$, how likely is
it that he could be assigned 17 times in 30 trials?

We already know that the events are *mutually exclusive* and the trial results
are *independent* of each other. We will make use of these two characteristics to
construct the binomial distribution, which is an arrangement that tells us what
each possible result of N trials is and its probability. If we begin with the
simplest cases, we may gain intuition about how the binomial distribution is
constructed for more complicated ones.

The simplest case in which there is more than one trial is when there are two
($N = 2$). If a fair coin is being used to assign Boris or Ingrid to reception duty,
then $P(B) = P(I) = \frac{1}{2}$. In two trials, there are four possible assignment
sequences that could occur. These are shown in the left-hand part of Table
4.5, along with the probability of each sequence. Since the two trials are
independent of each other, we may use the multiplication rule to obtain the
probability of each sequence. For instance, the probability of the B, I sequence
is $P(B \text{ and } I) = P(B)P(I) = (\frac{1}{2})(\frac{1}{2}) = \frac{1}{4}$.

The right-hand part of the table shows the binomial distribution for these
two trials, from Boris' standpoint. There is only one sequence that leads to
Boris getting no assignments, and that sequence is I, I, which has a probability
of $\frac{1}{4}$. So we may conclude that $P(0 \text{ B's}) = \frac{1}{4}$. Likewise, only the B, B sequence
leads to Boris getting two assignments, so $P(2 \text{ B's}) = \frac{1}{4}$. However, the sequences
I, B and B, I both lead to Boris getting one assignment in two trials, and since
these events are mutually exclusive the probability of one or the other
sequence occurring is just the sum of their probabilities. So, $P(1B) =
P(I, \text{ B}) + P(B, \text{ I}) = \frac{1}{4} + \frac{1}{4} = \frac{1}{2}$.

The same procedure may be used to construct the binomial distribution for
any value of N. Table 4.6 shows this distribution for $N = 3$. Fortunately, we

TABLE 4.5 Binomial distribution for $N = 2$

Sequence	Probability	Binomial distribution
I, I	$(\frac{1}{2})(\frac{1}{2}) = \frac{1}{4}$	$P(0 \text{ B's}) = P(I, \text{ I}) = \frac{1}{4}$
I, B	$(\frac{1}{2})(\frac{1}{2}) = \frac{1}{4}$	$P(1 \text{ B}) = P(I, \text{ B}) + P(B, \text{ I}) = \frac{1}{4} + \frac{1}{4} = \frac{1}{2}$
B, I	$(\frac{1}{2})(\frac{1}{2}) = \frac{1}{4}$	
B, B	$(\frac{1}{2})(\frac{1}{2}) = \frac{1}{4}$	$P(2 \text{ B's}) = P(B, \text{ B}) = \frac{1}{4}$

TABLE 4.6 Binomial distribution for $N = 3$

Sequence	Probability		Binomial distribution
I, I, I	$(\frac{1}{2})(\frac{1}{2})(\frac{1}{2}) = \frac{1}{8}$	←	$P(0 \text{ B's}) = \frac{1}{8}$
I, I, B	$(\frac{1}{2})(\frac{1}{2})(\frac{1}{2}) = \frac{1}{8}$		
I, B, I	$(\frac{1}{2})(\frac{1}{2})(\frac{1}{2}) = \frac{1}{8}$	←	$P(1 \text{ B}) = \frac{1}{8} + \frac{1}{8} + \frac{1}{8} = \frac{3}{8}$
B, I, I	$(\frac{1}{2})(\frac{1}{2})(\frac{1}{2}) = \frac{1}{8}$		
B, B, I	$(\frac{1}{2})(\frac{1}{2})(\frac{1}{2}) = \frac{1}{8}$		
B, I, B	$(\frac{1}{2})(\frac{1}{2})(\frac{1}{2}) = \frac{1}{8}$	←	$P(2 \text{ B's}) = \frac{1}{8} + \frac{1}{8} + \frac{1}{8} = \frac{3}{8}$
I, B, B	$(\frac{1}{2})(\frac{1}{2})(\frac{1}{2}) = \frac{1}{8}$		
B, B, B	$(\frac{1}{2})(\frac{1}{2})(\frac{1}{2}) = \frac{1}{8}$	←	$P(3 \text{ B's}) = P(B, B) = \frac{1}{8}$

do not have to go through this rather laborious process any time we want to use the binomial distribution. Tables for this distribution are commonly available, such as Table A.1 in the Appendix, and many statistical and spreadsheet programs enable computers to do the calculations for us.

Part of Table A.1 is displayed as Table 4.7. The number of trials, N, is listed in the left-hand column, and the number of events whose occurrences are of interest is listed in the next column to the right. The top row of numbers with '$P \leq 0.5$' above them are the probability of an event occurring. So far, we have considered only an event whose probability is $\frac{1}{2}$ (0.5 in this table). If we wished to find $P(0\text{B's})$ when $N = 2$, for instance, we would go to the left-most column and find '2' in the column for N, and then '0' in the 'No. of events' column. We would then move to the right along the '0' row until we got to the '0.50' column that corresponds to the probability of Boris being assigned reception duty, and find that the probability of 0 B's in two trials is 0.25000, or $\frac{1}{4}$ as in the table we constructed earlier. The relevant cell in the table has been highlighted in grey.

Let us try using Table A.1 in a situation where the probability of the event we are interested in is not $\frac{1}{2}$. An instructor is setting up part of an exam that will have multiple-choice questions. His questions each have five options from which students have to choose, only one of which is correct. If students get 50% or more of the questions right, then they have passed that section of the exam. He is interested in the probability that a student could pass that section by just randomly choosing answers. Since there are five options in each question, the student has a probability of 1/5 (0.2) of getting a question correct by random choice. If the section has only two questions, what is the probability that a student could pass the section?

The instructor consults Table A.1, using the section for $N = 2$ (Table 4.8). He reasons that the probability of a student getting 50% or better on the section is the probability of getting either 1 or 2 questions correct, which is

TABLE 4.7 Portion of table A.1

N	No. of events	0.05	0.10	0.15	0.20	0.25	0.30	0.35	0.40	0.45	0.50
						$P \leq 0.5$					
1	0	0.95000	0.90000	0.85000	0.80000	0.75000	0.70000	0.65000	0.60000	0.55000	0.50000
	1	0.05000	0.10000	0.15000	0.20000	0.25000	0.30000	0.35000	0.40000	0.45000	0.50000
2	0	0.90250	0.81000	0.72250	0.64000	0.56250	0.49000	0.42250	0.36000	0.30250	0.25000
	1	0.09500	0.18000	0.25500	0.32000	0.37500	0.42000	0.45500	0.48000	0.49500	0.50000
	2	0.00250	0.01000	0.02250	0.04000	0.06250	0.09000	0.12250	0.16000	0.20250	0.25000

TABLE 4.8 Part of table A.1 consulted by instructor

N	No. of events	0.05	0.10	0.15	0.20
1	0	0.95000	0.90000	0.85000	0.80000
	1	0.05000	0.10000	0.15000	0.20000
2	0	0.90250	0.81000	0.72250	0.64000
	1	0.09500	0.18000	0.25500	0.32000
	2	0.00250	0.01000	0.02250	0.04000

$P(1 \text{ correct}) + P(2 \text{ correct})$. The probability of a correct answer is 0.2, so he takes $P(1 \text{ correct})$ and $P(2 \text{ correct})$ from the column headed '0.20,' and finds $P(1 \text{ correct}) + P(2 \text{ correct}) = 0.32000 + 0.04000 = 0.36$. He should expect that a student who randomly chooses answers has a probability of 0.36 of passing this section of the exam.

A probability of 0.36 seems unacceptably high to the instructor. How could he decrease it? There are two ways: by increasing the number of choices in each question or by increasing the number of questions in the multiple-choice section. What if he used 14 questions instead of two? Table A.1 would reveal that the probability of a student getting seven or more questions out of 14 correct by random choice would be the sum of the probabilities highlighted in Table 4.9.

Those probabilities sum to only 0.01161, so a student would have only about a chance of 1 in 100 of passing the exam section by randomly choosing answers if 14 questions were used. And that is one reason why instructors set longer exams! Indeed, classical psychological test theory is based on, among other things, the insight that longer tests provide more reliable results.

We'll return to Boris and Ingrid's problem once more. If Boris wanted to find out the probability of being assigned 17 out of 30 times, he would find that Table A.1 does not go as far as $N = 30$, for reasons that we will learn about in

TABLE 4.9 Part of table A.1 for $N = 14$

N	No. of events	0.05	0.10	0.15	0.20
14	0	0.48767	0.22877	0.10277	0.04398
	1	0.35934	0.35586	0.25390	0.15393
	...	...	...	...	...
	7	0.00000	0.00016	0.00188	0.00921
	8	0.00000	0.00002	0.00029	0.00202
	9	0.00000	0.00000	0.00003	0.00034
	10	0.00000	0.00000	0.00000	0.00004
	11	0.00000	0.00000	0.00000	0.00000
	12	0.00000	0.00000	0.00000	0.00000
	13	0.00000	0.00000	0.00000	0.00000
	14	0.00000	0.00000	0.00000	0.00000

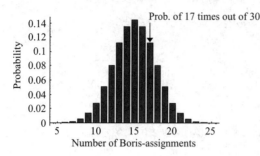

FIGURE 4.2 Binomial distribution for $P = 0.5$ and $N = 30$

Chapter 5. Ingrid, however, is statistically minded and produces a histogram of the binomial distribution when $N = 30$ and the probability of either event is $\frac{1}{2}$ (Figure 4.2). We can see from her histogram that 17 out of 30 times is not an unlikely occurrence, compared to the other possible outcomes. As you might expect, 15 out of 30 is the outcome with the highest probability, but others near to 15 are not all that much less likely. On the basis of this evidence, Boris does not have a clear-cut case that the boss is discriminating against him.

So far, we have dealt with **discrete distributions**, namely probability

DEFINITIONS distributions for discrete variables. Continuous variables may have **continuous distributions**, and one of the most widely used continuous distributions in psychological research is called the 'normal distribution.' The **normal distribution** is a symmetric, bell-shaped theoretical distribution with a specific shape that may be described in terms of its mean and standard deviation. Some naturally occurring phenomena have a distribution that corresponds fairly well to a normal distribution's shape (e.g., people's heights). In psychological research, some tests or quantitative measurement instruments are deliberately constructed so that their distributions approximate a normal curve. A standard IQ test is an example.

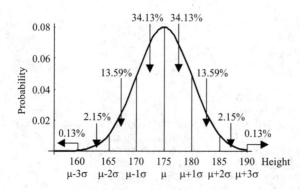

FIGURE 4.3 Normal distribution of men's heights

Suppose we have a population in which male heights are normally distributed with a mean of 175 cm and a standard deviation of 5 cm. Figure 4.3 displays some of the most important properties of the distribution, and provides the keys to understanding how those properties apply to any normally distributed variable. In any normal distribution, the percentage of the area under the curve between the mean (denoted by the Greek letter μ) and a score equal to the mean plus the standard deviation (denoted by the Greek letter σ) is 34.13%, so that 68.26% of the male heights are within one standard deviation above or below the mean. Likewise, the percentage of the area between $\mu + 1\sigma$ and $\mu + 2\sigma$ is 13.59%. And so on, for the other areas indicated in the graph.

Because the normal distribution has the same shape no matter what its mean and standard deviation, we do not have to construct a different normal distribution for every occasion. If we know that a variable has a normal distribution, then all we need to determine where and how wide the normal curve will be is the mean and standard deviation. For instance, if an IQ test had a normal distribution with a mean of 100 and standard deviation of 10, then an accurate display of the IQ probability distribution would simply substitute an IQ scale for the height scale in Figure 4.3 with 100 at μ, 110 at $\mu + 1\sigma$, 90 at $\mu - 1\sigma$, and so on.

Researchers often convert raw scores to the number of standard deviation units they are above or below the mean of the distribution. In so doing, they are transforming their raw scores into **standard scores** (also known as **z scores**). One of the reasons for this is so they can use a standardized normal distribution table such as Table A.2 in the Appendix. The **standardized normal distribution** has a mean of 0 and a standard deviation of 1, so it is scaled in terms of z-score values. For example, what percentage of the male population is taller than 183 cm? We cannot tell this from the graph. However, we can convert 183 cm into a z-score and consult Table A.2 to find out the area under the normal curve beyond that z-score. The relevant part of Table A.2 is displayed as Table 4.10. This table has three columns. The first one, labeled z, is the number of standard deviations a score is above the mean. The other two columns' entries are proportions (rather than percentages) of the area of the normal curve below z and beyond z. These two proportions add up to 1.

DEFINITION

TABLE 4.10 Portion of table A.2

z	Area below z	Area beyond z
1.60	0.9452	0.0548
1.61	0.9463	0.0537
1.62	0.9474	0.0526
1.63	0.9484	0.0516
1.64	0.9495	0.0505

Now our raw score, 183 cm, is 8 cm above the mean of 175 cm. Since the standard deviation is 5 cm, that is 8/5 (or 1.60) standard deviation units above the mean. In the z column we find 1.60 and go to the corresponding entry in the 'Area Beyond z' column because we want to know the proportion of the male population that is taller than 183 cm. The proportion is 0.0548, or 5.48%. Figure 4.4 shows what we have done in a somewhat more systematic way. First, we convert 183 cm to a z-score by subtracting the mean from it and dividing by the standard deviation: $z = (X - \mu)/\sigma = (183 - 175)/5 = 1.60$. The area beyond z that we found in Table A.2 is the shaded area in the graph.

Let us try another example. Suppose in a certain population, an IQ test has a normal distribution with a mean of 100 and standard deviation of 15. What proportion of the population has an IQ less than 95?

1. We convert the raw score of 95 to a z-score: $z = (X - \mu)/\sigma = (95 - 100)/15 = -0.33$.
2. Now go to Table A.2. This time, we seem to be in trouble because there are no negative z-score values in Table A.2. However, since the normal distribution is symmetric, we may use the entry in the table for $z = 0.33$. The area we want is "beyond z" because we are asking about scores below -0.33, which is just the mirror-image of the distribution of scores above $+0.33$.
3. The relevant entry in Table A.2 is 0.3707. So we may conclude that the proportion of the population with an IQ below 95 is 0.3707.

Familiarity with the normal distribution and other theoretical distributions can save us from some erroneous intuitions. One important class of such misapprehensions concerns the differences among subpopulations on quantifiable dimensions. By way of illustration, imagine that we now have two male subpopulations, the Yorbs and the Zorbs. Male Yorb heights are normally distributed with a mean of 175 cm and a standard deviation of 5 cm; and the

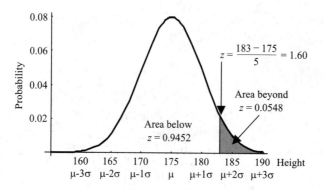

FIGURE 4.4 Proportion of men taller than 183 cm

male Zorb heights also are normally distributed but with a mean of 170 cm and a standard deviation of 5 cm.

Suppose the police force requires a minimum height of 175 cm for its male members. Assuming that the proportion of men interested in joining the police force is the same in both subpopulations, that they are a random sample of each subpopulation, and the police force is an equal opportunity employer, what ratio of male Y's to Z's we should expect to find in the police force? One way to approach this question is to line up two normal curves so that they are appropriately positioned along a common scale for height. Then we find the proportions of male Z's and male Y's who are taller than 175 cm. The proportion of Y's taller than 175 is just 0.5, since 175 is their mean height. The Z's, on the other hand, have a mean height of 170 and a standard deviation of 5, so 175 cm is one standard deviation above their mean. That gives a z-score of 1, and from Table A.2 we find that the proportion of Z's taller than 175 cm is 0.1587. This proportion is quite a bit smaller than 0.5, and their ratio is $0.5/0.1587 = 3.15$.

Given our assumptions, we should expect to find about 3.15 times as many Y's in the police force as Z's. Now, imagine that there is a national basketball squad whose minimum height requirement is 185 cm. Make the same assumptions about interest, random samples, and equal opportunity as before. What is the ratio of Y's to Z's on the basketball team that we should expect to find? Try making an intuitive guess before reading any further.

First, let us find the z-score associated with 185 cm for the Y's. We have

$$z = (X - \mu)/\sigma = (185 - 175)/5 = 2.$$

From Table A.2, we find that the area beyond a z-score of 2 is 0.0228, so only 2.28% of the Y's will be taller than 185 cm.

Now for the Z's. Their z-score is

$$z = (X - \mu)/\sigma = (185 - 170)/5 = 3.$$

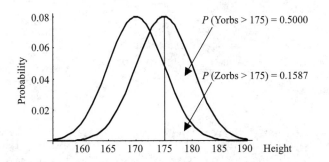

FIGURE 4.5 Proportion of Yorbs and Zorbs taller than 175 cm

From Table A.2, we find that the area beyond a z-score of 3 is 0.0013, so only 0.13% of the Z's will be taller than 185 cm.

The expected ratio of Y's to Z's is $0.0228/0.0013 = 17.54$! For every 17 or 18 Y's picked for the squad, we should expect to find only one Z being selected. So it might seem as if when it comes to selection for the basketball squad, the Z's are discriminated against more than they are for recruitment into the police force – but remember, this is simply due to chance and the properties of the normal distribution, rather than actual discrimination. If you are like most people, your intuitive estimate of this ratio will have been quite a bit lower than 17.54. However, as this example demonstrates, differences between populations are magnified at the extremes of normal distributions.

SUMMARY

A **probability distribution** presents the categories of a variable (or scores, for a quantitative variable) and the probability with which each occurs.
A **cumulative probability** associated with a particular score on a variable is the probability of occurrences at or below that score.
Observed distributions are based on a sample of data and therefore on empirical probabilities. **Theoretical distributions**, on the other hand, are based on a priori probabilities.
Discrete distributions are probability distributions for discrete variables. **Continuous distributions** are probability distributions for continuous variables.

The **binomial distribution** tells us the probability of getting a certain number of occurrences of an event out of N independent trials. There are only two possible events for each trial, and they are mutually exclusive events.
The **normal distribution** is a symmetric, bell-shaped theoretical distribution with a specific shape that may be described in terms of its mean and standard deviation.
Standard scores (also known as **z-scores**) are the number of standard deviation units a raw score is away from the mean. If X is the raw score, then its corresponding z-score is

$$z = (X - \mu)/\sigma,$$

where μ denotes the population mean and σ denotes the standard deviation.
The **standardized normal distribution** is a normal distribution with a mean of 0 and standard deviation of 1. The horizontal scale of this distribution corresponds to z-score values.

Where have we arrived and where are we going?

We've covered a lot of ground in this chapter. We began with the notions of internal, external, and statistical conclusion validity, all of which may be partially addressed through statistical inference. Statistical inference involves estimating a population characteristic from a sample of evidence, and then describing the degree of confidence we may have in those estimates. We also have learned that random sampling and randomized assignment in experiments each provide a basis for statistical inference.

In order to learn how statistical inferences may be made, we have had to find out about probability and probability distributions. Those are essential concepts, because they operate behind virtually any kind of statistical inference imaginable. Ingrid, for example, was able to tell Boris exactly how likely it was that he could get 17 receptionist duty assignments out of 30 by using the binomial distribution. She could infer on that basis that if Boris had exactly a (fair) probability of $\frac{1}{2}$ of being assigned, getting 17 assignments out of 30 was not an unlikely outcome. Likewise, given normal distributions of male adult heights in the Yorb and Zorb populations, with a couple more assumptions we were able to infer the expected ratio of Yorbs to Zorbs in the police force or on the national basketball squad.

Let's conclude this chapter by inquiring a bit further into these inferences. Boris asks Ingrid whether she can rule out the possibility that the boss really is assigning Boris to receptionist duty more often than half the time. She responds by pointing out that she cannot. After all, given 17 assignments out of 30, the *most plausible* value of Boris's probability of assignment is 17/30, which is bigger than $\frac{1}{2}$. However, she cannot rule out the possibility that the true probability is $\frac{1}{2}$ either, since it is also a plausible value on the basis of the evidence. What probabilities could she rule out, and why? How imprecise is the estimate of Boris' assignment probability, given the evidence?

Likewise, in the Yorb and Zorb example, imagine that we found that the ratio of Yorbs to Zorbs in the police force this year was 5 to 1 instead of our expected ratio of 3.15 to 1. Could we rule out the possibility that the three assumptions leading to that expected ratio are all true nevertheless? For a police force containing 500 men, how much variability should we expect in that ratio? In the next two chapters we will explore techniques for answering these sorts of questions.

Questions and exercises

Q.4.1. An educational linguist conducts a survey of adults in a community to find out the mean reading-age of adults in that community. She samples household addresses randomly from a complete list of households provided by the City Council. Once she has selected a household, she then goes there and finds out how many adults live in that household, and randomly selects one of them to test. She is then able to determine the reading-age of each adult in her sample.

(a) What is the sampling frame being used here?

(b) What kind of sample is being drawn?

(c) Does every adult in the community have an equal chance of being selected? Why or why not?

(d) What is the population parameter the linguist is trying to estimate?

(e) What is the population to which the linguist could statistically generalize?

Q.4.2. A psychologist in the Commonwealth Rehabilitation Service obtains permission from his superiors to investigate the extent and type of missing data in CRS client files. He is given an alphabetical list of client files, and he selects every 10th one to examine for missing data.

(a) What kind of sample is the psychologist getting?

(b) Is he sampling with or without replacement?

(c) Suppose that out of 10,000 clients, 1500 have a surname beginning with "S". What proportion of the sample should he expect will have surnames beginning with "S"?

Q.4.3. In an organizational psychological study using 40 managers, 20 managers were randomly assigned to take productivity training classes, and the remaining 20 had no training during the same period. The productivity of each manager's division was measured after the training period.

(a) Describe the kind of experimental design being used here.

(b) Discuss the potential threats to the internal validity of this study.

(c) Discuss whether it would be better to give all 40 managers the training and measure their divisions' productivity before and after the training.

Q.4.4. A psychologist conducts a survey in an organization and finds that the more pride an employee reports having in the organization, the higher their motivation to work beyond the call of duty. She concludes that increased pride causes increased work effort. Give *two* reasons for doubting her assertion.

Q.4.5. Two men and three women were short-listed for two positions with Cynosure Ltd. If Cynosure were to select them randomly, what is the probability that one man and one woman would be chosen to fill those positions? What is the probability that either two men or two women would be chosen?

Q.4.6. This question is an example from the 'simplest' problem option in the **StatPatch** module called **ProbPatch**, which may be used for an endless supply of practice problems of this kind. ProbPatch will provide you with explanations of the correct answers as part of its feedback. Suppose out of a population of 442 people, 135 are smokers and 185 are under 30.

(a) What is the probability of randomly selecting a smoker from this population?

(b) What is the probability of randomly selecting someone under 30?

(c) If smoking and being under 30 were independent of each other, what would be the probability of selecting someone who was both under 30 and a smoker?

Q.4.7. Now, for the population discussed in Q.4.6, suppose we also know that 40 people are both smokers and under 30.

(a) What is the probability of randomly selecting someone who is a smoker or under 30?

(b) What is the probability that someone is a smoker given that they are under 30?

(c) What is the probability that someone is under 30 given that they are a smoker?

Q.4.8. The scenario in this question is similar to the problems from the 'more complex' option in the **StatPatch** module called **ProbPatch**. Here are some probabilities for two characteristics of an adult population: exercise level and age group.

Exercise:

$$P(\text{None}) = 0.21 \quad P(\text{Light}) = 0.29 \quad P(\text{Moderate}) = 0.32$$
$$P(\text{Heavy}) = 0.18$$

Age group:

$$P(40\text{s}) = 0.43 \quad P(50\text{s}) = 0.35 \quad P(60+) = 0.22$$

(a) What is $P(\text{None or Light})$?

(b) What is the largest possible value of $P(\text{None and } 60+)$?

(c) Is it true that this information implies that at least someone in the $60+$ age group must be doing some exercise? Why or why not?

Q.4.9. This question is based on the **StatPatch** module called **AIDSPatch**. After the logo you'll see a welcome message screen. Click the **Continue** button and you'll be asked whether you've used the module before. Click the **No** radio button, and then click **OK**. Follow the instructions and answer the questions. AIDSPatch will provide explanations of the correct answers as part of its feedback. After you've worked through the scenario for the first time, you'll be asked by the program to nominate your own false positive and false negative criteria. Try 0.005 for the false positive and 0.01 for the false negative. Things to ponder and discuss:

(a) Why is the number of false positive diagnoses so much larger than the number of false negatives?

(b) Given that the probability of a false positive is so low, why is $P(\text{HIV}|\text{positive})$ so low? After all, that's the diagnosticity of the test!

(c) What are the implications for clinical diagnosis?

Q.4.10 A treatment for depression provides detectable improvement in 60% of clinically depressed people. A clinical psychologist administers this treatment to five depressed clients. What is the probability that fewer than three of them will show improvement?

Q.4.11. In a population where IQ is normally distribution with a mean of 100 and a standard deviation of 15, what is the probability of randomly selecting two people from that population whose IQs are both 115 or more?

Q.4.12. In the same population as in Q.4.11, imagine that we begin selecting 10 people at random and the first one we get has an IQ of 80. What should we expect the mean IQ of our sample will be?

Sampling Distributions and Confidence Intervals

5

CONTENTS

Estimating a population parameter from a sample

So far, we have examined the concepts of random samples and randomized assignment, both fundamental to designing psychological studies. We have also found that behind these concepts lies the notion of estimating probabilities from sufficiently long runs of independent observations. This chapter has three main goals. The first is to extend our knowledge of how to estimate things about populations on the basis of samples. In particular, we'll be investigating how to estimate widely used statistics such the mean, median, and standard deviation. The second goal is to set up a sensible framework for evaluating the quality of our sample estimates. This will entail addressing concerns such as bias and imprecision. The third goal is to address the question of how large a sample is 'good enough' for various purposes such as those of the researcher. The second and third goals involve judgments about how much *confidence* we may have in our estimates.

To anticipate where we are headed, it will turn out that we can attain all three goals by constructing an interval around our sample estimates that we can be reasonably confident will contain the true value (but unknown to us) of the parameter that we are trying to estimate. Moreover, we will be able to quantify the level of confidence. You may have seen intervals of this kind in media reports of social surveys or election poll results. A typical example is a polling company stating that the estimated percentage vote for a candidate in the forthcoming election is 38%, and claiming that they are 95% confident that this estimate is no further than 4% away from the true percentage vote. In this chapter we will find out how to construct similar kinds of intervals with associated confidence levels.

DEFINITION

We have already made the distinction between a **population** and a **sample**. Now we will extend that distinction to refer to statistics based on population data versus sample data, so that we'll know which one is being referred to. A **population statistic** (or sometimes **parameter**) is based on the entire population, whereas a **sample statistic** (or **estimate**) is based on a sample taken from a population.

Statisticians often use Greek letters to denote population statistics and Roman letters to denote sample statistics. We will follow that convention here because it is widely shared by psychologists and other social scientists. For instance, the Greek letter μ (pronounced 'mu') is used to denote the population mean, and the letter σ (pronounced 'sigma') is used to denote the population standard deviation. The sample mean, on the other hand, is usually denoted by $\bar{X}$ and the sample standard deviation by s.

DEFINITION

If we are going to estimate a population statistic with a sample statistic, then we need a **statistical model** of how we expect the sample statistic to behave. The key to such a model is knowing what the sampling distribution of the sample statistic is like. A **sampling distribution** includes the probability of getting each possible value that a sample statistic can take. Without knowing it, we have already looked at one such sampling distribution when we introduced the binomial distribution.

Let's return to a very simple example of this distribution, the one where $N = 3$. If we have a fair coin, then the population proportion of Heads we should expect when tossing this coin is 1/2. Moreover, on each toss, a Heads or a Tails is equally likely. So if we consider all the possible samples we could get from three tosses and find the sample proportion of Heads in each sample, we get the sampling distribution for that proportion shown in the next table.

As we saw in Chapter 4, there are eight possible samples. One of them produces all Heads, three produce two Heads, three produce one Head, and one produces no Heads. Each sample therefore corresponds to a sample estimate of the proportion of Heads in three tosses. As a result, we now have a sampling distribution for the sample proportion. There are four possible values for the sample proportion: 0, 1/3, 2/3, and 1. The probabilities of these values are 1/8, 3/8, 3/8, and 1/8 respectively.

Sample of $N = 3$

Sample	Proportion of heads
HHH	3/3
HHT	2/3
HTH	2/3
THH	2/3
HTT	1/3
THT	1/3
TTH	1/3
TTT	0/3
Average	$1.5/3 = 1/2$

You can see that three tosses do not provide us with a good sample estimate of the population proportion (which, remember, is 1/2) for at least one reason, namely 1/2 is not even one of the possible values! Nevertheless, there is one respect in which our sample estimate is good. If we took many repeated samples of three tosses and averaged the sample proportions obtained, that average would hover around 1/2. Another glance at the table of samples reveals why – the average of proportions from all possible samples is exactly 1/2. The theoretical average of any sample statistic, under repeated sampling, is known as its **expected value**. What we have found here is that the expected   DEFINITION value of the sample proportion of heads in three tosses of a fair coin is 1/2, which corresponds to the population proportion of heads.

It might seem obvious that the expected value of any sample statistic should turn out to be the corresponding population statistic's value. However, as you might expect by now, there are exceptions and so it always pays to check whether this is true. One important exception is the sample variance and standard deviation. Suppose we have a population whose IQ has a normal distribution with a mean of 100 and a standard deviation of 15. Table 5.1 shows sample estimates of the mean and standard deviation for 25 random samples of 10 each from this population. In fact, there are two estimates of the standard deviation. One of them uses the formula we saw back in Chapter 3:

$$\text{s.d.} = \sqrt{\frac{\Sigma(X - \bar{X})^2}{N}}$$

The other uses $N - 1$ in the denominator instead of N. Let's denote this one by s:

$$s = \sqrt{\frac{\Sigma(X - \bar{X})^2}{N - 1}}$$

Why would we ever want to use this second version?

The reason can be glimpsed by looking at the averages of these estimates across the 25 samples. Notice that while the average of the standard deviation using $N - 1$ (s) is quite close to the population value of 15 (14.972), the average of the standard deviation using N (s.d.) is too low (14.204). Although it is beyond the scope of this book to explain why this is so, in general the expected value of the standard deviation estimate using N in the denominator is not σ, but instead σ multiplied by the square root of $(N - 1)/N$. In our example that is the square root of 9/10, which is about 0.9487. So we should expect on average that a sample of 10 IQ scores from our population should give us an s.d. value of $15 \times 0.9487 = 14.231$. By using $N - 1$ in the denominator instead, s corrects for the bias in s.d.'s expected value so that its expected value is σ. That is why s is used as the sample estimate of σ.

If the expected value of a sample statistic is always the same as the corresponding population statistic's value, then the sample statistic is called an

TABLE 5.1 Sample means and two estimates of standard deviations for 25 random samples with $N = 10$

Sample	Mean	Std dev. using $N - 1$	Std dev. using N
1	94.466	10.479	9.942
2	97.151	17.922	17.002
3	98.418	16.692	15.835
4	100.077	23.705	22.489
5	102.212	5.726	5.433
6	99.417	14.955	14.187
7	102.117	14.660	13.907
8	101.463	17.555	16.654
9	104.596	16.505	15.658
10	114.369	10.779	10.226
11	87.590	11.797	11.192
12	94.969	17.940	17.019
13	93.708	19.234	18.247
14	105.246	12.598	11.952
15	99.942	9.247	8.773
16	99.186	12.708	12.056
17	94.636	12.598	11.951
18	97.816	18.317	17.377
19	99.020	11.959	11.345
20	94.173	15.230	14.448
21	98.938	17.311	16.423
22	99.016	14.733	13.977
23	102.509	10.870	10.312
24	96.745	23.490	22.285
25	105.063	17.296	16.409
Averages	99.314	14.972	14.204

unbiased estimator. We have seen in the above demonstration that s is unbiased, and it turns out that the mean also is unbiased. Sample percentiles, under some conditions, are unbiased estimators of population percentiles. In our IQ example, the population 25th percentile IQ is 89.883, the 50th percentile (Median IQ) is 100, and the 75th percentile is 110.117. Our 25 samples of 10 IQ scores produce estimates of 90.2971, 100.085, and 109.569 respectively for these three percentiles. These are all reasonably close to their expected values.

DEFINITION

You already know that sample statistics will vary if we take samples over and over again. The extent to which they vary around the population statistic's value is called **sampling error**. Note that you can have sampling error without measurement error, since the former simply depends on the 'luck of the draw.' Sample statistics with lower sampling error give more precise estimates of their corresponding population parameters. For instance, the standard deviation of the sample means from our 25 IQ samples is about 5.120 but the standard deviation of the sample medians turns out to be 5.851. The sample mean looks as if it has less sampling error than the sample median in this instance. In fact, it turns out that the sampling distribution for the mean generally has a smaller variance than the sampling distribution for the median.

DEFINITION

Before we can do much more with these ideas, we need to find out more about the sampling distributions of our sample statistics such as the mean and standard deviation. Fortunately, we already know something about those distributions because of the material we have covered on the binomial and normal distributions. The next section reveals how the binomial and normal distributions are related to sampling distributions for proportions and means.

A **population statistic** (or sometimes **parameter**) is a quantity based on data from the entire population, whereas a **sample statistic** (or **estimate**) is based on a sample of data taken from the population.

A **sampling distribution** of a sample statistic includes the probability of getting each possible value that the sample statistic can take.

The theoretical average of any sample statistic, under repeated sampling, is known as its **expected value**.

A sample statistic is an **unbiased estimator** if its expected value is always the same as the corresponding population statistic's value.

The extent to which sample statistics vary around the population statistic's value is called **sampling error**.

SUMMARY

Sampling distributions for proportions

Proportions and percentages (which are proportions multiplied by 100) are widely used in psychology, other social sciences, and in the popular media.

Quite often, proportions are estimated by samples drawn from a population. It is common practice, for instance, for pollsters to forecast election results by estimating the proportion of the electorate who will vote for each candidate on the basis of a random sample from that electorate. In order to know how precise their estimates are, they need to know the sampling distribution of a proportion.

Many psychological experiments require us to know the sampling distribution of a proportion for somewhat different reasons. Experiments and clinical trials usually involve making independent observations under identical conditions, rather like someone flipping a coin over and over again to see whether it is an unbiased coin. Even though there is no actual population from which a random sample is being taken, we may legitimately use the data from such experiments to estimate proportions (or other parameters) that would eventuate if we collected observations indefinitely.

Consider an experiment to test the 'social facilitation' hypothesis, which says that the mere presence of another person will motivate people to exert more effort in a task. Suppose we set up a tug-of-war task, in which pairs of participants are randomly assigned to an 'Observer Absent' or 'Observer There' condition. Each participant is in a small room. A rope goes through a hole in an opaque partition to the other participant (they can't see each other). In the Absent condition, no one is in the room but the participant. But the participant in the There condition has another person standing nearby in the same room, watching. The experimenter simply records which participant wins the tug-of-war, so each outcome is labeled 'A' if the Absent-condition participant wins and 'T' if the There-condition participant wins. If the social facilitation hypothesis is true, then more T's should occur than A's.

Suppose we somehow know in advance that the social facilitation hypothesis was false and a T is no more likely to occur than an A. Therefore, the true proportion of T's should be 1/2. Let us denote the true proportion by Π (upper-case 'pi'), in keeping with the standard practice of using Greek letters for population parameters. Now, consider a sample proportion, P, our estimate of Π when we have a random sample from a population in which P really is 1/2. What is the sampling distribution of P like?

One way of finding this out is to begin with very small samples which are fairly easy to understand. If we take a random sample of only three pairs of participants, can we ascertain the sampling distribution for P? Indeed we can, because we have seen what the sampling distribution of the proportion of heads is when $N = 3$. There are four possible values for the sample proportion: 0, 1/3, 2/3, and 1. The probabilities of these values are 1/8, 3/8, 3/8, and 1/8 respectively. This doesn't provide us with a very precise or reasonable estimate of the true proportion, but we can obtain a better one by taking larger samples. Figure 5.1 shows the sampling distribution of P for a sample size $N = 12$.

Notice that in this graph, 1/2 is the most likely value for the sample proportion, even though other values nearby 1/2 are fairly likely as well. If we try increasing N to 30, the sampling distribution turns out to be the one shown in Figure 5.2. By comparing these two graphs, you can see that we are more likely to obtain a sample proportion close to 1/2 when N is 30 than when N is 12. For example, the probability of getting $P = 0.333$ (i.e., 1/3) is about 0.121 when N is 12, but it is only 0.028 when N is 30.

In general, sampling error decreases as sample size increases. We get more precise and stable estimates with larger samples. This is a demonstration of a very important generalization called the **Law of Large Numbers**, which   DEFINITION
tells us that unbiased estimates will tend to be closer to the true population parameter value as we take larger samples. The Law of Large Numbers is what makes random sample estimates worthwhile.

A question arising from the Law of Large Numbers that might have already occurred to you is, how large a sample is large enough? This is a very reasonable question to ask, particularly before going out and collecting data. However, answering it requires that we know more than just the Law of Large Numbers. Perhaps the most important thing we need to know is how quickly sampling error declines as sample size increases, which in turn implies that we must find a way of measuring sampling error.

A simple way to measure the sampling error in our estimates of a proportion is to calculate the standard deviation of those estimates around the true proportion, P. The standard deviation of the estimate is known as the **standard**   DEFINITION
error, and fortunately the formula for it is very simple. Again letting P stand for the sample estimate of the true proportion, the standard error of the estimate is

$$s_P = \sqrt{\frac{P(1 - P)}{N}}$$

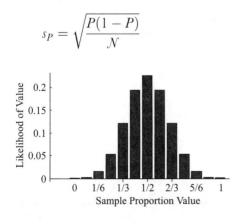

FIGURE 5.1 Sampling distribution of P when $N = 12$

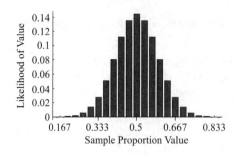

FIGURE 5.2 Sampling distribution of P when $N = 30$

We can see from this that the standard error decreases by the square-root of the sample size, N. In our example where $P = 1/2$, $P(1 - P) = 0.25$. When N is 3 then s_P is the square-root of $0.25/3 = 0.0833$, which is 0.289. When N is 12 then s_P is the square-root of $0.25/12 = 0.020833$, which is 0.144; and when N is 30, $s_P = 0.091$.

You may have noticed another trend as N gets larger, which is that the sampling distribution for a proportion begins to look more like a normal distribution. In fact, once N exceeds 20 the normal distribution is such a good approximation of the binomial distribution that it is used instead of the binomial distribution. Figure 5.3 shows a normal distribution with a mean of 1/2 and standard deviation of 0.091 superimposed on the binomial distribution for $N = 30$.

So, for a sample larger than 20 observations, the sampling distribution of a proportion may be approximated by a normal distribution with a mean of Π and a standard deviation of σ_Π. The tendency of the sampling distribution of a proportion to approximate a normal distribution as N becomes large is an

DEFINITION   example of the **Central Limit Theorem**, which says that the sampling distributions of certain sample statistics (proportions and means) converge to a normal distribution as N increases, even if the observations themselves are not normally distributed. Another somewhat more general way of putting this is that the normal distribution is the **limiting distribution** of a sample proportion as N increases.

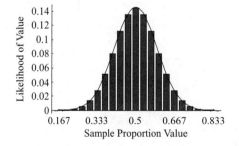

FIGURE 5.3 Normal approximation to the binomial distribution of P when $N = 30$

At this point, we have built up a statistical model for the sample proportion, incorporating the following components:

- A true population value for the proportion, Π;
- A sampling distribution that is a model of how the sample proportion varies around the true value of Π;
- A way of measuring sampling error, namely the standard error of the estimate of Π;
- A limiting distribution (the normal distribution) that can be used to approximate the sampling distribution as N becomes large.

All statistical models are based on these components, since all of them start from the concepts of a sampling distribution and sampling error. Let us consider how we may represent what happens to P if we take random samples repeatedly. We know that P will vary around Π, in a way that is governed by its sampling distribution. Each time we obtain a sample and compute P, the value of P will equal Π plus or minus some sample error. A somewhat more formal but concise way of expressing this model of a sampling distribution is the following formula:

$$P = \Pi + e,$$

where e denotes the sample error. Since we know what the sampling distribution of P is, we know that the sampling distribution of e must be the same, with P subtracted out. Remembering that the expected value of P is Π tells us that the expected value of e must be 0. In the next section, we will put all of this knowledge to work in solving a very useful problem, namely how to estimate a population proportion whose value we do not know in advance.

The standard deviation of a sample statistic is known as its **standard error**.   SUMMARY
The **Law of Large Numbers** tells us that unbiased sample statistics will tend to be closer to the true population parameter value as we take larger samples. In other words, the standard error decreases as sample size increases.
The **limiting distribution** of a sample statistic is the distribution that its sampling distribution converges to as sample size increases.
The **Central Limit Theorem** states that the limiting distribution of certain sample statistics (proportions and means) is a normal distribution.

A **statistical model** of a sample statistic incorporates the following components:
- A true population value (whether known or not) for the statistic;
- A sampling distribution that describes how the sample statistic varies around the true population value;

SUMMARY
- A way of measuring sampling error, such as the standard error of the sampling statistic;
- A limiting distribution that can be used to approximate the sampling distribution as N becomes large.

This model may be expressed in the following form:

Sample statistic value = population statistic value + sampling error.

Confidence intervals for proportions

One important practical limitation of our sampling distribution model is that we have been assuming that we know the true value of the proportion (Π) in advance. In real research that is often not the case. In fact, most experiments and correlational studies involve attempts to estimate population parameters whose values are unknown. Fortunately, our knowledge about the sampling distribution of a proportion provides everything we need for constructing such estimates and gauging how imprecise they are. Perhaps the best way to develop these ideas is to work with an example of a typical estimation problem in psychological research, in which we do not know the value of the relevant proportion beforehand.

In Chapter 4, we used the 'size–weight illusion' as an example of an experiment in which a guiding hypothesis is that most participants will perceive the larger of two objects as being the heavier even though both objects weigh the same and have the same cross-section for their lifting surface. A reasonable prelude to investigating why some people do this and others do not would be to estimate the proportion of people who pick the larger object.

In Chapter 4, we considered an experiment with 20 participants randomly sampled from a population of adults, in which 13 of them picked the larger object. Our estimate of the proportion would therefore be 13/20, but how far off might this be from the true proportion? One way we could set about addressing this question in a brute-force empirical way would be to run many experiments with random samples of 20 participants and examine the distribution of sample proportions. Figure 5.4 shows a histogram of the sample proportions obtained from 25 random samples of 20 individuals, and below that it shows the sample proportions descending in the order in which they occurred so that you can see how they vary from one experiment to another.

We do not know what the value of the population proportion is, but because we have a model of the sampling distribution of those estimates we can still say something about how far we would expect each of them to be from the true proportion, Π. Remember, our model may be expressed as

$$P = \Pi + e,$$

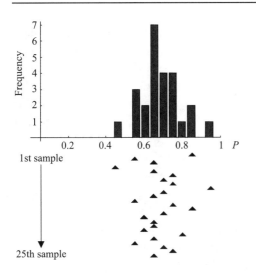

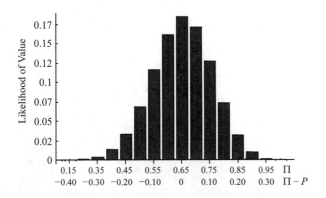

FIGURE 5.4 Two views of sample proportions from 25 random samples

where e has a sampling distribution that is the same as that for P with P subtracted out. We may rearrange this expression to represent the difference between P and Π by

$$\Pi - P = -e.$$

Now we may use the sampling distribution model to tell us how likely it is that this difference, $\Pi - P$, could be whatever value we choose. Figure 5.5 shows how to do this. The histogram is just the binomial distribution for $P = 13/20$ (or 0.65). We have two corresponding scales: one for Π, and one for $\Pi - P$. For example, the probability of getting 0.75 is the same as the probability that $\Pi - P = 0.10$, namely 0.1272.

FIGURE 5.5 Sampling distribution of $\Pi - P$ when $P = 13/20$

Better still, we can use the information in this model to ascertain how likely it is that $\Pi - P$ lies between two limits, by adding up the probabilities corresponding to every value of $\Pi - P$ between the limits. For instance, how likely is it that $\Pi - P$ is no less than -0.10 and no greater than 0.10? Using the tabulated sampling distribution (Table 5.2), we may ascertain this probability by summing the appropriate entries in the 'Prob.' column that correspond to the probabilities of $\Pi - P$ taking the values -0.10, -0.05, 0, 0.05, or 0.10 (the shaded rows in this table). We get $0.11584 + 0.16135 + 0.18440 + 0.17123 + 0.12720 = 0.76002$. In other words, the probability that $\Pi - P$ is no less than -0.10 and no greater than 0.10 is about 0.76. A standard way of expressing this result is $\Pr(-0.10 \leq \Pi - P \leq 0.10) = 0.76002$.

Yet another standard expression for what we have found is that we may be 76% *confident* that our sample estimate error e, or $\Pi - P$, lies in the interval from -0.10 to 0.10. All that has been done here is to multiply the probability, 0.76, by 100 to convert it into a percentage. The interval, $[-0.10, 0.10]$, is

DEFINITION   therefore called a 76% confidence interval for $\Pi - P$. A **confidence interval** for a statistic is a range of values that contains a specified percentage of the sampling distribution of that statistic. In terms of the experiment, we can say that if we repeated this procedure over and over again, $\Pi - P$ would be somewhere between -0.10 and 0.10, 76% of the time.

For practical purposes, researchers usually nominate the confidence level they would like before computing confidence intervals, rather than nominating lower and upper limits such as -0.10 and 0.10. As we shall see shortly, this practice has a certain wisdom to it. Conventionally acceptable confidence levels in psychological research are from 95% to 99%. Calculating a 95% confidence interval for $\Pi - P$ from a sample of 20 observations involves five steps.

1. Collect a sample of 20 observations.
2. Calculate the sample proportion P.

TABLE 5.2 Tabulated sampling distribution when $P = 13/20$

Π	$\Pi - P$	Prob.	Π	$\Pi - P$	Prob.	Π	$\Pi - P$	Prob.
0.00	-0.65	0.00000	0.35	-0.30	0.00449	0.70	$+0.05$	0.17123
0.05	-0.60	0.00000	0.40	-0.25	0.01356	0.75	$+0.10$	0.12720
0.10	-0.55	0.00000	0.45	-0.20	0.03359	0.80	$+0.15$	0.07382
0.15	-0.50	0.00000	0.50	-0.15	0.06861	0.85	$+0.20$	0.03226
0.20	-0.45	0.00004	0.55	-0.10	0.11584	0.90	$+0.25$	0.00998
0.25	-0.40	0.00026	0.60	-0.05	0.16135	0.95	$+0.30$	0.00195
0.30	-0.35	0.00121	0.65	0	0.18440	1.00	$+0.35$	0.00018

3. To ascertain the total proportion of the sampling distribution that will be excluded from the confidence interval, subtract 0.95 from 1 and get 0.05. Divide this proportion by 2 to get 0.025, earmarked for the lower and upper tails of the distribution.
4. Using the sampling distribution for P, find the limit below P such that the probabilities corresponding to all of the values below that limit add up to no more than 0.025.
5. Find the limit above P such that the probabilities corresponding to all of the values above that limit add up to no more than 0.025.

The lower and upper limits determined by this process then define a 95% confidence interval for $\Pi - P$.

If we use this procedure on our current example, we find that the resulting 95% confidence interval for $\Pi - P$ runs from -0.20 to 0.20. Using the tabulated sampling distribution, redisplayed as Table 5.3, in step 4 of our procedure we obtain -0.20 as the lower limit for $\Pi - P$ because the probabilities below that sum to $0.00004 + 0.00026 + 0.00121 + 0.00449 + 0.01356 = 0.01956$. If we moved the lower limit up one row to -0.15, then we would be adding 0.03359 to the lower tail which would exceed our limit of 0.025.

Likewise, in step 5 we obtain 0.20 as the upper limit for $\Pi - P$ because the probabilities above that sum to $0.00998 + 0.00195 + 0.00018 = 0.01211$, and moving the limit one row lower would exceed 0.025. The lower tail excludes 0.01956 and the upper tail excludes 0.01211 of the distribution, so this confidence interval contains $1 - 0.01956 - 0.01211 = 0.96833$, or 96.833% of the distribution. We may think of this interval as centered around the expected value of $\Pi - P$, namely 0, with a half-width of 0.20.

Now for the *most important argument* in this chapter: any confidence interval for $\Pi - P$ is also a confidence interval for Π. This is so because the expression for our confidence interval,

$$\Pr(-0.20 < \Pi - P < 0.20) = 0.96833,$$

TABLE 5.3 95% confidence interval when $P = 13/20$

Π	$\Pi - P$	Prob.	Π	$\Pi - P$	Prob.	Π	$\Pi - P$	Prob.
0.00	-0.65	0.00000	0.35	-0.30	0.00449	0.70	$+0.05$	0.17123
0.05	-0.60	0.00000	0.40	-0.25	0.01356	0.75	$+0.10$	0.12720
0.10	-0.55	0.00000	0.45	-0.20	0.03359	0.80	$+0.15$	0.07382
0.15	-0.50	0.00000	0.50	-0.15	0.06861	0.85	$+0.20$	0.03226
0.20	-0.45	0.00004	0.55	-0.10	0.11584	0.90	$+0.25$	0.00998
0.25	-0.40	0.00026	0.60	-0.05	0.16135	0.95	$+0.30$	0.00195
0.30	-0.35	0.00121	0.65	0	0.18440	1.00	$+0.35$	0.00018

may be rearranged by adding P to each of the terms inside the brackets to get

$$\Pr(P - 0.20 < \Pi < P + 0.20) = 0.96833.$$

Now we have a confidence interval for Π whose upper limit is $P + 0.20$, or 0.85, and whose lower limit is $P - 0.20$, or 0.45. The width of this interval is the upper limit minus the lower limit, or the distance from P to the lower limit plus the distance from P to the upper limit. In this case, both of those distances are 0.20, so the interval width is 0.40. If we repeated this procedure many times, our confidence interval would contain the true value of Π about 96.8% of the time, so we may be highly confident that Π is somewhere between 0.45 and 0.85.

We may also represent this confidence interval graphically, with a delta for the sample estimate and a bar showing the interval around it:

Graphically, it may be represented as follows.

Symbolically, our confidence interval statement is

$$\Pr(0.45 < \Pi < 0.85) = 0.96833.$$

Let's try this once more. Suppose we take another random sample of 20 subjects and this time 17 of them pick the heavier object, so our sample proportion P is $17/20 = 0.85$. Now we find the limits above and below P such that the probabilities corresponding to all of the values between those limits, including the limits themselves, add up to at least 0.95. From the tabulated sampling distribution (Table 5.4), see if you can confirm that the lower limit for this confidence interval must be $P - 0.15 = 0.85 - 0.15 = 0.70$, and it excludes 0.02192 of the distribution (or 2.192%). As for the upper limit, it has to be $P + 0.15 = 1$, since exclud-

TABLE 5.4 Confidence interval when $P = 17/20$

Π	$\Pi - P$	Prob.	Π	$\Pi - P$	Prob.	Π	$\Pi - P$	Prob.
0	−0.85	0.00000	0.35	−0.50	0.00000	0.7	−0.15	0.04537
0.05	−0.80	0.00000	0.4	−0.45	0.00000	0.75	−0.10	0.10285
0.1	−0.75	0.00000	0.45	−0.40	0.00003	0.8	−0.05	0.18212
0.15	−0.70	0.00000	0.5	−0.35	0.00021	0.85	0	0.24283
0.2	−0.65	0.00000	0.55	−0.30	0.00108	0.9	+0.05	0.22934
0.25	−0.50	0.00000	0.6	−0.25	0.00459	0.95	+0.10	0.13680
0.3	−0.55	0.00000	0.65	−0.20	0.01601	1	+0.15	0.03876

ing even the row corresponding to $P + 0.15$ would exclude 0.03876 of the distribution, which exceeds our limit of 0.025.

The lower tail excludes 0.02192 of the distribution and the upper tail excludes none of it, so this confidence interval contains $1 - 0.02192 = 0.97808$, or 97.808% of the distribution. More formally,

$$\Pr(P - 0.15 < \Pi < P + 0.15) = 0.97808$$

or

$$\Pr(0.70 < \Pi < 1) = 0.97808$$

Graphically, this interval is represented as

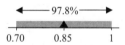

If we compare this confidence interval to the one we obtained from the earlier random sample, we can see that its *location* has changed insofar as P was 0.65 in the first sample and 0.85 in this one. The *width* of the interval also has changed, from 0.40 to 0.30.

Remember our original 25 random samples of 20 observations each? These data actually were artificially generated random samples from a population in which the proportion $\Pi = 0.65$. Figure 5.6 shows the 25 sample proportions as graphed earlier, but this time with 95% confidence intervals around each of them. The vertical line is positioned at 0.65. The locations and widths of these confidence intervals vary solely due to sampling error. As you can see, most of them contain 0.65 but three do not. If we repeated this sampling procedure a very large number of times, the percentage of intervals containing 0.65 would home in on 95%.

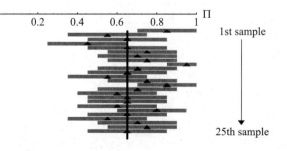

FIGURE 5.6 95% confidence intervals around 25 sample proportions

It is here that the wisdom of nominating a confidence level beforehand becomes apparent. Imagine repeatedly taking samples of 20 observations. If every time we took a sample we also followed the five-step procedure outlined above, then we could expect that on average at least 95% of our intervals around P would contain the true value of Π, whatever it may be. By fixing our confidence level criterion in advance at 95%, we can make good on the claim of 95% confidence. Technically speaking, the **confidence level** refers to the expected percentage of times that a confidence interval would contain the population value of the statistic being estimated, under repeated random sampling.

DEFINITION

Every confidence interval is characterized by its location (here this is the sample proportion), its confidence level, and the lower and upper limits. Understanding how these components are related is the key to using confidence intervals effectively. First of all, the greater the confidence level we require, the wider the interval will be. Greater confidence has a price, namely greater imprecision. For instance, recall that in our first sample of 20 observations in which P was 13/20 or 0.65, the 95% confidence interval for P had a range from 0.45 to 0.85 and therefore a width of 0.40. If we required a 99% confidence interval, however, then we would need a range from 0.35 to 0.90, or a width of 0.55. In fact, the only statement we can make about the population proportion with 100% confidence is that its value is somewhere between 0 and 1! Deciding how much confidence is sufficient requires careful judgments concerning the tradeoff between imprecision and confidence. We may be 100% confident that Π is somewhere between 0 and 1, but that is useless knowledge. In order to say anything useful about plausible values for Π, we must be prepared to live with less than 100% confidence. We will return to this issue toward the end of this chapter.

A second important property of confidence intervals is that their width decreases as sample size increases. Likewise, their location and width do not vary as much under repeated sampling. Both of these trends stem from the fact that sampling error decreases as samples become larger. This is just the Law of Large Numbers in another guise. Figure 5.7 demonstrates this by providing a comparison between 95% confidence intervals generated from 25 random samples with 50 observations and 25 random samples with 10 observations.

These samples all are taken from a population in which $\Pi = 0.65$. For $N = 50$, the locations 'dance around' less and the interval widths are both narrower and more uniform compared with $N = 10$. However, it is crucial to bear in mind that these are still 95% confidence intervals, and therefore under repeated sampling they will include the true value of Π around 95% of the time, regardless of sample size. Larger samples buy us greater precision *for the same confidence level.*

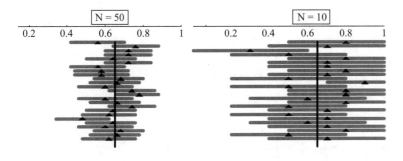

FIGURE 5.7 Confidence intervals for $N = 50$ and $N = 10$

So far, we have learned three important properties of confidence intervals:

- Both the *location* and *width* of confidence intervals vary because of sampling error.
- Greater confidence entails wider intervals. So there is a price for greater confidence, namely less precision.
- Larger sample size entails less variation in location, and narrower and more uniform intervals (and therefore more precise estimates).

Knowing how to construct confidence intervals for sample proportions enables us to deal with quite a few research questions and problems. Here are just two examples.

1. Medical practitioners have an agreed-upon level of blood pressure that is considered dangerous to exceed. Based on a random sample, what can we conclude about the proportion of people in a given population with dangerously high blood pressure?
2. In a random sample of laypeople presented with a vignette describing a clinically depressed person, only three out of 15 of the respondents correctly identified the person as being depressed. Could we be 99% confident in saying that less than half of the population from which the sample came would make the correct identification?

The first example repeats what we have already done, namely constructing a confidence interval around the sample proportion of people with high blood pressure. Nevertheless, it contains an interesting additional concept, namely that confidence intervals for proportions are the same as confidence intervals for quantiles. Blood pressure is measured on an interval-level scale, so it makes sense to use quantiles in describing a distribution of blood pressure scores. In this scenario we have chosen a cutoff point on the scale and are concerned with its quantile rank (the percentage or proportion of people whose scores lie at or below this point) or, equivalently, the proportion of people whose scores lie above the cutoff point. If a random sample of 10 people yielded three whose blood pressure exceeded the 'danger' cutoff point, our sample estimate of the population proportion would be $P = 3/10 = 0.3$. If we wanted to construct a 90% confidence interval and followed our five-step procedure, then we would find that it was the interval from 0.1 to 0.5 (which is actually a 92.44% confidence interval).

The second example is based on a real research project, concerning public mental health literacy (e.g., Jorm *et al.*, 1997), and we will come back to it later in this chapter. The investigators' question here amounts to whether they could be 99% confident in an interval that includes only proportions lower than 0.5. Since they do not care about excluding low values, they need to

DEFINITION   construct what is sometimes called a **one-sided confidence interval**. This kind of interval has only one limit (either the upper or lower one) that is free to vary, with the other limit fixed at one extreme of the distribution. In this case, the lower limit is fixed at 0, and the researchers want to know what upper limit would include at least 99% of the sampling distribution of the proportion of correct diagnoses. Table 5.5 demonstrates how to do this.

The sampling distribution when $P = 3/15 = 0.20$ is displayed in this table along with its corresponding cumulative distribution. The cumulative probability column tells us that the interval from 0 to 0.47 encompasses 99.576% of the distribution, whereas an interval from 0 to 0.40 includes only 98.194% of the distribution. So our 99% one-sided confidence interval ranges from 0 to 0.47, and therefore excludes 0.5. The investigators may claim that the interval they have constructed would contain Π 99% of the time if they carried out their procedure under repeated random samples of 15 each. So while they cannot be absolutely certain that half or more of the population would be able to make the correct diagnosis, they can claim that it is very unlikely given their evidence.

SUMMARY

A **confidence interval** for a statistic is a range of values containing a specified percentage of the sampling distribution of that statistic.
The **confidence level** refers to the expected percentage of times that a confidence interval would contain the population value of the statistic being estimated, under repeated random sampling.
A **one-sided confidence interval** has only one limit (either the upper or lower one) that is free to vary, with the other limit fixed at one extreme of the distribution.
A **two-sided confidence interval** has a lower and an upper limit that are free to vary.

TABLE 5.5 Confidence interval when $P = 3/15$

Π	Prob.	Cum. pr.	Π	Prob.	Cum. pr.	Π	Prob.	Cum. pr.
0	0.03518	0.03518	0.40	0.04299	0.98194	0.80	0.00000	1.00000
0.07	0.13194	0.16713	0.47	0.01382	0.99576	0.87	0.00000	1.00000
0.13	0.23090	0.39802	0.53	0.00345	0.99922	0.93	0.00000	1.00000
0.20	0.25014	0.64816	0.60	0.00067	0.99989	1	0.00000	1.00000
0.27	0.18760	0.83577	0.67	0.00010	0.99999			
0.33	0.10318	0.93895	0.73	0.00001	1.00000			

Confidence intervals for means

Now we will find out how to compute confidence intervals for sample means, which is the basis for the most popular statistical techniques in psychological research. As with the proportion, we will need a model of the sampling distribution of the mean, incorporating the following components:

- A true population value for the mean, μ;
- A sampling distribution that is a model of how the sample mean varies around the true value of μ;
- A way of measuring sampling error, namely the standard error of the estimate of μ;
- A limiting distribution that can be used to approximate the sampling distribution as N becomes large.

Our model is very similar to the one we used for the proportion. It is

$$\bar{X} = \mu + e,$$

so that the sample mean is modeled by the population mean plus sampling error, which may be either positive or negative. The **standard error** of the sample mean is

DEFINITION

$$s_{\bar{X}} = \frac{s}{\sqrt{N}}$$

where s is the sample standard deviation whose formula we examined earlier in this chapter. Like the standard error of the proportion, this standard error decreases with the square-root of the sample size, N. So the Law of Large Numbers applies to sample means just as it does to proportions, and we know that they will tend to be closer to the population mean's value as we take larger samples.

Likewise, for sufficiently large samples, the sampling distribution of a mean may be closely approximated by a normal distribution with a mean of μ and a standard deviation equal to the standard error of the mean. So the Central Limit Theorem applies to means, and the normal distribution is the limiting distribution of a sample mean as N increases. All this is well and good, but what about small samples?

DEFINITION   It turns out that the sample mean has what is called a **t-distribution** as a sampling distribution. Suppose we repeatedly take random samples of 10 IQ scores from a population whose mean and standard deviation are not known. Then the distribution of the sample mean IQ will be a *t*-distribution with a mean equal to the population mean IQ and a standard deviation equal to the standard error of the mean, which in this case will be $s/\sqrt{10}$. Figure 5.8 shows a graph of this distribution for a mean IQ of 100 and $s = 15$. The *t*-distribution is quite similar to a normal distribution, but as the next graph shows, the *t*-distribution has larger tails, which means that confidence intervals based on the *t*-distribution will be wider than they would be if they were based on the normal distribution. As sample size increases, this difference between the *t*- and normal distributions decreases until it is of no practical importance, just as it does for the binomial distribution.

Confidence intervals around the mean may be constructed along similar lines to those for proportions. We shall begin by constructing them for the difference between the sample and population means. The sampling distribution for this difference is just the same as that for the sample mean, as is illustrated in Figure 5.9. The *t*-distribution for $N = 10$ with a sample mean of 100 has been redrawn here with two scales, one for the sample mean and another for the difference between that and the population mean. This differ-

DEFINITION   ence is expressed in **standard error units**, i.e., the number of standard errors above or below the sample mean. Since $s = 15$, and the standard error for $N = 10$ is $s/\sqrt{10} = 15/\sqrt{10} = 4.74$, a value of 104.74 corresponds to one standard error unit above the mean of 100. Rescaling this way permits us to use *just one t-distribution for each sample size*, regardless of the value of our sample mean or standard error.

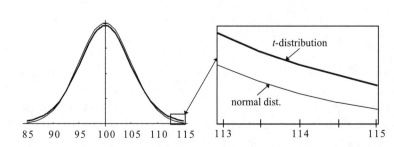

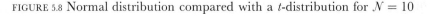

FIGURE 5.8 Normal distribution compared with a *t*-distribution for $N = 10$

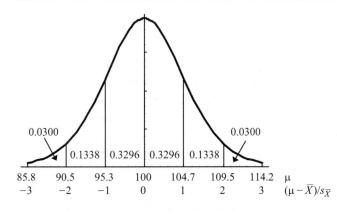

0.0300 0.1338 | 0.3296 | 0.3296 | 0.1338 0.0300

| 85.8 | 90.5 | 95.3 | 100 | 104.7 | 109.5 | 114.2 | μ |
| -3 | -2 | -1 | 0 | 1 | 2 | 3 | $(\mu - \bar{X})/s_{\bar{X}}$ |

FIGURE 5.9 Rescaled *t*-distribution for $N = 10$ and sample of mean 100

The numbers in between the vertical lines in the graph indicate the proportion of the distribution encompassed by adjacent lines. Moving from 0 to 1 standard deviation above the mean, for instance, includes 0.3296 (or 32.96%) of the distribution. We can use this information to construct confidence intervals. The interval ranging from three standard errors below the mean (−3 on the bottom scale in the graph) to three standard errors above the mean encompasses $0.0300 + 0.1338 + 0.3296 + 0.3296 + 0.1338 + 0.0300 = 0.9868$. That interval therefore includes 98.68% of the distribution and is a 98.68% confidence interval for the difference between the sample and population means. More formally,

$$\Pr(-3 < (\mu - \bar{X})/s_{\bar{X}} < 3) = 0.9868$$

As we saw in the section on proportions, we may rearrange this confidence interval into one that pertains to μ. Here, we do this by multiplying each of the terms inside the brackets by the standard error and then adding $\bar{x}$ to each of them to get

$$\Pr(\bar{X} - 3s_{\bar{X}} < \mu < \bar{X} + 3s_{\bar{X}}) = 0.9868.$$

By plugging in the numbers for the sample mean (100) and standard error (4.74), we get the confidence interval's lower and upper limits in terms of IQ scores. The lower limit is $100 - 3(4.74) = 85.8$ and the upper limit is $100 + 3(4.74) = 114.2$, as can be seen from the graphical representation below:

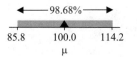

←——98.68%——→

| 85.8 | 100.0 | 114.2 |
| | μ | |

What do we do if we want a confidence level other than 98.68%, such as 95% or 99%? There are at least two options. One is to use a computer program such as SPSS or Excel to calculate how many standard errors above and below the mean we would need to go in order to encompass 95% or 99% of the distribution. Then we could simply substitute that for the '3' in the formula above. Another option is to use a *t*-distribution table such as Table A.3 in Appendix. That table is organized so that the rows correspond to sample size and the columns correspond to the proportion of the distribution that lies in the tail beyond the entries in that column. The entries in the cells of the table are standard error units. Because the *t*-distribution is symmetric, only positive entries are displayed in the table. Their negative counterparts have tails of exactly the same size. Table 5.6 shows part of Table A.3. For reasons that will be made clear later on, sample size is indexed by 'df,' which stands for 'degrees of freedom.' In this context, df is just $N - 1$, so the row corresponding to a sample of 10 is df = 9.

Suppose we want to construct a 99% confidence interval. Then we must find the table entry that tells us the number of standard errors above and below the mean required to encompass 99% of the distribution, which means it must exclude 1% of the distribution, or 0.5% in each of the tails. That corresponds to a two-tail area of 0.01 or a one-tail area of 0.005, which is the third column in Table 5.6. The corresponding cell entry for df = 9 and two-tail area = 0.01 is 3.2498, so we may conclude that

$$\Pr(\bar{X} - 3.2498s_{\bar{X}} < \mu < \bar{X} + 3.2498s_{\bar{X}}) = 0.99.$$

TABLE 5.6 Part of table A.3: *t*-distribution values

df	0.1 / 0.05	0.05 / 0.025	0.01 / 0.005	Two-tail area / One-tail area
1	6.3138	12.7062	63.6559	
2	2.9200	4.3027	9.9250	
3	2.3534	3.1824	5.8409	
4	2.1318	2.7764	4.6041	
5	2.0150	2.5706	4.0321	
6	1.9432	2.4469	3.7074	
7	1.8946	2.3646	3.4995	
8	1.8595	2.3060	3.3554	
9	1.8331	2.2622	3.2498	
10	1.8125	2.2281	3.1693	
11	1.7959	2.2010	3.1058	
12	1.7823	2.1788	3.0545	
13	1.7709	2.1604	3.0123	
...	...	...	...	

Compared with the 98.68% confidence interval we produced before, this one is a bit wider – we have had to go 3.2498 standard errors above and below the mean instead of just three. Translating back into IQ scores, our 99% confidence interval has a lower limit of $100 - (3.2498)(4.74) = 84.6$ and an upper limit of $100 + (3.2498)(4.74) = 115.4$.

At this point, we have a procedure for constructing two-sided confidence intervals around a sample mean. It is similar to the procedure for proportions, but uses the t-instead of the binomial distribution. We begin by deciding on our desired confidence level.

1. Collect a sample of N observations.
2. Calculate the sample mean, standard deviation, and standard error.
3. Then ascertain the total proportion of the sampling distribution that will be excluded from the confidence interval. Convert the confidence level to a proportion and subtract it from 1 to get this proportion. Denote the proportion by α.
4. Using Table A.3, find the cell entry in the row corresponding to df $= N - 1$ and the column corresponding to a two-tail area of α. Denote this cell entry by $t_{\alpha/2}$. Compute the half-width of the confidence interval,

$$w = t_{\alpha/2}s_{\bar{X}}.$$

5. The resulting confidence interval statement may be completed by plugging the sample mean, half-width w, and α into our formula

$$\Pr(\bar{X} - w < \mu < \bar{X} + w) = 1 - \alpha.$$

Let us try this procedure one more time before moving on. Suppose we take a random sample of 16 people from a population whose mean IQ we do not know, and we administer a standard IQ test. This test has been normed on another population in such a way as to make that population's mean IQ 100. What could we conclude about our population if the sample of 16 IQ scores produced a mean of 103 and a standard deviation of 9? We could elect to compute a 95% confidence interval, as a way of getting an idea of the range of plausible values for the population's mean IQ. We have already completed step 1, so we may proceed with the rest:

2. Calculate the sample mean, standard deviation, and standard error. We already know that the sample mean is 103 and the standard deviation is 9. The standard error is the standard deviation divided by the square-root of N (which is 16), so it is $9/4 = 2.25$.

CONSTRUC-
TING A
CON-
FIDENCE
INTERVAL
AROUND A
MEAN

3. Then ascertain the total proportion of the sampling distribution that will be excluded from the confidence interval. Convert the confidence level (95%) to a proportion (0.95) and subtract it from 1 to get this proportion (0.05). Denote the proportion by α, so $\alpha = 0.05$.

4. Using Table A.3, find the cell entry in the row corresponding to $\mathrm{df} = N - 1 = 16 - 1 = 15$, and the column corresponding to a two-tail area of $\alpha = 0.05$. The cell entry is $t_{\alpha/2} = 2.1314$. The half-width of the interval is

$$w = t_{\alpha/2} s_{\bar{X}} = (2.1314)(2.25) = 4.796.$$

5. The resulting confidence interval statement may be completed by plugging the sample mean, standard error, $t_{\alpha/2}$, and α into our formula

$$\Pr(\bar{X} - w < \mu < \bar{X} + w) = 1 - \alpha,$$

which gives us

$$\Pr(103 - 4.796 < \mu < 103 + 4.796) = 0.95,$$

or just

$$\Pr(98.2 < \mu < 107.8) = 0.95.$$

So the plausible values for the population's mean IQ range from 98.2 to 107.8. Clearly our sample mean of 103 is greater than 100, but that could be due to sampling error. The confidence interval contains 100, so 100 is a plausible value for the mean. Our confidence interval is telling us that we cannot rule out 100 as a plausible value for the mean, given that we want to be 95% confident that our interval will contain the population mean.

Earlier we saw how a *one-sided confidence interval* could be constructed for proportions. The same may be done for means as well. The procedure for constructing a one-sided confidence interval around the mean is quite similar to that for two-sided intervals. For one-sided intervals we exclude only one tail of the distribution from the interval. Therefore, steps 1–3 are as described above, while steps 4 and 5 are as follows.

4. Using Table A.3, find the cell entry in the row corresponding to d.f. $= N - 1$ and the column corresponding to a one-tail area of α. Denote this cell entry by t_α.

5. The resulting confidence interval statement may be completed by plugging the sample mean, standard error, t_α, and α into one of the formulas given below. The first formula is used when we want to exclude the lower tail of the distribution and the second is used when we want to exclude the upper tail.

$$\Pr(\bar{X} - t_\alpha s_{\bar{X}} < \mu) = 1 - \alpha \qquad \text{(excludes lower tail)}$$
$$\Pr(\mu < \bar{X} + t_\alpha s_{\bar{X}}) = 1 - \alpha \qquad \text{(excludes upper tail)}$$

For an example of a one-sided interval, we return to our most recent IQ example. Suppose the researchers are really interested only in whether the population's mean IQ might be below 99. Then they could construct a one-sided confidence interval that excludes only the lower tail of the distribution, to see whether 99 would be excluded and therefore implausible. As before, their desired confidence level is 95%. Their sample size is 16, with a mean of 103 and a standard deviation of 9, so as before the standard error is $9/4 = 2.25$.

Now we come to the new versions of steps 4 and 5 in the procedure. The fact that we want 95% confidence means that we must consult Table A.3 to find the cell entry in the row corresponding to d.f. $= 16 - 1 = 15$ and the column corresponding to a one-tail area of 0.05. The cell entry is $t_\alpha = 1.7531$. Since we are excluding the lower tail, we use the first formula of the pair given above, and get

$$\Pr(103 - (1.7531)(2.25) < \mu) = 0.95,$$

or

$$\Pr(99.1 < \mu) = 0.95.$$

Graphically, this confidence interval may be represented as follows:

According to this confidence interval, the plausible values for the population's mean IQ range from 99.1 upward. Since the lower limit of this one-sided confidence interval is 99.1, 99 lies just below the interval and is therefore not a plausible value for the population mean IQ. The researchers may conclude that the population mean IQ is likely to be above 99.

Note that this one-sided confidence interval *excludes* 99 whereas the two-sided confidence interval *includes* it. Why, and what are the implications? The reason for the different result is that our one-sided confidence interval cell excludes 5% of the lower tail in the sampling distribution while the two-sided interval excludes only 2.5% of it (and also 2.5% of the upper tail). Recall that for the one-sided interval, $t_\alpha = 1.7531$ but for the two-sided interval $t_{\alpha/2} = 2.1314$, so the one-sided interval's lower limit is $103 - (1.7531) \times (2.25) = 99.1$ and the two-sided interval's lower limit is $103 - (2.1314)(2.25) = 98.2$. Figure 5.10 shows this, with the one-sided confidence interval represented at the bottom of the figure and the two-sided interval just above it.

The upshot of all this is that any researcher should carefully decide what kind of confidence statement she or he wants to construct. One-sided confidence intervals are used mainly when the researcher has no reason to be interested in values in one of the distribution's tails or when such values would have no meaning. Later on we will encounter situations where such conditions hold, but in the meantime we will deal primarily with two-sided confidence intervals.

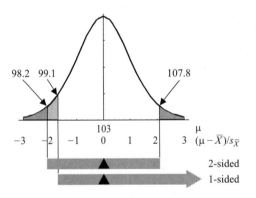

FIGURE 5.10 One-sided versus two-sided confidence intervals

SUMMARY

The sampling distribution of a mean is known as the **t-distribution** which has 'heavier' tails than the normal distribution does. As sample size increases, the *t*-distribution converges to a normal distribution, so that the normal distribution is the limiting distribution of the sample mean.

Standard error units refer to the number of standard errors above or below the sample mean, and are used in constructing confidence intervals.

Confidence intervals for means and proportions with larger samples

Having already seen that the normal distribution is a good approximation of the binomial distribution for samples of more than 20, a reasonable question is how we can use the normal distribution to provide confidence intervals for proportions from large samples. The key to the method for doing this is using our knowledge about the shape of the normal curve. In Chapter 4, we learned that the normal distribution curve has the same shape, no matter what its mean and standard deviation. We also learned that we could use z-scores to transform any normal distribution into one with a mean of 0 and a standard deviation of 1, thereby enabling us to use the information about the standardized normal distribution in Table A.2.

We have already seen that the standard error of P is

$$s_P = \sqrt{\frac{P(1-P)}{N}}$$

So for N larger than 20, the sampling distribution for P is approximately normal with a sample standard error of s_P. We may transform this distribution into a standardized normal distribution by rescaling it in exactly the same way as we did with the t-distribution, namely in terms of standard error units. Then we may construct confidence intervals by following a very similar procedure to the one we used with the t-distribution, employing the standardized normal distribution in its place.

To see how this works, let us return to the research example on public mental health literacy. Jorm and his colleagues (Jorm *et al.*, 1997) collected data from a nationally representative sample of Australian adults aged 18 to 74. Half of the respondents were presented with a vignette describing a person suffering symptoms of depression and the other half a vignette describing a person suffering symptoms of schizophrenia. The vignettes were based on ICD-10 (World Health Organization) and DSM-IV diagnostic criteria for each of these disorders. The respondents were asked to say, in their own words, what (if anything) was wrong with the person in the vignette. Their answers were then coded into diagnostic categories.

Among other things, the researchers were interested in the percentage (or proportion) of respondents who made a correct diagnosis. In fact, it turned out that 39% (a proportion of 0.39) of the respondents correctly identified the depressed person and 27% (a proportion of 0.27) correctly identified the schizophrenic one. Suppose Jorm and his colleagues had collected a random sample of 100 people, and they wanted to assess how precise their estimates of these percentages were. To do this, they could construct a two-sided 95% confidence interval around each sample proportion. They would need to determine how many standard error units on either side of the sample proportion they would need in order to encompass 95% of the sampling distribution.

Figure 5.11 shows the sampling distribution of a proportion of 0.39, with the sample standard error as its standard deviation. The standard error is computed with the formula we have used before, plugging in 0.39 for P and 100 for N:

$$s_P = \sqrt{\frac{P(1-P)}{N}} = \sqrt{\frac{0.39(1-0.39)}{100}} = 0.4877/10 = 0.04877.$$

The sampling distribution for P is approximately normal because N is fairly large. Remember, all normal distributions have the same shape regardless of their mean or standard deviation. So we may use the standard normal distribution with a mean of 0 and a standard deviation of 1 to tell us how many standard errors below and above 0.39 we would need to go in order to encompass 95% of the distribution. Figure 5.11 illustrates this with the bottom scale, which is in standard error (s_P) units.

As in the procedures we followed using the t-distribution, we may either get a computer package to help us find the answer to this question, or we may use a standard normal distribution table such as Table A.2. Part of this table is shown as Table 5.7. The number of standard error units corresponds to the column labeled 'z,' for reasons which will be explained shortly. The 'Area beyond z' column tells us how much of the tail of the normal distribution lies beyond the value of z given in the corresponding row. We want 0.025 (or 2.5%) of each tail of the distribution to be excluded from our 95% confidence interval, since a 95% confidence interval must exclude 5% of the

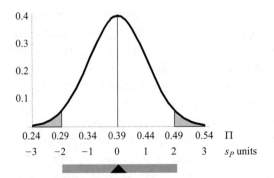

FIGURE 5.11 Normal distribution for $N = 100$ and $P = 0.39$

TABLE 5.7 Part of table A.2: Normal
distribution values

z	Area below z	Area beyond z
. . .	. . .	. . .
1.94	0.9738	0.0262
1.95	0.9744	0.0256
1.96	0.9750	0.0250
1.97	0.9756	0.0244
1.98	0.9761	0.0239
. . .	. . .	. . .

distribution in total. So we locate the value of z for which the area beyond it equals 0.025. That value turns out to be 1.96.

Our 95% confidence interval around 0.39 must therefore range from 1.96 standard errors below 0.39 to 1.96 standard errors above it. We have already calculated the standard error to be 0.04877. So the lower limit of the interval will be $0.39 - (1.96)(0.04877) = 0.39 - 0.09559 = 0.294$, and the upper limit will be $0.39 + 0.09559 = 0.486$. More formally, we may claim that

$$\Pr(0.39 - 0.09559 < \Pi < 0.39 + 0.09559) = 0.95,$$

or

$$\Pr(0.294 < \Pi < 0.486) = 0.95.$$

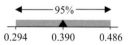

So, the plausible values of the population proportion of people correctly identifying the the depressed person range from 0.294 to 0.486. If you re-examine the normal distribution graph (Figure 5.11), you will see that the lower and upper limits of this confidence interval correspond to those of the gray bar at the bottom of the graph and the shaded tails of the distribution.

Having got this far, let us systematically generalize our procedure for constructing large-sample two-sided confidence intervals for proportions. First, we decide on the confidence level we want. Then, we follow this five-step routine.

CONSTRUC-
TING A CON-
FIDENCE
INTERVAL
AROUND A
PROPOR-
TION
1. Collect a sample of N observations.
2. Calculate the sample proportion and standard error.
3. Ascertain the total proportion of the sampling distribution that will be excluded from the confidence interval. Convert the confidence level to a proportion and subtract it from 1 to get this proportion. Denote the proportion by α.
4. Using Table A.2, find the value $\alpha/2$ in the column labeled 'Area beyond z,' and read off the value of z in the same row. Denote this z-value by $z_{\alpha/2}$. Calculate the half-width of the interval

$$w = z_{\alpha/2} s_P.$$

5. The resulting confidence interval statement may be completed by plugging the sample proportion, half-width w, and α into our formula:

$$\Pr(P - w < \Pi < P + w) = 1 - \alpha.$$

Almost exactly the same procedure may be used to construct confidence intervals for the mean when N is large. The only differences are that in step 2 we calculate the sample mean, sample standard deviation, and standard error; and these are used in the formula for step 4 so that it becomes

$$w = z_{\alpha/2} s_{\bar{x}}.$$

In this procedure, z has taken the role played by t when we use the t-distribution. The reason is simply that z denotes standard deviation units for the normal distribution, whereas t denotes standard deviation units for the t-distribution.

One way to appreciate this switch is to return to the last example involving IQ scores. In that example, a random sample of 16 IQ scores yielded a sample mean of 103 and a sample standard deviation of 9. We constructed a 95% confidence interval around the sample mean, finding a lower limit of 98.2 and an upper limit of 107.8. If instead of $N = 16$, we had a larger sample, say $N = 121$, then we could use the normal distribution to model sampling error and therefore employ the procedure outlined above. Since the square-root of 121 is 11, our standard error is $9/11 = 0.818$. Since our desired confidence level is 95%, we may use the same $z_{\alpha/2}$ value as in the depression diagnosis example, namely 1.96. Plugging the appropriate numbers into our formula for the half-width, we get $w = (1.96)(0.818) = 1.6$, so our interval is

$$\Pr(103 - 1.6 < \mu < 103 + 1.6) = 0.95,$$

or just

$$\Pr(101.4 < \mu < 104.6) = 0.95.$$

The next diagram shows how much more precise this second interval is.

Now, there are two reasons why this confidence interval is more precise than the one we obtained for $N = 16$. Both reasons stem from the larger N of 121, but they are none the less important to distinguish. The first reason is something that we already know, namely that the standard error decreases with larger sample sizes. In this case, when N is 16 the standard error is $9/4 = 2.25$, and when N is 121 it is $9/11 = 0.818$. The second reason, however, is that for $N = 16$ we used the t-distribution to model sampling error and found that for that sample size we had to use a $t_{\alpha/2}$ value of 2.1314, whereas for $N = 121$ we used the normal distribution and had to use a $z_{\alpha/2}$ value of 1.96, which is smaller. Using the t-distribution gives us wider, more conservative confidence intervals than using the normal distribution.

The difference between confidence intervals based on the t- and normal distributions decreases as sample size increases, but for small or moderate sample sizes the difference may be crucial. Table 5.8 illustrates this by displaying 95% confidence intervals for the sample mean IQ of 103 with a standard deviation of 9, based on $t_{0.025}$ vs. $z_{0.025}$ values. For small sample sizes, the confidence intervals based on t are considerably wider than those based on z. For instance, for $N = 5$, the t-based confidence interval ranges

TRY WORKING WITH DEM52 WHICH COMPARES CONFIDENCE INTERVALS BASED ON t VERSUS z

TABLE 5.8 Confidence intervals based on $t_{0.025}$ vs $z_{0.025}$ for increasing N

N	Std. err.	$t_{0.025}$	Based on t Confid. interval Lower	Upper	$z_{0.025}$	Based on z Confid. interval Lower	Upper
5	4.025	2.5706	92.7	113.3	1.96	95.1	110.9
10	2.846	2.2281	96.7	109.3	1.96	97.4	108.6
20	2.012	2.0860	98.8	107.2	1.96	99.1	106.9
50	1.273	2.0086	100.4	105.6	1.96	100.5	105.5
100	0.900	1.9840	101.2	104.8	1.96	101.2	104.8
200	0.636	1.9719	101.7	104.3	1.96	101.8	104.2
500	0.402	1.9647	102.2	103.8	1.96	102.2	103.8

from 92.7 to 113.3, whereas the z-based interval ranges from 95.1 to 110.9. From this table it is clear that for a sample of 50 or more, the differences between the lower and upper limits of these two confidence intervals are quite small. In fact, as indicated earlier in this chapter, a rule-of-thumb has it that the normal distribution is a good approximation of the sampling distribution of the mean for sample sizes above 30.

Confidence intervals and summary statistics

At this point, you have learned how to construct confidence intervals for proportions and means. Although it may not seem like it, you now possess some very powerful knowledge. Given a sample mean, standard deviation, and sample size, you now know how to construct a confidence interval around the mean. In summarizing a distribution of scores, if you are using the mean and standard deviation package, a confidence interval is essential for communicating the range of plausible values for the population mean.

For example, imagine that you are an educational psychologist with a mandate to construct national literacy tests for primary-school children. You have administered that test to a nationwide random sample of 1601 eight year olds and you want to be able to inform the Department of Education about the distribution of scores. The test has a range of scores from 0 to 1000, and the sample mean turns out to be 480 and the standard deviation is 120. Of course, you do not want the Department of Education to leap to the mistaken conclusion that the population mean score on your test is exactly 480, since it is only a sample estimate.

So you decide to construct a 99% two-sided confidence interval around this mean. The sample size is quite large ($N = 1601$), so you decide to use the normal distribution approximation of the sampling distribution for the mean. Having already completed the first step in the five-step procedure, you now complete step 2 by computing the standard error. The standard error of the mean is $s/\sqrt{N} = 120/\sqrt{1601} = 120/40.01 = 3.00$. For step 3, you convert 99% to the corresponding proportion of 0.99, which enables you to calculate the total proportion of the distribution to be excluded by your confidence interval, namely $\alpha = 1 - 0.99 = 0.01$. Step 4 entails finding $z_{\alpha/2}$, and since $\alpha = 0.01$, therefore $\alpha/2 = 0.005$. From Table A.2, you find $z_{0.005}$ is midway between 2.57 and 2.58, so $z_{0.005} = 2.575$. The half-width is therefore

$$w = z_{\alpha/2} s_{\bar{X}} = (2.575)(3.00) = 7.725.$$

Finally, for step 5 you plug the appropriate numbers into the formula for the confidence interval,

$$\Pr(\bar{X} - w < \mu < \bar{X} + w) = 1 - \alpha,$$

and get

$$\Pr(480) - 7.725 < \mu < 480 + 7.725) = 0.99,$$

or just

$$\Pr(472.275 < \mu < 487.725) = 0.99.$$

472.275   480   487.825

You are therefore able to report that the 99% confidence interval around the mean of 480 ranges from 472.275 to 487.725, and this range comprises plausible values for the true population mean.

Likewise, given a sample proportion and the sample size, you are now able to determine plausible lower and upper bounds on the value of the population proportion, with whatever confidence level you wish. Thus, any summary statistic from the percentile package can have a confidence interval associated with it. If you are reporting the *median* of a distribution, for instance, then you can also report a confidence interval around it because the median is just the score below which half of the observations fall. That score therefore corresponds to a sample proportion $P = 1/2$, with a standard error of

$$s_P = \sqrt{\frac{P(1 - P)}{N}} = \sqrt{\frac{0.5(1 - 0.5)}{N}} = 0.5/\sqrt{N}.$$

Returning to our literacy test example, suppose the sample median score is 460. If you want to report the median with a 99% two-sided confidence interval, since $N = 1601$ you can use the normal approximation to the sampling distribution for a proportion. The standard error is $0.5/\sqrt{N} = 0.5/\sqrt{1601} = 0.5/40.01 = 0.0125$. You already have $z_{0.005} = 2.575$ when constructing the 99% confidence interval for the mean, so you need only complete step 4 by plugging the standard error and $z_{0.005}$ into the formula

$$w = z_{\alpha/2}s_P = (2.575)(0.0125) = 0.032.$$

For step 5, you put P, w, and α into the confidence interval formula

$$\Pr(P - w < \Pi < P + w) = 1 - \alpha,$$

to get

$$\Pr(0.5 - 0.032 < \Pi < 0.5 + 0.032) = 0.99,$$

or just

$$\Pr(0.468 < \Pi < 0.532) = 0.99.$$

0.468   0.5   0.532

The 99% confidence interval that you have constructed pertains to the median score of 460, and is an interval around the score's **quantile (or percentile) rank**. That is, the population proportion of test scores that fall below 460 could plausibly range from 0.468 to 0.532 (in percentile terms, from 46.8% to 53.2% of the scores could fall below 460). This statement may not be what you had in mind for a confidence interval around the median. It would be useful to have a confidence interval for the median akin to the one you constructed for the mean, i.e., with a lower and an upper limit for the median score itself.

Fortunately, you already have everything you need to find that kind of confidence interval. You have found a 99% confidence interval for true proportion of test scores that fall below 460, namely the interval from 0.468 to 0.532. The way to convert this into a confidence interval around 460 is to find the scores whose quantile ranks are 0.468 and 0.532, respectively. Imagine that we have sorted the test scores from the lowest to the highest. Since $N = 1601$, the 801st score will correspond to the median.

First, we find which case corresponds most closely to a quantile rank of 0.468 by multiplying it by N, getting $(0.468)(1601) = 749.3$. We round this figure to the nearest integer, 749, which tells us that the 749th score is the lower limit of our 99% confidence interval. Next, we find the score that corresponds most closely to a quantile rank of 0.532, and get $(0.532)(1601) = 851.7$. Rounding this to the nearest integer, 852, tells us that the 852nd score is the upper limit on our confidence interval. So we have taken the confidence interval statement $\Pr(0.468 < \Pi < 0.532) = 0.99$, and converted it to

$$\Pr(749\text{th score} < \text{Median} < 852\text{nd score}) = 0.99.$$

As a final step, you inspect the sorted list of scores to identify the 749th and 852nd scores. Suppose you find that the value of the 749th score is 451 and the value of the 852nd score is 470. Then your 99% confidence interval for the median would have a lower limit of 451 and an upper limit of 470.

We have just discovered that there are two ways of representing confidence intervals for quantiles. One is a **quantile-rank-oriented** confidence interval around a population proportion. In the above example, the relevant interval is $\Pr(0.468 < \Pi < 0.532) = 0.99$. The other is a **quantile-score-oriented** confidence interval around the population score with a specified quantile rank. In our example, the relevant interval is $\Pr(749\text{th score} < \text{Median} < 852\text{nd score}) = 0.99$. Each of these confidence intervals is based on the same information, and they are simply two different expressions of the same findings.

DEFINITIONS

Which of them is the more useful depends on the research question that needs to be addressed. Generally, the quantile-rank-oriented confidence interval is useful when a variable has a preassigned cutoff value whose percentile or quantile rank is being estimated. The question about the proportion of a population whose blood pressure is above a designated danger-level is a case in point. A random sample of blood-pressure measurements from the population would enable us to construct a confidence interval around this proportion, so that we could speak of a range of plausible values for that proportion. Another example is in educational testing or assessment, in situations where policies prescribe specific pass-rates and the pass-level of the test has been established beforehand. In psychology, some clinical diagnostic tests have cut-off values that are used to distinguish those who suffer a disorder or symptom from those who do not. Quantile-rank-oriented confidence intervals would be useful in describing proportions of populations who would be diagnosed according to those tests.

The quantile-score-oriented confidence interval, on the other hand, is most useful when a particular quantile rank is the object of inquiry, such as the median or the quartiles. Here, the chief interest is in finding a range of plausible scores for the population median (or whatever quantile is being estimated). The literacy test example illustrates this kind of situation, hence the motivation for finding the 99% confidence interval for the median with a lower limit of 451 and an upper limit of 470.

It will be helpful if we can lay out the steps for converting a quantile-rank-oriented confidence interval into a quantile-score-oriented one in a generalizable way. We are familiar with the quantile-rank-oriented confidence interval statement because it is just the confidence interval around a sample proportion. We may represent such an interval generally by

$$\Pr(P - a < \Pi < P + b) = 1 - \alpha,$$

where $P - a$ is the lower limit and $P + b$ is the upper limit on the quantile rank of the score whose sample quantile rank is P.

In order to convert this confidence interval to a quantile-score-oriented one, we need some notation for denoting a score with a specific quantile rank. A standard notation for the score whose quantile rank is P is $X^{(P)}$, and in the same vein we may use $X^{(P-a)}$ to denote the score with a quantile rank of $P - a$ and $X^{(P+b)}$ to denote one with a quantile rank of $P + b$. We need one more bit of notation, namely the population score whose quantile rank is P. We will use the Greek letter θ (theta) for this purpose, with a subscript for its quantile rank. The resulting **quantile-score-oriented confidence interval** is

DEFINITION

$$\Pr(X^{(P-a)} < \theta_P < X^{(P+b)}) = 1 - \alpha,$$

which tells us that the confidence interval around the population score θ_P with a quantile rank of P has a lower limit of $X^{(P-a)}$ and an upper limit of $X^{(P+b)}$. We find the lower and upper limits by following these steps:

CONSTRUCT-ING A QUANTILE-SCORE CONFIDENCE INTERVAL

1. Sort the scores in ascending order.
2. To find $X^{(P-a)}$, first multiply $P - a$ by N and round the result to the nearest integer. Denote this integer by A. Then $X^{(P-a)}$ is the Ath score in the sorted list.
3. To find $X^{(P+b)}$, first multiply $P + b$ by N and round the result to the nearest integer. Denote this integer by B. Then $X^{(P+b)}$ is the Bth score in the sorted list.

The procedure outlined above should be used only on data-sets with samples of about 50 or more. Smaller sample-sizes render the procedure too 'coarse' to give reasonably accurate results. Let us try this procedure with a new example. Suppose we are studying a new test of general knowledge about probability and statistics, and we have administered this test to 101 subjects. The test scale ranges from 0 to 100, and we have sorted the subjects' scores in ascending order. The median is the 51st score in this sorted list, which turns out to be 63. The median has a percentile rank of 50%, or a quantile rank of 0.5. If we want to construct a 90% confidence interval around the median, then we may start by using the normal approximation to the sampling distribution to make a 90% confidence interval around the quantile rank of $P = 0.5$.

We calculate the standard error of $P = 0.5$ as before, namely $0.5/\sqrt{N} = 0.5/\sqrt{101} = 0.5/10.05 = 0.05$. Our desired confidence level is 0.10 and we are constructing a two-sided confidence interval, so we need to find $z_{0.05}$ from Table A.2, which turns out to be 1.645. Our half-width is therefore

$$w = z_{\alpha/2} s_P = (1.645)(0.05) = 0.082.$$

We then complete our procedure by plugging the sample proportion P, w, and $\alpha = 0.10$ into the formula

$$\Pr(P - w < \Pi < P + w) = 1 - \alpha,$$

to get

$$\Pr(0.5 - 0.082 < \Pi < 0.5 + 0.082) = 0.90,$$

or just

$$\Pr(0.418 < \Pi < 0.582) = 0.90.$$

Now we may follow the three-step procedure outlined above to convert this confidence interval into one around the median score of 63. Having already completed the first step by sorting the scores, we now do the second step by multiplying the lower quantile rank in our confidence interval by N, which is 101, to get $(0.418)(101) = 42.2$. We round this to the nearest integer which is 42, and find the 42nd score in our list. That score is 60, which becomes the lower limit for our confidence interval around the median. We then complete the third step by carrying out the same operations for the upper limit. The upper quantile rank is 0.582, which multiplied by 101 gives 58.8, which in turn may be rounded up to 59. The 59th score is 64, so that becomes our upper limit in the confidence interval for the median. We may now claim that

$$\Pr(60 < \theta_{0.5} < 64) = 0.90.$$

The next graph displays the cumulative frequency distribution with both the quantile-rank-oriented and quantile-score-oriented confidence intervals.

It might have occurred to you by now that there must be a simpler way of representing a confidence interval than the rather cumbersome-looking expressions such as $\Pr(472.275 < \mu < 487.725) = 0.99$. A few different conventions have been used in psychology and related fields. The abbreviation you are most likely to encounter in published research is 'CI' (short for 'confidence interval'), and sometimes writers use a subscript to indicate the confidence level. A 99% confidence interval might therefore be written as CI_{99} or $CI_{0.99}$. The interval itself is sometimes expressed as a lower limit and an upper limit enclosed by square brackets, so for our example here we would say $CI_{0.99} = [472.275, 487.725]$. Another expression for it is the sample estimate plus or minus half the width of the interval. In this case, the estimated mean is 480, and the amount being added or subtracted to obtain the upper or lower limit is 7.725, so we would say $CI_{0.99} = 480 \pm 7.725$. In this book we will

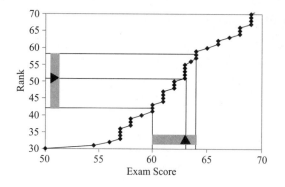

FIGURE 5.12 Quantile-rank-and quantile-score-oriented 90% confidence intervals

usually use the square-bracketed lower and upper limit representation, except when the alternative half-width version is particularly apt and the confidence interval is symmetric.

Students who are astute (or perhaps slightly obsessive) may have observed by now that we have confidence intervals for proportions or quantiles (and therefore any summary statistic in the percentile package) and for means, but we still do not have confidence intervals for the standard deviation or variance. It turns out that the variance has a readily understandable sampling distribution, but that distribution is important for other purposes as well and so we shall postpone the introduction of confidence intervals for the variance to a later chapter.

SUMMARY

A **quantile-rank-oriented** confidence interval is a statement of the form

$$\Pr(P - a < \Pi < P + b) = 1 - \alpha,$$

where $P - a$ is a lower limit and $P + b$ is an upper limit on the quantile rank of a score whose sample quantile rank is P.

A **quantile-score-oriented** confidence interval is a statement of the form

$$\Pr(X^{(P-a)} < \theta_P < X^{(P+b)}) = 1 - \alpha,$$

which tells us that the confidence interval around the population score with a quantile rank of P has a lower limit of $X^{(P-a)}$ and an upper limit of $X^{(P+b)}$.

There are two shorthand ways of expressing confidence intervals. The most generalizable version gives the lower and upper limits in square brackets, and has the form

$$CI_{1-\alpha} = [\text{lower limit, upper limit}].$$

The second way may be used when the confidence interval is symmetric, and has the form

$$CI_{1-\alpha} = \text{sample estimate} \pm w,$$

where w denotes the amount that must be added to obtain the upper limit and subtracted to obtain the lower limit.

How much confidence?

By now you probably are also wondering what confidence level is best to use. We have generally used fairly high levels such as 90%, 95%, and 99%. The latter two are the most commonly used in psychological research, but there is really no defensible reason for this convention. One of the main problems with choosing a confidence level is that there are seldom any clear guidelines for how much confidence is sufficient. We will return to this issue in Chapter 6 when we use confidence intervals for comparing rival models and deciding whether one of them is superior.

For now, we can at least gain some appreciation of the tradeoffs involved in deciding how much confidence we desire. We have already observed that there is a tradeoff between confidence and precision. Let us take a more detailed look at this tradeoff. Consider the construction of two-sided confidence intervals when our sample is large enough that we may use the normal distribution as an approximation to the sampling distribution of a proportion or mean. The higher the level of confidence we desire, the larger the value of $z_{\alpha/2}$ is required. Since half of the width of the confidence interval is $z_{\alpha/2}$ multiplied by the standard error, $z_{\alpha/2}$ directly determines how wide the interval will be.

However, the value of $z_{\alpha/2}$ does not increase in direct proportion to the confidence level. Instead, as we raise the confidence level the rate of increase in $z_{\alpha/2}$ accelerates, as the next graph shows. A confidence level of 0.85 requires that $z_{\alpha/2} = 1.44$, whereas a confidence level of 0.97 requires that $z_{\alpha/2} = 2.17$, which is an increase of about 0.73 in $z_{\alpha/2}$ in exchange for an increase of 0.12 in confidence level. However, a confidence level of 0.999 requires that $z_{\alpha/2} = 3.29$, an increase of 1.12 above 2.17 in exchange for an increase of only 0.029 in confidence. So a 97% confidence interval is slightly more than 1.5 times as wide as an 85% confidence interval, but a 99.9% confidence interval is slightly more than 1.5 times as wide as a 97% confidence interval.

Wider confidence intervals ensure that we are more likely to include the population parameter in them, but we end up not being able to be at all precise about where the parameter's true value might be. We will find in Chapter 6 that excessively wide confidence intervals also can prevent researchers from choosing between rival models or theories.

TRY WORKING WITH DEM 53, WHICH ALLOWS YOU TO COMPARE TWO CONFIDENCE INTERVALS

Another influence on the choice of a confidence level is the number of confidence intervals that are to be computed on the same data. At first glance, this might seem an odd point to raise because up to now we have dealt only with one confidence interval at a time. However, many kinds of statistical techniques and summaries involve more than one confidence interval. The percentile package provides an example with which we are familiar, namely the five-number summary that includes the 10th, 25th, 50th, 75th, and 90th percentiles.

If we compute, say, 99% confidence intervals for these five statistics to describe a distribution, then we encounter a problem with establishing how confident we can be about all five of the intervals simultaneously. For each interval, we have an expected chance of 1 in 100 (0.01) of the interval failing to include the population parameter value. Unfortunately, the probability that *one or more* of these intervals could fail to include its population parameter could be as high as $0.01 + 0.01 + 0.01 + 0.01 + 0.01 = 0.05$. So the probability that *none* of the five intervals will fail to include its population parameter could be as low as $1 - 0.05 = 0.95$ rather than the 0.99 we hoped for.

DEFINITION   A remedy for this problem was suggested by Bonferroni and is usually called a **Bonferroni correction**. Suppose our desired confidence level for k confidence intervals is $1 - \alpha$, in the sense that this is the probability we would prefer that none of the k intervals will fail to include its population parameter. In experimental psychological research, this probability is called a **family-wise** confidence level. Then each interval must be constructed with a confidence level of $1 - \alpha/k$. In the five-number summary, a 99% family-wise confidence level requires that we construct each interval with a confidence level of $1 - 0.01/5 = 1 - 0.002 = 0.998$, or 99.8%. This is a conservative way of guaranteeing a family-wise confidence level, since it is derived from the highest possible probability of one or more intervals excluding its population parameter. In later chapters we will examine some less conservative methods of dealing with family-wise confidence levels.

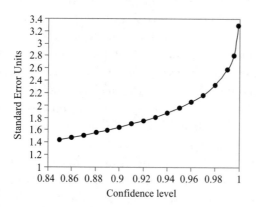

FIGURE 5.13 Increase in $z_{\alpha/2}$ as a function of confidence level

Human intuition about confidence levels

Having seen how our intuitions can fail us in probabilistic matters, perhaps you will not be surprised to learn that we may not be good at judging how confident we should be about our own predictions or guesses. In addition to the usual vagaries of wishful thinking (i.e., overestimating the probability of good outcomes and underestimating that of bad outcomes), psychological researchers claim that people are generally 'miscalibrated' in their estimates of probability. A large number of studies of laypeople on general knowledge (e.g., Fischhoff, Slovic & Lichtenstein, 1977), difficult tasks (Fischhoff & Slovic, 1980), performance tasks (Howell, 1972), and various experts (Christensen-Szalanski & Bushyhead's (1981) study of physicians, Oskamp's (1965) investigation of clinical psychologists, and Stael von Holstein's (1971) study of weather forecasters' judgments of relatively unfamiliar events) show a general tendency towards overconfidence.

Furthermore, overconfidence appears to increase with task difficulty and varies inversely with knowledge. A second widespread finding in calibration research is that when people are asked to provide quantile or other distributional estimates involving the spread of scores, they tend to construct distributions that are too tight (see Lichtenstein, Fischhoff & Phillips, 1982, for a review). Furthermore, training does not seem to reduce this tendency (Lichtenstein & Fischhoff, 1980). One plausible explanation for overconfidence is that we learn it from two other biases, namely the confirmation and hindsight biases, which seduce us into believing we are correct more often than we really are.

Here is an example of the kind of test used by experimenters to assess whether people are over- or underconfident. For each of the following 10 items, provide a low and high 'guesstimate' such that you are *70% confident* that the correct answer falls between the two. Your challenge is to be neither too narrow (i.e., overconfident) nor too wide (i.e., underconfident). If you successfully meet this challenge you should expect three misses in 10 (i.e., 30% misses).

1. Martin Luther King's age at death   Low ___ High ___
2. Length of the Nile River (in kilometers)   Low ___ High ___
3. Number of countries that are members of OPEC   Low ___ High ___
4. Number of books in the Old Testament   Low ___ High ___
5. Diameter of the moon (in kilometers)   Low ___ High ___
6. Weight of an empty Boeing 747 (in kilograms)   Low ___ High ___
7. Year of Wolfgang Amadeus Mozart's birth   Low ___ High ___
8. Gestation period (in days) of an Asian elephant   Low ___ High ___
9. Air distance from London to Tokyo (in kilometers)   Low ___ High ___
10. Deepest known point in the ocean (in meters)   Low ___ High ___

The answers are listed at the end of this chapter. To see whether you were over- or underconfident, count how many of the answers to the confidence exercise lie outside the intervals you nominated. If more than three were outside, you may have been overconfident in your estimations (of course, in self-defense you will want to construct an appropriate confidence interval around your proportion of missed answers!).

In his introductory statistics textbook, Robert Lockhart (1998: 352–353) proposes a confidence game as an entertaining way of gaining intuition about the tradeoff between confidence and precision. The game requires two or more players, one of whom is the dealer. The dealer selects a question on each turn and reads it to the players. The questions all require a numerical answer (e.g., 'How many movies did Victor Mature appear in?'). Players give their answers in the form of an interval that they believe contains the correct value. Lockhart even recommends that the questions be compiled from six Trivial Pursuit-like categories! The winning player is one who gives the shortest interval that contains the correct value. For a player who does not know the answer to the question, confidence may be increased only at the expense of increasing the interval's width; and likewise the width may be narrowed at the expense of lowering confidence.

SUMMARY

The **family-wise** confidence level associated with a collection of k confidence intervals is the probability we would prefer that none of the k intervals will fail to include its population parameter.

The **Bonferroni correction** for establishing a family-wise confidence level of at least $1 - \alpha$ for k confidence intervals requires that each interval must be constructed with a confidence level of $1 - \alpha/k$.

Answers to the confidence exercise

1. 39 years
2. 6632 km
3. 13 countries
4. 39 books
5. 3421 km
6. 177,270 kg
7. The year 1756
8. 645 days
9. 9439 km
10. 10,859 m

Questions and exercises

Q.5.1. Suppose you are running a replication of the size–weight illusion study, and out of 10 subjects, seven of them choose the larger object as the heavier of two objects. What is the 95% confidence interval around the sample proportion in this experiment?

Q.5.2. In a random sample of 15 IQ scores with a sample mean of 104 and a sample standard deviation of 18, what is the 90% confidence interval around the mean? What is the 99% confidence interval around the mean? (You may practice computing confidence intervals around means using either **ConfiPatch** or **Dem51**.)

Q.5.3. Which of the following are true and which are false?

(a) A 99% confidence interval around a sample mean is narrower than a 95% confidence interval.

(b) A 95% confidence interval around a sample proportion can have a width of 0.

(c) A confidence interval around a sample mean would be twice as wide if the sample size were 50 as it would be if the sample size were 100.

(d) The sampling distribution of the mean becomes normal as N gets large, only if the scores have a normal distribution.

(e) All else being equal, the narrower the confidence interval the lower the confidence level.

(f) Sampling error affects only the width of a confidence interval, not its location.

(g) When using a normal approximation, a confidence interval around a sample proportion is widest when $P = 0.5$.

Q.5.4. An industrial psychologist working for a large multinational corporation has created a new stress management program for executives, and wishes to assess its impact on (among other things) blood pressure. He randomly selects 13 executives from the corporation's personnel, and measures their blood pressure after they have gone through his program. The medical information in the corporate personnel records reveals a mean systolic blood pressure for executives of 125 mmHg. The mean for the 13 in the psychologist's study is 117 mmHg with a standard deviation of 9.2. Now, imagine what the population of executives' mean blood pressure might be if the psychologist had put all of the corporation's personnel through his program. Is 125 a plausible value for that hypothetical mean if the psychologist uses a 95% confidence interval for assessing the precision of this sample mean? Does the answer to this question shed any light on the issue of whether the psychologist's program lowers blood pressure?

Q.5.5. Suppose that you are going to conduct a poll prior to a national referendum and you want to ensure that a 99% confidence interval around your estimate of the proportion of people voting 'Yes' will have a half-width of less than 0.025. How big a sample you would need, and why?

Q.5.6. Compare the sample size required in Q.5.5 with the sample size for the same half-width if you use a confidence level of only 95% instead of 99%. You can explore what sample sizes are required for various half-widths and confidence levels by working with **Dem55**.

Q.5.7. Using **Dem53**, find out what sample sizes would yield confidence intervals of the same width for confidence levels of 99% and 90% when the sample mean IQ is 103 and sample standard deviation is 9. *Hint*: First try setting the sample size for the 90% confidence interval at around 300–350 and adjusting the second sample size.

Statistical Models and Significance Tests

Statistical models of a population statistic

In Chapter 5, we approached the concept of a confidence interval by starting with a statistical model of a sample statistic. This kind of model has the form

Sample statistic value = population statistic value + sampling error.

A statistical model of a sample mean, for instance, when we know what the value of m is in advance, may be expressed by

$$\bar{X} = \mu + e,$$

where e represents the sampling error in the model. In Chapter 5, we used the t-distribution as the sampling distribution of the mean for small samples, and the normal distribution for large samples.

    This statistical model could also be thought of as a *predictive model* in which the sample mean is being predicted on the basis of the population mean's value and sampling error. So μ is our predicted value for what the sample mean will be if we take a random sample from our population, and e represents the error we will make because of sampling. For example, if we know that an IQ test has been normed on a population so that the population mean is 100, then if we were to take a random sample of people from that population and give them the test, our predictive model of the sample mean would be

$$\bar{X} = 100 + e.$$

What if we do not know the value of μ beforehand, as is usually the case? If we were to guess a value for μ, then our predictions about sample means could very likely be contaminated by *two kinds of error*: sampling error and error due to how far off our guess is from the true value of μ. Researchers sometimes refer

DEFINITION   to this second kind of error as **model error**, since it arises from a mistaken model of reality. Suppose we denote a hypothetical value for μ by μ_h. Then we may represent our predictive model in this way:

$$\bar{X} = \mu_h + m + e,$$

where m represents model error, i.e., the difference between our hypothetical value μ_h and the mean's true value μ. All that has been done is to substitute $\mu_h + m$ in place of μ. More generally,

Sample statistic value = hypothetical population statistic value +

model error + sampling error.

The best possible model is one that has no model error, so that $m = 0$. The problem is, how do we know whether m might be 0 when all we have to go on is a sample statistic?

Most psychological research places researchers in this quandary. Their theories may provide them with hypothetical values for the population statistics of interest to them, but ultimately sample estimates are their only evidence of how accurate those hypothetical values are. Moreover, psychologists may have competing theories that yield competing models and therefore alternative hypothetical values. Quite reasonably, they want to be able to use their sample data to help them decide which model is the best one, or whether any of the competing models may be ruled out.

Confidence intervals may be used to address these problems, provided that researchers use them judiciously. In the last chapter, you may have noticed that the phrase 'plausible values' was used in the example where we estimated the mean IQ of a population by taking a random sample of 16 IQ scores. In that example, the population mean IQ was not known. Having obtained a sample mean of 103 and a standard deviation of 9, we computed a 95% confidence interval around this sample mean and found a lower limit of

98.2 and an upper limit of 107.8, so that $CI_{0.95} = [98.2, 107.8]$. On this basis, we concluded that the plausible values for the population's mean IQ ranged from 98.2 to 107.8.

In general, any value contained inside a confidence interval around a sample statistic is said to be a **plausible value** of the unknown population DEFINITION statistic, and any value outside the interval is said to be an **implausible value**. The term 'implausible' should not be confused with "impossible". We cannot say that it is *impossible* that the population mean IQ in our example could be 90, for instance, or 110. Remember, a confidence interval can fail to include the population statistic. Given our 95% confidence level, however, we can say that those values are implausible because they are quite unlikely on the basis of the evidence from our sample.

According to our sample's $CI_{.95}$ of [98.2, 107.8], it is plausible that the population's mean IQ could also be 100. However, it should be borne in mind that there are other plausible values as well. If someone hypothesized that this population's IQ is 105, that also would be a plausible value. On the other hand, the hypothesis that the mean IQ is 110 would be implausible.

Let us recast all of this in terms of model error, so we can see how the notion of plausible and implausible values for a population statistic may be used to determine whether the model error, m, could plausibly be 0. A **plausible** DEFINITION **model** is one for which 0 is a plausible value for model error. The formula for the confidence interval in our example is

$$\Pr(98.2 < \mu < 107.8) = 0.95.$$

Now recall that $\mu = \mu_h + m$, which implies that $\mu - \mu_h = m$. If we subtract μ_h from the three terms inside the brackets, we get a confidence interval around $\mu - \mu_h$, i.e., around m:

$$\Pr(98.2 - \mu_h < m < 107.8 - \mu_h) = 0.95.$$

The lowest value for μ_h that will enable 0 to be a plausible value for m is 98.2 and the highest such value is 107.8. These are just the lower and upper limits of our original confidence interval.

We have just discovered that *if a model of a sample statistic predicts values that lie inside the confidence interval, then it is a plausible model*. We may therefore decide whether a model is plausible by determining whether its prediction yields a plausible value. Before developing this concept any further, let us go through one more example to see how it works. We shall return to the size–weight illusion experiment developed in Chapter 5, because it is a simple but rather generalizable illustration of the concepts we have covered thus far. As you probably recall, in this experiment participants are presented with two objects, one larger than the other. If the size–weight illusion is operating, when asked to judge which of two objects is heavier, the majority of participants will pick the larger object even though both objects weigh the same and have the same cross-section for their lifting surface.

What if the size–weight illusion does not occur? Then because participants are forced to choose one object or the other, we would expect on average that half would select the larger object. If the size–weight illusion is not operating, then the appropriate hypothetical value for the proportion of people choosing the larger object would be $\Pi_h = 0.5$, and the resultant statistical model of the sample proportion P would use this hypothetical value:

$$P = 0.5 + m + e.$$

Is this a plausible model?

Recall that in Chapter 5 we considered an experiment with a random sample of 20 participants, and 13 of them chose the larger object. Therefore the sample proportion $P = 13/20 = 0.65$. We computed a 95% confidence interval for Π and obtained $CI_{0.95} = [0.45, 0.85]$. This confidence interval contains 0.5, so it is therefore a plausible value. Likewise, we can see that the corresponding confidence interval around model error m is

$$\Pr(0.45 - 0.5 < m < 0.65 - 0.5) = 0.95,$$

or

$$\Pr(-0.05 < m < 0.15) = 0.95.$$

This interval contains 0, so 0 is a plausible value of the model error. So, the model based on $\Pi_h = 0.5$ is a plausible model, and it is therefore plausible that the size–weight illusion does not occur in the population from which the sample came. Of course this does not mean we can conclude that the illusion really does not occur, but merely that its absence is not beyond the bounds of plausibility.

It is important to recognize that plausibility is not an all-or-nothing property. It is a matter of degree. Hypothetical values that are closer to the center of the confidence interval are more plausible, given the sample evidence, than those further away from the center. If we are using a sample statistic that is an unbiased estimator of the population statistic, then the most plausible hypothetical value of the population statistic is whatever value we obtained as the sample estimate. Given the sample data, the *most* plausible value for Π_h is 0.65 since that is the value of the sample proportion.

Model error is the difference between a hypothetical value of a population statistic and the true value of that statistic.

A **plausible hypothetical value of a population statistic** is one that lies inside the confidence interval that has been constructed around a sample estimate. It is **implausible** if it lies outside the interval. However, plausibility is a matter of degree. The closer to the center of the confidence interval, the more plausible the hypothetical value.

A **plausible model** is one for which 0 is a plausible value for model error. That is, a plausible model predicts plausible values.

SUMMARY

Making decisions with confidence intervals: Significance tests

In psychological research, as in any other science, progress is made partly through rivalry and disputation over competing theories and models. If everyone believes that one theory is unsurpassable, then there is little motivation to conduct research in hope of a better theory. Conversely, if everyone believes that any theory is as good as any other, then there is no motivation to design experiments to test alternative theories. Most psychologists hold a position somewhere in between these extremes, and they usually think that although some theories are better than others, even the best theories may be improved. It should come as no surprise, then, that pitting theories or at least hypotheses against one another has long dominated psychological research. In fact, for most researchers in the field, statistical methods have been used primarily for hypothesis testing.

While there is nothing intrinsically wrong with the idea of trying to decide in favor of one hypothesis (or theory) over another, some of the most damaging practices in psychologists' uses of statistics may be traced to an over-reliance on hypothesis testing. The position taken in this book is that hypothesis testing is a special case of decision making under risk. Usually the risks involve little more than being wrong about our own hypotheses. However, even those consequences can mount up. Researchers and theorists may take wrong turnings, thereby abandoning what would have been a productive line of inquiry or pursuing one that leads to a dead end. Therefore, decisions about hypotheses, like any decision under risk, should be made sparingly, carefully, and where possible, reversibly.

That said, we shall now examine how confidence intervals may be used to decide between rival hypotheses or models on the basis of a data sample. In the first section of this chapter, we saw how the boundaries on a confidence interval could be used to distinguish plausible hypotheses or models from implausible ones. If we must make a decision about which hypotheses we should retain and which ones we should reject, then the distinction between plausibility and implausibility could be used to make this decision.

Let's return to the social facilitation hypothesis, one of the earliest hypotheses in social psychological research. As you'll recall, this hypothesis states that the mere presence of another person is sufficient to motivate the participant to exert more effort in performing a task. There is a corresponding social inhibition hypothesis, which states that the presence of another person is sufficient to inhibit the participant from fully exerting themselves in the task. Imagine setting up an experiment to test these hypotheses using our tug-of-war contest described in Chapter 5, in which the two participants are randomly assigned to an 'Observer Absent' or an 'Observer There' condition. In the Absent condition, the participant is alone in a small room. A rope goes through a hole in an opaque wall to the other participant (so they cannot see each other). The other participant in the There condition is in an identical room, but has another person standing nearby who simply watches them pull on the rope.

We record which participant wins the tug-of-war, A (Absent) or T (There). If the presence of another person has no effect one way or the other, then the T-participants and A-participants should have the same chance of winning the tug-of-war. The population proportion of T-participants winning should be $\Pi = 0.5$. However, if the social facilitation hypothesis is correct then the T-participants should be motivated to tug harder and Π should be greater than 0.5. On the other hand, if the presence of another person inhibits the participant's performance then the T-participants should lose more often. In that case, Π would be less than 0.5.

If we were attempting to find out from this experiment whether there is any detectable effect at all from the presence of another person, it would make sense to combine the facilitation-effect and inhibition-effect possibilities together to create an 'effect hypothesis' which simply says that $\Pi \neq 0.5$. So we have two rival hypotheses:

- *No-effect hypothesis*: The presence of the other person has no effect, so $\Pi = 0.5$.
- *Effect hypothesis*: The presence of the other person has an effect, so $\Pi \neq 0.5$.

We can reject a hypothesis if we obtain evidence from our experiment such that all the values it predicts for Π end up being designated 'implausible.' For example the no-effect hypothesis predicts that $\Pi = 0.5$. If a confidence interval for Π excludes 0.5, then that value is implausible and the no-effect hypothesis therefore is implausible.

If we perform the experiment for 40 pairs of participants and find that 28 out of 40 times the T-participant wins, what can we decide? First, we must follow the procedure for constructing a confidence interval. Suppose we elect a confidence level of 95%. Since $N = 40$, we may use the normal approximation to construct our 95% confidence interval.

1. We have collected a sample of 100 observations.
2. We know the sample proportion is $P = 28/40 = 0.7$, and from that we may calculate the standard error. We substitute 40 for N and 0.7 for P in the formula for s_P:

$$s_P = \sqrt{\frac{P(1-P)}{N}} = \sqrt{\frac{0.7(1-0.7)}{40}} = 0.4583/6.32 = 0.0725.$$

3. Then we ascertain the total proportion of the sampling distribution that will be excluded from the confidence interval. We find this proportion by converting our 95% confidence level to the proportion 0.95, and subtracting that from 1 to get 0.05.
4. Since we are constructing a two-sided confidence interval, we will need to divide 0.05 into two halves. Using Table A.2, we find the value $0.05/2 = 0.025$ in the column labeled 'Area beyond z,' and read off $z_{.025} = 1.96$.
5. Finally, we complete the resulting confidence interval statement by plugging the sample proportion, standard error, $z_{\alpha/2}$, and α into our formula

$$\Pr(P - z_{\alpha/2}s_P < \Pi < P + z_{\alpha/2}s_P) = 0.95,$$

getting

$$\Pr(0.7 - (1.96)(0.0725) < \Pi < 0.7 + (1.96)(0.0725)) = 0.95,$$

or

$$\Pr(0.558 < \Pi < 0.842).$$

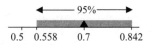

So our 95% confidence interval is $\text{CI}_{0.95} = [0.558, 0.842]$. We may consider any hypothetical value for Π from 0.558 to 0.842 to be plausible values, and any hypothetical values for Π below 0.558 and any above 0.842 to be implausible. This finding indicates that we should reject the no-effect hypothesis because *its predicted value for Π has been found to be implausible.* On the other hand, since the interval [0.558, 0.842] contains values in the range predicted by the effect hypothesis, we cannot reject the effect hypothesis.

DEFINITION

Let us pause here to summarize the procedure involved in deciding whether to reject a hypothesis or not. This procedure is traditionally called a **significance test**, which stems from a notion that we reject a hypothesis if the value of our sample statistic differs 'significantly' from the hypothetical value. All that is really meant by a 'significant difference' between the sample statistic and the hypothetical value is that the hypothetical value is implausible. We can set out a significance test fairly generally in four steps.

PROCEDURE
FOR A
SIGNIFIC-
ANCE TEST

1. Decide on the confidence level that you wish to use for distinguishing plausible from implausible values of the population statistic concerned.
2. For any hypothesis, ascertain its hypothetical (predicted) values of the population statistic.
3. On the basis of an appropriate random sample, construct a confidence interval for the population statistic.
4. If all the predicted values associated with a hypothesis lie outside the confidence interval (i.e., all of the predicted values are implausible), then the hypothesis may be **rejected**. Otherwise, we **fail to reject** it.

DEFINITIONS

When the statistic is a mean, the significance test is known as the ***t*-test**, because the *t*-distribution is used to model the sampling distribution of the mean for relatively small samples. Likewise, when the statistic is a proportion, the significance test is known as the **binomial test** for the reason that the binomial distribution is used to model the sampling distribution of proportions for small samples. In some psychological literature, the binomial test also is called the **sign test**. That name is associated with experiments along the lines of the social facilitation study, in which two different 'signs' are used to denote each of the two possible outcomes on each experimental trial.

A significance test involves making a decision based on a confidence interval. However, of course we may use confidence intervals without having to perform significance tests. In psychological research, however, conventional researchers almost always perform a significance test, often without even reporting the associated confidence interval. There are several reasons why this is not good practice, the most obvious of which is that a significance test focuses attention on only one hypothesis. Since confidence intervals display the entire range of plausible and implausible hypothetical values for a statistic, they help researchers and others focus on a variety of hypotheses, including any that have not been considered by the researchers themselves.

In principle, the significance test procedure outlined above places no limits on the number or variety of hypotheses that could be tested with a confidence interval. For instance, in our social facilitation example suppose we had four hypotheses instead of two:

- Strict inhibition effect: $\Pi < 0.5$;
- No effect: $\Pi = 0.5$;
- Weak facilitation effect: $0.5 < \Pi < 0.7$;
- Strong facilitation effect: $\Pi \geq 0.7$.

Then since $CI_{0.95} = [0.558, 0.842]$, we would know that we could reject the first two hypotheses (strict inhibition and no effect) because their hypothetical values all lie outside the interval and are therefore implausible. However, we could not reject the remaining two (weak and strong facilitation) since at least some of their hypothetical values lie inside the interval.

The conventional significance test, however, involves a decision on whether to reject one particular hypothesis. This hypothesis usually is constructed in such a way that the alternative to it is the state of affairs that the researcher hopes is valid. It is called the **null hypothesis** (usually abbreviated as H_0). DEFINITION Often in experimental work, the null hypothesis amounts to a hypothesis that the experimental manipulation has had no effect. If the null hypothesis is rejected then its alternative (the **alternative hypothesis**, usually denoted by H_1) must be plausible. In the social facilitation study, the null hypothesis is that the presence of another person has no effect, so $\Pi = 0.5$. By rejecting this hypothesis, the experimenter invites us to conclude that the only possible alternative, $\Pi \neq 0.5$, must be plausible, and that corresponds to the effect hypothesis.

It is crucial to realize that failing to reject a hypothesis does not entail believing it is true, even though the temptation is nearly irresistible when it so happens that there is only one hypothesis that has not been rejected. The reason why failing to reject does not imply truth becomes more obvious if we are unable to reject any hypotheses. What if only 24 out of 40 T-participants had won the tug-of-war? Then our sample P would be $24/40$, or 0.6, and our 95% confidence interval would be $CI_{0.95} = [0.448, 0.752]$. This interval contains both values predicted by the no-effect hypothesis (H_0: $\Pi = 0.5$) *and* values predicted by the effect hypothesis ($H_1 \neq 0.5$). Neither hypothesis can be rejected, but it would be silly to believe both or either of them.

A more important caution about significance testing without reporting confidence intervals arises in conjunction with the question of how we accumulate evidence about hypotheses from multiple studies. If we had two social facilitation experiments with the results described above, i.e., one with a sample P of $28/40$ and the other with a sample P of $24/40$, then simply reporting the significance test results would leave us in a misleading quandary. The first study would report a significant difference of P from 0.5, thereby rejecting the null (no-effect) hypothesis; but the second would report that P did not differ significantly from 0.5 and so the null hypothesis was not rejected. By itself, this looks as if we have one study favoring the effect hypothesis and another not favoring it, so the evidence for the effect hypothesis appears to be 50–50. However, such a conclusion is impoverished and can be downright misleading.

Confidence intervals place these findings in their proper perspective. In one study, $CI_{0.95} = [0.448, 0.752]$; and in the other $CI_{0.95} = [0.558, 0.842]$. As the next figure shows, these overlap considerably and clearly favor the hypothesis that there is an effect. The two studies really are presenting rather similar findings. A commonsensical approach to combining the evidence from these two studies would be to take the average of their sample proportions, which would give us an average of 0.65.

Now imagine that we have conducted 25 such studies, each with $N = 40$. Suppose significance tests based on 95% confidence intervals are carried out for each of the studies, and in 14 of the 25 studies we are able to reject the no-effect (null hypothesis) whereas for the remaining 11 we cannot reject it. If we paid attention only to whether each study's significance test rejected the null hypothesis, then we could fall into a trap that has snared many researchers and scholars trained in the significance testing framework instead of the confidence interval approach (cf. Schmidt, 1996). According to this simplistic vote-counting exercise, only a little over half of our studies reject the no-effect hypothesis and we might be inclined to say that the evidence for an effect is, at best, equivocal. We might even conclude that the evidence is conflicting.

We can avoid this trap by examining the sample proportions and the 95% confidence intervals for the studies. They are shown in the next graph, with the first two corresponding to the two studies we have considered so far. The left-hand vertical bar is at 0.5. You can see from the graph that although only 14 have rejected the no-effect hypothesis, the sample proportions for all 25 studies are above 0.5. If the evidence for an effect were truly equivocal, you would expect to see the sample proportions fairly evenly split between those above and those below 0.5, and you would expect their average to be very close to 0.5. However, the average of these sample proportions is nowhere near 0.5. The average P, and our best estimate of the true population value of Π, is 0.65. This is represented by the right-hand vertical bar. The evidence from these studies actually has accumulated quite convincingly in favor of the view that the presence of another person does cause the subject to have a greater probability of winning the tug-of-war than 0.5.

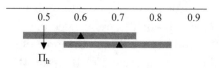

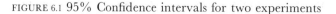

FIGURE 6.1 95% Confidence intervals for two experiments

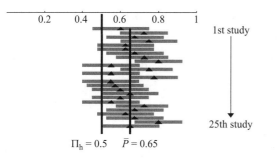

$\Pi_h = 0.5 \qquad \bar{P} = 0.65$

FIGURE 6.2 25 experiments with $N = 40$ and $\Pi = 0.65$

The lesson here is clear: Merely reporting whether a null hypothesis has been rejected or not is insufficient and potentially misleading. Contrary to long-standing traditions in psychological research, confidence intervals should be routinely presented in research reports, perhaps (but not always) in conjunction with significance tests.

A **significance test** is the procedure involved in deciding whether to reject a hypothesis or not on the basis of whether its predicted values of a statistic are plausible. When the statistic is a mean, the significance test is known as the *t*-**test**, and when it is a proportion the test is known as the **binomial test** or **sign test**.

A hypothesis is **rejected** if all of its predicted values of a statistic are implausible. Otherwise, we **fail to reject** it.

The **null hypothesis** (H_0) is the hypothesis tested in a significance test. Usually it is constructed in such a way that the alternative to it is the state of affairs that the researcher hopes is valid. If the null hypothesis is rejected then its alternative (the **alternative hypothesis**, or H_1) must be plausible.

SUMMARY

Making the wrong decision: Type I and Type II errors

The decision to reject or not reject a hypothesis may be correct or mistaken. There are two ways to err with the significance test procedure, because there are two choices for every hypothesis: reject or fail to reject. First, we could reject a null hypothesis when it really is true, which is called **Type I error**. Second, we could fail to reject a false null hypothesis, which is called **Type II error**. Table 6.1 summarizes the relationships between the two types of error, the decision to reject or retain the hypothesis, and the (unknown) state of reality.

DEFINITION

In Chapter 9, we will deal with the concepts of a false negative ersus false positive in clinical diagnosis, or a false conviction versus a false acquittal in a

TABLE 6.1 Type I and Type II errors

Decision	State of reality	
	Null hypothesis H_0 is true	Null hypothesis H_0 is false
Do not reject H_0	Correct decision	**Type II error**
Reject H_0	**Type I error**	Correct decision

legal trial. These errors are analogous to Type I and Type II error, and the analogies between them are shown in Table 6.2. Type I error can be seen to be a kind of false alarm in the sense that it is analogous to a false positive or a false conviction. This arises from the fact that the medical analog to a null hypothesis is that the patient is well, and likewise the null hypothesis in legal trials is that the defendant is innocent (in Western countries). Type II error, on the other hand, entails missing a real effect and is analogous to a false negative or a false acquittal. If you have mixed feelings about which is the worse kind of error, consider the fact that in conventional psychological research reporting, only Type I error is explicitly dealt with! The reasons for this practice turn out to be understandable, and they will become apparent shortly. Nevertheless, both kinds of error are important and if we must make decisions such as in significance tests, we ignore either kind at our peril.

In research, as in real life, we do not know whether we have committed a Type I or Type II error when we decide whether to reject a null hypothesis. We can, however, estimate the probability of committing either kind of error. Doing so for Type I error turns out to be straightforward. Returning to our social facilitation experiment, consider the no-effect hypothesis that predicts

TABLE 6.2 Type I and Type II errors and other testing or diagnostic errors

Diagnosis	State of reality	
	Patient is well	Patient is ill
Negative (clear)	Correct negative diagnosis	**False negative** (Type II error)
Positive (ill)	**False positive** (Type I error)	Correct positive diagnosis

Verdict	State of reality	
	Defendant is innocent	Defendant is guilty
Innocent (acquittal)	Correct acquittal	**False acquittal** (Type II error)
Guilty (conviction)	**False conviction** (Type I error)	Correct conviction

$\Pi_h = 0.5$. Our 95% confidence interval did not include 0.5 as a value, so we decided on that basis to reject this hypothesis. In so doing, we run a risk of making a Type I error. How large might this risk be?

To find out, we must ask how often we would (mistakenly) reject the no-effect hypothesis *if it really was true that* $\Pi = 0.5$. Since we have chosen a confidence level of 95%, we would reject this hypothesis if we obtained a 95% confidence interval that did not include 0.5. We should expect that to happen only 5% of the time, so our risk of making a Type I error is 5%. The conventional way to express this is as a probability, i.e., a 0.05 probability of making a Type I error. In general, if we decide to use a confidence level of $100(1 - \alpha)\%$, the **probability of making a Type I error** is α. It should   DEFINITION now be clear why Type I error is routinely reported in research based on significance tests, since it is so easy to ascertain. The probability of a Type I error is inversely related to confidence level, so the higher the confidence level the lower this probability will be.

Now let us turn to the **probability of making a Type II error**, i.e.,   DEFINITIONS failing to reject the null hypothesis when it really is false. This probability is commonly denoted by the Greek letter, β (beta). The probability of correctly rejecting the null hypothesis, on the other hand, is $1 - \beta$, and is called the **power** of a significance test. The closer power is to 1, the more likely we are correctly to reject null hypotheses. In our 25 social facilitation experiments, 11 of them failed to reject the null hypothesis even though the accumulated body of evidence indicated that H_0 is false and $\Pi \neq 0.5$. If the null hypothesis really is false, then we made a Type II error 11 times out of 25, which should seem uncomfortably high. How large might β really be?

We can get an idea of what this probability could be if we ask how often we would (mistakenly) fail to reject H_0 *if it really was true that* $\Pi = 0.65$. We will fail to reject H_0 whenever our 95% confidence interval includes 0.5. Since the 95% confidence interval around a sample proportion of 0.65 is $CI_{0.95} = [0.502, 0.798]$ and that just barely excludes 0.5, we will fail to reject H_0 whenever $P < 0.65$. Therefore, the probability of making a Type II error when $\Pi = 0.65$ is the same as the probability of getting a sample $P < 0.65$ when $\Pi = 0.65$. The sampling distribution for P when $\Pi = 0.65$ for a sample size of 40 is approximately normal with $s_P = 0.0754$. This distribution is graphed in Figure 6.3, with the white area indicating the probability that $P < 0.65$, which is 0.5. So the probability of a Type II error if $\Pi = 0.65$ is $\beta = 0.5$.

On the other hand, the power of our significance test under these conditions is the shaded area in the graph, which shows that $1 - \beta = 0.5$. We should expect to reject (correctly) the null hypothesis only half of the time. This result corroborates the impression we gained from the first two studies and subsequently the collection of 25 studies, since we ended up rejecting H_0 about half

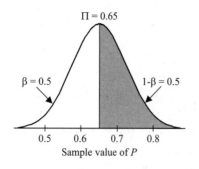

FIGURE 6.3 Probability of Type II error and power for $\Pi = 0.65$ and 95% confidence

of the time. If we are using significance tests to decide between H_0 and its rival H_1, we want the probability that we will reject H_0 to be high whenever H_0 is false. We surely want it to be higher than just 0.5. How can we increase our power?

What factors influence how large power is? The clues lie in a careful restatement of the definition of power provided in our example. Far from being a generalization, that definition contains important particulars. All we determined is that if $\Pi = 0.65$ and we use a confidence level of 95% for a random sample with $N = 40$, then the probability that we will (correctly) reject H_0 is 0.5. This statement specifies three things:

- The hypothetical value for Π,
- Confidence level,
- Sample size.

It turns out that power depends on all three. We will consider the hypothetical value of Π's effect first.

The alternative hypothesis includes all values of Π that are not 0.5, so we are free to ask what the probability of rejecting the null hypothesis would be if Π were any value other than 0.5. We already know that we will reject H_0 if we obtain a sample proportion of 0.65 *or more*. The larger that Π is, the more likely we are to reject H_0, and so the greater our power will be. The reason for this trend becomes apparent if we think in terms of sampling distributions and confidence intervals. Suppose we had run our 25 experiments on participants from a population where Π has a larger value than 0.65, say $\Pi = 0.75$. The left-hand part of Figure 6.4 shows the 95% confidence intervals for each of those experiments, and whether they include 0.5 or not. The right-hand part shows the confidence intervals that we have seen before from the 25 experiments in which $\Pi = 0.65$.

It is clear that when $\Pi = 0.75$ the confidence intervals do not contain 0.5 nearly as often as they do when $\Pi = 0.65$. In fact, only one out of 25 did so, whereas 11 out of 25 did when $\Pi = 0.65$. This suggests that we are more likely

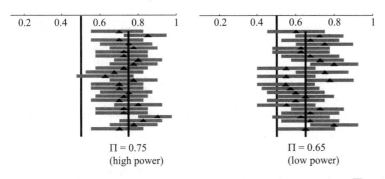

FIGURE 6.4 95% Confidence intervals for 25 experiments when $\Pi = 0.75$ vs. $\Pi = 0.65$

to correctly reject H_0 when $\Pi = 0.75$, and therefore our power must be higher. So, let us compare power when $\Pi = 0.75$ with power when $\Pi = 0.65$. We already know that power when $\Pi = 0.65$ is 0.5, so we can concentrate on finding out what power is when $\Pi = 0.75$. The sampling distribution for P when $\Pi = 0.75$ for a sample size of 40 is approximately normal with $s_P = 0.0685$. This distribution is graphed in Figure 6.5, with the shaded area indicating the probability that $P \geq 0.65$. The sampling distribution for P when $\Pi = 0.65$ is superimposed for comparison.

We can easily see that the shaded area is a lot larger than 0.5, but we still need to find out exactly how large it is. The number of standard errors that 0.65 is away from the mean, 0.75, is $0.1/s_P = 0.1/0.0685 = 1.46$. In Table A.2, we can find that the area in the tail of a normal distribution that starts at 1.46 standard error units from the mean is 0.0721. This tells us the size of the white (tail) area which is β, the probability of a Type II error. Therefore the size of the shaded area is $1 - 0.0721 = 0.9279$. So our power is $1 - \beta = 0.9279$. That means we should expect to (correctly!) reject the null hypothesis 92.79% of the time if $\Pi = 0.75$, and we will (incorrectly) fail to reject it only 7.21% of the time.

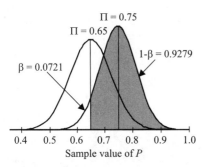

FIGURE 6.5 Probability of Type II error and power for $\Pi = 0.75$ and 95% confidence

The fact that power is greater when $\Pi = 0.75$ than when $\Pi = 0.65$ is due to the fact that 0.75 is further from the null hypothesis value of 0.5, demonstrating that the further Π is from 0.5, the more likely we are to reject H_0, and so the greater our power will be. Figure 6.6 shows how quickly power increases as Π gets further from 0.5. In terms that are both relevant to our social facilitation experiment and widely generalizable, the larger the experimental effect, the more likely we are to identify it by rejecting the null hypothesis.

Now we turn to confidence level and its influence on power. As mentioned in Chapter 5, higher confidence levels have a price in greater imprecision because they entail wider confidence intervals. Higher confidence also means a lower probability of a Type I error (α) and in fact it means that we are less likely to reject H_0 under any conditions. Being less likely to reject H_0 under any conditions implies that we are less likely to reject it when it is actually false. So more confidence entails lower power, and conversely less confidence entails higher power. There is a tradeoff: an increased confidence level is paid for by a loss in power.

If we reconsider how much power we have when $\Pi = 0.65$ and we use a confidence level of 99% instead of 95%, the tradeoff becomes clear. Recall that for $P = 0.65$, $CI_{0.95} = [0.502, 0.798]$ which barely excludes 0.5 and thereby enables us to reject H_0. But the corresponding 99% confidence interval around 0.65 is $CI_{0.99} = [0.456, 0.844]$, so we would have to obtain a value of P that is higher than 0.65 in order to reject H_0

In fact, we may reject H_0 only if $P \geq 0.7$, since the corresponding 99% confidence interval, $CI_{0.99} = [0.513, 0.887]$, just excludes 0.5. Therefore, the probability of making a Type II error when $\Pi = 0.65$ is the same as the probability of getting a sample where $P < 0.7$ from a population where $\Pi = 0.65$, shown in Figure 6.7. As mentioned before, the sampling distribution for P when $\Pi = 0.65$ for a sample size of 40 is approximately normal with $s_P = 0.0754$. A value of 0.7 is $0.05/s_P = 0.663$ standard errors above the mean. From Table A.2, we can ascertain that for $z = 0.663$ the corresponding area

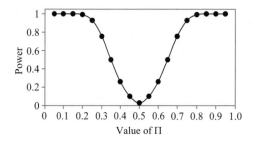

FIGURE 6.6 Power as a function of how far Π is from 0.5

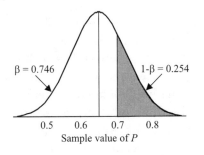

FIGURE 6.7 Probability of Type II error and power for $\Pi = 0.65$ and 95% confidence

under the normal curve in the tail beyond z is 0.254. So our power is $1 - \beta = 0.254$, which is substantially lower than 0.5.

Finally, let us examine the impact of sample size on power. Since we have already seen in Chapter 5 that larger samples give us more precise estimates and therefore narrower confidence intervals, we should expect that larger samples will increase power. This is certainly true. As an illustration, imagine that we ran another 25 social facilitation experiments in which the true value of Π was 0.65 as before, but this time we used samples of size $N = 160$. Our 95% confidence intervals would be about half as wide as those when $N = 40$. They would be far less likely to contain 0.5, as can be seen from a comparison between the two sets of 25 experiments in Figure 6.8.

We have had to spend some time on Type II error probability and power, because they are somewhat complicated. Nevertheless, our perseverance has paid off, because we now have a general picture of the factors that influence power. These may be summarized in the following way:

- The *further the alternative hypothesis value for a statistic is from the null hypothesis value*, the higher power will be.
- The *narrower the confidence intervals*, the higher power will be. Confidence intervals may be made narrower either by *lowering the confidence level* or *increasing sample size*.

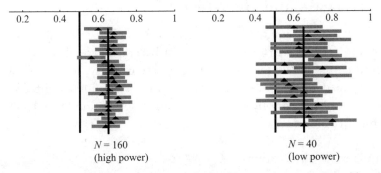

FIGURE 6.8 95% confidence intervals for 25 experiments when $N = 160$ vs. $N = 40$

The first point actually amounts to saying that if the null hypothesis and alternative hypothesis values are close together, then we are not likely to be able to correctly reject one in favor of the other. The further apart those values are, the better our chances of being correct when we reject the null hypothesis. The second point reinforces the observation that narrower confidence intervals permit us to be more decisive than wider ones do. The best way to narrow confidence intervals is to increase sample size. If our sample size has already been determined, then the only way we can narrow the confidence interval is to lower our confidence level.

SUMMARY

Type I error is rejecting a null hypothesis when it really is true.
Type II error is failing to reject a null hypothesis when it really is false.
The **probability of making a Type I error** is denoted by α. It is determined by using a confidence level of $100(1 - \alpha)\%$ for constructing confidence intervals.
The **probability of making a Type II error** is denoted by β.
Power is the probability of correctly rejecting the null hypothesis is $1 - \beta$. Power and β are influenced by how far an alternative hypothesis value for a statistic is from the null hypothesis value, and the width of the confidence interval (which in turn depends on the confidence level and the sample size).
The table below locates the two types of error and their probabilities in terms of whether the null hypothesis is true or not and what decision has been taken.

	State of reality	
Decision	Null hypothesis H_0 is true	Null hypothesis H_0 is false
Do not reject H_0	Correct decision	**Type II error**
Reject H_0	**Type I error**	Correct decision

Confidence intervals and the *t*-test

One of the most widely used significance tests in psychological research is the *t*-test. In this section, we will learn about the *t*-test by starting with what we have learned about confidence intervals for means. Accordingly, let us review the procedure developed in Chapter 5 for constructing a confidence interval around a sample mean. We begin by deciding on our desired confidence level, and then carry out five steps:

1. Collect a sample of N observations.
2. Calculate the sample mean, standard deviation, and standard error.

3. Then ascertain the total proportion of the sampling distribution that will be excluded from the confidence interval. Convert the confidence level to a proportion and subtract it from 1 to get this proportion. Denote the proportion by α.

4. Using Table A.3, find the cell entry in the row corresponding to d.f. = $N - 1$ and the column corresponding to a two-tail area of α. Denote this cell entry by $t_{\alpha/2}$. The half-width of the confidence interval is

$$w = t_{\alpha/2} s_{\bar{X}}.$$

5. The resulting confidence interval statement may be completed by plugging the sample mean, half-width w, and α into our formula

$$\Pr(\bar{X} - w < \mu < \bar{X} + w) = 1 - \alpha.$$

In the ***t*-test for one sample**, we compare the sample mean against a null DEFINITION
hypothesis value for the mean, and decide whether the null hypothesis may be rejected or not. The criterion for this decision is whether the null hypothesis value for the mean lies inside the interval or not (i.e., whether it is a plausible value or not).

One of the examples in Chapter 5 included all the essential steps. That example presumed that we had a random sample of 16 people from a population whose mean IQ was unknown. An IQ test was administered to them that had been normed on another population, whose mean IQ was 100. A reasonable null hypothesis would be that our population's mean IQ also is 100, and traditional researchers probably would wish to use the *t*-test to determine whether we could reject this hypothesis or not.

Our sample of 16 IQ scores produced a mean of 103 and a standard deviation of 9. We decided to compute a 95% confidence interval, to determine the range of plausible values for the population's mean IQ. Following the five-step procedure, in step 2 we found the standard error was $9/\sqrt{16} = 2.25$. In step 3 we established that our 95% confidence level implied $\alpha = 0.05$. In step 4, from Table A.3 we obtained the cell entry in the row corresponding to d.f. = $N - 1 = 16 - 1 = 15$, and the column corresponding to a two-tail area of $\alpha = 0.05$, to get $t_{\alpha/2} = 2.1314$. In step 5, we arrived at a confidence interval, $\text{CI}_{0.95} = [98.2, 107.8]$, which contained the null hypothesis value for the mean of 100. Therefore 100 is a plausible value, and we must fail to reject the null hypothesis.

The traditional way of reporting a *t*-test differs from this approach, because of its focus on significance testing rather than confidence intervals. Nevertheless, it is based on the same information and simply requires a bit of translation. Instead of using a confidence interval to display a range of

DEFINITION plausible values for the mean, the *t*-test employs a range of plausible values for the ***t*-statistic**, which has the formula

$$t(\mathrm{df}) = (\bar{X} - \mu)/s_{\bar{X}}$$

where $\mathrm{df} = N - 1$. The equivalent confidence interval around $t(\mathrm{df})$ is

$$\Pr(-t_{\alpha/2} < t(\mathrm{df}) < t_{\alpha/2}) = 1 - \alpha.$$

Demos

USE DEM61
TO GAIN
FAMILIARITY
WITH THE
t-TEST AND
ITS
RELATION-
SHIP WITH
CONFIDENCE
INTERVALS

If we put a null hypothesis mean, μ_{h}, in the place of μ, in the formula for $t(\mathrm{df})$, then we may ask whether the resulting value of $t(\mathrm{df})$ is a plausible one or not by finding out whether it lies inside the confidence interval. In our example, $\mu_{\mathrm{h}} = 100$. Our test-value for $t(\mathrm{df})$ is therefore $t(15) = (103 - 100)/2.25 = 1.3333$. The confidence interval around $t(15)$ is

$$\Pr(-2.1314 < t(\mathrm{df}) < 2.1314) = 0.95,$$

```
        ◄──── 95% ────►
     ▲
-2.1314    0    ▲ +2.1314
        +1.3333
```

so 1.3333 is contained in the interval and is a plausible value for $t(15)$. We must therefore fail to reject the null hypothesis that $\mu_{\mathrm{h}} = 100$. We could reject the null hypothesis that $\mu_{\mathrm{h}} = 100$ only if $t(15)$ lay outside this interval.

The way that this finding would be reported in many psychological research articles would be '$t(15) = 1.33$, $p > 0.05$.' The notation '$p > 0.05$' denotes the fact that the probability of making a Type I error (rejecting the null hypothesis when it is really true) is larger than 0.05, which is the criterion we have used in deciding whether to reject it or not. While this expression is admirably concise, it does not provide all of the information needed by serious readers. They would want to know the sample mean and standard deviation as well, so they could work out the confidence interval around the mean.

A closely related *t*-test is used on a very popular experimental design, based on measurements collected on two different occasions for the same partici-

DEFINITION pants. This design is a special case of the repeated measures experiment introduced in Chapter 4. The **within-subjects *t*-test** compares the mean difference between participants' scores on two occasions against a null hypothesis value and decides whether the null hypothesis may be rejected or not.

If a sports psychologist were to try improving on our social facilitation experiment, one of the first suggestions she might make is to use a more sensitive dependent variable than simply whether someone wins a tug-of-war or not. Following her suggestion, we design another experiment in which runners are automatically timed over 800 meters on two occasions:

when no one else is present, and when one person is present (we shall label these the Absent (A) and Present (P) conditions, respectively). We subject 12 athletes to these two conditions in random order, and record their 800-meter times in seconds.

We wish to ascertain whether their times differed between the A and P conditions, and that may be determined by taking the difference between the times for each athlete. The traditional procedure would be to compute the sample mean of the differences and compare that against a null hypothesis of no difference, which would be a mean difference of 0. We can do that and more, by computing a confidence interval around the sample mean difference.

The data are shown in Table 6.3, along with the differences (A − P) and their mean and standard deviation. Electing to use a 95% confidence level, we follow exactly the same procedure with the sample mean and standard deviation for the differences as we would for data from a single sample. Step 1 has already been completed, so we move on to step 2.

2. The mean difference is 0.983, and the standard deviation is 1.284. We compute the standard error, which is $1.284/\sqrt{12} = 0.371$.

3. Since the confidence level is 95%, we have $\alpha = 1 - (95/100) = 0.05$.

4. Using Table A.3, we find the $t_{\alpha/2}$ in the row corresponding to df = $N - 1 = 11$ and the column corresponding to a two-tail area of $\alpha = 0.05$. The resulting value is $t_{\alpha/2} = 2.201$. The half-width of the interval is

$$w = t_{\alpha/2}s_{\bar{x}} = (2.201)(0.371) = 0.817.$$

5. Finally, we substitute the sample mean difference, half-width w, and α into our formula

TABLE 6.3 The 800-meter times for athletes

Athlete	Absent	Present	A − P
1	112.3	111.2	1.1
2	110.7	111.9	−1.2
3	106.1	105.3	0.8
4	115.3	112.9	2.4
5	109.8	107.4	2.4
6	108.9	109.1	−0.2
7	106.0	106.2	−0.2
8	107.4	106.3	1.1
9	114.3	111.2	3.1
10	111.1	109.6	1.5
11	109.5	108.2	1.3
12	112.2	112.5	−0.3
			0.983 Mean
			1.284 s.d.

$$\Pr(\bar{X} - w < \mu < \bar{X} + w) = 1 - \alpha,$$

getting

$$\Pr(0.983 - 0.817 < \mu < 0.983 + 0.817) = 0.95,$$

or

$$\Pr(0.166 < \mu < 1.800).$$

The range of plausible values for μ, according to our confidence interval, is from 0.166 to 1.800. These are all potential hypothetical values for the mean difference that our study cannot rule out. The interval does not contain 0, however, so that is an implausible hypothetical value for μ and we may reject the null hypothesis of 0 difference.

Here is how the same test would be done using the t-statistic,

$$t(\mathrm{df}) = (\bar{X} - \mu)/s_{\bar{X}}$$

where $\mathrm{df} = N - 1$. The equivalent confidence interval around $t(\mathrm{df})$ is

$$\Pr(-t_{\alpha/2} < t(\mathrm{df}) < t_{\alpha/2}) = 1 - \alpha,$$

or

$$\Pr(-2.201 < t(11) < 2.201) = 0.95.$$

We put the null hypothesis mean, $\mu_{\mathrm{h}} = 0$, in the place of μ in the formula for $t(11)$, and ask whether the resulting value of $t(11)$ is a plausible one or not by finding out whether it lies inside the confidence interval. Our sample test-value for $t(11)$ is therefore

$$t(11) = (0.983 - 0)/0.371 = 2.650.$$

This value is outside the interval and is therefore an implausible value for $t(11)$. We may reject the null hypothesis that $\mu_{\mathrm{h}} = 0$.

If sample sizes are large enough, then the normal distribution may be used to approximate the t-distribution just as we did with confidence intervals in Chapter 5. Suppose that the study with the runners had a sample of 110 athletes and produced a mean difference of 0.983 seconds with a sample standard deviation of 4.494. Our standard error would then be $4.494/\sqrt{110} = 0.428$, and the sample test-value for $t(109)$ would be

$$t(109) = (0.983 - 0)/0.428 = 2.297.$$

The 95% confidence interval around $t(109)$ could be approximated by using $z_{\alpha/2}$ instead of $t_{\alpha/2}$, and Table A.2 tells us that the required $z_{0.025}$ value is 1.96. Our confidence interval statement would be

$$\Pr(-z_{\alpha/2} < t(\mathrm{df}) < z_{\alpha/2}) = 1 - \alpha,$$

or

$$\Pr(-1.96 < t(109) < 1.96) = 0.95.$$

We may now ask whether the sample value of $t(109) = 2.297$ is plausible or not. Since it does not lie inside the confidence interval it is implausible, and we may reject the null hypothesis that $\mu_{\mathrm{h}} = 0$.

Now that we have a procedure for assessing the size of an experimental effect in a repeated-measures design for two occasions (and deciding whether we think it differs from 0), it would be quite reasonable to ask whether either a confidence interval or a t-test can help us assess whether the effect is 'big' or 'important.' To some extent, the answer to this question inevitably will be subjective as well as depending on the beholder's purposes. To a national athletics coach who has seen his middle-distance runners suffer a string of defeats that involved margins of less than half a second, a mean difference of 0.983 seconds might seem very important indeed.

In psychological research, however, often the issue of what constitutes a large effect is adjudicated according to the sizes of effects that other researchers have found in similar studies of the same phenomenon. In the next section, we will apply what we have learned about confidence intervals and significance tests to this problem, and also to the question of how to effectively compare studies with one another.

The **_t_-statistic** has the formula   SUMMARY

$$t(\mathrm{df}) = (\bar{X} - \mu)/s_{\bar{X}}$$

and its sampling distribution is a t-distribution with $N - 1$ degrees of freedom, a mean of 0 and a standard deviation of 1. A confidence interval around $t(\mathrm{df})$ has the form

$$\Pr(-t_{\alpha/2} < t(\mathrm{df}) < t_{\alpha/2}) = 1 - \alpha.$$

For large samples, we may use the normal distribution as an approximation, and the confidence interval is

$$\Pr(-z_{\alpha/2} < t(\mathrm{df}) < z_{\alpha/2}) = 1 - \alpha.$$

SUMMARY

The *t*-test for one sample compares a sample mean against a null hypothesis value for the mean, and decides whether the null hypothesis may be rejected or not. The procedure is to substitute null hypothesis mean, μ_h, in the place of μ, in the formula for $t(df)$ and ascertain whether the resulting value of $t(df)$ is contained in the confidence interval or not. If the value is in the interval, then we cannot reject the null hypothesis because it is a plausible value. If the value of $t(df)$ is outside the interval then we may reject the null hypothesis because it is an implausible value.

The within-subjects *t*-test compares the mean difference between participants' scores on two occasions against a null hypothesis value and decides whether the null hypothesis may be rejected or not. The procedure is identical to that for the *t*-test for one sample.

Differences between models and effect sizes

How big should a difference between a sample statistic and a hypothetical value be for it to seem important or worthwhile? There are at least two ways to evaluate how big such a difference is. One is *relative to the range of the scale itself* (**scale-based evaluation**) and another is *relative to the dispersion of scores* (**distribution-based evaluation**).

Scale-based evaluation may take into account the scale range, coarseness, and position on the scale. Taking the range into account makes sense when the scale is bounded at both ends. Doing so requires computing what percentage of the scale-range has been covered by the difference. For instance, suppose the average improvement for participants after a self-esteem enhancing experiment is a three-point increase in scores on a self-esteem test. Is this increase small or large? If the test has a scale range of five points, it seems very large, since it spans 60% of the range. If the scale range is from 0 to 300 points, on the other hand, the three-point increase covers only 1% of the scale range and seems very small.

Taking scale coarseness into account is relevant when the scale is discrete and has only several possible values. The general idea is to evaluate a difference in terms of the proportion of the distance between successive points on the scale spanned by it. Consider the widely used Agree–Disagree scale scored {1 = Strongly Disagree, 2 = Disagree, 3 = Neutral, 4 = Agree, 5 = Strongly Agree}. Suppose we find in an experiment that the mean agreement level moves up by 0.5. This average increase of 0.5 shifts the mean halfway from one point (Neutral, say) up to the next (Agree). That is equivalent to 50% of the participants ticking one point higher on the scale on the second occasion than they did on the first.

Finally, in situations where we have a ratio-level scale and it makes sense to think of the scale in terms of quantity, then the size of an effect may be evaluated relative to position on the scale. For instance, suppose an earning effectiveness program produces a mean increase of $2000 in annual incomes of its participants. If their original average income was $3000, that is very substantial. If their original average income was $30,000, it is less so. In these situations, researchers often express the difference as a percentage of the baseline figure. Thus, an increase from $3000 to $5000 is an increase of $2000, which is about a 66.7% increase over $3000. However, a $2000 increase is only a 6.7% increase over $30,000.

Distribution-based evaluation of effects usually employs standard deviation units. We will examine why this is the case, and build up a conceptual understanding of what the 'size of an effect' is and how to assess it. Returning to the *t*-statistic,

$$t(\mathrm{df}) = (\bar{X} - \mu)/s_{\bar{X}}$$

and its confidence interval

$$\mathrm{Pr}(-t_{\alpha/2} < t(\mathrm{df}) < t_{\alpha/2}) = 1 - \alpha,$$

we will reassemble them in terms of three things: a measure of effect size in standard deviation units, confidence level, and sample size. All we need do is recall that the standard error is the $s/\sqrt{N}$, and rewrite the $t(\mathrm{df})$ formula as

$$t(\mathrm{df}) = \frac{\bar{X} - \mu}{s/\sqrt{N}} = d\sqrt{N},$$

where d stands for the difference between the sample mean and the population mean divided by the sample standard deviation:

$$d = \frac{\bar{X} - \mu}{s}$$

This is known as **Cohen's *d***, and it measures the difference between the DEFINITION
sample mean and the population mean in *standard deviation units*. A Cohen's *d* of 2.5, for instance, means that the sample mean is 2.5 standard deviation units above the population mean; and a *d* of -0.5 means that the sample mean is 0.5 standard deviation units below the population mean. Now we may rewrite our confidence interval around $t(\mathrm{df})$ by replacing $t(\mathrm{df})$ with $d\sqrt{N}$:

$$\mathrm{Pr}(-t_{\alpha/2} < d\sqrt{N} < t_{\alpha/2}) = 1 - \alpha.$$

Suppose we have a value for d based on a null hypothesis mean, μ_h, denoted by d_h. When a null hypothesis mean, μ_h, replaces μ in the formula for d, it indicates how many standard deviation units the sample mean is away from the null hypothesis mean μ_h. Three things will determine whether $d_h\sqrt{N}$ will lie inside or outside the confidence interval:

1. The number of standard deviation units between the sample mean and null hypothesis mean (d_h),
2. The confidence level $(1 - \alpha)$,
3. The sample size (N).

Cohen's d is useful because it provides a measure of the difference between a hypothetical value for a mean and the sample mean that is *independent of the scale* used for our variable. In the context of an experiment for which the null hypothesis amounts to a 'no effect' hypothesis, Cohen's d is a scale-free measure of the experiment's **effect size**.

To illustrate this point, let us return to our sport psychologist's social facilitation experiment and imagine that a psychologist at another institute has decided to try replicating it. But this psychologist decides to test his runners over a distance of 1500 meters rather than 800. Moreover, he has only nine runners to test instead of 12 as in the first study. He times his nine runners under the Absent and Present conditions, and obtains a mean difference in their times of 1.967 seconds, with a standard deviation of 2.568.

Like the first psychologist, he decides to ascertain whether he can reject a null hypothesis of a mean difference of 0, and he uses a confidence level of 95%. Using Table A.3, he finds the $t_{\alpha/2}$ in the row corresponding to df $= N - 1 = 8$ and the column corresponding to a two-tail area of $\alpha = 0.05$. The resulting value is $t_{\alpha/2} = 2.306$. He decides to use the $d\sqrt{N}$ version of the confidence interval around $t(\text{df})$. His 95% confidence interval is therefore

$$\Pr(-2.306 < d\sqrt{N} < 2.306) = 0.95.$$

Now, he calculates his null hypothesis value for d_h using $u_h = 0$:

$$d_h = (1.967 - 0)/2.568 = 0.766.$$

He finds that the value $d_h\sqrt{N} = 0.766\sqrt{9} = 2.298$, which is inside the confidence interval and is therefore a plausible value. Unlike the other psychologist, he cannot reject the null hypothesis of no difference.

He is puzzled, but curious as to how the effect yielded in his study compares with the effect obtained by the first psychologist, so he computes Cohen's d for her study as well. In her study, the 800-meter runners' times differed by an average of 0.983 seconds with a standard deviation of 1.284. Since her null hypothesis also was $u_h = 0$, he gets

$d_h = (0.983 - 0)/1.284 = 0.766.$

Her sample mean was the same number of standard deviation units above u_h as his is! Cohen's d_h is identical in both studies. Relative to the mean and standard deviation, his study has produced *the same size of effect* as hers. Far from contradicting her findings, his study has replicated them very closely and, taken together, they provide quite consistent evidence that the presence of an observer enables runners to go faster. However, his study has less power than hers because his has a smaller sample.

As you can see, Cohen's d enables us to compare results from studies that use different sample sizes and even different scales (as long as they are measuring the same thing, of course). Since it is employed in confidence intervals around the mean and uses the mean and standard deviation, Cohen's d is associated with the mean and standard deviation package that we introduced in Chapter 3. What about a measure of an effect size for proportions or the quantile package?

Demos

USE DEM62 TO GAIN FAMILIARITY WITH COHEN'S d AND THE t-STATISTIC

Cohen's d may be used for proportions, and therefore with the binomial (or sign) test. In our social facilitation experiment, as you'll recall, the null hypothesis value of the proportion of T-participants winning was $\Pi_h = 0.5$, and the sample proportion was $P = 28/40 = 0.70$. The 95% confidence interval was $CI_{0.95} = [0.558, 0.842]$, so 0.5 lay outside the interval and was found to be an implausible value. We could reject the null hypothesis of $\Pi_h = 0.5$. Given that this null hypothesis was a no-effect hypothesis, it makes sense to evaluate how large the effect was. Cohen's d for proportions is

$$d = \frac{P - \Pi}{s} = \frac{P - \Pi}{\sqrt{P(1 - P)}}$$

Substituting $\Pi_h = 0.5$ for Π and $P = 0.7$ into this formula, we get $d_h = (0.7 - 0.5)/\sqrt{0.21} = 0.2/0.458 = 0.436$. That is, the sample proportion ($P = 0.7$) is 0.436 sample standard deviation units above the null hypothesis proportion ($\Pi_h = 0.5$).

All this may be well and good, but how do we know when Cohen's d is 'small,' 'medium,' or 'large'? There is no simple answer to this question. In one situation, a sample proportion $P = 0.55$ may be an important, substantial departure from a null hypothesis of $\Pi_h = 0.5$; and in another it could be trivial. In Western democratic elections, for example, a politician who gets 55% of the vote is said to have won by a 'landslide.' Yet Cohen's d in this case is just

$$d_h = (0.55 - 0.5)/\sqrt{0.248} = 0.05/0.497 = 0.100.$$

The question of how big a 'worthwhile' effect size should be is related to a question we raised briefly in Chapter 5 about how large our sample size should be, and also related questions about how much confidence we should wish for and how wide we should want our confidence intervals to be. We have already seen suggestions that confidence level, sample size, and effect size have some kind of tradeoff relationship with one another. In fact, you will encounter this tradeoff in every statistical technique that you learn about or use. The concluding section of this chapter is therefore devoted to examining this tradeoff and its implications for planning research and interpreting research findings.

SUMMARY

The size of the difference between a sample statistic and a hypothetical value may be evaluated in two ways. One is *relative to the range of the scale itself* (**scale-based evaluation**) and another is *relative to the dispersion of scores* (**distribution-based evaluation**).

Scale-based evaluation takes into account the scale range, coarseness, and position on the scale.

Distribution-based evaluation of effects usually employs standard deviation units.

A popular distribution-based measure of **effect size** is **Cohen's d**, and it measures the difference between the sample mean and the population mean in *standard deviation units*:

$$d = \frac{\bar{X} - \mu}{s}$$

The t-statistic may be rewritten in terms of Cohen's d multiplied by $\sqrt{N}$:

$$t(\mathrm{df}) = \frac{\bar{X} - \mu}{s/\sqrt{N}} = d\sqrt{N}$$

and the corresponding confidence interval around $d\sqrt{N}$ is

$$\Pr(-t_{\alpha/2} < d\sqrt{N} < t_{\alpha/2}) = 1 - \alpha,$$

or for large samples it is

$$\Pr(-z_{\alpha/2} < d\sqrt{N} < z_{\alpha/2}) = 1 - \alpha.$$

When a null hypothesis mean, μ_h, replaces μ in the formula for d, we use d_h to denote the effect size.

Confidence level, precision, and effect size tradeoffs

In Chapter 5, we saw that the width of confidence intervals is influenced by the confidence level we choose and the sample size. We pay for greater confidence by having wider (less precise) intervals around our sample estimates, and the higher the confidence level the greater the rate of increase in width. Larger sample size entails less variation in location, and narrower and more uniform intervals. In fact, the width of the confidence intervals we have studied so far decreases with the square root of the sample size. Now that we have introduced hypothesis testing, we also know that narrower confidence intervals give us greater statistical power. Likewise, any study has greater power to detect large effects than small effects.

The concern with effect size, then, is directly related to both estimation and hypothesis testing. In some situations, researchers may know how big an effect size should interest them. A political pollster, for example, who knows that a 7% swing against the incumbent party will unseat it from government in the next election is in a good position to figure out how large a sample she needs. Likewise, a marketing researcher evaluating an advertising campaign has a readymade criterion scale of increase in profits that can be linked to effect size.

Most of the time, however, researchers just do not have clear-cut criteria by which they can judge the importance of effect sizes. Cohen (1988: 25–27) offers benchmarks that have proved popular with some researchers:

- Small: $d = 0.2$,
- Medium: $d = 0.5$,
- Large: $d = 0.8$.

Many studies would not enable us to reliably detect small effect sizes, either because their statistical power is too low or their confidence intervals are too wide.

Cohen's ground-breaking (1962) survey of articles in a volume of the *Journal of Abnormal and Social Psychology* found that none of the studies reported in those articles had better than a 50–50 chance of correctly rejecting the null hypothesis for a small effect size ($d = 0.2$), and the mean power level for a medium effect size ($d = 0.5$) was only 0.48. Twenty years later, a similar survey by Sedlmeier & Gigerenzer (1989) concluded that the statistical power of a typical study in social psychology or abnormal psychology had not increased since the publication of Cohen's paper. The main culprits, these authors claimed, were small sample sizes and a widespread failure to report confidence intervals or power.

Why do so many researchers use small sample sizes? Aside from practical reasons such as difficulty in finding participants for experiments, one possible explanation is that researchers (and the rest of us) have erroneous intuitions about adequate sample sizes. In a widely cited study, Tversky & Kahneman (1971) studied experienced researchers' intuitive judgments on these matters. They found that researchers greatly underestimated the sample sizes that would be required to obtain certain levels of statistical power because they believed that even small samples would mimic their parent populations far more closely than random samples do. This was termed a 'belief in the law of small numbers' by Tversky & Kahneman, who averred that the most obvious remedy would be reporting confidence intervals and power. That was in 1971, and their advice has only just begun to be heeded by the editors of psychological research journals.

Another obvious remedy is to educate the upcoming generation of researchers about confidence intervals from the start! Accordingly, let us investigate the sample size requirements of studies that would stand a reasonable chance of identifying small effect sizes. It is easiest to start by asking what sample sizes would be required for confidence interval widths to be narrow enough to reject a null hypothesis if d really is 0.2. We are going to be dealing with moderately large sample sizes, so we will use the normal distribution as an approximation (and also to keep things as simple as possible).

Consider the confidence interval around $d\sqrt{N}$ again:

$$\Pr(-z_{\alpha/2} < d\sqrt{N} < z_{\alpha/2}) = 1 - \alpha.$$

If we decide to use a confidence level of 95%, or $\alpha = 0.05$, then the required $z_{\alpha/2}$ value is 1.96. If our null hypothesis is the no-effects one where $d_h = 0$, then a value of $d\sqrt{N}$ larger than 1.96 would be an implausible value and would enable us to reject the null hypothesis. If $d = 0.2$, then we could reject the null hypothesis only if N is large enough for $0.2\sqrt{N}$ to be at least 1.96. Therefore, N would have to be at least $(1.96/0.2)^2$, which is about 96.

Unfortunately, if $d = 0.2$ and $N = 96$, our power to correctly reject the null hypothesis is only 0.5. The graph below shows why this is so. If the null hypothesis is true then the $\mathrm{CI}_{0.95}$ for $d_h\sqrt{96}$ is $[-1.96, 1.96]$ and any sample value of $d\sqrt{96}$ outside that interval will enable us to reject the null hypothesis. The normal distribution shown in Figure 6.9 shows how likely it is that we would get a value of $d\sqrt{96}$ outside the interval if the real effect size d was 0.2,

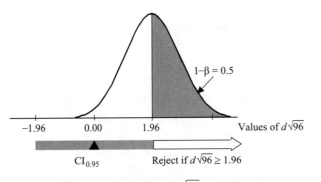

FIGURE 6.9 Power $= 0.5$ when $d\sqrt{96} = 1.96$

so that the population mean of $d\sqrt{96}$ was 1.96. Half of the distribution lies above the mean, so the probability of correctly rejecting the null hypothesis under these conditions would be only 0.5.

In general, if $d\sqrt{N} = z_{\alpha/2}$ then power is always 0.5. To increase power, we would have to make $d\sqrt{N}$ bigger than $z_{\alpha/2}$. In fact, if we set power to be $1 - \beta$ then we would need $d\sqrt{N} = z_{\alpha/2} + z_\beta$, where z_β is the z-score whose area under the normal curve beyond it is β. You can see this in Figure 6.10. This figure is somewhat complicated, but it is worthwhile becoming familiar with it. Most of its components are from the example we just went through. We have a confidence interval around $d_h\sqrt{N}$, whose half-width is $z_{\alpha/2}$. We may reject the null hypothesis that $d_h\sqrt{N} = 0$ if we get a sample value of $d\sqrt{N}$ outside this interval. If the *true* value of $d\sqrt{N}$ is $z_{\alpha/2} + z_\beta$ as shown below, then the probability of getting a sample value of $d\sqrt{N}$ greater than $z_{\alpha/2}$ is the shaded area under the normal curve beyond $-z_\beta$, which is $1 - \beta$. That is *the statistical power of the study to detect an effect size of d.*

Imagine that we decided we would like power to be at least 0.9. Given that $1 - \beta = 0.9$, we know that $\beta = 0.1$. From Table A.2, we find that our best candidate is $z_\beta = 1.29$, for which $\beta = 0.0985$. As you can see in the figure, the shaded area under the normal curve beyond $-z_\beta$ is $1 - \beta$, which in this example is $1 - 0.0985 = 0.9015$. If we are using a confidence level of 95% so that $\alpha = 0.05$ as before, then $z_{\alpha/2} = 1.96$, and we have

$$d\sqrt{N} = z_{\alpha/2} + z_\beta = 1.96 + 1.29 = 3.25.$$

If our sample size were still $N = 96$, then d would have to be 0.33, which is a little less than midway between Cohen's 'small' and 'medium' benchmarks of 0.2 and 0.5.

How large a sample size would we need in order for power to be 0.9015 when $d = 0.2$? We use our formula $d\sqrt{N} = 0.2\sqrt{N} = 3.25$ and solve for $\sqrt{N}$,

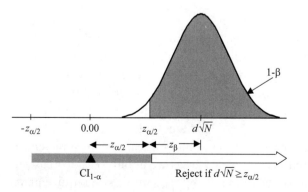

FIGURE 6.10 Power $= 1 - \beta$ when $d\sqrt{N} = z_{\alpha/2} + z_\beta$

getting $\sqrt{N} = 3.25/0.2 = 16.25$. So $N = (16.25)^2 = 264.1$. Our sample size would need to be about 264 to attain a power level of 0.9015 for a small effect ($d = 0.2$).

We have finally arrived at an answer to the question of how large a sample we need. Unfortunately, the answer is not a simple one and requires several crucial judgments to be made in planning a study. First, we need to decide what confidence level $(1 - \alpha)$ we want to use for our confidence intervals. If we are hypothesis-testing then we may wish to think of this in terms of setting α directly, by deciding how large a risk of making a Type I error we can afford. Second, we must decide the smallest size of effect we would be interested in detecting (e.g., Cohen's 'small' value of 0.2 for d). Third, we must choose the level of power $(1 - \beta)$ we wish to have for detecting our smallest effect. Once we have done all of that, we are in a position to calculate sample size. Our chosen values for α and β enable us to find $z_{\alpha/2}$ and z_{β}. We already know that

$$d\sqrt{N} = z_{\alpha/2} + z_{\beta},$$

so we can find N by the following rearrangement of this formula:

$$N = [(z_{\alpha/2} + z_{\beta})/d]^2.$$

Let us try one more example. Suppose we decided we were content with an effect size of $d = 0.3$ instead of 0.2, but wished to maintain the same confidence and power levels as before. The required sample size would be

$$N = [(z_{\alpha/2} + z_{\beta})/d]^2 = [(1.96 + 1.29)/0.3]^2 = [3.25/0.3]^2$$

$$= (10.83)^2 = 117.36.$$

Or about 117. That is quite a bit less than 264, and demonstrates how sharp the tradeoff is in effect size. The next table shows sample size requirements as a function of three different values of confidence level, power, and effect size.

This table illustrates the three-way tradeoff quite clearly. You can see that there is nearly an even tradeoff between confidence level and power. For example, the sample sizes required for a confidence level of 0.95 and power of 0.90 are nearly identical to those required for a confidence level of 0.90 and power of 0.95. On the other hand, a relatively small increase in d is sufficient to greatly reduce sample size requirements, whereas a similar size decrease in either power or confidence (or both) does not reduce sample size requirements nearly as much.

TABLE 6.4 Sample size as a function of confidence, power, and effect size

| | | | | Sample sizes for | | |
Confidence	Power	$z_{\alpha/2}$	z_β	$d = 0.2$	$d = 0.3$	$d = 0.5$
0.99	0.95	2.576	1.645	445	198	71
0.99	0.90	2.576	1.282	372	165	60
0.99	0.85	2.576	1.036	326	145	52
0.95	0.95	1.960	1.645	325	144	52
0.95	0.90	1.960	1.282	263	117	42
0.95	0.85	1.960	1.036	224	100	36
0.90	0.95	1.645	1.645	271	120	43
0.90	0.90	1.645	1.282	214	95	34
0.90	0.85	1.645	1.036	180	80	29

Oftentimes a researcher will not be able to dictate sample size, but instead will be stuck with a limit on N. In that case, her best option is to find out how much power her study will have to detect effects of various different sizes. Again, we may use a rearrangement of our formula

$$d\sqrt{N} = z_{\alpha/2} + z\hat{\beta},$$

to find d:

$$d = (z_{\alpha/2} + z_\beta)/\sqrt{N}.$$

Demos

The value of d we obtain here is the *smallest effect size that our study can detect* with a sample size of N, power of $1 - \beta$, and confidence level $1 - \alpha$.

Many researchers conduct this kind of 'power analysis' after the fact in an attempt to ascertain how sensitive their study was. A better practice would be to do this while planning the study, particularly if already aware that N may be limited for whatever reasons. Given a sample size of 60, for instance, the researcher who would like a confidence level of 0.99 and power of 0.90 will be able to detect an effect size of no less than about $d = 0.5$ with her desired level of power (Cohen's 'medium' size of effect):

USE DEM63 TO DESIGN YOUR OWN STUDY, OR TO GAIN FAMILIARITY WITH THESE TRADEOFFS

$$d = (z_{\alpha/2} + z_\beta)/\sqrt{N} = (2.576 + 1.282)/\sqrt{60} = 3.858/7.746 = 0.498.$$

Even if she were willing to drop her confidence level to 0.90 and her power to 0.85, she would still not be able to detect effect sizes of less than 0.35 or so, as Table 6.5 illustrates.

TABLE 6.5 Effect size as a function of confidence, power, and sample size

Confidence	Power	Effect sizes for		
		$N = 30$	$N = 60$	$N = 240$
0.99	0.95	0.771	0.545	0.272
0.99	0.90	0.704	0.498	0.249
0.99	0.85	0.660	0.466	0.233
0.95	0.95	0.658	0.465	0.233
0.95	0.90	0.592	0.418	0.209
0.95	0.85	0.547	0.387	0.193
0.90	0.95	0.601	0.425	0.212
0.90	0.90	0.534	0.378	0.189
0.90	0.85	0.490	0.346	0.173

As in the earlier table, effect size and sample size have a very strong inverse relationship. Since $d = (z_{\alpha/2} + z_\beta)/\sqrt{N}$, keeping confidence level and power constant and increasing your sample size by a factor of 4 enables you to detect an effect size half as small with the same power level. You can verify this not only via the formula, but also by comparing the column in the above table where $N = 60$ with the column where $N = 240$, which is 4×60.

SUMMARY

Cohen's **benchmarks for effect size** as measured by d:

- Small: $d = 0.2$,
- Medium: $d = 0.5$,
- Large: $d = 0.8$.

Given a confidence level of $1 - \alpha$, we reject the null hypothesis that $d_h\sqrt{N} = 0$ if we get a sample value of $d\sqrt{N}$ outside the confidence interval around $d_h\sqrt{N}$, whose half-width is $z_{\alpha/2}$. If the *true* value of $d\sqrt{N}$ is $z_{\alpha/2} + z_\beta$, then the probability of getting a sample value of $d\sqrt{N}$ greater than $z_{\alpha/2}$ is the area under the normal curve beyond $-z_\beta$, which is $1 - \beta$.

This is the **statistical power of the study to detect an effect size of d**.

Given a confidence level of $1 - \alpha$, the **required sample size** for the study to detect d with power of $1 - \beta$ is

$$N = [(z_{\alpha/2} + z_\beta)/d]^2.$$

Given a confidence level of $1 - \alpha$ and sample size N, the **smallest effect size** that the study can detect with power of $1 - \beta$ is:

$$d = (z_{\alpha/2} + z_\beta)/\sqrt{N}.$$

Questions and exercises

Q.6.1. Government spokespeople are claiming that technicians are overpaid, and have claimed that the average qualified technician earns an income before tax 'in excess of $45,000 per year.' A large union conducts a survey of qualified technicians to estimate their mean annual income. A random sample of 100 technicians yields a mean income before tax of $44,000 and a standard deviation of $3400. Is the Government figure plausible, if the unionists construct a 95% confidence interval around their sample mean? Discuss how the Government would make a case for plausibility and the union for implausibility on the basis of this evidence.

Q.6.2. Imagine that you are called upon to adjudicate a dispute among clinical psychological researchers concerning the effectiveness of a new antidepression treatment. There are three competing claims concerning the proportion of clinically depressed people who show improvement after 6 months under this course of treatment:

    A. No more than half of the people improve;
    B. The proportion who improve is between 0.5 and 0.7;
    C. The proportion who improve is higher than 0.7.

You have conducted a clinical trial on a representative sample of 169 depressed clients, and 104 of them improved after 6 months. What could you conclude about these three claims?

Q.6.3. Given a null hypothesis that $\Pi = 1/2$ and a Type I error probability of $\alpha = 0.05$, which of the following is true?

    (a) Power would be greater if Π really was 0.2 than if Π really was 0.1.
    (b) Power would be greater if $N = 15$ than if $N = 10$.
    (c) Power would be greater if $\alpha = 0.01$ instead of 0.05.
    (d) We would be more likely to reject the null hypothesis if $\alpha = 0.01$ instead of 0.05.

Q.6.4. In Q.6.1, suppose the union survey had a sample of only 20 instead of 100. Perform a *t*-test to determine whether you could reject the Government's hypothetical mean income of $45,000. You may check your own calculations via **Dem61**.

Q.6.5. In the data-file called **Heart**, 50 patients' cholesterol levels are measured at the end of the first year of the study (the variable is called Chol1yr) and the second year (the variable is Chol2yr). Using SPSS, Excel, or another statistics package, test against the null hypothesis that the mean cholesterol level has not changed from the end of the first year to the end of the second. Then test against the null hypothesis that the mean cholesterol level at the end of the second year (Chol2yr) does not differ from the mean level at the end of the third year (Chol3yr). Use a 99% confidence level, so that $\alpha = 0.01$.

Q.6.6. Using Cohen's d, compare the size of the change in mean cholesterol level from the end of year 1 to year 2 (Chol2yr vs. Chol1yr) with the change from year 2 to year 3 (Chol3yr vs. Chol2yr).

Q.6.7. A 4-month-long reading enrichment program for Grade 3 students has been tested on a random sample of 24 Grade 3's. A test reveals that the mean reading age of this sample has increased by 6.2 months by the end of the program, with a standard deviation of 4.5. Given that the mean reading age ordinarily should have increased by 4 months, test against the null hypothesis that the program has not accelerated an increase in reading age.

Q.6.8. Another 4-month-long reading enrichment program tested on another random sample of 24 Grade 3's also yields a mean increase of 6.2 months in reading age, with a standard deviation of 3.2. Has this program had the same size effect as the first one? Why or why not?

Q.6.9. The developmental psychologists who have been testing the reading enrichment program are planning another study. This time, they want to be able to detect an effect size of at least 0.3 with power = 0.90. They also want to use a confidence level of 99% (0.99) for their confidence interval when they estimate the increase in reading age. What is the smallest sample size they will need to accomplish these goals?

Q.6.10. Suppose the developmental psychologists can only obtain a sample size of 120. With everything else remaining the same as in Q.6.9, what size of effect can they detect with power = 0.90? You may find **dem63** helpful for answering this question.

Predicting a Quantitative Variable from a Categorical Variable: The *t*-Test and Analysis of Variance

CONTENTS

Comparing means from two independent samples

In Chapter 4, we compared within-subjects designs with between-subjects designs as alternative approaches to planning experiments. Between-subjects experiments are those in which participants are randomly assigned to one experimental condition only. The key to understanding statistical inference in between-subjects experiments is randomized assignment. It enables researchers to analyze the data from such experiments as if the experimental conditions provided two **independent random samples**. The same may be said of nonexperimental studies in which we have split a random sample into categories. The subsamples may also be treated as independent random samples. DEFINITION

In most between-subjects experiments or nonexperimental studies, the independent samples are compared via summary statistics such as the sample means. In this section, we will find out how to construct confidence intervals for the difference between two means and then we will explore how they may be applied to a variety of research questions. You have learned virtually all of the concepts required during Chapters 5 and 6. As always, it helps to begin with a simple example.

Suppose we have two groups of participants in a classic experimental design with a Training group and a Control group (T and C). The object of the study is training in client interviewing skills; the participants are clinical psychology students; and the treatment is a special intensive training program. The inventors of this program want to evaluate its effectiveness, so they have randomly assigned 12 clinical psychology students in a Ph.D. program to these two groups. They would like to find out whether the trained group scores higher on a 10-point skills rating judgment scale than the untrained group. One obvious way of doing this would be to compare the two group means on this scale, and to estimate how different they are from one another.

The data are shown in Table 7.1. It turns out that five clinical students were assigned to the T group and seven to the Control group. As you can see from the summary statistics beneath the table, the mean for the T group is higher than that for the C group. Our estimate of the difference between the means is 2.0. How precise is this estimate? Based on what we have seen in Chapters 5 and 6, you might come up with the following idea. If the sampling distribution of a mean is a t-distribution, perhaps the sampling distribution of the difference between two means also is a t-distribution. In fact, that turns out to be the case. If we were to investigate the sampling distributions of the difference between two sample means, we would find that it has a t-distribution, with the mean at the population value of this difference, $\mu_1 - \mu_2$.

TABLE 7.1 Clinical training experiment

Trained X_1	Control X_2
8	5
6	6
7	8
6	3
8	4
	6
	3

Trained: $N_1 = 5$, $\bar{X}_1 = 7.0$, $s_1^2 = 1.0$.
Control: $N_2 = 7$, $\bar{X}_2 = 5.0$, $s_2^2 = 3.3$.
$\bar{X}_1 - \bar{X}_2 = 7.0 - 5.0 = 2.0$

If the difference between two sample means has a t-distribution, then why not construct a confidence interval around the difference between those two means of the form

$$\Pr(\bar{X}_1 - \bar{X}_2 - w < \mu_1 - \mu_2 < \bar{X}_1 - \bar{X}_2 + w) = 1 - \alpha,$$

with $w = (t_{\alpha/2})$(standard error)? If you did come up with this, congratulations – you are quite close to the mark. The only really problematic aspect of this approach is figuring out what the 'standard error' should be.

As it turns out, the standard error for the difference between two means is not a difficult problem to solve. The main insight required is that the two means are free to vary independently of one another, so their difference will vary quite a bit more than each mean does. In fact, the variance of the difference between two means is based on a weighted *sum of the variances* of each mean, called the **pooled variance**. The weights are determined by the DEFINITIONS size of each sample. This is what its formula looks like:

$$s^2_{\text{pooled}} = \frac{(N_1 - 1)s_1^2 + (N_2 - 1)s_2^2}{(N_1 - 1) + (N_2 - 1)}$$

The resulting **pooled standard error** shall be denoted s_{err}, and its formula is

$$s_{\text{err}} = \sqrt{s^2_{\text{pooled}}\left[\frac{1}{N_1} + \frac{1}{N_2}\right]}.$$

There is one catch, however. In order for the pooled variance to be a sensible estimate, we must assume that the two sample variances differ only because of sampling error. In other words, the population variances are assumed to be the same. This assumption is referred to as the **homogeneity of variance** assumption, and we will encounter it on a few more occasions.

We are almost done. The remaining issue is how to decide on the degrees of freedom so as to enable us to select the appropriate sampling distribution and therefore the value for $t_{\alpha/2}$. The degrees of freedom turn out to be $(N_1 - 1) + (N_2 - 1)$, or to make things simpler, just $N_1 + N_2 - 2$. The **confidence interval for the difference between two means**, $\mu_1 - \mu_2$, may be constructed in the following steps:

PROCEDURE
FOR A
CONFIDENCE
INTERVAL

1. Collect two independent random samples of size N_1 and N_2.
2. Calculate the means and standard deviations for each sample, and the pooled standard error s_{err}.
3. Then ascertain the total proportion of the sampling distribution that will be excluded from the confidence interval. Convert the confidence level to a

FOR THE
DIFFERENCE
BETWEEN
TWO MEANS

proportion and subtract it from 1 to get this proportion. Denote the proportion by α.

4. Using Table A.3, find the cell entry in the row corresponding to df $= N_1 + N_2 - 2$ and the column corresponding to a two-tail area of α. Denote this cell entry by $t_{\alpha/2}$. The half-width of the confidence interval is

$$w = t_{\alpha/2} s_{\text{err}}.$$

If the df value is larger than any of the values in Table A.3, use the normal distribution instead and find the appropriate value of $z_{\alpha/2}$ from Table A.2. For larger samples such as these, the half-width is

$$w = z_{\alpha/2} s_{\text{err}}.$$

5. The resulting confidence interval statement may be completed by plugging the sample means, half-width w, and α into our formula

$$\Pr(\bar{X}_1 - \bar{X}_2 - w < \mu_1 - \mu_2 < \bar{X}_1 - \bar{X}_2 + w) = 1 - \alpha.$$

Let us see how this works with our example. We have completed step 1 and part of step 2. The pooled variance is

$$s_{\text{pooled}}^2 = \frac{(N_1 - 1)s_1^2 + (N_2 - 1)s_2^2}{(N_1 - 1) + (N_2 - 1)} = \frac{(5 - 1)(1.0) + (7 - 1)(3.3)}{(5 - 1) + (7 - 1)}$$

$$= \frac{4 + 20}{4 + 6} = 2.4,$$

and the standard error is

$$s_{\text{err}} = \sqrt{s_{\text{pooled}}^2 \left[\frac{1}{N_1} + \frac{1}{N_2} \right]} = \sqrt{2.4 \left[\frac{1}{5} + \frac{1}{7} \right]} = 0.907.$$

Step 3 requires us to decide on a confidence level. For now, we will use the conventional 95% confidence level, so that $\alpha = 0.05$. In step 4, we use Table A.3 to find the cell entry in the row corresponding to df $= N_1 + N_2 - 2 = 7 + 5 - 2 = 10$, and the column corresponding to a two-tail area of α. The value is $t_{0.025} = 2.228$. The half-width of our confidence interval is

$$w = t_{\alpha/2} s_{\text{err}} = (2.228)(0.907) = 2.021,$$

and the confidence interval statement is

$$\text{Pr}(\bar{X}_1 - \bar{X}_2 - w < \mu_1 - \mu_2 < \bar{X}_1 - \bar{X}_2 + w) = 1 - \alpha,$$

and if we put in $w = 2.021$ and the difference between the sample means of 2.0, we get

$$\text{Pr}(2.0 - 2.021 < \mu_1 - \mu_2 < 2.0 + 2.021) = 0.95,$$

or just

$$\text{Pr}(-0.021 < \mu_1 - \mu_2 < 4.021) = 0.95.$$

As with the confidence intervals we have used before, we may use the shorter expressions $\text{CI}_{0.95} = 2.0 \pm 2.021$, or $\text{CI}_{0.95} = [-0.021, 4.021]$ as long as it is clear which confidence intervals are being represented. The interpretation of the confidence interval for $\mu_1 - \mu_2$ is quite similar to that for a population mean. Values lying inside the interval are considered plausible and those outside are considered implausible. In this example, $\mu_1 - \mu_2 = 0$ is in the interval and is therefore a plausible value. It is plausible that the two samples of students did not differ after all on their mean scores. However, it is also plausible that the T group mean may have been as much as 4.021 points higher than the C group mean. Remember, 'plausibility' is always specified with respect to the level of confidence. The higher the confidence level, the wider the confidence interval and therefore the greater the range of 'plausible' values.

It may have occurred to you that we could just as easily have swapped the places of the two samples, so that the difference between our means was negative $(5.0 - 7.0 = -2.0)$ instead of positive. This poses no real problem, as long as you keep track of which sample each mean is from. Everything else remains the same, and in this example we would end up with a confidence interval of $\text{CI}_{0.95} = -2.0 \pm 2.021$, or $\text{CI}_{0.95} = [-4.021, 0.021]$. In psychological research, a widespread convention is to subtract the smaller mean from the larger one so that the sample difference between the two means is positive. Nevertheless, there are situations in which a researcher might wish to represent a negative difference because it has special theoretical or substantive meaning.

As you may have surmised, there is a **between-subjects *t*-test** that is traditionally used for comparing the difference between the sample means against a null hypothesis difference (usually the 'no-effects' null hypothesis, $\mu_1 - \mu_2 = 0$). If the null hypothesis difference is an implausible value then the null hypothesis may be rejected; otherwise it is a plausible value and the null hypothesis cannot be rejected. Like the *t*-test for one sample, the *t*-test for two independent samples uses a **t-statistic**, which compares the difference between the sample means against the null hypothesis difference, and divides that by the pooled standard error. Its formula looks like this:

$$t(\mathrm{df}) = \frac{(\bar{X}_1 - \bar{X}_2) - (\mu_1 - \mu_2)}{s_{\mathrm{err}}}$$

where $\mathrm{df} = N_1 + N_2 - 2$. The equivalent confidence interval around $t(\mathrm{df})$ is the same as for the one-sample version of $t(\mathrm{df})$:

$$\Pr(-t_{\alpha/2} < t(\mathrm{df}) < t_{\alpha/2}) = 1 - \alpha.$$

USE ANOVA-
PATCH TO
GAIN
FAMILIARITY
WITH THE
BETWEEN
SUBJECTS
t-TEST

In our example, we already know that we would not be able to reject a null hypothesis of no effect, since 0 is contained in the confidence interval around the difference between the means and is therefore plausible. The way this would be done using the *t*-test is to replace $\mu_1 - \mu_2$ in the formula for $t(\mathrm{df})$ with 0, and then ask whether the resulting value of $t(\mathrm{df})$ is a plausible one or not by finding out whether it lies inside the confidence interval around $t(\mathrm{df})$. Our test-value for $t(\mathrm{df})$ in this example is $t(10) = (2.0 - 0)/0.907 = 2.205$. Our value for $t_{\alpha/2}$ is $t_{0.025} = 2.228$. The confidence interval around $t(10)$ is

$$\Pr(-2.228 < t(10) < 2.228) = 0.95,$$

so 2.205 is contained in the interval and is a plausible value. We must therefore fail to reject the null hypothesis that $\mu_1 - \mu_2 = 0$.

Let us try another example, this time a somewhat more complex one from a real data-set. Mr. Bernd Heubeck (at the Division of Psychology in the Australian National University) compared a sample of 89 children, aged 8–14, from Western Sydney with a sample of 89 children from the same area who had been referred to a child psychiatric clinic. One of the measures on which he wanted to compare the two samples was the Aggressive Behavior subscale from the Child Behavior Checklist (CBCL), as published in the *Manual for the Child Behavior Checklist 4–18 and 1991 Profile* (Achenbach, 1991).

The CBCL Aggressive Behavior subscale is completed by the child's parents, independently, so that there are separate assessments of the child's behavior by the mother and the father. This subscale asks the parents to indicate the extent to which their child's behavior during the past 6 months is typified by fighting, arguing, threatening, displaying jealousy, and the like. Individual items are scored

0 = Never or not at all
1 = Sometimes or somewhat
2 = Often or a lot

and these numbers are then added up to provide that parent's Aggressive Behavior subscale score. There are 20 items with each given a score of 0, 1, or 2, so the subscale score may range from 0 to 40. A higher score indicates more aggressive behavior, at least as rated by the parent.

If we wanted to compare how the two samples of children were rated by their mothers on the CBCL Aggressive Behavior subscale, one reasonable way to do so would be to estimate the difference between the sample mean scores on that subscale and then construct a confidence interval around it. Let us try this out with a confidence level of 99%, using our five-step procedure.

1. We have two independent samples of size $N_1 = 89$ and $N_2 = 89$.
2. The means and standard deviations for each sample are shown below.

Community	Clinic
$N_1 = 89$	$N_2 = 89$
$X_1 = 6.107$	
	$X_2 = 15.797$
$s_1^2 = 18.982$	$s_2^2 = 52.251$

$\bar{X}_1 - \bar{X}_2 = 6.107 - 15.797 = -9.690.$

Note that in this case, the difference between the two means is negative. That reflects the fact that mothers of the children who were referred to the clinic rated their behavior as more aggressive than the mothers of the nonreferred children. Now, we compute the pooled variance estimate:

$$s_{\text{pooled}}^2 = \frac{(N_1 - 1)s_1^2 + (N_2 - 1)s_2^2}{(N_1 - 1) + (N_2 - 1)} = \frac{(89 - 1)(18.982) + (89 - 1)(52.251)}{(89 - 1) + (89 - 1)}$$

$$\frac{6268.504}{176} = 35.617,$$

and then the standard error:

$$s_{\text{err}} = \sqrt{s_{\text{pooled}}^2 \left[\frac{1}{N_1} + \frac{1}{N_2} \right]} = \sqrt{35.617 \left[\frac{1}{89} + \frac{1}{89} \right]} = 0.895.$$

3. Then we ascertain the total proportion of the sampling distribution that will be excluded from the confidence interval. Converting the 99% confidence level to a proportion, we have $\alpha = 1 - 0.99 = 0.01$.

4. Now, the df $= N_1 + N_2 - 2 = 176$. Since this value is larger than any of the values in Table A.3, we may use the normal distribution instead and find the appropriate value of $z_{0.005}$ from Table A.2, which turns out to be $z_{0.005} = 2.576$. For larger samples such as these, the half-width is

$$w = z_{0.005}s_{\text{err}} = (2.576)(0.895) = 2.306.$$

5. The resulting confidence interval statement may be completed by plugging the sample means, half-width w, and α into our formula

$$\Pr(\bar{X}_1 - \bar{X}_2 - w < \mu_1 - \mu_2 < \bar{X}_1 - \bar{X}_2 + w) = 1 - \alpha,$$

so that we get

$$\Pr(-9.690 - 2.306 < \mu_1 - \mu_2 < -9.690 + 2.306) = 0.99,$$

or just

$$\Pr(-11.996 < \mu_1 - \mu_2 < -7.384) = 0.99.$$

So we may claim that the mean Aggressive Behavior scores given by mothers of nonreferred children is between 7.384 and 11.996 points lower than the mean scores given by mothers of children referred to the clinic. This time, a difference between the means of 0 is clearly not a plausible value. Now that we have our sample estimate of the difference between the two samples' mean scores and a 99% confidence interval, how do we assess the size of this difference?

As we saw in Chapter 6, there are at least two ways of doing this: scale-based evaluation and distribution-based evaluation. Let us try scale-based evaluation first. Recalling that the Aggressive Behavior subscale score may range from 0 to 40, we could represent the magnitude of the sample difference between the means as a percentage of the scale range of 40. To get the magnitude of the difference, we just ignore the negative sign. The difference was -9.690, and so its magnitude is 9.690. That is $100(9.690/40) = 24.225\%$ of the scale range, which is a very sizeable difference.

For distribution-based evaluation of the difference, we may use Cohen's d in a suitably modified form. In Chapter 6, we defined d as the difference between the sample mean and the population mean divided by the sample standard deviation. Its formula is

$$d = \frac{\bar{X} - \mu}{s}$$

and the version of Cohen's d we will use here is quite similar. Instead of the sample and population means, we have the difference between two sample means and the difference between two population means. Likewise, instead of one sample standard deviation, we use the pooled standard deviation (which is the square root of s^2_{pooled}). The result is **Cohen's d for two independent** DEFINITION **samples**:

$$d = \frac{(\bar{X}_1 - X_2) - (\mu_1 - \mu_2)}{s_{\text{pooled}}}$$

As with the one-sample version of Cohen's d, usually a 'no-effects' null hypothesis value of $\mu_1 - \mu_2 = 0$ is substituted into the formula for d, so as to assess how many pooled standard deviation units the difference between the sample means is from 0. Also, the magnitude of d is what most researchers are interested in, so any negative sign for d is usually ignored. In the children's Aggressive Behavior example, the difference between the sample means is -9.690, and the pooled standard deviation is $\sqrt{35.617} = 5.968$. Substituting these into the formula for d, we get

$$d = \frac{(\bar{X}_1 - \bar{X}_2) - (\mu_1 - \mu_2)}{s_{\text{pooled}}} = \frac{-9.690 - 0}{5.968} = -1.624.$$

The magnitude of d is 1.624, which is very large by Cohen's standards (remember, a value of d of 0.8 is considered by him to be a large effect).

Data from between-subjects experiments with randomized assignment to two SUMMARY conditions are analyzed as if the experimental conditions provided two **independent random samples**. The same may be said of nonexperimental studies in which we have split a random sample into categories. The subsamples may also be treated as independent random samples.

A **confidence interval for the difference between two means** has the form

$$\Pr(\bar{X}_1 - \bar{X}_2 - w \leq \mu_1 - \mu_2 \leq \bar{X}_1 - \bar{X}_2 + w) = 1 - \alpha.$$

where

- $w = t_{\alpha/2} s_{\text{err}}$ for small to moderate sample sizes;
- $w = z_{\alpha/2} s_{\text{err}}$ for large samples.

Homogeneity of variance is required for this confidence interval to be properly constructed. That is, we assume that the sample variances differ only because of sampling error.

SUMMARY

The **pooled variance** estimate for the difference between the means is

$$s_{\text{pooled}}^2 = \frac{(N_1 - 1)s_1^2 + (N_2 - 1)s_2^2}{(N_1 - 1) + (N_2 - 1)}.$$

and the **pooled standard error**, s_{err}, is

$$s_{\text{err}} = \sqrt{s_{\text{pooled}}^2 \left[\frac{1}{N_1} + \frac{1}{N_2} \right]}.$$

The corresponding **between-subjects *t*-test** is based on this ***t*-statistic**:

$$t\,(\text{df}) = \frac{(\bar{X}_1 - \bar{X}_2) - (\mu_1 - \mu_2)}{s_{\text{err}}}$$

where df $= N_1 + N_2 - 2$. The equivalent confidence interval around $t(\text{df})$ is the same as for the one-sample version of $t(\text{df})$:

$$\Pr(-t_{\alpha/2} \leq t(\text{df}) \leq t_{\alpha/2}) = 1 - \alpha.$$

For a distribution-based evaluation of the size of an effect, we use **Cohen's *d* for two independent samples**:

$$d = \frac{(\bar{X}_1 - \bar{X}_2) - (\mu_1 - \mu_2)}{s_{\text{pooled}}}$$

Comparing proportions from two independent samples

Sometimes researchers need to compare proportions instead of means. The most common reason for this is simply that they are interested in a nominal variable with only two categories. For instance, in the size–weight illusion study the researcher simply records whether the participant chooses the larger or smaller object. However, even when the dependent variable is quantifiable, researchers may not always be interested in using the mean for comparisons between two samples or experimental conditions. For instance, the CBCL Aggressive Behavior subscale has a 'Clinical Borderline' cutoff score of 20. A developmental or clinical psychologist might be interested in comparing the proportions of clinically referred and nonreferred children who score beyond this cutoff.

Now we will translate the confidence interval for the difference between two means into a **confidence interval for the difference between two proportions**. This interval has the form

$$\Pr(P_1 - P_2 - w \leq \Pi_1 - \Pi_2 \leq P_1 - P_2 + w) = 1 - \alpha.$$

This just replaces the sample means with the sample proportions P_1 and P_2 and the population means with the population proportions Π_1 and Π_2. The half-width is either

- $w = t_{\alpha/2} s_{\text{err}}$ for small to moderate sample sizes, or
- $w = z_{\alpha/2} s_{\text{err}}$ for large samples.

The formula for s_{err} differs from the one for the difference between means. It is

$$s_{\text{err}} = \sqrt{\frac{P_1(1 - P_1)}{N_1} + \frac{P_2(1 - P_2)}{N_2}}$$

and is based on the sum of the variances of the proportions.

Suppose we return to the example of comparing how the clinically referred and nonreferred samples of children were rated by their mothers on the CBCL Aggressive Behavior subscale. We have already done this by estimating the differences between the means. Another way would be to estimate the difference between the proportions of each sample who score at or below some cutoff criterion. The previously mentioned 'Clinical Borderline' cutoff score of 20 is one possibility, and it provides a vivid comparison indeed.

In the clinically referred sample, 22 mothers out of 89 gave their children scores of 20 or more, whereas only two out of 89 mothers did in the nonreferred sample. That gives us sample proportions

$$P_1 = 22/89 = 0.247$$

and

$$P_2 = 2/89 = 0.022.$$

The difference between these proportions is

$$P_1 - P_2 = 0.225.$$

To construct, say, a 99% confidence interval around this difference, we use $w = z_{\alpha/2} s_{\text{err}}$ as our half-width, since we have sufficiently large samples, where

$$s_{\text{err}} = \sqrt{\frac{P_1(1 - P_1)}{N_1} + \frac{P_2(1 - P_2)}{N_2}} = \sqrt{\frac{0.247(0.753)}{89} + \frac{0.022(0.978)}{89}}$$

$$= 0.48$$

and from Table A.2, $z_{0.005} = 2.576$. So, we get a half-width of

USE DEM71 TO GAIN FAMILIARITY WITH CONFIDENCE INTERVALS FOR DIFFERENCES OF MEANS AND PROPORTIONS

Demos

$$w = z_{\alpha/2} s_{\text{err}} = (2.576)(0.048) = 0.125.$$

Our resulting 99% confidence interval statement is

$$\Pr(0.225 - 0.125 \le \Pi_1 - \Pi_2 \le 0.225 + 0.125) = 0.99,$$

or

$$\Pr(0.100 \le \Pi_1 - \Pi_2 \le 0.350) = 0.99.$$

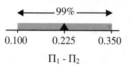

Somewhat less formally, we could say $\text{CI}_{0.99} = 0.225 \pm 0.125$, or $\text{CI}_{0.99} = [0.100, 0.350]$. We can claim that the two samples differ markedly in the proportions of children whose mothers give ratings over the Clinical Borderline cutoff on the CBCL Aggressive Behavior subscale. In fact, as you can see from the boxplots in Figure 7.1, the distributions of scores for these two samples of children overlap only to a small extent.

The same procedure may be used to fashion a reasonably effective comparison of proportions at any cutoff score we choose. For example, we may find out whether the medians of these two samples differ by constructing a confidence interval for the difference between proportions at the cutoff score nearest to the median for the combined samples. In the CBCL data, the

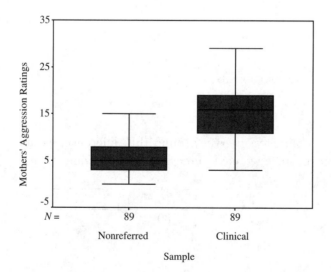

FIGURE 7.1 Boxplots of CBCL Aggressive Behavior scores

mothers' Aggressive Behavior subscale median is 9. Out of the combined sample of 178, 93 (or 52.2%) rated their children at 9 or below on this subscale. How do the children in the two samples compare in terms of the proportions whose mothers rated them at 9 or below?

In the clinically referred sample, 18 mothers out of 89 gave their children scores of 9 or less, whereas 75 out of 89 mothers did in the nonreferred sample. That gives us sample proportions $P_1 = 18/89 = 0.202$ and $P_2 = 75/89 = 0.843$. The difference between these proportions is $P_1 - P_2 = -0.641$. To construct a 99% confidence interval around this difference, we use $w = z_{\alpha/2}s_{err}$ as before. We already know from the previous example that $z_{0.005} = 2.576$, and it turns out that $s_{err} = 0.057$. So, we get a half-width of $w = (2.576)(0.057) = 0.148$. Our 99% confidence interval is $CI_{0.99} = -0.641 \pm 0.148$, or $CI_{0.99} = [-0.789, -0.493]$. This is a very large difference, reflecting the fact that the distributions of scores for these two samples of children have relatively little overlap.

The **confidence interval for the difference between two proportions** SUMMARY
begins with the sample estimate of that difference, namely the difference between the two sample proportions

$$P_1 - P_2.$$

In constructing a $100(1 - a)\%$ confidence interval for the population difference, we use a half-width that is either

- $w = t_{\alpha/2}s_{err}$ for small to moderate sample sizes, or
- $w = z_{\alpha/2}s_{err}$ for large samples,

where the pooled standard error, s_{err}, is

$$s_{err} = \sqrt{\frac{P_1(1 - P_1)}{N_1} + \frac{P_2(1 - P_2)}{N_2}}$$

The resulting confidence interval statement is

$$\Pr(P_1 - P_2 - w \leq \Pi_1 - \Pi_2 \leq P_1 - P_2 + w) = 1 - \alpha.$$

Multiple confidence intervals

What happens when we have more than two independent samples? After all, while some experiments require only two conditions, many require more; so this is a situation that any researcher is bound to encounter. Consider, for instance, an educational psychologist who wishes to compare three methods of teaching students to recognize Chinese characters (Hanzi). She randomly assigns five students to each of the three methods and gives them a comprehension test at

TABLE 7.2 Hanzi experiment

	Method 1	Method 2	Method 3
	2	1	12
	1	8	8
	6	7	9
	5	8	13
	7	5	11
Sums	21	29	53
Means	4.2	5.8	10.6
Variances	6.7	8.7	4.3

the end of their respective periods of instruction. Given that the test yields an interval-level measure of their ability to recognize Hanzi, she wishes to compare the mean test-scores for each instructional method.

The concepts and techniques we have covered so far would lead us to advise the psychologist to construct confidence intervals for the three possible differences between pairs of means: $\mu_1 - \mu_2$, $\mu_1 - \mu_3$, and $\mu_2 - \mu_3$. Because of the homogeneity of variance assumption, the pooled standard error for these comparisons is based on a pooled variance of all three samples, rather than each pair of them. The formula for the pooled variance is a weighted sum of variances just like the one for two samples, with terms added on in the numerator and denominator for the third sample variance and sample size:

DEFINITION

$$s_{pooled}^2 = \frac{(N_1 - 1)s_1^2 + (N_2 - 1)s_2^2 + (N_3 - 1)s_3^2}{(N_1 - 1) + (N_2 - 1) + (N_3 - 1)}$$

The **pooled standard error** has the same formula as before, with this new s_{pooled}^2 employed in it.

Let us try this with our example. The psychologist's Hanzi recognition test has a scale ranging from 0 to a maximum score of 15. She considers it to be an interval-level measure of Hanzi recognition ability. The students' scores are displayed in Table 7.2, along with the sums of the scores, means, and variances for the students studying under each method.

Given that her main interest is in whether any of these methods is more effective than any other, she has decided in advance that a comparison between every possible pair of methods is a reasonable undertaking. The mean scores for these three conditions do appear to differ. Method 3 has the highest mean by a fairly large margin, and the means for Method 1 and Method 2 are rather similar. The three possible pairs of means yield these differences:

$$\bar{X}_1 - \bar{X}_2 = -1.6$$
$$\bar{X}_1 - \bar{X}_3 = -6.4$$
$$\bar{X}_2 - \bar{X}_3 = -4.8$$

The pooled variance estimate for these three conditions is

$$s^2_{\text{pooled}} = \frac{(N_1 - 1)s^2_1 + (N_2 - 1)s^2_2 + (N_3 - 1)s^2_3}{(N_1 - 1) + (N_2 - 1) + (N_3 - 1)} = \frac{(4)6.7 + (4)8.7 + (4)4.3}{4 + 4 + 4}$$

$$= 78.8/12 = 6.6.$$

Since there are the same number of participants in each condition, the pooled standard error for the difference between each pair of means is also the same:

$$s_{\text{err}} = \sqrt{s^2_{\text{pooled}}\left[\frac{1}{N_1} + \frac{1}{N_2}\right]} = \sqrt{6.6\left[\frac{2}{5}\right]} = 1.62.$$

Assuming that we already have decided on a confidence level, the next step is finding the appropriate value for $t_{\alpha/2}$ from Table A.3 to include along with s_{err} in the formula for the half-width of the confidence interval,

$$w = t_{\alpha/2}s_{\text{err}}.$$

Now, since three independent sample variances were used in estimating s_{err}, the appropriate degrees of freedom for all three confidence intervals is $(N_1 - 1) + (N_2 - 1) + (N_3 - 1)$. A simpler way to compute this is just to take the total number of participants in the experiment, N, and subtract the number of samples, k, so that df $= N - k$. In our example, df $= 15 - 3 = 12$. If our desired confidence level is 0.95, then the relevant $t_{0.025}$ value is 2.1788.

We may now ascertain the half-width of the three intervals:

$$w = t_{0.025}s_{\text{err}} = (2.1788)(1.62) = 3.53.$$

The resulting confidence intervals are listed below.

- For $\mu_1 - \mu_2$, $CI_{0.95} = -1.6 \pm 3.53 = [-5.13, 1.93]$;
- For $\mu_1 - \mu_3$, $CI_{0.95} = -6.4 \pm 3.53 = [-9.93, -2.87]$;
- For $\mu_2 - \mu_3$, $CI_{0.95} = -4.8 \pm 3.53 = [-8.33, -1.27]$.

The first confidence interval indicates that 0 is among the plausible values for the difference between the means for Methods 1 and 2, as are negative values down to -5.13 and positive ones up to 1.93. It is therefore unclear whether there really is a difference between those two means, and if so, whether it is positive or negative. On the other hand, the other two intervals tell us that the range of plausible values for the difference between Method 3's mean and that of either Method 1 or 2 does not include 0 and consists entirely of negative numbers. This evidence suggests that Method 3 yields higher test-scores on average than either of the other two methods.

All we have done here is to extend our familiar procedure for calculating confidence intervals to a situation where we construct a simultaneous collection of them. However, there is a very good reason for us to pause and consider this procedure carefully. Because we are setting up three confidence intervals from the same experiment, we are actually running the risk of failing to include the true population parameter in our interval *three times*. If our confidence level is 95%, for example, we have a 0.95 probability of including the true difference between a pair of means in its confidence interval; but we do not have a 0.95 probability of including *all three* differences in their respective intervals. In Chapter 5, we encountered this issue and briefly introduced the **Bonferroni correction** for the confidence level as a way of getting around it. As you may recall, if we are constructing k confidence intervals simultaneously and wish to have a **family-wise** confidence level of $1 - \alpha$, then each interval must be constructed with a confidence level of $1 - \alpha/k$.

DEFINITION

Returning to our example, $k = 3$ so if we wish to have a 0.95 family-wise confidence level, then α is 0.05 and we will need a confidence level of $1 - 0.05/3 = 0.983$ for each interval. Table A.3 does not include a column that corresponds to a confidence level of 0.983, but it does have one corresponding to 0.99 which is even more conservative. A confidence level of 0.99 entails a two-tailed area of 0.01 (i.e., with 0.005 in each tail). In our example, df $= 15 - 3 = 12$, and the relevant $t_{0.005}$ value is 3.0545.

So, the half-width of the three intervals is bigger than the value of 3.53 we had before:

$$w = t_{0.005} s_{\text{err}} = (3.0545)(1.62) = 4.95.$$

Our more conservative confidence intervals are:

- For $\mu_1 - \mu_2$, $\text{CI}_{0.99} = -1.6 \pm 4.95 = [-6.55, 3.35]$;
- For $\mu_1 - \mu_3$, $\text{CI}_{0.99} = -6.4 \pm 4.95 = [-11.35, -1.45]$;
- For $\mu_2 - \mu_3$, $\text{CI}_{0.99} = -4.8 \pm 4.95 = [-9.75, 0.15]$.

Notice that the picture has changed somewhat. The confidence interval for the difference between Methods 2 and 3 now includes 0, casting some doubt on whether Method 3's mean really is the higher.

The main purpose of this illustration has been to highlight the distinction between simultaneous confidence intervals and individual confidence intervals. **Simultaneous confidence intervals** are those for which the confidence

DEFINITION

level refers to the entire collection of intervals. This is the **family-wise** confidence level referred to earlier in the Bonferroni procedure. In the example we just completed, the second collection of confidence intervals permits us to claim that under repeated random sampling, at least 95% of the time all three of them would contain their respective population values.

Researchers differ on whether simultaneous confidence intervals are preferable to individual ones. The Bonferroni procedure clearly suits the more cautious researcher, but it can also result in low statistical power and a genuine difference between means may be obscured by the wide confidence intervals that this procedure tends to produce. Researchers may offset the conservative effects of the Bonferroni procedure via two strategies:

- *Minimizing the number of comparisons* in their collection;
- Combining samples to *include as much of the data as possible.*

Some researchers adhere to a rule that if the number of comparisons planned is fewer than $k - 1$, where k is the number of experimental conditions (or independent samples) then a Bonferroni correction need not be used.

Back in our example, imagine that our psychologist has a theoretical strategy behind her experimental setup. Her theory is that students learn Hanzi recognition best if they are given a combination of visual component-based instruction and semantically based mnemonics. Method 1 has only visual component-based instruction; Method 2 has only semantically based mnemonics; and Method 3 combines the two.

Her best strategy for comparing these methods would involve just two comparisons rather than three. The first comparison would be between Methods 1 and 2. The second would be between Method 3 and the combined samples of Methods 1 and 2. Suppose her preferred confidence level is 98% instead of 95%. She decides to use the Bonferroni correction to set the confidence level for the individual confidence intervals. Since $1 - \alpha = 0.98$, and $k = 2$, she will need to use $1 - \alpha/2 = 0.99$ as her confidence level for each comparison.

Now she sets up the comparisons themselves. The first comparison is identical to the one we already have made between Method 1 and Method 2. The comparison between Method 3 and the combination of Methods 1 and 2 requires that she combine the Methods 1 and 2 data and treat them as if they are a single sample. So their combined mean is $(4.2 + 5.8)/2 = 5.0$ and their combined sample size is 10. The resulting two comparisons are:

$$\bar{X}_1 - \bar{X}_2 = -1.6$$

$$\frac{\bar{X}_1 + \bar{X}_2}{2} - \bar{X}_3 = -5.6.$$

The first comparison has the same confidence interval as before. For the second comparison, however, although the relevant $t_{0.005}$ value is still 3.0545, the pooled standard error s_{err} has changed because instead of two samples of 5 each we have one sample of 10 and one of 5. So s_{err} for the second confidence interval is

$$s_{err} = \sqrt{s_{pooled}^2 \left[\frac{1}{N_1} + \frac{1}{N_2}\right]} = \sqrt{6.6\left[\frac{1}{10} + \frac{1}{5}\right]} = 1.40,$$

which is *smaller* than 1.62. Therefore, the half-width of this interval is *narrower*:

$$w = t_{0.005}s_{err} = (3.0545)(1.40) = 4.29.$$

The two confidence intervals are:

- For $\mu_1 - \mu_2$, $CI_{0.99} = -1.6 \pm 4.95 = [-6.55, 3.35]$;
- For $(\mu_1 + \mu_2)/2 - \mu_3$, $CI_{0.99} = -5.6 \pm 4.29 = [-9.89, -1.31]$.

The picture is very clear now. Method 3 does seem superior to the average of Methods 1 and 2. By using only two comparisons that in turn use all of the data, the psychologist has a higher family-wise confidence level (98%) and a more precise confidence interval for the comparison involving Method 3.

The practice of strategically selecting comparisons in advance and then constructing the appropriate confidence intervals for them is called 'planned comparisons.' **Planned comparisons** are decided on by the researcher before conducting the experiment. They are often based on a specific theory or hypothesis that the experimenter would like to test. There are several viable approaches to conducting planned comparisons, and we have only described one of them here. Most statistical authorities agree that if the main point of your research is captured by planned comparisons, you should simply carry them out and nothing more is needed in the way of analysis.

However, quite often interesting but unexpected findings crop up, and so there are comparisons that researchers want to make after they have seen the data. These are **post-hoc comparisons**, and since there is no way to specify how many or what kind are going to be made, a Bonferroni-style approach to handling family-wise confidence levels cannot be applied here. It is beyond the scope of this introductory textbook to describe the variety of methods that have been developed for making post-hoc comparisons. Many of them are based on alternatives to or variations on the *t*-test. The oldest and most influential solution, however, to the post-hoc comparison problem is a technique known as the 'analysis of variance.' That is the topic of a section later in this chapter.

DEFINITION

DEFINITION

Comparisons are differences between means of independent samples (usually experimental conditions) in a study.

Confidence intervals for these differences are a generalized version of the confidence interval for the difference between two means:

$$\Pr(\bar{X}_1 - \bar{X}_2 - w \leq \mu_1 - \mu_2 \leq \bar{X}_1 - \bar{X}_2 + w) = 1 - \alpha$$

where

- $w = t_{\alpha/2}s_{\text{err}}$ for small to moderate sample sizes;
- $w = z_{\alpha/2}s_{\text{err}}$ for large samples.

The **pooled standard error** for these comparisons is based on a pooled variance of all independent samples in the study. The formula for the pooled variance estimate is:

$$s_{\text{pooled}}^2 = \frac{(N_1 - 1)s_1^2 + (N_2 - 1)s_2^2 + \ldots + (N_k - 1)s_k^2}{(N_1 - 1) + (N_2 - 1) + \ldots + (N_k - 1)}$$

where k is the number of independent samples (usually the number of experimental conditions) in the study. Then for a comparison between the means from samples i and j, the pooled standard error is

$$s_{\text{err}} = \sqrt{s_{\text{pooled}}^2 \left[\frac{1}{N_i} + \frac{1}{N_j} \right]}$$

where N_i and N_j may be from *single or combined* samples.

In the formula for the half-width of the confidence interval,

$$w = t_{\alpha/2}s_{\text{err}},$$

the appropriate number of degrees of freedom for $t_{\alpha/2}$ is $N - k$, where N is the total number of sampling units in the study and k is the number of independent samples. For large samples, the normal distribution is a good approximation, so $z_{\alpha/2}$ may be used.

Post-hoc comparisons are comparisons that researchers elect to make after they have seen the data.

Planned comparisons are decided on by the researcher before conducting a study. They involve the construction of simultaneous confidence intervals.

Simultaneous confidence intervals are those for which the confidence level refers to the entire collection of intervals, i.e., a **family-wise** confidence level. The **Bonferroni correction** for the confidence level stipulates that if we are constructing k confidence intervals simultaneously and wish to have a *family-wise* confidence level of $1 - \alpha$, then each interval must be constructed with a confidence level of $1 - \alpha/k$.

SUMMARY
Researchers may offset the *conservative effects* of the Bonferroni procedure via two strategies:

- *Minimizing the number of comparisons* in their collection;
- Combining samples to *include as much of the data as possible.*

Comparing variances from two independent samples

Can differences between sample means or proportions detect all differences between two independent samples? No, since the difference between two groups might be solely due to difference in their variances. Consider, for instance, a treatment designed to restrict the mood swings of people suffering bipolar disorder. Table 7.3 shows some artificial data from a hypothetical study in which a self-report mood scale ranging from 0 (extreme depression) to 10 (extreme elation) was used. In the Treatment condition, the participants had taken a drug designed to stabilize mood swings, and in the Control condition the participants had no treatment.

Clearly the most plausible difference between the means is 0, since the two sample means are equal. Nevertheless, the distributions of mood scores clearly differ from one another. The treatment group has far less variance (the variance of the scores in the Treatment condition is 1.6, while the variance in the Control condition is 20.0), which is what one might hope for in view of the goals of the study. The mood scores for the C group participants are 'all over the place' and the large sample variance reflects that. The T group participants, on the other hand, have mood scores near the middle of the scale and with low variance, so they probably are not experiencing mood swings. The point here is that researchers must mindfully select their analyses, most importantly on the basis of whether they can reveal what the researcher is looking for.

TABLE 7.3 Clinical training experiment

Control	Treatment
1	3
9	6
10	5
0	6
8	4
2	6

Control: $N_1 = 6$, $\bar{X}_1 = 5.0$, $s_1^2 = 20.0$.
Treatment: $N_2 = 6$, $\bar{X}_2 = 5.0$, $s_2^2 = 1.6$.
$\bar{X}_1 - \bar{X}_2 = 5.0 - 5.0 = 0$.

We will now find out how to compare the variances from these two samples. Instead of using the difference between the means, as we did in comparing two means, we will use the *ratio* of the variances, s_1^2/s_2^2, where s_1 and s_2 are the sample standard deviations. This ratio is compared with its population value σ_1^2/σ_2^2 via the **F-statistic**, which has the form   DEFINITION

$$F = \frac{s_1^2/s_2^2}{\sigma_1^2/\sigma_2^2}.$$

The convention is to assign the larger variance to be s_1^2 in the ratio s_1^2/s_2^2, so in our example we would put $s_1^2/s_2^2 = 20.0/1.6$. F can range from 0 to infinity. If $s_1^2/s_2^2 = \sigma_1^2/\sigma_2^2$, then $F = 1$; but clearly F could stray above or below 1 because of sampling error.

F has a sampling distribution which is called (oddly enough) the **F-dis-** DEFINITION **tribution**. This distribution is positively skewed. F has two degrees of freedom associated with it that determine its shape. One is for the numerator (s_1), and is $\mathrm{df}_1 = N_1 - 1$. The other is for the denominator (s_2), namely $\mathrm{df}_2 = N_2 - 1$. Conventionally, these degrees of freedom are listed in brackets after the letter F, i.e., $F(\mathrm{df}_1, \mathrm{df}_2)$. For instance, if $\mathrm{df}_1 = 5$ and $\mathrm{df}_2 = 60$, we would write $F(5, 60)$. When it is possible to avoid confusion, however, we will drop the df's and just use F. Figure 7.2 shows an example of this kind of distribution, for $F(5, 60)$.

If we want to indicate a value of F and refer to the area under the F-curve beyond it, we may use the same kind of notation we did with t and z. Thus, F_α is the value of F beyond which the area under the F-curve is equal to α. For example, in Figure 7.2 '$F_{0.05} = 2.3683$' tells us that the area under the F-curve beyond 2.3683 is 0.05. We can get these values from Table A.4, for three values of α: 0.05, 0.01, and 0.005. Table A.4 is organized so that the rows are grouped in threes, each corresponding to $\alpha = 0.05$, 0.01, and 0.005. Each *group of rows* is indexed by degrees of freedom for the *denominator* (df_2). The

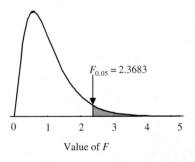

FIGURE 7.2 F distribution with $\mathrm{df}_1 = 5$ and $\mathrm{df}_2 = 60$; $F_{0.05} = 2.3683$

columns correspond to the degrees of freedom for the *numerator* (df_1). The relevant part of Table A.4 is displayed as Table 7.4, so that you can see where the value for $F_{0.05}(5, 60)$ comes from.

DEFINITION   Just as the *t*-statistic is associated with a *t*-test for hypothesis testing, the *F*-statistic has a corresponding **F-test** associated with it. The *F*-test involves evaluating whether some hypothetical value for σ_1^2/σ_2^2 is plausible or not, by ascertaining whether the corresponding value for the *F*-statistic lies inside a confidence interval. Since the convention is to assign the larger variance to be s_1^2 in the ratio s_1^2/s_2^2, a **one-sided confidence interval** around the *F*-statistic is used:

$$\Pr\left(\frac{s_1^2/s_2^2}{\sigma_1^2/\sigma_2^2} < F_\alpha\right) = 1 - \alpha,$$

or more compactly,

$$\Pr(F(df_1,\ df_2) < F_\alpha) = 1 - \alpha.$$

Graphically, we may represent this interval as follows:

The 'no effects' null hypothesis that usually is used is that $\sigma_1^2 = \sigma_2^2$, which is equivalent to saying that $\sigma_1^2/\sigma_2^2 = 1$. Whenever $\sigma_1^2/\sigma_2^2 = 1$, $F(df_1,\ df_2)$ is just s_1^2/s_2^2. If s_1^2/s_2^2 lies outside the confidence interval then we may reject the null hypothesis and conclude that the two variances are unequal, but otherwise we cannot.

In our fictitious mood-swing study since we would like to know whether σ_1^2 is larger than σ_2^2, we are interested in whether it is plausible that $\sigma_1^2/\sigma_2^2 = 1$.

TABLE 7.4 Part of table A.4 with $F_{0.05}(5, 60) = 2.3683$

df denominator	α: Area under *F*	df numerator						
		1	2	3	4	5	6	7
55	0.05	4.0162	3.1650	2.7725	2.5397	2.3828	2.2687	2.1813
	0.01	7.1194	5.0132	4.1591	3.6809	3.3700	3.1493	2.9834
	0.005	8.5538	5.8432	4.7727	4.1813	3.8000	3.5309	3.3296
60	0.05	4.0012	3.1504	2.7581	2.5252	2.3683	2.2541	2.1665
	0.01	7.0771	4.9774	4.1259	3.6491	3.3389	3.1187	2.9530
	0.005	8.4947	5.7950	4.7290	4.1399	3.7600	3.4918	3.2911

Suppose we decide on a confidence level of 99%, so that $\alpha = 0.01$. Then we take the following steps.

1. First we need to find $F_{0.01}$. Our degrees of freedom for the numerator are

   $$df_1 = N_1 - 1 = 6 - 1 = 5,$$

   and for the denominator,

   $$df_2 = N_2 - 1 = 6 - 1 = 5.$$

   We consult Table A.4 to obtain $F_{0.01}$ and locate the column corresponding to $df_1 = 5$, the group of rows corresponding to $df_2 = 5$, and the row in that group for $\alpha = 0.01$. There, we find that $F_{0.01} = 10.9671$.
2. Now, putting $F_{0.01}$ into the formula for the confidence interval we have $\Pr(F(5, 5) < 10.9761) = 0.99$.

   ```
   ─────── 99% ──────→
   ┌──────────────────────┬─────┐
   │▓▓▓▓▓▓▓▓▓▓▓▓▓▓▓▓▓▓▓▓▓▓│     │
   └──────────────────────┴─────┘
   0            10.9761  12.5
   ```

3. When $\sigma_1^2/\sigma_2^2 = 1$, then $F(5, 5) = s_1^2/s_2^2 = 20.0/1.6 = 12.5$, which is our hypothetical value for $F(5, 5)$. It is clear that our hypothetical value of 12.5 is larger than 10.9761 and lies outside the confidence interval. We may therefore reject the null hypothesis that $\sigma_1^2 = \sigma_2^2$.

We may conclude that the variances of the mood scores in the two experimental conditions probably differ, and therefore the treatment probably does decrease manic-depressive mood swings.

SUMMARY

Comparisons between two sample variances use their ratio, s_1^2/s_2^2, as the basis for such a comparison.

The **F-statistic** has the form

$$F(df_1,\ df_2) = \frac{s_1^2/s_2^2}{\sigma_1^2/\sigma_2^2}.$$

Its sampling distribution is known as the **F-distribution** with degrees of freedom $df_1 = N_1 - 1$ associated with the numerator (s_1), and $df_2 = N_2 - 1$ with the denominator (s_2).

Since the conventional practice is to make s_1 the larger of the two standard deviations, researchers usually use only a **one-sided confidence interval for $F(df_1,\ df_2)$**,

$$\Pr(F(df_1, df_2) < F_\alpha) = 1 - \alpha.$$

SUMMARY

The *F*-statistic has an **F-test** associated with it. The usual 'no effects' null hypothesis is $\sigma_1^2 = \sigma_2^2$, which is equivalent to saying that $\sigma_1^2/\sigma_2^2 = 1$. The corresponding hypothetical value of $F(\mathrm{df}_1, \mathrm{df}_2)$ is just s_1^2/s_2^2. If s_1^2/s_2^2 lies outside the confidence interval then we may reject the null hypothesis, but otherwise we cannot.

The analysis of variance

In this section, we will introduce the 'analysis of variance.' This is still perhaps the most popular statistical technique in psychological research, and it is traditionally used to test whether there are any differences among the mean scores of experimental conditions (or independent samples). At first, it may seem as if this technique has little to do with comparing means. By the end of this section, however, the connection should be clear.

In an experiment such as the Hanzi recognition study, if the experimental conditions do not have an effect on the experimental variable, we should expect the mean scores for the conditions to differ from one another simply because of sampling error. After all, even though they are all estimates of the same population mean, we should not expect them to all be exactly the same. However, if the experimental conditions *do* have an effect, then those means should differ to a greater extent than we would expect from sampling error alone.

How much variance should we expect from sampling error? If we make the homogeneity of variance assumption, as we did when constructing simultaneous confidence intervals, then the pooled variance estimate, s_{pooled}^2, gives us a reasonable estimate of variance due to sampling error. In other words, s_{pooled}^2 is an estimate of the population variance of the scores, σ^2.

Now, s_{pooled}^2 is a weighted average of the variances of scores *within* each experimental condition. In the analysis of variance, s_{pooled}^2 is usually denoted by s_{w}^2, where the 'w' stands for 'within experimental conditions.' The sample estimate of the variance *between* experimental conditions is denoted by s_{b}^2, and it also is an estimate of the population variance, σ^2. In the next paragraph we will get an intuitive grasp of what it is.

In experiments where each condition has an equal number of participants, we can estimate the *squared standard error of the means* by just treating them as if they are raw scores and plugging them into the formula for a sample variance. Since there are k experimental conditions, we would divide by $k - 1$ instead of $N - 1$. Our estimate is

$$s_{\bar{x}}^2 = \frac{\Sigma(\bar{X}_i - \bar{X})^2}{k - 1}.$$

However, we know that the sampling distribution of the mean has a variance that equals the variance of the scores divided by the size of the sample. To convert this squared standard error into an estimate of the population variance σ^2, we must multiply the squared difference between each condition's mean and the overall mean by N_i, the number of participants in its condition. The steps we have taken here may be summarized in this way:

- standard error = standard deviation$\sqrt{N}$,
- squared standard error = (standard error)$^2/N$ = variance$/N$, so
- variance = N(squared standard error).

*The result is our sample estimate of the variance **between** experimental conditions:*   DEFINITION

$$s_b^2 = \frac{\Sigma N_i(\bar{X}_i - \bar{X})^2}{k - 1}$$

and the sum in the numerator often is abbreviated as SS_b, which stands for the **sum of squares between conditions**.

The **analysis of variance** (usually abbreviated as ANOVA) uses an F-statistic to compare the variance *between* experimental conditions against the   DEFINITION
variance of scores *within* conditions. This **F-statistic** has the form

$$F(\mathrm{df_b},\ \mathrm{df_w}) = \frac{s_b^2/s_w^2}{\sigma_b^2/\sigma_w^2}$$

so that the between-conditions variance is always on top (in the numerator). Its sampling distribution is an F-distribution with degrees of freedom $\mathrm{df_b} = k - 1$ associated with the numerator (s_b^2), and $\mathrm{df_w} = N - k$ with the denominator (s_w^2). Conventionally, researchers refer to the ratio s_b^2/s_w^2 as the 'F-ratio.' In fact, usually the F-ratio is itself called 'F.'

The corresponding **F-test** associated with ANOVA posits a 'no effects' null   DEFINITION
hypothesis that sets $\sigma_b^2 = \sigma_w^2 = \sigma^2$, which is equivalent to saying that $\sigma_b^2/\sigma_w^2 = 1$. Why is this a 'no effects' hypothesis? We started off with the claim that if the experimental conditions have no effect on the experimental variable, we should expect the mean scores for the conditions to vary only as much as sampling error would predict. We developed s_b^2, based solely on the variance of the means, to compare against s_w^2, which is an estimate of σ^2. If the means' variability is influenced only by sampling error, then s_b^2 and s_w^2 should both be σ^2. If, on the other hand, the means' variability is also influenced by experimental effects, then s_b^2 should be bigger than s_w^2.

Another way to think of this is that s_b^2 is a matter of effects + sampling error, whereas s_w^2 is a matter of sampling error alone. Schematically, the F-ratio s_b^2/s_w^2 may be expressed this way:

$$\frac{s_b^2}{s_w^2} = \frac{\text{effects} + \text{error}}{\text{error}}.$$

If the null hypothesis of no effects is true, then this ratio should be 1. If it is false, then the ratio should be larger than 1.

Let us revisit the Hanzi recognition study, and try this out on it. The data are redisplayed in Table 7.5. The **within-conditions variance**, s_w^2, is the same as the pooled variance estimate that we calculated back in the section on simultaneous confidence intervals. Recapitulating, we have

$$s_w^2 = \frac{(N_1 - 1)s_1^2 + (N_2 - 1)s_2^2 + (N_3 - 1)s_3^2}{(N_1 - 1) + (N_2 - 1) + (N_3 - 1)}$$

$$= \frac{(4)6.7 + (4)8.7 + (4)4.3}{4 + 4 + 4}$$

$$= 6.57.$$

Now for the between-conditions variance, s_b^2. The overall mean of the scores is 6.87, so as shown in Table 7.6, we need to obtain the squared differences between each condition's mean and the overall mean. Each squared difference is multiplied by its N_i (which is 5 for all of the conditions) to get the SS_b terms. The resulting SS_b is 110.933, and the value of s_b^2 is

$$s_b^2 = \frac{\Sigma N_i (\bar{X}_i - \bar{X})^2}{k - 1} = \frac{SS_b}{k - 1} = \frac{110.933}{2} = 55.47.$$

TABLE 7.5 Hanzi experiment revisisted

	Method 1	Method 2	Method 3	
	2	1	12	
	1	8	8	
	6	7	9	
	5	8	13	
	7	5	11	Totals
Sums	21	29	53	103
Means	4.2	5.8	10.6	6.87
Variances	6.7	8.7	4.3	$s_w^2 = 6.57$

Having obtained s_b^2 and s_w^2, we need only follow the procedure for the F-test that we learned in the previous section. Suppose we have decided on a confidence level of 95%, so that $\alpha = 0.05$. Then we take the following steps.

1. First we need to find $F_{0.05}$. Our degrees of freedom for the numerator are

$$df_b = k - 1 = 3 - 1 = 2,$$

   and for the denominator

$$df_w = N - k = 15 - 3 = 12.$$

   We consult Table A.4 and locate the column corresponding to $df_b = 2$, the group of rows corresponding to $df_w = 12$, and the row in that group for $\alpha = 0.05$. There, we find that $F_{0.05} = 3.8853$.

2. Now, putting $F_{0.01}$ into the formula for the confidence interval

$$Pr(F(df_b, \ df_w) < F_a = 1 - \alpha,$$

   we have

$$Pr(F(2, 12) < 3.8853) = 0.95.$$

3. When $\sigma_b^2 / \sigma_w^2 = 1$, then $F(2, 12) = s_b^2 / s_w^2 = 55.47/6.57 = 8.45$, which is our hypothetical value for $F(2, 12)$.

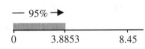

   It is clear that our hypothetical value of 8.45 is larger than 3.8853 and lies outside the confidence interval. We may therefore reject the null hypothesis that $\sigma_b^2 = \sigma_w^2$.

   In rejecting that null hypothesis, we may conclude that the method of instruction has influenced students' Hanzi recognition ability. The reason we may do this is that s_b^2 is a matter of effects + sampling error, whereas s_w^2 is a matter of sampling error alone. If the means' variability is influenced only by sampling error, then s_b^2 and s_w^2 should be approximately the same. If, on the

TABLE 7.6 Squared differences for means

	Means	Diff.	Sq. diff.	N_i	SS$_b$ terms
Method 1	4.2	−2.667	7.111	5	35.556
Method 2	5.8	−1.067	1.138	5	5.689
Method 3	10.6	3.733	13.938	5	69.689
Total	6.867				110.933

other hand, the means' variability is also influenced by experimental effects, then s_b^2 should be bigger than s_w^2.

The traditional way of reporting the F-test for an ANOVA is to mention the value of the F-ratio s_b^2/s_w^2 and its significance level, e.g., '$F(2, 12) = 8.45$, $p < 0.05$.' This statement may be translated in much the same way as we did with the t-test. Instead of using the confidence interval statement, the significance-testing approach just uses F_α as a cutoff point for deciding whether $F(\text{df}_b, \text{df}_w)$ is large enough to reject the null hypothesis.

One of the chief drawbacks of the F-test in ANOVA is that by itself, $F(\text{df}_b, \text{df}_w)$ tells us hardly anything useful about what effects our experiment has had. It does not inform us of which condition's mean is larger than another, or how much larger it is. Many researchers therefore report means, standard deviations, and simultaneous confidence intervals to convey more information about their experiments' outcomes. This is a good habit for you to adopt in communicating about your own research.

Let us try one more example, but this time to tie up a loose end. It may already have occurred to you to wonder whether ANOVA may be used when there are only two experimental conditions, and if so, what relationship it has to the t-test for two samples that we covered earlier in this chapter. Historically, the t-test was invented before ANOVA, and there is a very simple relationship between them. The easiest way to understand the relationship is to take an example from the t-test for two samples, such as our clinical training experiment, and reanalyze it using ANOVA.

In that experiment, we had a Training and Control group. The object of the study was training in client interviewing skills; the participants were clinical psychology students; and the training group underwent a special intensive program. The researchers had randomly assigned 12 clinical psychology students in a Ph.D. program to these two groups. They wanted to find out whether the trained group scores higher on a 10-point skills rating judgment scale than the untrained group. The data are redisplayed in Table 7.7.

The within-conditions variance, s_w^2, is the same as the pooled variance estimate that we calculated for these data at the start of this chapter:

$$s_w^2 = \frac{(N_1 - 1)s_1^2 + (N_2 - 1)s_2^2}{(N_1 - 1) + (N_2 - 1)} = \frac{(5 - 1)1.0 + (7 - 1)3.33}{(5 - 1) + (7 - 1)} = 2.4.$$

The components needed for computing the between-conditions variance, s_b^2, are shown in Table 7.8. The overall mean of the scores is 5.833, so we need to obtain the squared differences between each condition's mean and the overall mean. Each squared difference is multiplied by its N_i (which is 5 for the Trained and 7 for the Control group) to get the SS_b terms.

(margin note) **StatPatch**

USE ANOVA-
PATCH TO
GAIN
FAMILIARITY
WITH
ONE-WAY
ANOVA

TABLE 7.7 Clinical training experiment revisited

	Trained	Control	
	8	5	
	6	6	
	7	8	
	6	3	
	8	4	
		6	
		3	Totals
Sum	35	35	70
Means	7	5	5.833
s_i^2	1.000	3.333	$s_w^2 = 2.4$

The resulting SS_b is 11.667, and the value of s_b^2 is

$$s_b^2 = \frac{\Sigma N_i(\bar{X}_i - \bar{X})^2}{k-1} = \frac{SS_b}{k-1} = \frac{11.667}{1} = 11.667.$$

Having obtained s_b^2 and s_w^2, we need only follow the procedure for the F-test. For this example we use a confidence level of 95%, so that $\alpha = 0.05$. Then we take the following steps.

1. First we need to find $F_{0.05}$. Our degrees of freedom for the numerator are

   $$df_b = k - 1 = 2 - 1 = 1,$$

   and for the denominator

   $$df_w = N - k = 12 - 2 = 10.$$

   We consult Table A.4 and locate the column corresponding to $df_b = 1$, the group of rows corresponding to $df_w = 10$, and the row in that group for $\alpha = 0.05$. There, we find that $F_{0.05} = 4.9646$.

2. Now, putting $F_{0.01}$ into the formula for the confidence interval

   $$\Pr(F(df_b, df_w) < F_\alpha) = 1 - \alpha,$$

we have

TABLE 7.8 Components of s_b^2

	Means	Dev.	Sq. Dev	N_i	SS_b terms
Trained	7	1.167	1.361	5	6.806
Control	5	−0.833	0.694	7	4.861
Total	5.833		2.056		11.667

$$\Pr(F(1, 10) < 4.9646) = 0.95.$$

3. When $\sigma_b^2/\sigma_w^2 = 1$, then $F(1, 10) = s_b^2/s_w^2 = 11.667/2.4 = 4.861$, which is our hypothetical value for $F(1, 10)$.

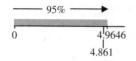

It is clear that our hypothetical value of 4.861 is smaller than 4.9646 and lies inside the confidence interval. We therefore cannot reject the null hypothesis that $\sigma_b^2 = \sigma_w^2$.

Now, let us compare the outcome of this F-test with the outcome of the t-test we conducted on these same data at the beginning of this chapter. There, we set up a confidence interval around the t statistic, $t(\mathrm{df})$:

$$\Pr(-t_{\alpha/2} < t(\mathrm{df}) < t_{\alpha/2}) = 1 - \alpha,$$

where $\mathrm{df} = 7 + 5 - 2 = 10$ and $\alpha = 0.05$. We found that the required value for $t_{0.025}$ was 2.228. The hypothetical value for $t(10)$ turned out to be 2.205. The confidence interval around $t(10)$ is

$$\Pr(-2.228 < t(10) < 2.228) = 0.95,$$

and 2.205 is contained in the interval. We were therefore unable to reject the null hypothesis that $\mu_1 - \mu_2 = 0$. So both tests reach the same conclusion.

The crucial comparison here is between the t- and F-statistics. In general, whenever F has only one degree of freedom for the numerator (i.e., when there are only two experimental conditions), $\boldsymbol{F} = \boldsymbol{t}^2$. Thus,

$$F_{0.05} = 4.9646 = (t_{0.025})^2 = (2.228)^2,$$

and

$$F(1, 10) = 4.861 = (t(10))^2 = (2.205)^2.$$

Any t-test for two samples therefore may be duplicated by an F-test for a two-condition experiment. Why worry about the t-test at all, then? There are three reasons. First, much of the traditional literature reports t-tests for experiments with two conditions. Second, the t-statistic is directly related to the confidence interval for a difference between means, which often is more informative than the F-statistic is. Third, as we shall see in the next chapter, the t-statistic is useful in helping us interpret the overall magnitude of an effect.

The **analysis of variance** (usually abbreviated as **ANOVA**) uses an   SUMMARY
F-statistic to compare the variance *between* experimental conditions against
the variance of scores *within* conditions. This **F-statistic** has the form

$$F(\mathrm{df_b}, \mathrm{df_w}) = \frac{s_b^2/s_w^2}{\sigma_b^2/\sigma_w^2}$$

so that the between-conditions variance is always on top (in the numerator).
Its sampling distribution is an F-distribution with degrees of freedom $\mathrm{df_b} =$
$k - 1$ associated with the numerator (s_b^2), where k is the number of conditions,
and $\mathrm{df_w} = N - k$ with the denominator (s_w^2), where N is the total number of
participants.

The **between-conditions variance estimate** is

$$s_b^2 = \frac{\Sigma N(\bar{X}_i - \bar{X})^2}{k - 1} = \frac{\mathrm{SS_b}}{k - 1}$$

when N_i is the number of participants in the ith experimental condition, and $\mathrm{SS_b}$
stands for the **sum of squares between conditions**.
Under the **homogeneity of variance assumption**,
the **within-conditions variance estimate** is

$$s_w^2 = \frac{(N_1 - 1)s_1^2 + (N_2 - 1)s_2^2 + \ldots + (N_k - 1)s_k^2}{(N_1 - 1) + (N_2 - 1) + \ldots + (N_k - 1)}$$

The corresponding **F-test** associated with ANOVA posits a 'no effects' null
hypothesis that sets $\sigma_b^2 = \sigma_w^2 = \sigma^2$, which is equivalent to saying that $\sigma_b^2/\sigma_w^2 = 1$.
The corresponding hypothetical value of $F(\mathrm{df_1}, \mathrm{df_2})$ is just s_1^2/s_2^2.
If s_1^2/s_2^2 lies outside the confidence interval

$$\Pr(F(\mathrm{df_1}, \mathrm{df_2}) < F_\alpha) = 1 - \alpha,$$

then we may reject the null hypothesis, but otherwise we cannot.
When there are just two experimental conditions, the F-test and t-tests are
mathematically equivalent.
In general, when there are only two experimental conditions, $\boldsymbol{F = t^2}$.

The size of effect in ANOVA

Another type of information that researchers often convey to supplement the
F-test is the size of the experimental effect. Thus far, we have seen how
Cohen's d may be used for this purpose when an experiment has only two
conditions. What should we do when there are more than two conditions?
Although the F-statistic itself does not tell us how big the overall effect is, its
components turn out to provide just the measure we need.

At the start of Chapter 6, we saw that the sampling statistical model of a sample mean could also be thought of as a *predictive model* in which the sample mean is being predicted on the basis of the population mean's value and sampling error. We may apply the same idea to predicting an individual score. An individual score randomly selected from a population could be represented by a sampling model with the form

$$X = \mu + e,$$

where X is the score, μ is the population mean score, and e represents sampling error.

Consider this simple model in terms of prediction. In Chapter 3, we observed that the mean produces the smallest sum of squared differences between scores and any value. If you had to choose one value as your 'best guess' for each of the 15 test scores from the Hanzi data as they were being pulled out of a hat, and if the error in your guesses were measured by the squared difference between each guess and the actual score, then your best strategy would be to guess the mean every time. The total amount of error you would accumulate in using the mean as your guess would be the sum of the squared differences between the mean and each score, which is called the **total**

DEFINITION   **sum of squares** and denoted **SS$_t$**:

$$SS_t = \Sigma(X - \bar{X})^2.$$

By using the model

$$X = \mu + e,$$

DEFINITIONS the amount of error we make in predicting the X's is SS_t. If the experimental conditions have no effects, then this **null model** should do a reasonable job of prediction because taking into account which condition a score comes from should make no difference in how accurately we could predict it.

If the experimental conditions have effects, however, then this simple model is inadequate because it does not take into account which condition a score comes from. An alternative **effects model** would be

$$X = \mu_i + e,$$

where μ_i is the mean score for the ith experimental condition. Let us consider this effects model from the standpoint of predicting the X's. One way to do this is to imagine that you are subjected to a similar kind of guessing-game regarding the 15 test scores from the Hanzi data, but this time the scores are allocated to three hats, labeled Method 1, Method 2, and Method 3. The mean of the scores in Method 1 would be your best guess for a score being taken from the Method 1 hat, the Method 2 mean for a score from the Method 2 hat, and the Method 3 mean for scores from the Method 3 hat.

The total amount of error you would accumulate for each condition in using these means as your guesses would be the sum of the squared differences between each score and the mean of the scores in that condition. These sums of squares are abbreviated SS_i and may be expressed in both ways shown in the formula below:

$$SS_i = \Sigma(X - \bar{X}_i)^2 = (\mathcal{N}_i - 1)s_i^2.$$

Adding all those component SS_i's together gives us the total **sum of squares within conditions**, SS_w:

DEFINITION

$$SS_w = \Sigma SS_i = (\mathcal{N}_1 - 1)s_1^2 + (\mathcal{N}_2 - 1)s_2^2 + \ldots + (\mathcal{N}_k - 1)s_k^2.$$

What SS_w measures is the total amount of error you would make by using the model

$$X = \mu_i + e,$$

i.e., guessing each score by using the mean score for the condition from which the score comes. SS_w is also the numerator from the formula for s_w^2, the within-conditions variance estimate.

If the experimental conditions' means differ from one another, then you should make smaller errors by using each condition's mean as your guess than by using the overall mean. In other words, if the *effects model* is better than the *null model*, then SS_w should be less than SS_t. The conventional way of measuring how much smaller the SS_w error is than the SS_t error is by taking the difference between them as a proportion of SS_t. Conventionally, this proportional difference is denoted by R^2:

DEFINITION

$$R^2 = \frac{SS_t - SS_w}{SS_t}$$

R^2 can range as high as 1, since SS_w can be as small as 0 (when the experimental condition means perfectly predict each score, so there is no error). Conversely, R^2 can go as low as 0, because SS_w can be as large as SS_t (no improvement in prediction, no reduction in error). Thus, R^2 is an example of what is called a **proportional reduction in error** (or PRE) measure of effect.

DEFINITIONS

There is just one more piece of the puzzle to put in place before we try all of this on an example. Before introducing SS_w and SS_t, we had already worked with SS_b, which stands for the **sum of squares between conditions**. It is just the numerator from the formula for s_b^2, the between-conditions variance estimate:

$$SS_b = \Sigma N_i(\bar{X}_i - \bar{X})^2.$$

There is a very useful relationship involving SS_b, SS_w and SS_t:

$$SS_t = SS_b + SS_w.$$

This relationship enables us to represent R^2 in two ways, the one already introduced above and this alternative:

$$R^2 = \frac{SS_b}{SS_t}.$$

Returning once more to the Hanzi recognition study, let us try using R^2 to measure the size of the overall experimental effect. In calculating s_b^2, we found earlier that

$$SS_b = 110.933.$$

As for SS_w, from the calculations for s_w^2, we can redo the numerator separately:

$$SS_w = (N_1 - 1)s_1^2 + (N_2 - 1)s_2^2 + (N_3 - 1)s_3^2 = (4)(6.7) + (4)(8.7)$$
$$+ (4)(4.3) = 78.800.$$

Finally,

$$SS_t = SS_b + SS_w = 110.933 + 78.800 = 189.733.$$

We are all set. We may plug in the appropriate numbers to obtain R^2:

$$R^2 = \frac{SS_t - SS_w}{SS_t} = \frac{SS_b}{SS_t} = \frac{110.933}{189.733} = 0.585.$$

This result says that by using the effects model instead of the null model for predicting the scores, we reduce the total error ($SS_t = 189.733$) by 58.5% (i.e., by

$$SS_t - SS_w = 189.733 - 78.800 = 110.933).$$

DEFINITION   A second interpretation for R^2 frequently used in the research literature is to say that it is a **proportion of variance accounted for** by the experimental effects. After all, SS_t is a measure of how much the scores vary about the mean, and SSb is the component of that variation due to variability in the condition means. So, if we think of R^2 in terms of SS_b/SS_t then we can see that it is the proportion of variation in the scores that is accounted for by variation in the means, i.e., due to experimental effects. In the Hanzi recognition study, $R^2 = 0.585$ could be translated to mean that 58.5% of the variation in test scores is accounted for by experimental effects (i.e., the different learning methods used).

Unfortunately, many researchers do not report R^2 along with their F-test results. This is a pity, because like Cohen's d, R^2 does not depend on sample size whereas the F-statistic does. One implication is that if you read a research report that tells you only what the F-statistic is, you cannot get much of an idea of how big the effect is.

There are ways around this problem. Some researchers present 'source' tables that summarize their ANOVA results in a tabular form. Table 7.9 shows the Hanzi study ANOVA results in such a form. This table is read essentially from left to right, starting with the sums of squares (SS), divided by their respective df's to produce the between and within variance estimates (s^2), whose ratio then yields the F-statistic. This table contains everything needed to figure out what R^2 is, since all of the SS terms are included there.

What about articles in which the researcher simply reports the F-statistic? Even there, they usually report the value of the statistic and the degrees of freedom (since they surely need to tell us how many participants and conditions the experiment had!). As it happens, the laconic statement '$F(2, 12) = 8.45$, $p < 0.05$' contains everything we need in order to convert that F value into R^2. Given a value for $F(df_b, df_w)$, we may convert it into R^2 by this formula:

$$R^2 = \frac{df_b F}{df_w + df_b F}$$

We may test this by plugging in the appropriate numbers from the ANOVA table below:

Demos

$$R^2 = \frac{2(8.45)}{12 + 2(8.45)} = 16.9/28.9 = 0.585.$$

USE DEM72
TO EXPLORE
THE
RELATION-
SHIP
BETWEEN **F**,
ITS DEGREES
OF FREEDOM,
AND **R**^{2}

TABLE 7.9 ANOVA table for Hanzi study

Source	SS	df	s^2	F
Between	110.933	2	55.47	8.45
Within	78.800	12	6.57	
Total	189.733	14		

Armed with this formula, you can range at will through classic studies by famous psychologists and reveal how big (or small) their effect sizes were!

Near the end of the previous section, we observed that a drawback of the F-test is that by itself, $F(\mathrm{df_b}, \mathrm{df_w})$ tells us hardly anything useful about what effects our experiment has had. Now that we do have a measure of effect size, can we use it to help us understand anything more about the F-statistic? Indeed we can, because the F-statistic can be decomposed into *two components*. One is based on R_2, and the other is based on the number of participants and experimental conditions (i.e., the df's). The decomposition formula is

$$F = \frac{R^2}{1 - R^2} \times \frac{N - k}{k - 1}$$

This formula is worthy of a moment's contemplation because it tells us about everything that is going to influence the size of F. The left-hand part is based on R^2, the size of the effect. If R^2 is close to 0, then this component also will be close to 0 and F will be small unless the right-hand part is very big. However, if R^2 is close to 1, this component will be very large and so will F. The right-hand part is the ratio of $N - k$ ($\mathrm{df_w}$) to $k - 1$ ($\mathrm{df_b}$), which becomes big only when N (the total number of participants) is quite a bit larger than k (the number of conditions). So this right-hand component reflects the *size of the sample relative to the size of the experiment*. Thus, a large value of F is obtainable from studies with large effects and/or sufficiently large sample sizes.

Let us consider one more example to conclude with, this time taken from a real study that is not experimental. During the late 1980s, I was a member of an interdisciplinary project investigating health-related issues in remote Indigenous communities in Northeastern Australia. As a basis for comparison with people living in these communities, we obtained random samples of both Indigenous and Nonindigenous people living in a medium-sized urban center in the region. One of the psychologically relevant scales used in the study was a short form of the Rosenberg Self-Esteem scale, and in this example we will compare how members of the remote communities scores on this scale compare with the scores from the other two samples.

DATA FILE NAME: ESTEEM

The scale itself has a range from 6 to 15, with a higher score indicating higher self-esteem. In this analysis, we have three independent samples: 159 Nonindigenous urbanites, 94 Indigenous urbanites, and 191 Indigenous remote community members. As you can see in Table 7.10, the mean score for the Nonindigenous urbanites is a bit higher than that for the Indigenous urbanites, which in turn is somewhat higher than the mean for the Indigenous remote sample. As the standard errors for the means indicate, the means are rather precise estimates because of the relatively large sample sizes.

TABLE 7.10 Summary statistics for self-esteem data

	Means	N	s_i^2	s_{error}
Nonind. Urban	13.198	159	1.817	0.107
Indig. Urban	12.66	94	1.774	0.137
Indig. Remote	12.257	191	2.117	0.105

Table 7.11 shows how these three samples compare on the Rosenberg scale according to ANOVA. There are three samples, and the total number of people in the entire sample is 444. Our degrees of freedom are

$$df_b = k - 1 = 3 - 1 = 2,$$

and

$$df_w = N - k = 444 - 3 = 441.$$

If we want to form a 99% confidence interval for F, then we need to find the appropriate value for $F_{0.01}$. The nearest we can get to it via Table A.4 is to use the group of rows for $df_w = 400$, which give us $F_{0.01} = 4.6586$. Our resulting confidence interval is

$$\Pr(F(2, 441) < 4.6586) = 0.99.$$

As you can see from Table 7.11 below, our value for $F(2, 441) = 17.414$. This is large enough to lie outside the 99% confidence interval, so according to the F-test procedure we may reject the null hypothesis and conclude that there is an effect on self-esteem attributable to differences between the samples.

Having rejected the null hypothesis, the next reasonable step is to ask what the size of effect is. In doing so, we may use R^2 to ascertain how much of the total error in predicting self-esteem scores may be reduced by taking into account which sample the respondents come from. From the ANOVA table, we can see that the total error for the null model is $SS_t = 921.816$. The error for the effects model is $SS_w = 854.344$, and the difference between them is $SS_b = 67.472$. We plug SS_t and SS_b into the formula for R^2:

$$R^2 = \frac{SS_t - SS_w}{SS_t} = \frac{SS_b}{SS_t} = \frac{67.472}{921.964} = 0.073.$$

The value for R^2 indicates that only about 7.3% of the total error in predicting self-esteem scores (as measured by $SS_t = 921.816$) has been reduced by taking into account which sample the respondents come from. So, the effects model is better than the null model, but not by much. This is not a

TABLE 7.11 ANOVA table for self-esteem data

Source	SS	df	s^2	F
Between	67.472	2	33.736	17.414
Within	854.344	441	1.937	
Total	921.816	443		

large effect by many researchers' standards, and the sizeable value of F is clearly due to the large samples in this study. If we put R^2, $N - k$, and $k - 1$ into the conversion formula for F, we can see that the relative size of the study makes a huge contribution to the value of F:

$$F = \frac{R^2}{1 - R^2} \times \frac{N - k}{k - 1} = 0.079 \times 220.5 = 17.414.$$

The reason that this study can detect this relatively small effect is because of its large sample size.

SUMMARY

Assessments of the size of an experimental effect are based on comparing the amount of predictive error in a no-effects (null) model against the amount of error in an effects model.
The **null model** is

$$X = \mu + e,$$

where μ is the mean score of the entire sample. By using this model to predict scores, the amount of error we accumulate is called the **total sum of squares, SS_t**:

$$SS_t = \Sigma(X - \bar{X})^2.$$

If the experimental conditions have effects, however, then the null model is inadequate because it does not take into account which condition a score comes from. An alternative **effects model** is

$$X = \mu_i + e,$$

where μ_i is the mean score for the ith experimental condition. Using this model, the amount of error we accumulate is the **sum of squares within conditions, SS_w**:

$$SS_w = \Sigma SS_i = (N_1 - 1)s_1^2 + (N_2 - 1)s_2^2 + \ldots + (N_k - 1)s_k^2.$$

The difference between SS_t and SS_w is SS_b, the **sum of squares between conditions**. That is,

$$SS_t = SS_b + SS_w.$$

The conventional way of measuring how much smaller the SS_w error is than the SS_t error is by taking the difference between them as a proportion of SS_t, i.e., the **proportional reduction in error** (or PRE):

$$R^2 = \frac{SS_t - SS_w}{SS_t} = \frac{SS_b}{SS_t}.$$

A second interpretation for R^2 frequently used in the research literature is to say that it is a **proportion of variance accounted for** by the experimental effects.

Given a value for $F(df_b, df_w)$, we may convert it into R^2 by this formula:

$$R^2 = \frac{df_b F}{df_w + df_b F}$$

Likewise, we may decompose the F-statistic into two components:

$$F = \frac{R^2}{1 - R^2} \times \frac{N - k}{k - 1}$$

with the left-hand component reflecting effect size and the right-hand component reflecting the size of the sample relative to the size of the experiment.

SUMMARY

Questions and exercises

Q.7.1. A clinical psychologist is concerned that the percentage of her clients successfully completing therapeutic programs last year (56.6%) is lower than the percentage from the year before that (62.9%). She turns to you for statistical advice on this matter. Last year she saw 83 clients, of whom 47 completed. The year before that, she saw 89 clients, of whom 56 completed. She wants to know whether it is possible that this apparent decline in completion rate could be a 'chance fluctuation'. What advice would you give, and why?

Q.7.2. This question concerns the data-file called **Skull**. You should find that it has two variables: *species* and *length*. The latter are measurements of the lengths of skulls, in millimeters, from *Homo erectus* (species 1) and *Neanderthal* (species 2). A physical anthropologist wants to use these data to assess an hypothesis that says the difference in mean skull lengths between these two species should be between 5 and 10 mm. Is this hypothesis plausible, given her data? What other kinds of hypotheses would be plausible?

Q.7.3. Use **ANOVAPatch** to practice completing an ANOVA table, by choosing the appropriate type of problem.

Q.7.4. You may use **ANOVAPatch** (the exploration option) to address the following problem. Alternatively, you may use a spreadsheet or a statistics package.

A neuropsychologist has run two identical learning experiments involving 15 monkeys randomly assigned to one of three learning methods (A, B, and C). The number of correct choices by each animal out of 20 trials is the experimental variable. The first experiment's data are shown below. Using a 95% confidence level, can the experimenter rule out the null hypothesis that there is no difference among the three methods?

Method A	Method B	Method C
1	7	15
1	15	8
7	1	13
13	8	13
13	9	6

The second experiment's data are shown in the next table. Using a 95% confidence level, can the experimenter rule out the null hypothesis for this experiment? How would you explain the difference in conclusions between the first and second experiments?

Method A	Method B	Method C
6	7	8
7	8	6
7	8	15
7	8	13
8	9	13

Q.7.5. Suppose you want to construct confidence intervals for all possible mean differences in an experiment that has four experimental conditions, and you would like a family-wise confidence level of 99%. What confidence level would you need for each interval?

Q.7.6. A therapist working with alcoholic patients decides to test two treatments for alcoholism: a drug that induces illness when alcohol is consumed, and a behaviour modification approach. She randomly assigns her 24 volunteers from her clinic to three groups, one of which receives no therapy during the period of the experiment. Her dependent measure is alcohol consumption in terms of standard drink equivalents per day over a one-week period. The data are in a file called **Drink**. For the treatment variable,

1 = No therapy
2 = Drug treatment
3 = Behaviour modification

(a) Test the hypothesis that there is a difference in the consumption levels of the three groups, using a confidence level of 95% for the F-statistic.

(b) Which is the most effective treatment, and how do you know?

(c) What is the size of the treatment effect on alcohol consumption?

Q.7.7. Imagine that you are reading about an experiment comparing four treatments for post-trauma stress, and the research report claims to have found a statistically significant difference among the effectiveness of the four treatments at three weeks post-trauma. As a clinician with a professional interest in post-trauma stress management, this claim piques your interest. However, the report simply reports that '$F(3, 213) = 4.32$, $p < 0.05$,' without offering any further relevant information about the differences among these treatments. What can you deduce about the size of the experimental effect here? You may wish to use **dem72** to help you with this.

Quantitative Predictors: Regression and Correlation

8

CONTENTS

Predicting a quantitative variable with a quantitative predictor

Toward the end of Chapter 7, we considered ANOVA from the standpoint of a prediction model. The variable being predicted was always a quantitative variable (such as scores on the Hanzi test), and the predictor was a categorical variable, such as the experimental condition to which the participant had been assigned. While ANOVA is a reasonable technique for assessing how well a categorical variable predicts a quantitative one, using a quantitative variable as a predictor requires a somewhat different approach.

In this chapter, we will apply our predictive model approach to the problem of how to predict one quantitative variable from another. We will also use the squared correlation, R^2, to describe the strength and accuracy of the predictive relationship between two quantitative variables. When prediction is the main goal of a study, this kind of analysis is usually referred to as a **regression**

analysis. A **regression model** is a description of a predictive relationship DEFINITIONS
between two quantitative variables. When the emphasis is on strength of
relationship between the variables, then it is often called a **correlation**
analysis.

Let us begin with an example in an experimental setting, where prediction is
the main goal. Dr. Chris Burt, a cognitive psychologist at the University of
Canterbury in New Zealand, conducted a study in which each participant was
given a sum of money in payment for participation. As the participants left the
experimental room, each was asked to donate to a charity. Although they were
not aware of it at the time, this was part of the study. The amount of money
they were given was randomly determined, and Dr. Burt was interested in
whether that amount would predict how much they were willing to donate.

We will start with a somewhat simplified version of this experiment. DATA
Imagine that each of the 36 participants in the study has been randomly FILENAME
allocated one of six amounts of money, as shown in 'Given' columns in DONDAT
Table 8.1. The amounts they then donated to the charity are listed in the
'Gave' columns. Both amounts are in cents.

You can probably see that participants who were given larger amounts gave
more. Nevertheless, a graphical display of these two variables in a 'scatterplot'
is indispensable for understanding the relationship between them. In a **scat-** DEFINITION
terplot, the scale for the *predictor* variable (in this case, 'Given') is represented
on a *horizontal* axis and the scale for the *predicted* variable ('Gave') is represented on a *vertical* axis. Each pair of values for the two variables is represented
by a dot, whose location is appropriately determined using each axis. The
scatterplot in Figure 8.1 shows that the amount given by participants increases
in a regular fashion as a function of the amount they were given.

The relationship between Gave and Given is **positive**, since an increase in DEFINITIONS
the value of one variable predicts an increase in the other. A **negative** relationship is one in which an increase in the value of one variable predicts a
decrease in the other. We will see an example of a negative relationship later
on. It also looks as if it would be well-described by a straight line running

TABLE 8.1 Data from simplified version of donation study

| Group 1 | | Group 2 | | Group 3 | | Group 4 | | Group 5 | | Group 6 | |
Given	Gave	Given	Gave	Given	Gave	Given	Gave	Given	Gave	Given	Gave
124	49	317	106	463	204	608	257	741	301	902	350
124	56	317	149	463	209	608	264	741	315	902	354
124	64	317	168	463	214	608	262	741	318	902	359
124	74	317	180	463	228	608	286	741	321	902	362
124	91	317	189	463	252	608	280	741	330	902	366
124	100	317	192	463	253	608	296	741	344	902	370

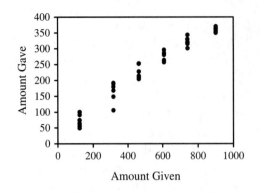

FIGURE 8.1 Scatterplot of amounts Given vs. Gave

DEFINITIONS through the groups of points. A relationship between two quantitative variables that can be represented by a straight line is called a **linear relationship**.

A linear relationship may also be represented by a linear equation. In regression, the predicted variable is conventionally denoted by Y and the predictor variable by X. A linear equation that represents the prediction of the value of Y from the value of X has the form

$$Y' = a + bX.$$

This equation is usually said to represent a linear regression **model**, in the sense that it is a model of how Y is predicted by X. The '$'$' sign after Y denotes that this is a predicted value of Y and not actual data. The reason for this notation is so that we may compare predicted values (Y') with observed ones (Y) in assessing how good the regression model is.

The values of a and b are determined so as to minimize the predictive error of the resulting regression model in a special way. For any regression model, we may assess how far off each observed value of Y is from the value that is predicted by the model by taking the difference between them:

$$Y - Y' = Y - (a + bX).$$

DEFINITION   This difference is known as a **residual** in regression terminology. For example, suppose our model is $Y' = 50 + 0.25X$. When participants are given 124 cents, so $X = 124$, our model's predicted value of Y is

$$Y' = 50 + 0.25(124) = 50 + 31 = 81 \text{ cents.}$$

The first participant listed in the table above gave only 49 cents, so the residual (i.e., the error in prediction) for that participant would be

$$Y - Y' = 49 - 81 = -32.$$

In evaluating a model of this kind, we square these residuals and add them up. Regression finds the values of a and b that *minimize the sum of the squared residuals* in the model, as measured by

$$SS_e = \Sigma(Y - Y')^2.$$

For this reason, it is often referred to as **least-squares** regression.   DEFINITION

The least-squares regression model for the Donation data turns out to be the equation

$$Y' = 41.4 + 0.371X.$$

Let us take a moment to understand a bit about what these numbers mean. The value of the first parameter, $a = 41.4$, may be understood in two ways. First, it is the value predicted for Y when X is 0. The parameter a is often called the **intercept**, because it indicates where the regression line will inter- DEFINITION cept the Y axis when $X = 0$. According to our model, if someone was given no payment at all for participating in the study, they would nevertheless donate 41.4 cents in response to the charity request. In some situations this kind of prediction makes sense because X could have a value of 0 (for instance, it is possible for a participant to be given no payment). In other settings, however, it might not be possible or meaningful for X to be 0 and in that case this interpretation of a is not helpful.

There is another interpretation that almost always makes sense, however. It relies on the fact that *the regression line always passes through the mean of X and the mean of Y*. The reason for this is that both means and regression lines minimize squared errors, so the only possible value of Y that can be predicted by a regression model for the mean of X is the mean of Y. As a result, if we know what b is, then a can be found by this formula: FORMULA

FOR

$$a = \bar{Y} - b\bar{X}.$$

INTERCEPT

Since the regression line always pivots around the mean of X and the mean of Y, the parameter a tells us something about where this 'pivot' is located. In our example, the mean of X, the amount given to participants, was 525.833 cents; while the mean of Y, the amount donated, was 236.472 cents. We already know that $b = 0.371$, so we may plug these numbers into the formula above to get

$$a = 236.472 - (0.371)(525.833) = 41.4.$$

Now let us find out more about b. Perhaps the most important thing about b
DEFINITION   is that it is the 'slope' of the regression line. The **slope** of the line is the amount
of change in Y that we can expect from each unit of increase in X. Figure 8.2
provides a diagrammatic illustration of this interpretation. In our example,
$b = 0.371$ tells us that for every additional cent given to a participant (an
increase of one unit in X), we should expect an increase by 0.371 cents in the
donation made by the participant (the amount of increase in Y). The larger b is,
the steeper the slope.

The formula for b involves two quantities. You are already familiar with one
of them, namely the sum of squares for X:

$$SS_X = \Sigma(X - \bar{X})^2.$$

DEFINITION   The other quantity is called the **sum of the products** (or sometimes the sum
of the 'cross-products'), and is the sum of the difference between each participant's X score and the mean of X multiplied by the difference between the
participant's Y score and the mean of Y. Its formula is:

$$SS_{XY} = \Sigma(X - \bar{X})(Y - \bar{Y}).$$

Each of the terms in SS_{XY} indicates how far away from the mean of X and the
mean of Y each participant is, and it is this term that determines whether the
slope of the line is going to be positive or negative. If a participant who is
above the mean of X is also above the mean of Y, or if a participant who is
below the mean of X also is below the mean of Y, then that participant's
product term will make a positive contribution to SS_{XY}. On the other hand,
if every time a participant is above the mean of X they are below the mean of
Y, and vice versa, then the products will make a negative contribution to
SS_{XY}. The first participant, for instance, in our data set was given 124

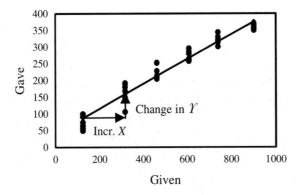

FIGURE 8.2 Regression line: $Y' = 41.4 + 0.371X$

cents. The mean amount given to participants was 525.833 cents, so the difference between X and the mean of X for this participant is

$$X - \bar{X} = 124 - 525.833 = -401.833.$$

Likewise, this participant gave 49 cents. The mean donation was 236.472 cents, so for this participant

$$Y - \bar{Y} = 49 - 236.472 = -187.472.$$

The product term for this participant is therefore

$$(X - \bar{X})(Y - \bar{Y}) = (-401.833)(-187.472) = 75,332.586.$$

The sum of all these products is $\text{SS}_{XY} = 897,775.833$.

The slope, finally, is the ratio of SS_{XY} to SS_X :

FORMULA
FOR SLOPE

$$b = \text{SS}_{XY}/\text{SS}_X.$$

In our example, $\text{SS}_X = 2,421,473$, so

$$b = \frac{\text{SS}_{XY}}{\text{SS}_X} = \frac{897,775.833}{2,421,473} = 0.371.$$

Now we are in a position to find out what the regression model predicts Y will be for each of the six different values of X used in the experiment. Table 8.2 below displays the predicted donations (Y') that correspond to each amount given to the participants (X), according to our regression model

$$Y' = 41.4 + 0.371X.$$

For instance, if a participant is given 463 cents, then the amount that participant is predicted to donate is

$$Y' = 41.4 + 0.371(463) = 213.2.$$

TABLE 8.2 Predicted donations from regression model

Group 1		Group 2		Group 3		Group 4		Group 5		Group 6	
Given X	Pred. Y'	Given X	Pred. Y'	Given X	Pred. Y'	Given X	Pred. Y'	Given X	Pred. Y'	Given X	Pred. Y'
124	87.5	317	159.1	463	213.2	608	267.1	741	316.4	902	376.2

Linear regression models involve four requirements:

1. Both variables have interval-level scales.
2. The best description of the relationship between the variables is a linear relationship.
3. Both variables have normal distributions.
4. Homogeneity of variance.

The first requirement merely says that we need an appropriate level of measurement in order for regression to make any sense, given that a regression model requires both variables to be quantitative.

The second requirement reminds us that the regression model we have investigated here is only a *linear* model. There are many other kinds (e.g., curvilinear ones), and researchers should always examine a scatterplot of X and Y before deciding to proceed with a linear regression. Here is an example to illustrate this point. Gerrity, Earp & DeVellis (1992) asked physicians to rate their degree of agreement (or disagreement) with 61 items about their attitudes towards uncertainty in their own medical practice. Figure 8.3 shows the item means plotted against the item dispersions (as measured by their variances). You can see that the items with high means (strong agreement with the item) or low means (strong disagreement with the item) have the lowest dispersion values. The items in the middle have the largest dispersion

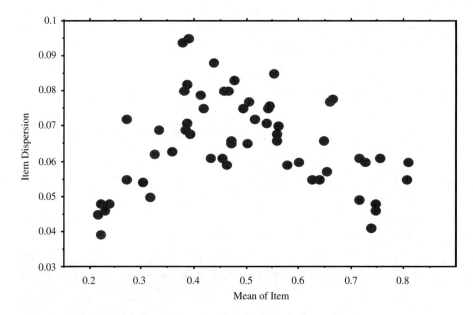

FIGURE 8.3 Means and dispersions for Gerrity's scale items

values. We would use a type of *curvilinear regression* to model this trend rather than linear regression.

The third and fourth requirements for linear regression are very similar to the assumptions for ANOVA. The normal distribution requirement stipulates that the distributions of X and Y are normal, and that for any value of X the distribution of Y values is normal as well. Homogeneity of variance in regression has much the same meaning as it does in ANOVA, but in regression it amounts to saying that the variance of Y is the same throughout the range of X. A schematic illustration of these two requirements in the setting of our example is shown in Figure 8.4. The six identical normal distribution curves represent the distribution of the donation values (Y) for each of the six amounts given to participants (X).

If you inspect the original scatterplot and compare it with Figure 8.4, you should find that the real data look as if they approximately satisfy the homogeneity of variance requirement. There are statistical tests for homogeneity of variance, but they are beyond the scope of this introductory textbook. However, you can often spot any serious violation of this requirement simply by examining a scatterplot. Figure 8.5 shows the scatterplot for a fictitious data set in which participants' donations varied more widely the more they were given. You can see that homogeneity of variance has been violated here because the data 'fan out' as X increases.

Let us introduce another example before proceeding any further. This time, we will examine a nonexperimental study. The data are from a study reported in a *Scientific American* article by Nathan Keyfitz (1989), entitled 'The growing human population.' He presents data from 58 developing countries, and among other things records their annual birthrate and the estimated percentage of adults using contraception. The main goal here is prediction, namely predicting national birthrates from contraceptive usage rates.

DATA FILENAME CON-TRACEP

A scatterplot of the data is shown in Figure 8.6, along with the linear regression line. Each point in this graph represents a country, and clearly

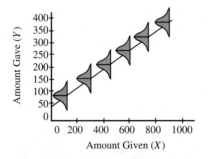

FIGURE 8.4 Normality and homogeneity of variance for regression example

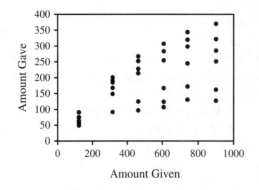

FIGURE 8.5 Hypothetical example of heterogeneity of variance

the higher the percentage of contraceptive use (X) for a country, the lower its birthrate (Y). X and Y are *negatively* related. The regression model is

$$Y' = a + bX = 49.936 - 0.401X,$$

and the negative value for b (-0.401) reflects the negative relationship between X and Y.

Inspection of the scatterplot should satisfy you that the relationship between these two variables is well-represented as a linear relationship, and that there does not appear to be any gross violation of the homogeneity of variance requirement. There are at least three other pertinent questions that any researcher should ask of a regression model:

1. Does the model predict beyond the range of the data? In other words, does it predict 'silly' or impossible values for Y?

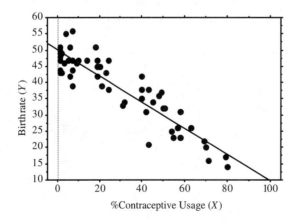

FIGURE 8.6 Countries' birthrates and contraceptive usage rates

2. Is it based on a truncated range of values for either X or Y?

3. Over what range of X can we trust this model?

For the first question, our best tests are the most extreme values possible for X, the contraceptive usage rate, which are 0% and 100%. For 0%, the model predicts a birthrate of:

$$Y' = 49.936 - 0.401(0) = 49.936.$$

For 100%, the model predicts

$$Y' = 49.936 - 0.401(100) = 8.936.$$

Neither of these are impossible or 'silly' values for birthrates, so the model performs reasonably well on this criterion.

As for the second and third questions, the range over which we may trust this model is somewhat limited, because there are no countries included in the sample with a contraception usage rate higher than about 80%, so predictions of birthrates for contraception usage rates beyond 80% should be treated cautiously. There is much more to evaluating regression models than these three criteria, and we will take up that topic in the next section.

A **regression model** is a description of a predictive relationship between two quantitative variables. When prediction is the main goal of a study, this kind of analysis is usually referred to as a **regression** analysis. When the emphasis is on strength of relationship between the variables, then it is often called a **correlation** analysis.

In a **scatterplot**, the scale for the *predictor* variable (X) is represented on a *horizontal* axis and the scale for the *predicted* variable (Y) is represented on a *vertical* axis. Each pair of values for X and Y is represented by a dot, whose location is appropriately determined using each axis.

A relationship between two quantitative variables that can be represented by a straight line is called a **linear relationship**. A linear equation that represents the prediction of the value of Y from the value of X has the form

$$Y' = a + bX.$$

The parameter a is often called the **intercept**, because it indicates where the regression line will intercept the Y axis when $X = 0$.

The parameter b is is the **slope** of the regression line, and it is the amount of change in Y that we can expect from each unit of increase in X.

If b is positive then the relationship between X and Y is **positive**, since an increase in the value of X predicts an increase in Y. If b is negative then the relationship between X and Y is **negative**, whereby an increase in the value of X predicts a decrease in Y.

SUMMARY

StatPatch

REGRESS-
PATCH
PROVIDES
PRACTICE
WITH COM-
PUTATIONS
INVOLVED IN
REGRESSION

SUMMARY

The formula for b is

$$b = \mathrm{SS}_{XY}/\mathrm{SS}_X,$$

where SS_X is the sum of squares for X:

$$\mathrm{SS}_X = \Sigma(X - \bar{X})^2,$$

and SS_{XY} is the **sum of the products** (or sometimes the sum of the 'cross-products'):

$$\mathrm{SS}_{XY} = \Sigma(X - \bar{X})(Y - \bar{Y}).$$

The regression line always passes through the mean of X and the mean of Y. If we know what b is, then a can be found by this formula:

$$a = \bar{Y} - b\bar{X}.$$

Regression finds the values of a and b that *minimize the sum of the squared residuals* in the model, as measured by

$$\mathrm{SS}_e = \Sigma(Y - Y')^2.$$

For this reason, it is often referred to as **least-squares** regression.

Linear regression models involve four requirements:

1. Both variables have interval-level scales.
2. The best description of the relationship between the variables is a linear relationship.
3. Both variables have normal distributions.
4. Homogeneity of variance.

Evaluating linear regression models

Besides ascertaining that the four requirements have been met, and that the regression model gives sensible predictions over whatever range of X is relevant, researchers usually also ask how precise the regression model is and how strongly related X and Y are. These two evaluative criteria are connected so we will pursue both of them in this section, starting with the issue of measuring the strength of the relationship between X and Y.

In the last section, it was claimed that regression minimizes the squared error in the linear regression model. This squared error is measured by

$$\mathrm{SS}_e = \Sigma(Y - Y')^2,$$

which is the sum of the squared residuals (i.e., the squared differences $Y - Y'$). In ANOVA, we compared the squared errors for an *effects model* against the squared errors for a *null model*, and we may do exactly the same thing here.

If we did not use anything to predict Y, then the value that would minimize the squared error in predicting Y would be just its mean. So our **null model** DEFINITION for predicting Y is

$$Y' = \mu_Y + e,$$

where μ_Y is the population mean of Y and e is sampling error.

The estimated total squared error for the null model is just the sum of the squares for Y:

$$SS_Y = \Sigma(Y - \bar{Y})^2.$$

The effects model in regression is just the linear regression model, since it presumes that X effectively predicts Y. Now, we may express the effects model in a way that is directly comparable with the null model. First, we add an 'e' term to represent sampling error, so our regression model is

$$Y' = a + bX + e.$$

We already know that the regression line passes through the mean of X and the mean of Y, so in terms of their population means we may say

$$a = \mu_Y - b\mu_X.$$

Substituting the right-hand expression for a in our regression model, we get an **effects model** of the form DEFINITION

$$Y' = \mu_Y - b\mu_X + bX + e = \mu_Y + b(X - \mu_X) + e.$$

Notice that this model includes the terms in the null model (i.e., $\mu_Y + e$) plus the additional term $b(X - \mu_X)$, which represents the effect of X. The effects model is more *complex* than the null model.

The estimated total squared error for the effects model is SS_e. If X does not help us predict Y, then SS_e should be as big as SS_Y. Otherwise, SS_e should be smaller. We may measure how much smaller SS_e is than SS_Y by doing the same with them as we did with SS_w and SS_t in ANOVA. That is, we may use them to construct a proportional reduction of error measure, R^2:

$$R^2 = \frac{SS_Y - SS_e}{SS_Y}$$

DEFINITION   In regression, R^2 is known as the **squared correlation coefficient**, or sometimes the 'coefficient of determination.' Its interpretations are the same as R^2 in ANOVA. Thus, we may think of R^2 as the proportion of SS_Y that has been reduced by using X to predict Y. We may also think of R^2 as measuring the proportion of variance in Y accounted for by X via the linear regression model.

In our first example (the donation study), it turns out that the sum of squares for Y is

$$SS_Y = \Sigma(Y - \bar{Y})^2 = 349,563.$$

The sum of the squared residuals is

$$SS_e = \Sigma(Y - Y')^2 = 16,707.13.$$

Plugging these numbers into the formula for R^2, we get

$$R^2 = \frac{SS_Y - SS_e}{SS_Y} = \frac{349,563 - 16,707.13}{349,563} = \frac{332,855.87}{349,563} = 0.952.$$

So, we may say that about 95.2% of the variance in Y (the amounts donated by subjects) has been accounted for by X (the amounts they were given). That is nearly all of the variance, so this is a very good predictive model.

In our second example (the birthrate study), the sum of squares for Y is

$$SS_Y = \Sigma(Y - \bar{Y})^2 = 6568.28.$$

The sum of the squared residuals is

$$SS_e = \Sigma(Y - Y')^2 = 1045.86.$$

Plugging these numbers into the formula for R^2, we get

$$R^2 = \frac{SS_Y - SS_e}{SS_Y} = \frac{6568.28 - 1045.86}{6568.28} = \frac{5522.41}{6568.28} = 0.841.$$

So, we may say that about 84.1% of the variance in Y (the birthrates of the countries) has been accounted for by X (their contraceptive usage rates). That is also quite high by social science standards.

Given that we have SS_e and SS_γ playing the same roles in R^2 for regression as SS_w and SS_t did in ANOVA, it should come as no surprise that regression has a version of SS_b as well. We will denote it by $\mathbf{SS_r}$, and it is defined as the DEFINITION sum of the squared differences between the predicted values of Y and the mean of Y:

$$SS_r = \Sigma(Y' - \bar{Y})^2.$$

SS_r measures the amount of variation in Y about the mean that is predicted by the regression model, and so the 'r' subscript is an abbreviation of 'regression'. As is the case for ANOVA, in regression we have

$$SS_\gamma = SS_r + SS_e.$$

Unless X is an error-free predictor of Y, SS_r will always be less than SS_γ. One important implication of this fact is that regression models *underestimate* the true variance of Y. Indeed, they do this in a systematic way, namely by underestimating extreme deviations away from the mean of Y. To understand how this occurs, we will examine a scatterplot of the residuals against the observed values for birthrate. Notice in the scatterplot of Figure 8.7 that there is a slight *positive relationship* between the residual and birthrate. The positive residuals occur mainly for higher birthrates and most of the negative residuals occur for lower birthrates.

What does this mean? It means that for countries with high birthrates, the predicted birthrate tends to be *lower* than the actual value, while for countries with low birthrates, the predicted birthrate tends to be *higher* than the actual value. In other words, the regression model underestimates how far the extreme values of birthrate are away from the mean. This is generally the

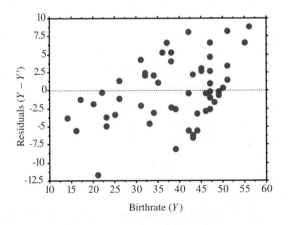

FIGURE 8.7 Birthrates versus residuals

case with any linear model that fits the data imperfectly. It arises directly from the fact that the independent and dependent variables are less than perfectly related, and that regression automatically minimizes the squared deviations from the regression line.

DEFINITION   Another important and counter-intuitive consequence of all this is called **regression to the mean**. This is the tendency for scores that are at the extremes of a distribution on one occasion to fall back towards the mean of the distribution on the next occasion. The reason for this is simple. If measurement on the two occasions is not perfectly reliable, then the scores on the first occasion do not perfectly predict the scores on the second. Thus, some scores are extremely high (or low) on the first occasion partly because of *chance*. That means that on the next occasion some of them are likely to no longer be at the extremes, whereas some other people who scored close to the mean on the first occasion may be at the extremes on the second.

Intuitively, however, we tend to overlook this phenomenon in many settings. Consider instructors or anyone else who rewards good performance and punishes poor performance. They will observe that the highest performers on one occasion generally do not do as well on the second (despite having been rewarded) whereas the poorest performers generally do not do as badly on the second occasion (which the instructor may erroneously attribute to their having been punished). The upshot is that punishment appears to be more effective than reward.

Moreover, samples selected on the basis of their extremity can mislead researchers into thinking that a treatment or intervention has had an effect. People selected because of their extreme scores on a depression scale will score as less depressed when measured on a second occasion, but that may be because of regression to the mean rather than the impact of any treatment or intervention. Likewise, children designated as 'gifted' on the basis of their high scores on an IQ test will be likely to appear less 'gifted' as a group when retested.

The extent of regression to the mean is directly related to how much a regression model underestimates the true variance in Y, which is measured by how much smaller SS_r is than SS_Y. Since $R^2 = SS_r/SS_Y$, $1 - R^2$ is an indication of how severe regression to the mean will be.

Now that we have seen R^2 in action as an effect measure for both ANOVA and regression, it would seem justifiable to ask how big R^2 should be before we would regard it as important. One popular (but misconceived and unsatisfactory) answer to this question is to perform a significance test on R^2 using a null hypothesis that it is 0. We will briefly examine this test, which is identical to the F-test associated with R^2 in ANOVA.

Most computer statistical packages report an **F-test** associated with R^2. It amounts to a test of whether R^2 differs from 0, so it is quite frequently used to assess whether X is a 'significant' predictor of Y. The F-test for the donation study example is shown in Table 8.3, as it would be reported by a statistical package such as SPSS.

The SS entries are SS_r (Regression), SS_e (Residual), and SS_Y (Total). There is always one degree of freedom associated with the predictor X and therefore with SS_r, while SS_e has df $= N - 2$, where N is the sample size. The reasons for this will be explained a bit more in the next section, but for now suffice it to say that SS_r is the estimate of the variance in Y about the mean that is predicted by the regression model, and it is being compared with an estimate of the variance in Y about the regression line based on SS_e, the sum of the squared deviations away from that line. The procedure for this F-test is almost exactly the same as in ANOVA. The only specific difference here is that the df associated with the numerator is 1, and the df associated with the denominator is $N - 2$.

As we saw in the self-esteem study at the end of Chapter 7, however, a large sample size can result in a small R^2 being found to differ significantly from 0. As in any statistical technique, 'statistical significance' does not tell us anything much about theoretical, practical, or other kinds of significance. Of course, how large a value of R^2 is considered to be 'small' or 'large' will depend to some extent on the values of R^2 that researchers are accustomed to finding in their studies, and so standards will vary considerably from one field to another.

Cohen (1988: 79–81) once again has provided benchmarks for R^2 that are based primarily on the magnitudes of squared correlations that his reviews found in the so-called 'softer' areas in psychology (his examples include clinical, personality and social psychology):

- Small: $R^2 = 0.01$,
- Medium: $R^2 = 0.09$,
- Large: $R^2 = 0.25$.

However, these proposals have not met with anything like universal acceptance, even in the areas nominated by Cohen.

Judgments of how important or 'strong' a value of R^2 is are bound to be influenced by research contexts and researchers' purposes and values; and they

TABLE 8.3 ANOVA table for donation study regression

Source	SS	df	MS	F
Regression	332,855.87	1	332,855.87	677.382
Residual	16,707.13	34	491.386	
Total	349,563	35		

are likely to be controversial in any unsettled research area. Some of the bitterest debates in psychology (for instance, in the field of intelligence testing) have hinged on disagreements about whether certain R^2 values were 'big enough.' In a recent exchange over whether empirical evidence supports the claim that cultural factors are important influences on risk perceptions, Sjoberg (1997) weighed in with a claim that they are not, basing his argument on the fact that the relevant R^2 values from pertinent studies ranged from only 0.01 to 0.07 (i.e., between 1% and 7% of variance accounted for). By Cohen's standards, these values do indeed fall below a 'medium' effect size. Nevertheless, Slovic & Peters (1998) came back at Sjoberg with a reasoned case for claiming that these R^2 values indicate sizeable effects of theoretical and practical importance.

Indeed, some methodologists have proposed using measures of effect size other than R^2 on the grounds that seemingly small R^2 values may mislead researchers into discounting or ignoring important findings. Rosenthal (1990), for instance, argues that psychologists are doing themselves a disservice by relying on R^2 as a measure of effect size. He produces examples of effects that were of great importance despite being 'smallish' even by Cohen's standards. One of his more intriguing examples is the finding of a reduction in deaths of AIDS patients by the administration of AZT from 61.5% to 38.5%, sufficient to lead to the termination of the clinical trial on the grounds that it would be unethical to withhold the drug from patients in the control group. Yet, the R^2 value for this study was only 0.05!

SUMMARY

Regression may be seen in terms of comparing a null model against an effects model.

The **null model** for predicting Y is

$$Y' = \mu_Y + e,$$

where μ_Y is the population mean of Y and e is sampling error.

The **effects model** is

$$Y' = \mu_Y + b(X - \mu_X) + e.$$

The error rates for these two models are SS_Y and SS_e, respectively.

These error rates are compared via the **squared correlation coefficient**, R^2, whose formula is

$$R^2 = \frac{SS_Y - SS_e}{SS_Y}$$

SS$_r$ measures the amount of variation in Y about the mean that is predicted by the regression model:

$$SS_r = \Sigma(Y' - \bar{Y})^2.$$

It is related to SS_e and SS_Y in the following way: SUMMARY

$$SS_Y = SS_r + SS_e.$$

Whenever X is an imperfect predictor of Y, SS_r will always be less than SS_Y. One implication of this fact is that regression models *underestimate* the true variance of Y. A consequence of this implication is called **regression to the mean**, the tendency for scores that are at the extremes of a distribution on one occasion to fall back towards the mean of the distribution on the next occasion.

There is an ***F*-test** associated with R^2, ordinarily used to test whether R^2 differs from 0. Procedurally, it is identical to the F-test for ANOVA.

Assessing the accuracy of prediction

One popular alternative approach to evaluating regression models involves focusing on how accurately the model predicts Y. Although the statistics used to measure predictive error (or accuracy) are closely related to the components of R^2, they are worthy of attention in their own right. Because SS_e measures the amount of variation in Y away from Y', it is used as the basis for an estimate of the variance in Y around the regression line, known as the **squared standard error of the estimate**. The squared standard error of   DEFINITION the estimate is usually denoted by $s^2_{Y|X}$ (where $s_{Y|X}$ is read as the 'standard deviation of Y given X'), and its formula is

$$s^2_{Y|X} = SS_e/(N-2).$$

where N is the size of the sample. Many computer statistical packages report the standard error of the estimate or its squared counterpart. It is this variance that is compared with SS_r in the F-test outlined in the previous section. Sometimes researchers compare $s^2_{Y|X}$ with s^2_Y as a way of indicating how much the variability in Y is reduced by using X as a predictor, although this comparison provides very similar information to that conveyed by R^2.

The main role played by $s^2_{Y|X}$, however, is as a component in the *confidence interval around the regression slope*, b. As it is beyond the scope of this textbook to derive the sampling distribution for b, we will just state it. It has a t-distribution, which is well approximated by the normal distribution when the sample size is large. The **standard error for b** is   DEFINITION

$$s_{\text{err}b} = \sqrt{\frac{s^2_{Y|X}}{SS_X}}$$

The df associated with this standard error are $N - 2$, and the half-width of the confidence interval is

$$w = t_{\alpha/2} s_{errb}.$$

DEFINITION   The resulting **confidence interval for b** is of a kind that should look familiar to you by now, and may be expressed as

$$CI_{1-\alpha} = b \pm w$$

or alternatively

$$CI_{1-\alpha} = [b - w, b + w].$$

This confidence interval becomes narrower (more precise) as $s^2_{Y|X}$ becomes small, or in other words as X becomes a better predictor of Y.

Returning to the donation study example, suppose we wish to construct a 95% confidence interval for $b = 0.371$. First, we need to find the components for the standard error for b, s_{errb}. We have

$$s^2_{Y|X} = SS_e/(N - 2) = 16{,}707.13/34 = 491.386,$$

and

$$SS_X = 2{,}421{,}473.$$

We plug the values of $s^2_{Y|X}$ and SS_X into the formula for s_{errb}:

$$s_{errb} = \sqrt{\frac{s^2_{Y|X}}{SS_X}} = \sqrt{\frac{491.386}{2{,}421{,}473}} = 0.014.$$

Now we need to find $t_{\alpha/2}$. Since $df = N - 2 = 36 - 2 = 34$, the nearest approximation we can get from Table A.3 is for $df = 35$, for which $t_{0.025} = 2.0301$. So,

$$w = t_{\alpha/2} s_{errb} = (2.0301)(0.014) = 0.028,$$

and our 95% confidence interval is

$$CI_{0.95} = b \pm w = 0.371 \pm 0.028,$$

or alternatively

$$CI_{0.95} = [b - w, b + w] = [0.343, 0.399].$$

This confidence interval is quite precise because X is a very good predictor of Y, as we have already seen.

Let us try this once more, using the birthrate example. Suppose we wish to construct a 99% confidence interval for $b = -0.401$. First, we need to find the components for the standard error for b, s_{errb}. We have

$$s^2_{Y|X} = SS_e/(N-2) = 1045.86/56 = 18.676,$$

and the sum of squares for X is

$$SS_X = 34{,}260.91.$$

We plug the values of $s^2_{Y|X}$ and SS_X into the formula for s_{errb}:

$$s_{errb} = \sqrt{\frac{s^2_{Y|X}}{SS_X}} = \sqrt{\frac{16.676}{34{,}260.91}} = 0.023.$$

Now we need to find $t_{\alpha/2}$. The df $= N - 2 = 58 - 2 = 56$, so the nearest approximation we can get from Table A.3 is for df $= 50$, for which $t_{0.025} = 2.6778$. So,

$$w = t_{\alpha/2}s_{errb} = (2.6778)(0.023) = 0.062,$$

and our 99% confidence interval is

$$CI_{0.99} = b \pm w = -0.401 \pm 0.062,$$

or alternatively

$$CI_{0.99} = [b - w, b + w] = [-0.463, -0.339].$$

The fact that b has a t-distribution (approximated by the normal distribution when the sample size is large) not only enables researchers to construct confidence intervals for b, but also permits them to use all of the statistical techniques that we learned about in Chapter 7 for comparing means from independent samples. An exposition of the use of the t-test and ANOVA for comparing regression slopes from independent samples is beyond the scope of this textbook, but I mention it here because these techniques are pertinent for quite a few commonly encountered research problems in psychology. In fact, they are a component of an elaborated version of ANOVA known as the 'analysis of covariance' (or ANCOVA).

Imagine, for instance, that Dr. Burt extended his donation study into the cross-cultural domain by replicating the experiment with a sample of Japanese subjects. Suppose a linear regression model turned out to describe the relationship between the amount given and amount donated for the Japanese sample. He would want to compare these findings with those from the New Zealand sample. Did subjects in one sample donate more generously than in the other? A crucial part of that comparison would be assessing the difference between the regression slopes. Likewise, Keyfitz might divide the countries in his birthrate study according to cultural regions, and might predict that in some cultures contraceptive usage rate would have a greater impact on birthrates than in others. He could test his prediction by comparing the regression slopes among the regions.

Despite their usefulness, the confidence interval around b has some important limitations. One of them is that it cannot be straightforwardly used to construct a confidence interval around Y'. At first glance, it might seem that since our effects model in regression is

$$Y' = \mu_Y + b(X - \mu_X) + e,$$

putting a confidence interval around b would automatically put one around Y'. A complete explanation of why this is not the case would overly complicate matters for our purposes here, but we can gain an intuitive understanding by contemplating the effects model formula from the standpoint of sample estimations. The sample data are being used not only to estimate b, but also the mean of X and the mean of Y. As a result, Y' has three sources of sampling error rather than just the error involved in estimating b.

Moreover, since b is multiplied by the difference between X and the mean of X, the sampling error for Y' is going to be larger as X gets further from its mean. Therefore, *the confidence interval around Y' becomes wider (less precise) the further X is from its mean.* The greatest precision affordable in predicting Y occurs at the mean of X (and therefore the mean of Y). Earlier, we observed that using a regression model to predict beyond the range of its data is unwise. Here, we are adding to this admonition by pointing out that predictions out towards the extremes of the data range are less precise (and therefore shakier) than predictions where the bulk of the data lie. For example, a 99% confidence interval around birthrate predictions for Keyfitz' data results in a halfwidth for the interval of about 12.1 for countries with high contraceptive usage rates versus 11.6 for those with contraceptive rates near the mean.

Demos

TRY

EXPLORING

THIS

CONCEPT

USING

DEM82

SUMMARY

> The **squared standard error of the estimate** is denoted by $s^2_{Y|X}$ (where $s_{Y|X}$ is read as the 'standard deviation of Y given X'), and its formula is
>
> $$s^2_{Y|X} = SS_e/(N - 2).$$

The main role played by $s^2_{Y|X}$ is as a component in the *confidence interval around*   SUMMARY
the regression slope, b.

The sampling distribution for b is a t-distribution (approximated by the normal distribution when the sample size is large). The **standard error for b** is

$$s_{errb} = \sqrt{\frac{s^2_{Y|X}}{SS_X}}$$

The df associated with this standard error are $N - 2$, and the half-width of the confidence interval is

$$w = t_{\alpha/2} s_{errb}.$$

The resulting **confidence interval for b** may be expressed as

$$CI_{1-\alpha} = b \pm w$$

or alternatively

$$CI_{1-\alpha} = [b - w, b + w].$$

The fact that b has a t-distribution permits researchers to use the statistical techniques in Chapter 7 (i.e., the t-test and ANOVA) for comparing regression slopes from independent samples.

The *confidence interval around* Y' is based on the confidence interval for b but becomes wider (less precise) the further X is from its mean.

More about the correlation coefficient

We have already seen that the squared correlation coefficient, R^2, plays an important role in evaluating effects models in both ANOVA and linear regression. At the beginning of this chapter the remark was made that when *prediction* is the main goal of a study, researchers refer to **regression** analysis, but when the emphasis is on *strength of relationship* between the variables, then it is often called a **correlation** analysis. In a correlation analysis, the interpretation of R^2 as the proportion of variance in Y accounted for by X is employed in somewhat modified form. Researchers say that R^2 *measures the proportion of*   DEFINITION
variance shared between X and Y. R^2 may therefore be used as a measure of the magnitude or strength of the *linear relationship* between X and Y.

It is crucial to bear in mind always that R^2 *pertains only to a linear relationship* and that all of the requirements for linear regression apply to the use of R^2 as well. All too often you will find published research articles in which writers conclude that a low value of R^2 implies that two variables are not related in any way whatsoever, but this is a gross fallacy. The only sensible conclusion based on a low value of R^2 is that X and Y are not *linearly* related to a strong degree.

Moreover, R is not the only kind of correlation coefficient, although it is the most popular among psychologists and social scientists. To distinguish it from other correlation coefficients, R is called the **product-moment correlation** or sometimes **Pearson's correlation** (after the statistician Karl Pearson). We will learn about some other correlation coefficients in Chapter 9.

We already know one formula for R^2, namely

$$R^2 = \frac{SS_Y - SS_e}{SS_Y} = \frac{SS_r}{SS_Y}$$

Other equivalent formulas are often used for R^2 and R. We will briefly examine two of them here, since they cast some light on the relationship between R and the regression slope (b), as well as alerting you to a few related concepts that are frequently referred to in the research literature.

ALTERN-
ATIVE
FORMULA
FOR R

One such formula expresses R in terms of the sum of the products, SS_{XY}:

$$R = \frac{SS_{XY}}{\sqrt{SS_X SS_Y}}$$

and this is the version that reveals something about the relationship between b and R. Earlier in this chapter, we learned that

$$b = SS_{XY}/SS_X.$$

Substituting b for SS_{XY}/SS_X in the formula for R^2, we get

$$R^2 = \frac{SS_{XY} SS_{XY}}{SS_X SS_Y} = b^2 \frac{SS_X}{SS_Y}$$

RELATION-
SHIP
BETWEEN
R AND b

An equivalent version of this relationship that is more commonly used in textbooks and the research literature relates R instead of R^2 to b:

$$R = b \frac{s_X}{s_Y}$$

where s_X is the standard deviation of X and s_Y is the standard deviation of Y. The main reason that this second version is more popular is that standard deviations are more likely to be included in research reports than sums of squares such as SS_Y.

There is also a pedagogical reason for spending time on this formula. If s_X and s_Y are identical then $R = b$. One circumstance under which this will occur is if X and Y have both been converted to standard scores, or z-scores. These were introduced at the end of Chapter 4 as a way of converting any distribution of scores to one that has a mean of 0 and a standard deviation of 1. To convert X to a z-score, for instance, we subtract the mean of X from it and divide the result by s_X. If we denote the z-score for X by z_X and the z-score for Y by z_Y, then the regression equation

$$Y' = a + bX$$

may be rewritten as

$$z_{Y'} = R z_X.$$

The reason why there is no 'a' term in the z-score equation is that the means of z_X and z_Y are both 0 and the regression line always passes through the means (so $a = 0$). Since z_X and z_Y may also be thought of in terms of standard deviation units, in this version of the regression equation R *tells us how many standard deviation units' change in Y would be predicted for one standard deviation unit increase in X.*

In the z-score version of the regression equation, R is referred to as the **standardized regression coefficient**. The standardized regression coefficient is the slope when the variables in the regression have been converted to standard scores. An **unstandardized regression coefficient** is the slope associated with raw scores. Standardized regression coefficients often are used to make comparisons between regression models using different variables. For example, suppose there were two studies that used linear regression to predict anxiety from self-esteem, but they used different scales to measure anxiety and self-esteem. We could still assess whether a change of one standard deviation unit in self-esteem predicts the same amount of change in anxiety standard deviation units for both studies, by converting the data in both of them to z-scores. Unstandardized coefficients usually are used in comparisons between models with the same variables but different samples, especially where the researcher is concerned to replicate a previous study. DEFINITIONS

The second alternative formula for R uses variances in the denominator and something called the 'covariance' in the numerator. The **covariance** is the sum of the products, SS_{XY}, divided by $N - 1$, just as the variance of X, say, is SS_X divided by $N - 1$. The covariance is a measure of the extent to which X and Y covary, relative to their respective scales. It is denoted by Cov_{XY}, and its formula is DEFINITION RELATION-SHIP BETWEEN R AND COVARIANCE

$$Cov_{XY} = SS_{XY}/(N - 1).$$

The corresponding formula for R is

$$R = \frac{Cov_{XY}}{s_X s_Y}$$

As you learn more about regression or read research that uses multivariate regression techniques, you will encounter covariance. However, we will not deal any further with it in this book.

SUMMARY

In a **correlation** analysis, we say that R^2 *measures the proportion of variance shared between X and Y.* R^2 may therefore be used as a measure of the magnitude or strength of the *linear relationship* between X and Y.

R is called the **product-moment correlation** or sometimes the **Pearsonian correlation**.

If we denote the z-score for X by z_X and the z-score for Y by z_Y, then the regression equation may be rewritten as

$$z_{Y'} = R z_X.$$

In this context, R is a **standardized regression coefficient**, which is the slope when the variables in the regression have been converted to standard scores. R tells us how many standard deviation units' change in Y would be predicted for one standard deviation unit increase in X.

An **unstandardized regression coefficient** is the slope associated with raw scores.

The **covariance** is a measure of the extent to which X and Y covary, relative to their respective scales, and its formula is

$$\text{Cov}_{XY} = \text{SS}_{XY}/(N-1).$$

Evaluating the magnitude of a correlation

There are several things to take into account when evaluating a correlation between two variables. The most obvious one is simply the size of the correlation. Another that we have already touched on is nonlinearity. Two additional issues are outliers and 'range restriction effects.' We will start with some more thoughts about size, and then proceed to the latter two concerns.

We already have two ways of interpreting R^2: as a proportion of reduction in error and as a proportion of variance shared between X and Y. What about R? Let us return to the interpretation of R as a standardized regression coefficient, since it gives us another point of view about benchmarks for assessing the magnitude of R. To repeat the major point in that interpretation, R tells us how many standard deviation units' change in Y would be predicted for one standard deviation unit increase in X. Thus, we have a way of interpreting the size of R that is similar to Cohen's d. Earlier in this chapter, we learned about Cohen's benchmarks for R^2, and these may be translated into benchmarks for R. I have added a 'Very Large' benchmark to his list, to make it more exhaustive.

	Shared variance	Std. dev. units change in Y'
Small	$R^2 = 0.01$	$R = 0.10$
Medium	$R^2 = 0.09$	$R = 0.30$
Large	$R^2 = 0.25$	$R = 0.50$
Very Large	$R^2 = 0.64$	$R = 0.80$

One very good way to gain intuition about the meaning of these benchmarks is to examine scatterplots of variables whose correlations have these magnitudes. It is also a good idea to practice doing this, because our intuitive judgments of correlation sizes from scatterplots is usually not very accurate. In fact, we tend to underestimate the size of the correlation if we try to estimate it by examining a scatterplot. Figures 8.8–8.10 show scatterplots for variables whose correlations are 0.1, 0.5 and 0.8. You probably will find it difficult to believe that the first scatterplot shows any sort of relationship at all. Human visual intuition generally does not spot linear relationships in scatterplots between variables correlated at less than about 0.2.

The scatterplot for $R = 0.5$ should appear to you as if there is a relationship between X and Y, but you may feel that it hardly warrants Cohen's label of 'Large.' Again, this is because most of us underestimate correlations when examining scatterplots.

The scatterplot for $R = 0.8$, on the other hand, probably looks as if X and Y are fairly strongly related. The data lie in a tight band running diagonally across the plot area. Nevertheless, it is worth considering the fact that in many research areas in psychology (and the other human sciences) a correlation of this size is rare.

Now that we have some visual as well as numerical benchmarks to work with, we will move on to consider two important extraneous influences on the

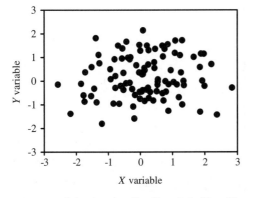

FIGURE 8.8 Scatter plot for $R = 0.1$ (Small)

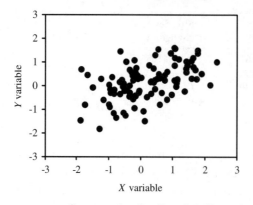

FIGURE 8.9 Scatter plot for $R = 0.5$ (Large)

size of a correlation. The first of these is outliers. In Chapter 3, we learned that the mean and standard deviation can be dramatically influenced by outliers. The same is true of the product-moment correlation. To demonstrate this, we will use a real research example.

In Chapter 7, we introduced a data-set collected by Bernd Heubeck (at the Division of Psychology in the Australian National University) comparing a sample of 89 children, aged 8–14, from Western Sydney with a sample of 89 children from the same area who had been referred to a Child Psychiatric Clinic. We concentrated on analyzing the CBCL Aggressive Behavior subscale as completed by the child's mother. However, aggressiveness ratings were obtained independently from both parents, so there were separate assessments of the child's behavior by the mother and the father.

A reasonable question to ask of these data is whether the mothers' and fathers' Aggressive Behavior ratings agree with one another. One way of addressing this question is to assess how strongly correlated they are. The

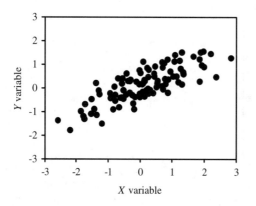

FIGURE 8.10 Scatterplot for $R = 0.8$ (Very Large)

scatterplot for the mothers' and fathers' ratings of the 89 nonreferred children is displayed in Figure 8.11. Notice that some of the points on this graph have 'spines' on them. The spines are there to represent cases that have identical values on X and Y and therefore have indistinguishable positions in the scatterplot. The spiny points are called 'sunflowers' and each spine denotes a case. A sunflower with three spines, for example, represents three cases with identical values of X and Y.

It turns out that for these data, $R = 0.560$, so $R^2 = 0.314$, meaning that the mothers' and fathers' ratings share about 31.4% of the variance. This would be called a 'Large' effect according to Cohen's benchmarks. Nevertheless, before we leap to any conclusions we should examine that scatterplot more closely and ask whether the correlation has been inflated by the two outliers in the upper right-hand corner of the plot.

If we omit those two outliers and recompute the correlation, we get $R = 0.384$ instead of 0.560, which is a substantial drop. That means the shared variance declines from 31.4% to 14.7% (since $R^2 = (0.384)^2 = 0.147$), less than half of its original amount. We would have to conclude that the correlation is being unduly inflated by the two outliers. Outliers can either *inflate* or *deflate* correlation coefficients. If instead of lying in the upper right-hand corner of the graph, the two outliers were in the lower right-hand or upper left-hand corner, they would decrease the correlation from 0.384 to a substantially lower value. The difficulty posed by outliers is that we have no idea of where the points would fall if we collected more cases with high Aggressiveness ratings

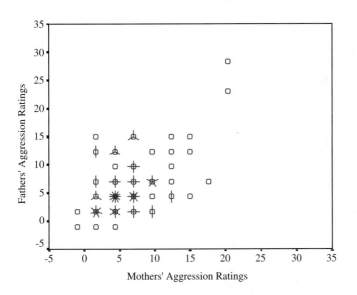

FIGURE 8.11 Scatterplot for nonreferred children

StatPatch

EXPLORE THE
EFFECTS OF
OUTLIERS
AND RANGE
RESTRICT-
IONS USING
REGRESS-
PATCH

from mothers and/or fathers. If we were writing a research paper based on these results, the most honest practice would be to report the correlations with and without the outliers.

This same example may be used to illustrate **range restriction effects** on correlations. If the range of values is truncated on one or both variables, then the correlation will be reduced. Notice that in the scatterplot above, except for the two outliers, the Aggressiveness ratings for both fathers and mothers vary from 0 to less than 20. However, when this example was introduced in Chapter 7 we noted that this subscale had a range from 0 to 40. The data in the scatterplot cover less than half of the scale range.

Let us compare that scatterplot and its correlation with one that also includes the sample of 89 children who were referred to a Child Psychiatric Clinic. Remember, these children generally had higher Aggressiveness ratings from their mothers than the nonreferred children did. The scatterplot of the fathers' and mothers' ratings incorporating both samples is shown in Figure 8.12. The ratings vary from 0 to about 35, thereby covering much more of the scale's range than the nonreferred sample alone.

The correlation for these data is $R = 0.685$, so $R^2 = 0.469$. The percentage of variance shared between the mothers' and fathers' ratings has therefore increased from 31.4% to 46.9%. If we recall that R was 0.560 with the outliers and 0.384 without them, we can see that the restriction of the range in the nonreferred sample has a dramatic effect on the size of the correlation. Moreover, the correlation between mothers' and fathers' ratings for the Clinical sample is $R = 0.521$, again substantially less than the correlation when both samples are combined. The reason is the same: children from the

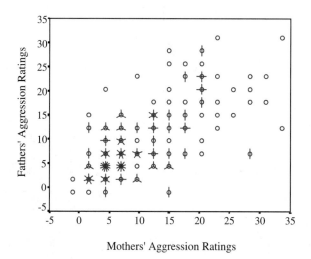

FIGURE 8.12 Scatterplot for nonreferred and clinical children

Clinical sample tended to receive high Aggressiveness ratings from their parents, and so that sample also has a restricted range.

Range restrictions are easy to overlook, especially if researchers do not draw readers' attention to them. An important question to bear in mind when reading articles that report correlations or regression results is whether those results might be contaminated by range restrictions. Unfortunately, most psychology research articles do not report ranges. Nevertheless, you can sometimes gain a fairly good idea if means and standard deviations have been given and if there is enough information about the range of the scale. You should be especially wary of studies whose samples come from 'special' populations that lie at the extremes on the variables being correlated, as in our example here.

The final part of this section introduces a confidence interval for R. It may be skipped without much adverse effect if you are unfamiliar with logarithms and exponents. We will need them because it turns out that a particular transformation of R is required to change it into a statistic that has an approximately normal sampling distribution. First, denote the **population correlation coefficient** by ρ, to distinguish it from the sample correlation, R. Our goal is to construct a confidence interval around ρ.

The required transformation of R is known as **Fisher's z**, but to avoid DEFINITIONS confusion we will denote it by R':

$$R' = \tfrac{1}{2}\ln\left(\frac{1+R}{1-R}\right)$$

where 'ln' stands for the natural logarithm. It turns out that the standard error of R' is

$$s_{R'} = \frac{1}{\sqrt{N-3}}.$$

Demos

We may now obtain a **confidence interval around ρ'**, the transformed population correlation. For a confidence level of $100(1-\alpha)$, the half-width of a confidence interval around ρ' is

USE DEM81 TO GAIN FAMILIARITY WITH FISHER'S z AND THE CI FOR R

$$w = z_{\alpha/2}s_{R'},$$

and so our confidence statement is

$$\Pr(R' - w < \rho' < R' + w) = 1 - \alpha.$$

To convert this confidence interval back to an interval around ρ, we need the inverse of the transformation we used originally:

$$R = \frac{e_1^{2R'} - 1}{e^{2R'} + 1}$$

which may be used to transform the lower and upper limits of the confidence interval.

Let's try all of this on an example. Consider the sample correlation between mothers' and fathers' aggressiveness ratings in Heubeck's data. We had $R = 0.685$, with a sample size of $N = 178$. The Fisher's z-transformation of R gives us

$$R' = \tfrac{1}{2}\ln\left(\frac{1 + R}{1 - R}\right) = 0.5\ln\left(\frac{1.685}{0.315}\right) = 0.5\ln(5.349) = 0.8385.$$

The standard error of R' is

$$s_{R'} = \frac{1}{\sqrt{N - 3}} = \frac{1}{\sqrt{175}} = 0.0756.$$

Now, suppose we wish to use a confidence level of 95%. Then $z_{0.025} = 1.96$, and the half-width is

$$w = z_{\alpha/2}s_{R'} = (1.96)(0.0756) = 0.1482.$$

Our confidence interval around ρ' is

$$\Pr(R' - w < \rho' < R' + w) = \Pr(0.6903 < \rho' < 0.9866) = 0.95.$$

If we apply our inverse transformation formula to convert this interval back to an interval around ρ, we get

$$\Pr(0.5982 < \rho < 0.7559) = 0.95.$$

One important characteristic about the confidence interval around ρ is that it is usually not symmetric with respect to R, even though the interval around ρ' is with respect to R'. In our example, $R = 0.685$ is closer to the upper limit of 0.7559 than it is to the lower limit of 0.5982.

There are two important extraneous influences on the size of a correlation. Correlation sizes can be dramatically influenced by **outliers**, which may either inflate or deflate correlations.
Range restriction on one or both variables will reduce the correlation between those variables.

A **confidence interval** around the **population correlation coefficient** ρ requires a transformation known as **Fisher's** z, denoted by R':

$$R' = \tfrac{1}{2}\ln\left(\frac{1+R}{1-R}\right)$$

The standard error of R' is

$$s_{R'} = \frac{1}{\sqrt{N-3}}$$

and the half width is $w = z_{\alpha/2}s_{R'}$, so the confidence interval statement is

$$\Pr(R' - w < \rho' < R' + w) = 1 - \alpha.$$

The formula for transforming R' back to R is

$$R = \frac{e^{2R'} - 1}{e^{2R'} + 1}$$

which is used to convert the confidence interval around ρ' into one around ρ.

Correlation, prediction, determinism, and causation: A mildly philosophical interlude

Most often, researchers are interested in relationships between two variables when they wish to *predict*, *explain*, or even *control* one variable by its association with another. In order to handle these concepts adroitly and responsibly, we need to make sure that we understand the distinctions among them and the conditions under which we may infer one from the other.

In Chapter 4, we reviewed three widely held rules for establishing that one thing causes another:

1. **Covariation rule**: The cause and effect co-occur.
2. **Temporal precedence rule**: The cause always precedes the effect.
3. **Rival cause discount rule**: Plausible rival causes must be ruled out.

We may think of these rules in terms of their analogies with correlation, prediction, and causation in the context of linear regression. The covariation rule is akin to establishing that there is a correlation between two variables. The temporal precedence rule is tantamount to being able to predict one variable from another.

While it is tempting to leap from finding a correlation to the conclusion that X causes Y, these three rules make it clear that no such leap is warranted. Put baldly, **correlation is not causation**. The number of fire engines arriving on the scene of the fire predicts the cost of the damage to the building. Does this mean fire engines cause the damage? No, since there is a third variable that predicts and causes both of these variables, namely the size of the fire. In many areas of psychological research, the causal linkages (if any) among key theoretical constructs are open to debate. As many researchers found to their chagrin in the debate throughout the 1970s in social psychology over whether attitudes cause behavior or the other way around, even experiments seldom provide unequivocal evidence concerning causation when some of the constructs (such as attitudes) are not directly observable.

A related topic of debate throughout the human sciences concerns determinism versus free will or sentience. Sometimes predictability or lack thereof is erroneously brought in as evidence for one side or the other in this debate. For some people, evidence that X predicts Y counts as evidence that Y is *determined* by X. Thus, predictability in human behavior counts for them as evidence in favor of determinism and against free will. Conversely, some people argue that unpredictability in human behavior is evidence in favor of free will.

Both of these arguments are fatally and obviously flawed. Again putting matters baldly, **predictability is not determinism**. It is easy to find counterexamples against claims that it is. We all have habits, for instance. These make some of our behaviors very predictable. Does that mean we cannot change or break our habits if we wish to? Of course not. Even consciously directed behavior may be quite predictable, in some cases because we are choosing to behave logically or in accordance with what we and others know.

Likewise unpredictability does not indicate indeterminism, nor is it evidence for 'free will' or sentience. A random process such as tossing a coin is unpredictable, but no one would claim that the coin has free will. The computer chess-playing program that beats the world's best human player is unpredictable (to us) but deterministic. In fact, if you are as poor a chess-player as I am, many computer chess-playing programs are unpredictable. There are many simple, deterministic, but chaotically behaved systems for which long-range prediction is impossible. None of those systems can be said to have free will or sentience, nor do they need those qualities in order to behave unpredictably.

So (un)predictability and (in)determinism have no necessary association with each other. Searching for one psychological variable to predict another does not mean you are subscribing to a deterministic view of human nature. Likewise, belief in free will does not mean you have to abandon all searches for predictability. Such world-views become relevant only at the point where we attempt to interpret and explain whatever predictive relationships between variables that we have found or failed to find.

A third widespread intuition about prediction is that if X does cause Y, then we are better able to predict Y from X than vice versa. If X causes Y and we believe that Y may be influenced by other things as well, then we become even more confident that we can predict Y from X more accurately than we can predict X from Y. Here is a quick test of your own intuitive sense about this. Which would you be more confident in doing:

1. Predicting someone's height if you were told their weight, or
2. Predicting someone's weight if you were told their height?

If you are like most of us, you will have chosen 2. We know that height and weight are positively correlated, we think that height causes weight (Does anyone attend Height-Watchers? Are you too short for your weight?), and we believe that weight is influenced by other things (such as diet or exercise). So height seems like a better predictor of weight than weight is of height.

However, if height and weight really are linearly related, then the strength of that relationship is measured by R^2, which does not distinguish between which is the predictor and which is the predicted variable. Accordingly, we will be able to predict height from weight just as accurately as we can predict weight from height. **The fact that X causes Y does not mean we can predict Y from X more accurately than X from Y**. A good real-world example to contemplate here is the birthrate study. There is a strong negative linear relationship between birthrate and contraceptive usage rate, as indicated by $R^2 = 0.841$. That means 84.1% of the variance in birthrate is accounted for by contraceptive usage rate, but it *also means the reverse –* 84.1% of the variance in contraceptive usage rate is accounted for by birthrate. We can predict either one equally accurately from the other, even though we know that contraceptive usage influences birthrate.

Finally, there are three common misidentifications of cause with other matters. First **causality is not controllability**. There are plenty of examples of phenomena for which we know a great deal about the causes but lack the means to influence them (e.g., the orbital paths of planets). The assumption that finding causes enables us to seize control is behind the repeated call to identify the 'root causes' of crime, substance abuse, and so on. While we may be able to control some root causes, finding a root cause does not in itself guarantee controllability. Likewise, looking for an 'ultimate' cause involves a greater fallacy still. Searching for the 'ultimate' cause long enough will take you back to the Big Bang. Unfortunately, it does none of us much instrumental good to gain the insight that the Big Bang caused everything in the universe.

Second, from time to time we may fall prey to relabeling something and claiming that the new label is a cause (e.g., a suicide attempt is a 'cry for help'). Even when it is true that someone attempts suicide as a way of calling attention to themselves in the hope that others will come to their aid, a complex suite of causes is probably at work there and the 'cry for help' label may well conceal more than it reveals. **A label is not a cause**.

Third, **tautologies are not causal relationships**. A tautology amounts to circular reasoning, whereby the argument already assumes what it purports to demonstrate. A certain crude version of behaviorism, for example, holds that behaviors increase in frequency by being reinforced (by a reward, for instance). We know that X is a reinforcer of behavior Y if it increases the frequency of behavior Y. But why does it have that effect? Because it is a reinforcer. And so around we go. The problem here is that in principle we can never find an instance where a reinforcer of Y does not increase the frequency of Y, because anything that does not do that is not a reinforcer of Y. So this version of behaviorism is *untestable* because it is circular. Another older (and perhaps more familiar) example is the vulgar version of instinct theory. Observations of females nurturing their young are used evidence of a 'maternal instinct,' but this instinct is then used to explain why the nurturing behavior occurs in the first place. Male nurturing likewise is simultaneously evidence of and explained by a 'paternal instinct.'

SUMMARY

> The object of this section has been to point out crucial distinctions between correlation, prediction, causation, and other concepts that are frequently confused with them. The main points that have been argued here are as follows:
>
> 1. Correlation is not causation.
> 2. Predictability is not evidence for determinism, and unpredictability is not evidence for free will or sentience.
> 3. The fact that X causes Y does not mean we can predict Y from X more accurately than X from Y.
> 4. Causality is not controllability.
> 5. A label is not a cause.
> 6. Tautologies are not causal relationships.

Regression, ANOVA, and the general linear model

In Chapter 7 and this chapter, we have seen that the F-statistic is equivalent to t^2. We have also learned that R^2 may be used to compare effects with null models in ANOVA and linear regression. These signs might seem to point to some underlying relationship between the t-test, ANOVA, and regression. Let us pursue this matter further to resolve this 'mystery' here. Table 8.4 displays data from a small-scale experiment in which 15 students were randomly assigned to two teaching methods (Method 1, the 'Old way' and Method 2, the 'New way').

TABLE 8.4 Data for teaching
experiment

	Old	New
	68	50
	56	75
	59	65
	57	71
	50	62
	48	69
	50	74
		77
Means	55.43	67.88
s_i^2	47.95	77.84

The methods were compared for their effectiveness by how well the students scored on an examination after the period of instruction ended. If we were to compare the exam scores for the two methods, many psychologists would advise us to use a *t*-test for comparing two means from independent samples. This would be a reasonable choice. However, we could also perform an ANOVA. Since we already know from Chapter 7 that $F = t^2$ we will proceed with the ANOVA first.

The summary ANOVA table is laid out as Table 8.5. If we use the SS terms to calculate R^2, then we can see that the proportion of error in the null model that has been reduced by using the effects model is reasonably substantial:

$$R^2 = SS_b/SS_t = 578.344/1410.933 = 0.410.$$

Now let us see what happens when we analyze the same data using regression. Yes, regression! The variable Method is just a binary variable, and we may turn it into a suitable predictor for regression by coding 0 for 'Old,' say, and 1 for 'New.'

Thus, X is an indicator variable that switches on to 1 when Method = New and switches off to 0 when Method = Old. This kind of variable is sometimes known as a **dummy variable**. The recoded data-set is shown in Table 8.6.

TABLE 8.5 ANOVA table for teaching experiment

Source	df	SS	MS	*F*
Between	1	578.344	578.344	9.030
Within	13	832.589	64.045	
Total	14	1410.933		

TABLE 8.6 Teaching study data recoded for regression

Method X	Exam Y	Method X	Exam Y
0	68	1	50
0	56	1	75
0	59	1	65
0	57	1	71
0	50	1	62
0	48	1	69
0	50	1	74
		1	77

If we perform a regression with Method as X and Exam as Y, we get the ANOVA table shown as Table 8.7 as part of the the regression output. This table is exactly the same as the other one, except for the labeling of the 'between groups' effect as 'regression' and the 'within groups' term as 'residual.' The point here is that ANOVA is just a special case of regression, even though the two techniques look very different. ANOVA is a linear model just as regression is, and when the independent variable is binary (i.e., just two categories) then ANOVA and regression will produce exactly the same R^2 value ($R^2 = 0.410$ here) and F-test results ($F = 9.030$).

What about the regression equation for these data? What could it possibly mean? It turns out that the regression equation is

$$Y' = a + bX = 55.43 + 12.45X.$$

This model predicts that when $X = 0$ then $Y' = 55.43$. Recall that Old was coded as 0. If you examine the first table in which the data were presented for this study, you will find that the mean exam score for students working with the Old Method was 55.43. Likewise, when $X = 1$, $Y' = 55.43 + 12.45 = 67.88$, which is the mean for the students working with the New Method, and New was coded as 1. So the regression model actually *predicts* the means of the two groups. That is precisely what the effects model in ANOVA does!

TABLE 8.7 ANOVA table for teaching experiment

Source	df	SS	MS	F
Regression	1	578.344	578.344	9.030
Residual	13	832.589	64.045	
Total	14	1410.933		

The effects models in ANOVA and regression for these data are exactly the same.

One last connection between ANOVA and regression will conclude the tale. Earlier in this chapter we learned that the squared standard error of the estimate has the formula

$$s_{Y|X}^2 = \mathrm{SS_e}/(\mathcal{N} - 2).$$

In the ANOVA table, $\mathrm{SS_w} = \mathrm{SS_e}$, so $s_w^2 = s_{Y|X}^2$. We now know that the variance within groups in ANOVA is the squared standard error of the estimate in the equivalent regression analysis.

Having learned that the t-test is a special case of the F-test in ANOVA (F is t^2), we have now learned that ANOVA is a special case of regression. These techniques all belong to a broad class known as the **General Linear Model**, because they all are based on the evaluation of linear effects models against null models. If you advance your study of research methods and statistics to the point where you are dealing with more than one predictor variable at a time, you will encounter the General Linear Model many times.

SUMMARY

In this section, we compared ANOVA with regression by using a technique for converting binary variables into **dummy variables** that take a value of 0 for one category and 1 for the other. The regression model then becomes

$$Y' = a + bX,$$

where X is either 0 or 1. This model *predicts the mean of Y for each of the two samples*, just as the effects model in ANOVA does. That is, when $X = 0$ then $Y' = a$, and when $X = 1$ then $Y' = a + b$.

The regression analysis produces the same R^2 value and F-test results as the ANOVA does, and indeed ANOVA is a special case of regression.

They are both members of a class of techniques known as the **General Linear Model**, because they all are based on the evaluation of linear effects models against null models.

Questions and exercises

Q.8.1. The director of a counseling center has a hunch that employee ill health and stress in her organization are predictable according to the casework load that each psychologist has. She decides to investigate this notion by examining the employees' files for information on how many days of sick leave each has taken and their average weekly caseload during the past 6 months. Here are the data:

Case-load	Days Absent
35	4
48	7
39	3
33	3
45	6
42	5
40	4

Do these two variables seem to be linearly related? Why or why not? Is the relationship positive or negative? There is a data-file named **Caseload** containing these data, if you prefer using a computer to analyze them.

Q.8.2. Which of the following is (or are) true?

(a) The regression coefficient measures how much X causes Y.
(b) A correlation of 0 means there is no relationship between X and Y.
(c) A correlation coefficient of -0.9 indicates a strong positive relationship between X and Y.
(d) The regression line always passes through the point located at 0 for X and 0 for Y.
(e) Regression minimizes the average squared deviation of the data from the regression line.

Q.8.3.   In any year during modern times, there has been a very strong positive relationship between the per-capita Gross Domestic Product of a country and its per-capita energy consumption (actually, a strong linear relationship between the log of each of these variables). The relationship holds for any kind of economy at any level of technological development. Provide at least two plausible explanations for this relationship, at least one of which introduces a third intervening variable.

Q.8.4. In the donation study, consider the regression model's prediction that if a person is given $X = \$0$ by the experimenter the amount that person is predicted to donate is $Y = \$41.4$. Describe *two* respects in which this prediction is problematic.

Q.8.5. Let's return to the **Caseload** data again. Either by hand or using a statistics package, compute the linear regression model for predicting days absent from counselor caseload.

- How many days absence would be predicted for a counselor with a caseload of 38?
- Does the model make any 'silly' predictions?
- Given an increase of 5 in someone's caseload, how many more days' absence would be predicted by this model?
- Can we reject the 'null' (no-effects) model if we use a confidence level of 99%? Why or why not?
- How large is the effect that caseload has on days' absence?
- Construct a 95% confidence interval around b.

Q.8.6. Launch **RegressPatch**. When you are offered a choice among three different kinds of problems, choose 'Compute a predicted value for Y from X in a regression model' and work through the problem.

Q.8.7. As long as you are in **RegressPatch**, choose the appropriate option to explore what happens in a scatterplot when data-values are altered. You'll be presented with a scatterplot that has moveable points.

- Try dragging the white point to the upper left-hand corner of the graph. What happens to the correlation? What are the implications for the influence of outliers on regression and correlation?
- Now try dragging all of the blue points into the lower left-hand corner and the white point to the upper right-hand corner of the graph. Compare the correlation that you get there with the correlation when the white point has been dragged close to where the blue points are bunched.

Q.8.8. The table below displays four famous data sets that are 'replications' of one another. Use SPSS or any suitable statistical package to predict Y from X for each of these. The required data-file is called **Replicant**. Do the four studies yield the same findings concerning the relationship between Y and X? Are

Study 1		Study 2		Study 3		Study 4	
X	Y	X	Y	X	Y	X	Y
10.0	8.04	10.0	9.14	10.0	7.46	8.0	6.58
8.0	6.95	8.0	8.14	8.0	6.77	8.0	5.76
13.0	7.58	13.0	8.74	13.0	12.74	8.0	7.71
9.0	8.81	9.0	8.77	9.0	7.11	8.0	8.84
11.0	8.33	11.0	9.26	11.0	7.81	8.0	8.47
14.0	9.96	14.0	8.10	14.0	8.84	8.0	7.04
6.0	7.24	6.0	6.13	6.0	6.08	8.0	5.25
4.0	4.26	4.0	3.10	4.0	5.39	19.0	12.50
12.0	10.84	12.0	9.13	12.0	8.15	8.0	5.56
7.0	4.82	7.0	7.26	7.0	6.42	8.0	7.91
5.0	5.68	5.0	4.74	5.0	5.73	8.0	6.89

they equally reliable findings? Does the linear model apply equally well to the four studies? Justify your conclusions.

Q.8.9. (This question is for those who have covered the material on the confidence limit for R.) The data-file named **Aggro** contains data from Heubeck's study involving 178 mothers' and 178 fathers' ratings of their children's characteristics. We have already seen that the correlation between both parents' ratings of their children's aggressiveness is 0.685. The data-set also contains their ratings of the children's depression and anxiety levels (in one subscale). The correlation between mothers' and fathers' ratings on this subscale turns out to be 0.546. Construct a 95% confidence interval for this correlation. If a researcher hypothesized that the correlation between parents' ratings would not fall below 0.5, would you consider that hypothesis to be plausible based on your confidence interval? Why or why not?

Predicting Categorical Variables: Contingency Tables and Chi-Square

9

Tabulations and contingency tables

Predicting categorical variables involves working with tables, and tables (or tabulations) are among the most widely used ways of displaying data. In Chapter 3, we saw that categorical variables could be described quite well with frequency distributions presented in a tabular format. The frequency distribution of a variable presents the categories of that variable and the frequency with which each of them occurs. Usually, percentages are also provided in such tables.

Here is an example. A medical researcher is interested in outcomes and survival rates of female patients who have had tumors in their breasts. She has obtained data on this kind of patient from a large-scale survey of hospitals in a region where the risk of breast cancer is reputed to be high. Suppose she has decided to categorize patient outcomes in three categories: benign, malignant/survived, and malignant/died. Then she might tabulate the data in a frequency distribution table like Table 9.1.

Now, suppose the medical researcher wonders whether hospitals in an urban center have a similar outcome distribution to those in a rural hinterland where

TABLE 9.1 Breast-cancer patient outcomes

Outcome	Frequency	Percentage
Benign	300	43.5
Survived	70	10.1
Died	320	46.4
Total	690	100

breast cancer rates are reputedly higher. How would she compare the rates for each of these outcomes between the two regions? What would be an effective way for her to display the outcome distributions for urban and rural hospitals separately?

DEFINITION

The medical researcher would turn to the categorical equivalent to a scatterplot, namely the 'contingency table.' A **contingency table** is a tabulation of the frequency with which cases occur in combinations of categories from two or more variables. One way to think of a contingency table is as a *cross-classification* of the categories in the variables. In our example, the three categories of outcomes would be cross-classified with the two hospital locations (urban and rural). For this reason, a contingency table is also called a 'cross-tabulation' in some research traditions.

Another way to think of a contingency table is in terms of *conditional distributions*. The medical researcher really is interested in the distribution of patient outcomes conditional on whether they are urbanites or ruralites. She would probably think of displaying the frequency distributions of outcomes in the two regions side by side. The result would be the contingency table displayed as Table 9.2. Both the cross-classification and conditional distribution interpretations of contingency tables are valid. The cross-classification interpretation is analogous to a correlation analysis, and the conditional distribution interpretation is analogous to a regression analysis.

DEFINITIONS

Contingency tables have a terminology all their own. The numbers inside each of the **cells** of this table are called the **cell frequencies**. For instance,

TABLE 9.2 Contingency table of tumor outcome by hospital location

Outcome	Hospital location		Row total
	Urban	Rural	
Benign	220	80	300
Survived	40	30	70
Died	200	120	320
Column total	460	230	690

TABLE 9.3 Frequencies (and column percentages) for hospital data

Outcome	Hospital location		Row total
	Urban	Rural	
Benign	220 (47.8%)	80 (34.8%)	300
Survived	40 (8.7%)	30 (13.0%)	70
Died	200 (43.5%)	120 (52.2%)	320
Column total	460 (100%)	230 (100%)	690

the cell frequency of Benign tumor cases from Urban hospitals is 220. The totals on the right-hand side are the sums of the cell frequencies in each of the rows, and therefore known as the **row totals**. The total number of Benign cases, for example, is $220 + 80 = 300$. Likewise, the totals at the bottom of the table are the sums of the cell frequencies in each column, and therefore called **column totals**. A generic term for these totals is the **marginal frequencies**, which refers to the margins of the table. The number 690 down in the lower right hand corner is the **grand total** and of course equals N, the number of cases in the data.

But how do we get comparative information out of such a table? For example, are Benign cases more or less likely in the Urban than the Rural hospitals? There are two ways to answer this question. The most popular way is to compare percentages of Benign cases out of the total caseloads from each hospital location. Because we are using the *column total* to do this, it is called a **column percentage**. So, for the 220 Benign cases in the Urban hospitals, we DEFINITION compute $100 \times (220/460) = 47.8\%$, which is the number in parentheses in the Benign–Urban cell in Table 9.3. The other percentages in this table were computed in the same way, i.e.,

$$\text{column } \% = 100 \frac{\text{cell frequency}}{\text{column total}}$$

The column percentages should add up to 100% in each column. Notice that this table gives a rather different appearance to the information than the raw frequencies do. We can see that the Rural hospitals have a lower percentage of Benign cases (34.8%) and somewhat higher percentages of both types of malignant outcomes (13.0% and 52.2%) than the Urban hospitals.

What if you wanted to find out the percentages of deaths among these patients that occurred in Urban as opposed to the Rural hospitals? This time you would want to compute a **row percentage**. For instance, the per- DEFINITION centage of all deaths that occurred in Urban hospitals is $100 \times (200/320) = 62.5\%$. In general, the formula for this is

$$\text{row } \% = 100 \frac{\text{cell frequency}}{\text{row total}}$$

DEFINITION

StatPatch

CROSSPATCH
PROVIDES
PRACTICE IN
WORKING
WITH PER-
CENTAGES
IN CONTIN-
GENCY
TABLES

Finally, there is a third kind of percentaging that can be done, namely **percentaging across rows and columns** (cell percentages), which amounts to simply dividing each cell frequency by N and then multiplying by 100. Here is another example, taken from social psychological research on helping behavior (Smithson, Amato & Pearce, 1983). Many social psychological studies of helping behavior have used helping between strangers in situations that arise spontaneously and quickly. But how common is this kind of helping in everyday life? It seems that most helping occurs between friends or in families, and involves pre-planning or organization. In a survey designed to investigate this issue, respondents were asked to recall five instances of helping they had engaged in during the past week and to classify them in two ways: Whether it was helping a stranger or not; and whether it was in a spontaneous situation or not.

The results are shown in Table 9.4. As we are interested in what percentage of helping episodes is both between strangers and spontaneous, we want to compute the *cell percentages*. For instance, the percentage of episodes where people spontaneously helped a stranger is $100 \times (117/474) = 24.7\%$, which is only about one-fourth of the total. The cell percentages are displayed in parentheses in this table.

We can see from the column totals and their percentages that there is a tendency for helping to be spontaneous more often (68.4%) than planned (31.6%). The row totals and percentages tell us that the majority of episodes are between friends or with family. Fully 70.5% of helping episodes in this sample involve friends or family members. The most common kind of helping in our cross-classification is spontaneous and with friends/family (43.7%). Thus, the social psychological studies dealing with spontaneous helping between strangers cover only a minority of the kinds of helping that people engage in (24.7%).

Now, we started our discussion of percentaging with the observation that there were two ways to obtain comparative information from a contingency

TABLE 9.4 Frequencies (and cell percentages) for helping data

Recipient	Type of Helping		Row total
	Planned	Spontan.	
Friends/Family	127 (26.8%)	207 (43.7%)	334 (70.5%)
Strangers	23 (4.8%)	117 (24.7%)	140 (29.5%)
Col. total	150 (31.6%)	324 (68.4%)	474 (100%)

table, and percentages are the most popular method. The less popular method may already have occurred to you. We could use probabilities. In contingency tables (as in many other situations), probabilities are just percentages divided by 100. In fact, they are just proportions. So row percentages, column percentages, and so on may be converted to row probabilities, column probabilities, and the like by dividing the percentages by 100.

There is an additional important connection between probabilities and percentaging in contingency tables. Row and column percentages are both *conditional* probabilities multiplied by 100. Likewise, cell percentages are *compound event* probabilities multiplied by 100. Returning to our helping example, imagine randomly sampling a helping episode from the 474 episodes in the sample. The probability of obtaining an episode that is between strangers and spontaneous is $117/474 = 0.247$, since 117 of the episodes fall into both of these categories. We could say P(strangers and spontaneous) $= 0.247$. The corresponding cell percentage, 24.7%, is just this probability multiplied by 100.

Now consider the conditional probability of randomly selecting an episode that is between strangers given that it is spontaneous. We could recall from Chapter 4 the formula for a conditional probability and work this out by using it. We already know that

$$P(\text{strangers and spontaneous}) = 117/474 = 0.247.$$

From Table 9.4 we could also figure out that

$$P(\text{spontaneous}) = 324/474 = 0.684.$$

Using the formula for conditional probabilities, we would then calculate

$$P(\text{between strangers}|\text{spontaneous})$$

$$= \frac{P(\text{between strangers and spontaneous})}{P(\text{spontaneous})}$$

$$= \frac{0.247}{0.685} = 0.361$$

However, a quicker way would be to simply compute the column percentage without multiplying it by 100:

$$P(\text{between strangers}|\text{spontaneous}) = 117/324 = 0.361.$$

Table 9.5 shows how conditional probabilities may be presented in a contingency table format. The upper table displays conditional probabilities that correspond to column percentages, and the lower table displays conditional

TABLE 9.5 Conditional probabilities for helping data

| | Conditional on Help | | |
	Planned	Spontaneous	Row total
Friends/Family	127 (0.847)	207 (0.639)	334 (0.705)
Strangers	23 (0.153)	117 (0.361)	140 (0.295)
Column total	150 (1.000)	324 (1.000)	474 (1.000)

| | Conditional on Recipient | | |
	Planned	Spontaneous	Row total
Friends/Family	127 (0.380)	207 (0.620)	334 (1.000)
Strangers	23 (0.164)	117 (0.836)	140 (1.000)
Column total	150 (0.316)	324 (0.684)	474 (1.000)

probabilities that correspond to row percentages. Just as row or column percentages must sum to 100% for each row or column, row or column probabilities must sum to 1 for each row or column. These tables present a fairly large quantity of information coherently in a small space, and they are much easier to comprehend than a list or a narration of the same information.

These two tables also provide different kinds of information about the relationship between type of helping and recipient. The upper table enables us to make statements about the likelihood that the recipient will be a stranger (versus friend or family member) given that the type of helping is spontaneous or planned. The probability of the help being given to a stranger is 0.361 if it is spontaneous, but only 0.153 if it is planned. So the upper table is useful for predicting recipient on the basis of type of helping. This tells us something important about column percentages too, namely that *column percentages (and their corresponding conditional probabilities) are used when we want to predict the row variable*.

The lower table, on the other hand, is useful for predicting type of helping based on whom the recipient is. The probability of planned helping is 0.380 if the recipient is a friend or family member, but only 0.164 if the recipient is a stranger. So, *row percentages (and their corresponding conditional probabilities) are used when we want to predict the column variable*. We will work more with these two kinds of tables later in this chapter as we learn more about predicting one categorical variable from another.

We are well-equipped now to display and interpret data for two categorical variables. We have found that contingency tables allow us to present joint and conditional frequency distributions, percentages, and probabilities. Contingency tables are not only very effective for two variables, but they may be used for three or more. Researchers often refer to contingency tables in terms of the number of variables involved. A two-way table displays two variables, a three-way table has three, and so on. We will investigate some uses of higher-order contingency tables in Chapter 10.

A **contingency table** is a tabulation of the frequency with which cases occur in combinations of categories from two or more variables.

One way to think of a contingency table is as a *cross-classification* of the categories in the variables, and this is analogous to a correlation analysis.

Another way is in terms of *conditional distributions*, which is analogous to a regression analysis.

The frequencies for each combination of categories are called **cell frequencies**.

The **marginal frequencies** are **row totals** or **column totals**.

A **column percentage** is a cell frequency divided by its column total and multiplied by 100.

A **row percentage** is a cell frequency divided by its row total and multiplied by 100.

Column and row percentages are *conditional probabilities* multiplied by 100.

Column percentages (and their corresponding conditional probabilities) are used when we want to *predict the row variable*.

Row percentages (and their corresponding conditional probabilities) are used when we want to *predict the column variable*.

SUMMARY

Working with one categorical variable

In Chapter 6, we used the binomial distribution to test hypotheses about sample proportions. In effect, what we were doing was making predictions about proportions for categorical variables with only two categories (hence the term 'binomial'). Quite often, researchers find themselves wanting to test predictions about proportions for variables that have more than two categories. We will start with a fictitious but realistic example, involving a question about whether discrimination is occurring.

In a certain region there are three distinct ethnic groups, which we shall call A, B, and C. It is widely believed that the C's receive preferential treatment at the expense of the A's and B's in many spheres, including employment. A hotly contested claim by the A's spokespeople is that the unemployment rate is higher for A's and B's than for C's.

The regional council has hired an independent research consultant to assess whether this claim has any justification. The consultant collects data on a random sample of 800 unemployed and records, among other things, their ethnic identities. He finds that there are 335 A's, 196 B's, and 269 C's in his unemployed sample. What benchmark could he use against which to compare these frequencies? Are they anything like what he should expect to find if unemployment occurred in a nondiscriminatory fashion?

The consultant could use census information to find out what the distribution of A's, B's, and C's is among those eligible for employment. Suppose he ascertains that the population eligible for employment contains 33% A's, 22% B's, and 45% C's. If unemployment operates in an indiscriminate fashion, the number of A's, B's, and C's in his sample of 800 unemployed should approximately correspond to those percentages when one is converted into the other.

He elects to translate the percentages into frequencies out of 800. For example, 33% of 800 is $800 \times (33/100) = 264$, so the number of A's he would expect to find in his sample of 800 would be about 264. Instead, he found 335 A's, which is 71 more than 264. He tabulates these **expected frequencies**, denoted by f_e, along with the **observed frequencies**, denoted by f_o, and their differences $(f_o - f_e)$. The results are shown in Table 9.6.

On the basis of mere description, the evidence appears to favor the A's claim. There are more unemployed A's and B's, and fewer unemployed C's, than would be expected according to population figures. The consultant knows better than to leap to the conclusion of discrimination, since he knows that his sample is subject to sampling error. His unemployment figures are only sample estimates. Without confidence intervals around the A's unemployment figure of 335, for instance, he cannot say whether 264 is an implausible value or not.

In Chapter 7, we found that if we wanted to compare more than two sample means, then we had to use simultaneous confidence intervals or ANOVA. The F-test in ANOVA was based on the sums of squared errors in predicting scores. When we are predicting frequency distributions for a categorical variable, we face similar alternatives. One possibility would be to use simultaneous confidence intervals for the sample proportions in each category. Although that is not a widely used technique, it is legitimate under the same provisos that simultaneous confidence intervals for means or any other sample statistic are. Our consultant could, for example, convert his observed frequencies to sample proportions (by dividing them by 800) and compute confidence inter-

TABLE 9.6 Population percentages compared with unemployment frequencies

	Populat. %	Expected f_e	Observed f_o	Diff. $f_o - f_e$
A's	33	264	335	71
B's	22	176	196	20
C's	45	360	269	−91
Total	100	800	800	

vals for each of them. He could use a Bonferroni correction to ensure that the family-wise confidence level was, say, 95%.

The second possibility is somewhat analogous to ANOVA, and involves measuring predictive error, squaring it and adding it up. The error in this case is between the f_e, the frequencies predicted by a model that assumes there is no discrimination, and the f_o, the observed frequencies. Since the $f_o - f_e$ sum to 0, we must use the same trick we did with deviations from the mean, namely squaring these differences. Finally, instead of dividing the sum of the squared differences by $N - 1$ to get a variance, the technique we are going to learn about here divides each of the squared difference by f_e. The result when we add them up is a statistic that is known as a **chi-square statistic** (chi is DEFINITIONS pronounced 'kai') and denoted by the Greek letter chi (χ):

$$\chi^2 = \sum \frac{(f_o - f_e)^2}{f_e}$$

Each of the $(f_o - f_e)^2/f_e$ terms is called a **squared standardized residual**, which means that the 'residual' model error, $f_o - f_e$, has been squared and then standardized relative to the size of f_e.

The chi-square statistic measures the total amount of squared error from the predictive model that has provided the expected frequencies (f_e). The *larger the value* of χ^2, the larger the total squared error and therefore the *worse the fit between the model and the data*. In our example,

$$\chi^2 = \sum \frac{(f_o - f_e)^2}{f_e}$$
$$= \frac{(71)^2}{264} + \frac{(20)^2}{176} + \frac{(-91)^2}{360}$$
$$= 19.10 + 2.27 + 23.00$$
$$= 44.37$$

In order to know whether 44.37 is large or not, we need to know something about the sampling distribution of χ^2.

The chi-square statistic's sampling distribution is known as (surprise!) the DEFINITION **chi-square distribution**. Since χ^2 is the sum of squared quantities, it is never negative and its distribution resembles the F-distribution in general shape and range. As with the t- or F-statistics, the sampling distribution of χ^2 depends on degrees of freedom. For the chi-square distribution there is only one df parameter, and when we are dealing with one categorical variable df $= k - 1$, where k is the number of categories. In our example, since there are three ethnic groups, $df = 3 - 1 = 2$. The df parameter is customarily placed in parentheses after the χ^2, so in our example we would put $\chi^2(2) = 44.37$. Like the F-distribution, the chi-square distribution is positively skewed. As the degrees of freedom increase, the skewness decreases also. In Figure 9.1, you can see that for $df = 2$ the chi-square distribution is very highly skewed, but for $df = 4$ the skew is noticeably less extreme.

To indicate a value of χ^2 that denotes the area under the curve beyond it, we use the same α-subscript as we have for F, t, and z. So, χ^2_α is the value beyond which the area under the curve is equal to α. In the $df = 2$ graph, for instance, '$\chi^2_{0.05} = 5.9915$' tells us that the area under the curve beyond 5.9915 is 0.05. We can get these values from Table A.5, which is organized in a similar way to the t-distribution table. The rows correspond to the degrees of freedom, and the columns correspond to α levels. The relevant part of Table A.5 is shown here as Table 9.7, with the row for $df = 2$ and column for $\alpha = 0.05$ highlighted.

Like the F-statistic, most of the time the chi-square statistic is assessed via a

DEFINITION   **one-sided confidence interval** of the form

$$\Pr(\chi^2(df) < \chi^2_\alpha) = 1 - \alpha.$$

$$\xleftarrow{\text{---}100(1-\alpha)\%\longrightarrow}$$

0   χ^2_α

The 'no effects' hypothesis usually is that the expected frequencies are close enough to the observed ones that $\chi^2(df)$ is small. If the sample $\chi^2(df)$ value lies outside the confidence interval, then we may reject the null hypothesis and conclude that the observed and expected frequencies differ.

In our example since $\chi^2_{0.05} = 5.9915$, the 95% confidence interval is

$$\Pr(\chi^2(2) < 5.9915) = 0.95.$$

$$\xleftarrow{\text{---}95\%\longrightarrow}$$

0   5.9915

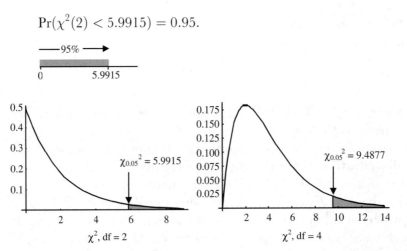

FIGURE 9.1 Chi-square distributions with $df = 2$ and $df = 4$

TABLE 9.7 Part of Table A.5: $\chi^2_{0.05} = 5.9915$

df	0.99	0.95	0.9	0.8	0.2	0.1	0.05	0.01
1	0.0002	0.0039	0.0158	0.0642	1.6424	2.7055	3.8415	6.6349
2	0.0201	0.1026	0.2107	0.4463	3.2189	4.6052	5.9915	9.2104
3	0.1148	0.3518	0.5844	1.0052	4.6416	6.2514	7.8147	11.3449
4	0.2971	0.7107	1.0636	1.6488	5.9886	7.7794	9.4877	13.2767

However, our sample chi-square value is $\chi^2(2) = 44.37$, and since that lies outside the confidence interval we may reject the null hypothesis, whose expected frequencies were derived from the assumption that unemployment operates in an indiscriminate fashion. We would therefore conclude that unemployment does discriminate and that at least two of the ethnic groups have unemployment rates that do not correspond closely with their respective proportions of eligible employees.

Usually, when a chi-square statistic reveals a bad fit between the expected and observed frequencies, researchers try to ascertain the sources of the poor fit. If we re-examine the differences between the observed and expected frequencies in our example, it seems likely that the C's are underrepresented and A's are overrepresented among the unemployed. The B's are somewhat over-represented, but how does that compare with the A's or C's? This is a situation in which a careful examination of the standardized residuals pays off.

Table 9.8 includes the standardized residuals in the right-most column. Each of these has the formula $(f_o - f_e)/\sqrt{f_e}$, and tells us how large the difference between the observed and expected frequency is relative to the magnitude of the expected frequency. In this example, both the **raw residuals** (that is, $f_o - f_e$) and standardized residuals provide much the same information, indicating that the $f_o - f_e$ magnitudes are considerably higher for the A's and C's than for the B's. However, in situations where there are large and small expected values, standardized residuals can provide a very useful supplement to the chi-square statistic and the raw residuals.

The chi-square statistic requires only two assumptions for its proper use. The first one is that the observations must be mutually independent. This

TABLE 9.8 Raw and standardized residuals

	Expected f_e	Observed f_o	Raw res. $f_o - f_e$	Std. res. $(f_o - f_e)/\sqrt{f_e}$
A's	264	335	71	4.37
B's	176	196	20	1.51
C's	360	269	−91	−4.80
Total	800	800	0	

assumption underlies nearly all of the techniques we have mentioned thus far, but it is worthwhile mentioning it here specifically. The second assumption is that the expected frequencies for each category must not be too small. A widely accepted rule of thumb in this regard is that the expected frequencies should be at least 5 for each category.

In instances where expected frequencies are below 5, sometimes a remedy is to combine the sparse category with another in some sensible way. When the variable has a categorical ordinal scale, adjacent categories may be combined. For example, suppose a Likert-style Agree–Disagree scale has the following categories and expected frequencies:

- Strongly Agree   3
- Agree   12
- Neutral   27
- Disagree   19
- Strongly Disagree   9

The Strongly Agree category has an expected frequency below 5, but it could be combined with the Agree category whose combined expected frequency would be $3 + 12 = 15$. For variables that are nominal, the choice of which categories to combine depends on research goals and theoretical considerations.

The chi-square statistic may be used to compare observed frequency distributions with theoretical ones. We will investigate an example that uses the binomial distribution. Suppose we are pilot-testing a short seven-item test of basic First Aid knowledge for use in a survey of public beliefs and perceptions about health-related issues. The seven items consist of questions that are scored either 'Correct' or 'Incorrect,' so each person's score on the test could range from 0 to 7. Imagine that we have administered this test to a random sample of 270 people from the population we are concerned with.

What kind of distribution could we expect these scores to have? One possibility is the binomial distribution, since the questions have only two outcomes and each person's score is the number of 'Correct' responses out of 7. In order for the binomial distribution to describe these scores adequately, everyone's knowledge about First Aid would have to be about the same, so that they all had the same probability of getting a question correct. In other words, we would need to assume that our population was *homogeneous* when it came to First Aid knowledge. However, you may already have thought of a good reason why this model is unlikely to fit the distribution of scores very well. People probably differ considerably in their knowledge about First Aid, so the assumption that they all have the same probability of getting a question correct is unlikely to be true.

However, faced with a skeptic who wanted us to produce convincing evidence that the levels of First Aid knowledge in this population do vary, what could we do? We could use the chi-square statistic to measure how good (or bad) the fit is between our sample score distribution and the binomial distribution, thereby determining whether the homogeneity of knowledge assumption is plausible. The next table displays the outcomes of the required calculations for this procedure. The observed frequencies of each score (from 0 to 7) are shown in the 'f_o' row, and these frequencies sum to 270. The last column combines the scores of 6 and 7 and shows that there were 15 people who scored 6 and 12 who scored 7. The reason for this will be explained shortly.

The mean score on this test turns out to be 2.8 for our sample, so our estimate of the average probability of getting a question correct is $2.8/7 = 0.4$. The 'Probability' row contains the binomial probabilities of getting a score of 0, 1, 2, and so on out of 7, assuming that every person in the sample has a probability of 0.4 of getting a question correct. The 'f_e' row contains the expected frequencies. These are derived by taking the probability of each score and multiplying it by the number of people in the sample. For instance, the expected frequency for a score of 0 is $(0.0280)(270) = 7.56$ which agrees with 7.558 within roundoff error. It might seem odd that we could have expected frequencies that are fractional, but these are theoretical *average* frequencies (i.e., the average that we would get if we took many random samples of 270). Notice that the expected frequency for a score of 6 or 7 is 5.076, which is just above the statutory limit of 5. This is the reason for combining those two scores, since otherwise we would have two score categories whose expected frequencies were less than 5.

Once we have the expected frequencies, the next part of the procedure amounts to computing the chi-square statistic and then putting a confidence interval around it. Suppose we have decided to use a confidence level of 99%.

TABLE 9.9 Chi-square layout for first-aid test scores

	No. correct							
	Score = 0	1	2	3	4	5	6 or 7	Total
Observed freq. (f_o)	30	37	64	55	33	24	15 + 12	270
Probability	0.0280	0.1306	0.2613	0.2903	0.1935	0.0774	0.0188	1
Expected freq. (f_e)	7.558	35.272	70.544	78.382	52.255	20.902	5.076	
$(f_o - f_e)$	22.442	1.728	−6.544	−23.382	−19.255	3.098	21.924	$\chi^2 =$
$(f_o - f_e)^2/f_e$	66.633	0.085	0.607	6.975	7.095	0.459	94.693	176.547

Then we may obtain our confidence interval in the following steps.

1. Compute the differences between the observed and expected frequencies, i.e., the raw residuals. These are tabulated in the '$f_o - f_e$' row in the table.
2. Compute the squared standardized residuals, which are the $(f_o - f_e)^2/f_e$ terms, as displayed in the next row. Sum these to find the value of the chi-square statistic, which is $\chi^2 = 176.547$.
3. The degrees of freedom for chi-square are $k - 1$, where k is the number of categories. Since we have combined the scores of 6 and 7, we have 6 categories, so df $= 5$. Since we are using a confidence level of 99%, the proportion of the tail in the chi-square distribution we want to exclude is $1 - 0.99 = 0.01$. From Table A.5, we find that the appropriate chi-square value for df $= 5$ is $\chi^2_{0.01} = 15.0863$. Now we can complete a confidence interval statement of the form

$$\Pr(\chi^2(\mathrm{df}) < \chi^2_\alpha) = 1 - \alpha$$

namely

$$\Pr(\chi^2(5) < 15.0863) = 0.99.$$

4. Our sample chi-square value is 176.547, which is well outside of the confidence interval because it exceeds the upper bound of 15.0863 by a large amount. So we may conclude that it is an implausible value given the original hypothesis, which was that everyone in the population had the same chance of getting a question correct on the First-Aid test. Therefore, it is quite unlikely that everyone in the population has the same chance of getting a question correct.

Having arrived at this conclusion, we are now in a position to meet the skeptic's strictest reasonable standards of evidence. We have compared a theoretical distribution derived from an assumption that people's knowledge of First Aid is homogeneous against our sample distribution of scores on the seven-item test, and found that the fit is poor enough to justify our claim that people differ in their knowledge about First Aid. There is also a bonus payoff for computing all those squared standardized residuals (i.e., $(f_o - f_e)^2/f_e$). If we look back at the table and examine the row containing those residuals, we can see that there are two very large ones: 66.633 in the '0' column and 94.693 in the '6 or 7' column. These account for almost all of the chi-square statistic's magnitude. The reason why the homogeneous-knowledge model fits the distribution so poorly at these extreme scores is that some people know quite a bit less and others know considerably more than the typical person in the sample, so the distribution of scores is much more spread out than the homogeneous-knowledge model would predict.

It might seem as if we have labored long and hard to get to an obvious point (people differ; so what?), but there are two good reasons for going about this the 'hard way.' First, in many situations it is not obvious whether individual or subpopulation differences exist, and entire approaches to psychological phenomena may stand or fall on just this point (e.g., almost any area in cognitive psychology). Second, we were able to address the question of whether individual differences exist *without knowing anything about those differences*. All we had to do was establish that the scores were not distributed as they would be if everyone had the same level of knowledge. This example demonstrates that the chi-square statistic is quite useful for a variety of purposes. It is no surprise that comparisons between theoretical and sample distributions are at the heart of many sophisticated statistical techniques, and you will encounter the chi-square statistic in many diverse circumstances.

The chi-square statistic for one variable compares **expected frequencies**, denoted by f_e, with the **observed frequencies**, denoted by f_o. The expected frequencies are generated by a model, so the comparison amounts to an evaluation of how well the model fits the sample evidence in the form of the observed frequencies.

This comparison is done by converting the **raw residuals**, $f_o - f_e$, into **squared standardized residuals** $(f_o - f_e)^2/f_e$, which are summed to form the **chi-square statistic**:

$$\chi^2 = \sum \frac{(f_o - f_e)^2}{f_e}$$

The *larger the value* of χ^2, the larger the total squared error and therefore the *worse the fit between the model and the data*.

The chi-square statistic's sampling distribution is the **chi-square distribution**, whose shape depends on the degrees of freedom. When we are dealing with one categorical variable, $\mathrm{df} = k - 1$, where k is the number of categories.

The chi-square statistic is considered to be dependable as long as the *expected frequency in each category is at least 5*.

Most of the time the chi-square statistic is assessed via a **one-sided confidence interval** of the form

$$\Pr(\chi^2(\mathrm{df}) < \chi^2_\alpha) = 1 - \alpha.$$

SUMMARY

StatPatch

CHIPATCH

PROVIDES

PRACTICE IN

WORKING

THROUGH

ONE WAY

CHI-SQUARE

PROBLEMS

Working with two categorical variables

We have learned how to use the chi-square statistic to assess the fit between a predictive model and sample data for one categorical variable. The predictive models, however, were theoretical or hypothetically-based predictions about distributions that did not allow for any contingencies or circumstances. Many psychological models make predictions about one variable that depend on another variable. Fortunately, the chi-square statistic may be readily adapted to this purpose.

In Chapter 7, we found out how to use ANOVA to determine whether the *mean* of a *quantitative variable* differs across the categories of a categorical variable. In this section, we will learn how the chi-square statistic may be used to determine whether the *frequency distribution* of a *categorical variable* differs across the categories of another categorical variable. In ANOVA, we compared a null model (no differences between the means) with an effects model (differences between the means) via the *F*-statistic. The chi-square technique does much the same, by comparing a **null model** (no differences between distributions) against an **effects model** (differences between distributions). The terminology of the chi-square technique is somewhat different but the concepts are very similar to ANOVA.

To begin with, let us return to the helping episode example. Earlier we observed that the probability of help being given to strangers versus friends/ family members differed when the type of helping was spontaneous from when it was planned. Are those differences merely due to sampling error, or does the distribution of helping to strangers versus friends/family members differ when it is spontaneous from when it is planned? The chi-square statistic can assist us here.

First, we need to calculate what a null model would predict for our f_e values. Fortunately, we have already learned how to do this in the material that we covered on probability. Back in Chapter 4, we learned that events A and B are *independent* if $P(A|B) = P(A)$. We may apply this concept of independence to specify our null model. If there are no differences between the probability of helping a stranger given that the help is spontaneous versus helping a stranger given that the help is planned, then both of those conditional probabilities should be the same. If Str = stranger, Spo = spontaneous, and Pl = planned, then the null model predicts that $P(\text{Str}|\text{Spo}) = P(\text{Str}|\text{Pl}) = P(\text{Str})$.

DEFINITION   It is for this reason that the null model in the chi-square technique often is called the 'independence model.' The **independence model** assumes that helping type and helping recipient are independent events. How do we get expected frequencies from an independence model? If two events are independent, then the probability of both of them occurring is the product of their probabilities. In our example, the probability of the recipient being a stranger

TABLE 9.10 Helping example f_o and f_e

| | Observed frequencies | | |
	Planned	Spontaneous	Row total
Friends/Family	127	207	334
Strangers	23	117	140
Column total	150	324	474

| | Expected frequencies | | |
	Planned	Spontaneous	Row total
Friends/Family	105.7	228.3	334 (0.705)
Strangers	44.3	95.7	140 (0.295)
Column total	150 (0.316)	324 (0.684)	474

is $140/474 = 0.295$. Likewise, the probability of the helping being spontaneous is $324/474 = 0.684$. So, the independence model predicts that the probability of spontaneous helping between strangers is $(0.684)(0.295) = 0.202$. Therefore, the expected frequency for this cell is this cell probability multiplied by the number of people in the sample, or $(0.202)(474) = 95.7$.

In general, the expected frequency for any cell is the product of its row probability and column probability, multiplied by N. There is a simpler way to calculate the expected frequencies if you are doing it by hand, however:

$$f_e = \frac{\text{Row total} \times \text{Column total}}{N}$$

We will use this formula here. Table 9.10 shows the f_o and f_e for the helping data. The f_e are obtained in the following way:

$$\{\text{Frnd/Fam, Planned}\} \quad f_e = (334 \times 150)/474 = 105.7$$

$$\{\text{Frnd/Fam, Spontaneous}\} \quad f_e = (334 \times 324)/474 = 228.3$$

$$\{\text{Stranger, Planned}\} \quad f_e = (140 \times 150)/474 = 44.3$$

$$\{\text{Stranger, Spontaneous}\} \quad f_e = (140 \times 324)/474 = 95.7$$

The χ^2 statistic is calculated in the same way as for the setup for one variable. In our example here, the calculations are as follows:

$$\chi^2 = \sum \frac{(f_o - f_e)^2}{f_e} = \frac{(21.3)^2}{105.7} + \frac{(-21.3)^2}{228.3} + \frac{(-21.3)^2}{44.3} + \frac{(21.3)^2}{95.7}$$

$$= 4.29 + 1.99 + 10.24 + 4.74 = 21.27.$$

The next thing we want to do is to establish whether this chi-square value is plausible if our independence model is assumed to be true. In order to do that, we need to construct a confidence interval around $\chi^2(\mathrm{df})$ based on the independence model, of the form

$$\Pr(\chi^2(\mathrm{df}) < \chi^2_\alpha) = 1 - \alpha.$$

DEFINITION

    The key missing ingredient here is the **degrees of freedom**. For contingency tables, the expected frequencies are calculated by using the marginal (row and column) frequencies. Since these are being treated as if they do not vary, the only frequencies left to vary are those inside the contingency table. For a table such as in our example with only two rows and two columns (a 2×2 table), once one f_e has been calculated all of the others are predetermined because the sum of each row or column must equal its row or column total. So we conclude that a 2×2 table has only one degree of freedom. For larger tables with r rows and c columns (an $r \times c$ table), this line of argumentation generalizes to the conclusion that $\mathrm{df} = (r - 1)(c - 1)$.

    Returning to our example, we now know that our confidence interval requires $\mathrm{df} = 1$. If we were to use a confidence level of 99%, in Table A.5 we would find that for $\mathrm{df} = 1$, $\chi^2_{0.01} = 6.6349$. The resulting confidence interval statement is

$$\Pr(\chi^2(1) < 6.6349) = 0.99.$$

Our sample value of χ^2 was 21.27, which lies outside this interval. We may therefore reject the null (independence) model and conclude that helping type and helping recipient are *not* independent of each other.

    What does this conclusion tell us? It implies that the apparent difference between the probability of helping a stranger when the help is spontaneous and the probability of helping a stranger when the help is planned is unlikely to be due to sampling error. We can confidently claim that the evidence from the study shows that the distribution of helping to strangers versus friends/family members differs when it is spontaneous from when it is planned.

    Note that being able to reject the independence model does *not* provide any information about how spontaneity of help is related to recipient status. All it tells us is that these two variables are related in some fashion, because they are not independent. For that reason, the chi-square significance test associated

DEFINITION

with a contingency table is often called a **test of independence**.

Let us try a somewhat more complex example. In the research project where I was a member of a team investigating suicidal and self-destructive behavior in Trust-Area Indigenous communities, one issue we tried to address was the extent to which being Indigenous and having made suicide attempts was connected with the likelihood of being arrested. To start with, we grouped the respondents in our study into four categories: Urban Nonindigenous, Urban Indigenous, Trust-Area Indigenous, and Trust-Area Attempter (i.e., those who attempted suicide). The data in the upper part of Table 9.11 show the number of respondents in our samples who had been arrested within the previous month before being interviewed and the number of respondents who had not been arrested.

Now, if the probability of being arrested depends on which population a person belongs to, then a comparison of the observed frequencies in this table with expected frequencies based on an independence model should reveal a poor fit between them. The expected frequencies are shown in the lower half of the table.

If you focus on the frequencies in the 'Arrested' row, you should be able to quickly see that the expected frequencies are higher than the observed frequencies for the Urban Nonindigenous and Urban Indigenous samples, and vice versa for the two Trust-Area samples. In other words, the independence model overestimates the number of arrests for the two Urban samples and underestimates the arrests for both Trust-Area samples. The upper half of Table 9.12 displays this trend in the raw residuals, $f_o - f_e$.

The second half of this table shows the squared standardized residuals, $(f_o - f_e)^2 / f_e$, whose sum is the sample χ^2 statistic of 55.62. We want to

TABLE 9.11 Arrest frequencies for four samples

	Observed frequencies				
	Urban NonInd.	Urban Indig.	Trust-A. Indig.	Trust-A. Attempter	Total
Arrested	6	10	27	24	67
Not Arr.	164	99	114	35	412
Total	170	109	141	59	479

	Expected Frequencies				
	Urban NonInd.	Urban Indig.	Trust-A. Indig.	Trust-A. Attempter	Total
Arrested	23.78	15.25	19.72	8.25	67
Not Arr.	146.22	93.75	121.28	50.75	412
Total	170	109	141	59	479

TABLE 9.12 Residuals and chi-square for arrest data

	Raw residuals $f_o - f_e$:				
	Urban NonInd.	Urban Indig.	Trust-A. Indig.	Trust-A. Attempter	Total
Arrested	−17.78	−5.25	7.28	15.75	0
Not Arr.	17.78	5.25	−7.28	−15.75	0
Total	0	0	0	0	0

	Squared standardized residuals $(f_o - f_e)^2/f_e$ and chi-square			
	Urban NonInd.	Urban Indig.	Trust-A. Indig.	Trust-A. Attempter
Arrested	13.29	1.81	2.69	30.05
Not Arr.	2.16	0.29	0.44	4.89

$$\chi^2 = 55.62$$

know whether 55.62 could be a plausible value of χ^2, if the independence model were true. Our degrees of freedom are df $= (r-1)(c-1) = (2-1)(4-1) = 3$. If we were to use a confidence level of 99%, in Table A.5 we would find that for df $= 3$, $\chi^2_{0.01} = 9.2104$. The resulting confidence interval statement is

$$\Pr(\chi^2(3) < 9.2104) = 0.99.$$

Our sample value of χ^2 is 55.62, which lies outside this interval. We may therefore reject the null (independence) model and conclude that arrest and community sample are *not* independent of each other. The trend we detected for arrest-rates to be higher in the Trust-Area communities is probably real.

SUMMARY

The chi-square technique for assessing the independence of two categorical variables compares a **null model** (no differences between distributions) against an **effects model** (differences between distributions).
The null model is really an **independence model**, which asserts that the two variables are statistically independent of each other. Since they are independent, the expected frequency (f_e) for any cell in a contingency table is the product of its row probability and column probability, multiplied by N. A more convenient way of computing f_e is

$$f_e = \frac{\text{Row total} \times \text{Column total}}{N}$$

The **chi-square statistic** is the same as the version for one variable:

$$\chi^2 = \sum \frac{(f_o - f_e)^2}{f_e}$$

For a table with r rows and c columns (an $r \times c$ table), if the independence model is true, then the sampling distribution of the chi-square statistic is a chi-square distribution with degrees of freedom

$$\mathrm{df} = (r - 1)(c - 1).$$

The corresponding confidence interval has the same form as the version for one variable:

$$\mathrm{Pr}(\chi^2(\mathrm{df}) < \chi^2_\alpha) = 1 - \alpha.$$

In the chi-square significance **test of independence**, if the sample chi-square value lies outside the confidence interval then it is an implausible value according to the independence model, and we may reject the null hypothesis that the independence model is true. We then conclude that the two variables are related (although this test says nothing about how they are related).

SUMMARY

CHIPATCH PROVIDES PRACTICE IN WORKING THROUGH TWO-WAY CHI-SQUARE PROBLEMS

Chi-square, effect size, and association

In this section, we will examine ways of using the chi-square statistic as a **measure of the association** (or strength of the relationship) between two categorical variables. In Chapters 7 and 8 we saw how R^2 measures the degree of linear association between two variables. Here, statistics based on chi-square perform a similar role because the value of chi-square increases as the observed frequencies depart farther from the independence model (meaning that the variables are more strongly related).

Although the chi-square statistic is very useful, it does not tell us how strong a relationship between two variables is. There are two reasons for this. First, all things remaining equal, the greater the number of cells the larger the chi-square. This is because chi-square is a sum rather than an average. Second, chi-square increases with sample size. Indeed, if we double all the observed frequencies the chi-square will double; if we triple them the chi-square will triple, and so on.

The second problem is easy enough to deal with: simply divide chi-square by N, the sample size. For 2×2 contingency tables this works perfectly well, and is known as the ϕ^2 **coefficient** (pronounced 'phi-squared'). The ϕ^2 coefficient's formula is

DEFINITION

$$\phi^2 = \chi^2/N.$$

Its value ranges from 0 (independence) to 1 (complete dependence). A value of 1 occurs only if the 2×2 contingency table has a 0 in two diagonally opposite cells, which implies that if we know which category an observation falls in for one variable, we can predict with perfect accuracy which category it will fall in for the other variable.

It turns out that ϕ^2 can be thought of as a squared correlation coefficient, provided that we also think of each variable in binary terms as having an 'on' category with a value of 1 and an 'off' category with a value of 0. It often does not matter which category we assign 1 and which we assign 0, but sometimes these values correspond with the category meanings (e.g., 'present' $= 1$; 'absent' $= 0$). The main benefit of this interpretation of ϕ^2 is that it can be interpreted as an effect size in the same way as R^2. Likewise, Cohen's (1988) benchmarks for the magnitude of R^2 may be applied to judging the size of ϕ^2. Remember, in Chapter 8 we saw that these benchmarks were 0.01 for a small effect, 0.09 for a medium one, and 0.25 for a large effect.

In the helping behavior example, our sample value of χ^2 was 21.27 and the sample size was 479. The ϕ^2 coefficient has the value

$$\phi^2 = \chi^2/N = 21.27/479 = 0.04,$$

which is small even by Cohen's standards. The relatively large sample has enabled us to detect what, according to ϕ^2, is a subtle effect. We will reconsider the interpretation of effect sizes later in this chapter.

If the sample size, N, is regarded as fixed, then any confidence interval for χ^2 can be changed into a confidence interval for ϕ^2 simply by dividing the upper limit of the interval by N. In our helping behavior example, the 99% confidence interval for χ^2 under the independence model was

$$\Pr(\chi^2(1) < 6.6349) = 0.99.$$

So we may divide 6.6349 by N, which was 474, and also say that under the independence model,

$$\Pr(\phi^2 < 0.014) = 0.99.$$

DEFINITION

The fact that chi-square increases with the number of rows and columns in a table is a drawback that is not dealt with by ϕ^2, but long ago Cramer came up with a suitable modification of ϕ^2 for larger tables. It is called **Cramer's V^2**, and it divides ϕ^2 by the number of rows or columns minus 1, whichever is smaller. If we denote this quantity by $m - 1$, the formula for V^2 is

$$V^2 = \chi^2/N(m-1).$$

Cramer's V^2, unlike ϕ^2, cannot be interpreted as a squared correlation coefficient. It has no other effect size interpretation, so it is difficult to know what any particular value of V^2 means. There are other measures of effect size for contingency tables that do not suffer this disadvantage.

Let us recycle an example from Chapter 7. In the last section of that chapter, we used ANOVA to compare mean self-esteem scores from three samples taken from northeastern Australia: Nonindigenous urbanites, Indigenous urbanites, and Indigenous remote community members. However, as with many samples from Western societies, the majority of the people have high self-esteem and so the self-esteem scores are strongly skewed with most people scoring quite highly. In fact, although our scale ranged from 6 to 15, more than four-fifths of the people in our study scored 12, 13, or 14. A reasonable alternative approach would be to categorize scores in four groups (<12, 12, 13, and 14) and to compare the distribution of the three samples across those four groups. Table 9.13 shows these distributions in the form of a contingency table. A chi-square statistic will tell us whether sample is independent of self-esteem score, and since this table has more than two rows and two columns, Cramer's V^2 is the appropriate measure of effect size.

Without going into the computational detail, the value of chi-square for this table is $\chi^2 = 57.813$. There are four rows and three columns, so $m - 1 = 3 - 1 = 2$ and

$$\text{Cramer's } V^2 = \chi^2/N(m-1) = 57.813/444(2) = 0.065.$$

That is fairly close to the R^2 value of 0.073 that we obtained when we used ANOVA for comparing these three samples, so these two techniques give us about the same effect sizes.

Having said that Cramer's V^2 has limited interpretive value, it is still decidedly preferable to using chi-square in many situations. In the self-esteem example, we obtained a chi-square value of 57.813. Remember if we doubled

TABLE 9.13 Three samples of self-esteem scores

Esteem Score	Urban NonInd.	Urban Indig.	Trust-A. Indig.	Total
<12	19	15	52	86
12	13	19	41	73
13	36	32	58	126
14	91	28	40	159
Total	159	94	191	444

the frequencies in the table above, that chi-square value would also double, but V^2 would remain the same. If we are comparing two or more studies that have different sample sizes, Cramer's V^2 is much less misleading than chi-square.

Likewise, chi-square can mislead us when we are comparing sizes of effects that involve tables of different sizes. In our arrest example (taken from the same data-set as the self-esteem example), we found $\chi^2 = 55.62$ when we tested whether likelihood of arrest was independent of sample. This value is just slightly less than 57.813 and so it might seem as if the strength of association between arrest and sample is similar to that between self-esteem and sample. Cramer's V^2 tells us otherwise. The arrest example involves a 2×4 table, so $m - 1 = 2 - 1 = 1$. For those data, $N = 479$, and $V^2 = 55.62/479(1) = 0.116$, which is about 1.8 times *larger* than the V^2 of 0.065 that we obtained for the self-esteem example.

Cramer's V^2 and ϕ^2 are not the only measures of association based on chi-square, but they are the most popular. All measures of association based on chi-square share some of its limitations. Like chi-square, they are vulnerable to *sparseness* in contingency tables. Some computer programs warn users about this. Earlier in this chapter, we mentioned a rule-of-thumb that chi-square is dependable only when every *expected* cell-frequency in the contingency table is at least 5. If a table has too few cases in one or more cells, then one remedy is to collapse columns and/or rows by combining categories which make sense to put together.

Chi-square and its affiliated measures of association also are affected by *skewed marginal totals*, so if the skewness is very large then they should be used with caution. A related, but more subtle issue is the fact that chi-square changes if a row or column is multiplied by a constant. We can see why this might be a problem by reconsidering the arrest example and imagining that we had obtained twice as many suicide attempters as we did in the study, so that we had 118 of them instead of 59. If the proportion of attempters arrested in the previous month remained the same, the contingency table would be like Table 9.14, with 48 attempters arrested and 70 not arrested.

TABLE 9.14 Twice as many attempters

	Urban NonInd.	Urban Indig.	Trust-A. Indig.	Trust-A. Attempt.	Total
Arrested	6	10	27	48	91
Not Arr.	164	99	114	70	447
Total	170	109	141	118	538

Everything else in the table has remained the same and the probability of arrest for each sample has remained the same, but chi-square has changed. Instead of 55.62, its value has increased to 74.24 and therefore Cramer's V^2 has increased from 0.116 to 0.155. The problem is that by merely increasing the size of one of the samples, we have made the association between sample and arrest appear stronger (as measured by Cramer's V^2). This makes no sense when relative sample sizes are arbitrary, as in clinical studies using cases and controls. The only time when this would not be a problem would be when the sample sizes are proportional to population sizes. In the next section we will examine some ways of getting around this difficulty.

SUMMARY

In this section we examined two popular **measures of the association** (or strength of the relationship) between two categorical variables, both based on the chi-square statistic.

For 2×2 contingency tables, the ϕ^2 coefficient is equivalent to a squared correlation coefficient and has the formula

$$\phi^2 = \chi^2/N.$$

If the sample size, N, is regarded as fixed, then any confidence interval for χ^2 can be changed into a confidence interval for ϕ^2 simply by dividing the upper limit of the interval by N.

Cramer's V^2 is used for tables with more than two rows or columns, and it divides ϕ^2 by the number of rows or columns minus 1, whichever is smaller. If we denote this quantity by $m - 1$, the formula for V^2 is

$$V^2 = \chi^2/N(m - 1).$$

The main limitations on the valid use of these measures of association are those that pertain to chi-square, namely *skewness* in the marginal totals and *sparseness* in the table.

Using percentages and proportions to interpret associations

Thus far, we have found that the chi-square statistic and its affiliated measures of association tell us whether two categorical variables are related in some way, without informing us very much about the nature or strength of the association between them. In this section we will examine some popular methods for 'dissecting' contingency tables that employ proportions or percentages. None of them are panaceas, and choosing one approach over another requires the researcher to consider what kind of question about the data is to be addressed.

Before reading on, try answering the following question intuitively, i.e., without calculating anything. As the hospital chief investigating a new flu virus, you have tabulated the occurrence of two symptoms, nasal congestion and stomach cramps, in patients diagnosed with this flu. According to the data in Table 9.15, which conclusion are you able to reach?

- There is a positive association between the two symptoms.
- There is no association between the two symptoms.
- There is a negative association between the two symptoms.

Now, try answering the next question in the same intuitive way. In a nation with a population of 20 million adult employees, HIV blood tests have been made mandatory as a workplace health and safety measure. The initial screening test has been extensively tested for several years and is quite accurate, but like all tests it is not perfect. Two percent of those who do not have the virus will be *false positives* (i.e., their test result will be positive, saying that they have the virus when they do not) and 4% of those who have the virus will be *false negatives* (i.e., their test result will be negative even though they have the virus). Imagine that out of the 20 million employees, 50,000 are HIV-positive. What percentage of the people whose test is positive will actually have the disease?

The first question usually trips us into thinking that there is a positive association between stomach cramps and nasal congestion, because there are 120 people who have that combination of symptoms, whereas the other cell frequencies are much smaller. If your intuition led you there, then you have fallen prey to the same *confirmation bias* that we encountered in Chapter 2 with the Wason–Johnson-Laird card task. A chi-square statistic computed for that table yields a value of 0, so the two symptoms are unrelated. Somewhat more intuitively, the row percentages are identical for both rows. That is, the percentage of patients with stomach cramps who also have nasal congestion is $100 \times (120/140) = 85.7\%$, and likewise the percentage of patients without stomach cramps who also have nasal congestion is $100 \times (30/35) = 85.7\%$. So, those who have stomach cramps have no greater likelihood of having nasal congestion than those without stomach cramps.

The second question is subtler and raises several issues that we will consider in this section. The best way to approach it systematically is by laying the problem out in a contingency table like the one displayed as Table 9.16. To start with, we know that 4% of the 50,000 who have the virus will test

TABLE 9.15 Flu symptoms

	Nasal congestion	
Stomach cramps	Present	Absent
Present	120	20
Absent	30	5

TABLE 9.16 **HIV preventative testing scenario**

Has HIV	Test result		
	Positive	Negative	
Yes	48,000	2,000	50,000
No	399,000	19,551,000	19,950,000
	447,000	19,553,000	20,000,000

negative, so that gives us $0.04 \times 50,000 = 2000$ false negatives (they are in the Yes–Negative cell). If 50,000 have the virus, then 19,950,000 do not. Moreover, 2% of them will test positive, which is $0.02 \times 19,950,000 = 399,000$ false positives (in the No–Positive cell). How many *true* positives are there? Out of the 50,000 who have the virus, 2000 test negative so that leaves 48,000 employees who both have the disease and test positive.

The total number of positive test results is $48,000 + 399,000 = 447,000$, of which only 48,000 (or about 10.74%) actually have the disease! The probability that a randomly selected employee whose test is positive really has the virus is only $48,000/447,000 = 0.1074$. In contrast, the percentage of the 19,553,000 employees with negative tests who really do not have the disease is a whopping 99.99%. Remember, this test has a *higher* false negative rate (4%) than false positive rate (2%). Moreover, there is the tragic and costly magnitude of the social injustice to be considered, whereby nearly 400,000 employees are falsely labeled as HIV-positive, with all of the dreadful consequences that follow.

How could such a straightforward exercise in preventative testing go so spectacularly wrong? To many of us, this outcome is quite counter-intuitive unless we examine the contingency table fairly closely. The main clue is the relatively small number of HIV-infected people (50,000) and the very large number of people who do not have the virus (19,950,000). If we wanted the probability that a randomly selected employee whose test is positive really has the virus to be 0.9, say, then instead of 399,000 false positives we could afford only about 5333. That is only about 0.027% of the 19,950,000 people who do not have the virus! The test would have to err about 75 times less often on positive tests than it does.

The first problem illustrates how easily misled we can become when trying to 'eyeball' even a simple 2×2 table of frequencies to detect a relationship between two variables. The second problem alerts us to the fact that even a very strong association between two variables (in this case, a test for HIV and HIV status) does not guarantee high predictive accuracy in all respects. Fortunately, there are some helpful ways of pulling a contingency table apart that enable us to avoid pitfalls such as these.

StatPatch

AIDSPATCH
INVITES
FURTHER
EXPLORA-
TION OF
THIS ISSUE

Perhaps the easiest and most obvious method is to use row or column percentages (and their equivalent conditional probabilities). Row percentages were sufficient to tell us that the symptoms in the flu-symptom data were unrelated. Likewise, our understanding of the HIV-testing scenario relied on the use of conditional probabilities. It turns out that comparing percentages or conditional probabilities can help us interpret a wide variety of relationships between categorical variables.

Row or column percentages are at their best when we want to compare two categories of a dependent variable across the categories of an independent variable. The arrest data provides a good example. Table 9.17 redisplays the arrest data for the four samples. We already know that there is an association between arrest and sample. In the original study, we treated arrest as a dependent variable, that is, to be predicted on the basis of which sample people came from. The best way to interpret this association is to use column percentages, the percentage of people from each sample who were arrested or not.

The second part of this table shows the percentages of people arrested and not arrested from each sample. It is easy to see that the percentage of people arrested increases as we move from left to right in this table. Urban Indigenes are more likely to be arrested than Urban Nonindigenes, Trust-Area Indigenes

TABLE 9.17 Arrest data revisted

	Observed frequencies				
	Urban NonInd.	Urban Indig.	Trust-A. Indig.	Trust-A. Attempter	Total
Arrested	6	10	27	24	67
Not Arr.	164	99	114	35	412
Total	170	109	141	59	479

	Column percentages				
	Urban NonInd.	Urban Indig.	Trust-A. Indig.	Trust-A. Attempter	Total
Arrested	3.53%	9.17%	19.15%	40.68%	13.99%
Not Arr.	96.47%	90.83%	80.85%	59.32%	86.01%
Total	100%	100%	100%	100%	100%

	Percentage difference				
	Urban NonInd.	Urban Indig.	Trust-A. Indig.	Trust-A. Attempter	Total
Arrested		5.64%	9.97%	21.53%	
Not Arr.		−5.64%	−9.97%	−21.53%	

more likely still, and Trust-Area suicide attempters most likely. One effective way of assessing these effects is to simply take the **percentage differences** between adjacent samples. The percentage of arrests increases from 3.53% for Urban Nonindigenes to 9.17% for Urban Indigenes, for a difference of 5.64% which is recorded in the lower section of the table. Likewise, Trust-Area Indigenes are 9.97% more likely to be arrested than Urban Indigenes, and Trust-Area suicide attempters 21.53% more likely than Trust-Area Indigenes who have not attempted suicide. Note that since there are only two rows, the second row of percentage differences is redundant.

Percentage differences range from −100% to +100%, and they are easy to interpret by virtue of being percentages. They are fairly easy to communicate to nonspecialists. Percentaging and percentage differences also generalize readily to larger tables. The self-esteem example is redisplayed as Table 9.18, with

TABLE 9.18 Self-esteem data revisited

| Esteem score | Observed frequencies | | | |
	Urban NonInd.	Urban Indig.	Trust-A. Indig.	Total
< 12	19	15	52	86
12	13	19	41	73
13	36	32	58	126
14	91	28	40	159
Total	159	94	191	444

| Esteem score | Column percentages | | | |
	Urban NonInd.	Urban Indig.	Trust-A. Indig.	Total
< 12	11.95%	15.96%	27.23%	19.37%
12	8.18%	20.21%	21.47%	16.44%
13	22.64%	34.04%	30.37%	28.38%
14	57.23%	29.79%	20.94%	35.81%
Total	100%	100%	100%	100%

| Esteem score | Percentage difference | | | |
	Urban NonInd.	Urban Indig.	Trust-A. Indig.	Total
< 12		4.01%	11.27%	
12		12.04%	1.25%	
13		11.40%	−3.68%	
14		−27.45%	−8.84%	
Total				

column percentages and percentage differences between adjacent samples shown in the middle and lower parts of the table, respectively. These percentages show that there is a marked decline in high self-esteem scores and a corresponding increase in lower scores as we move from the left to the right in the table.

Before we leave the topic of percentage differences, we must explore the connections between them and the sections in Chapter 7 on the difference between two proportions and multiple confidence intervals. Returning to the arrest data, we found a 5.64% difference in the percentage of people arrested between Urban Nonindigenes and Urban Indigenes, a 9.97% difference between Urban and Trust-Area Indigenes, and a 21.53% difference between Trust-Area nonattempters and attempters. In reporting these sample estimates, it would make sense to construct confidence intervals for them so that we (and others) have some idea of how precise those estimates are. In Chapter 7 we learned how to construct confidence intervals for a difference between two proportions. Since a proportion is a percentage divided by 100, we may use those methods here.

First, we need to recall how to construct a confidence interval for the difference between proportions. This interval has the form

$$\Pr(P_1 - P_2 - w \le \Pi_1 - \Pi_2 \le P_1 - P_2 + w) = 1 - \alpha,$$

where P_1 and P_2 are the sample proportions for samples 1 and 2, and Π_1 and Π_2 are the population proportions. The half-width is either

- $w = t_{\alpha/2} s_{\text{err}}$ for small to moderate sample sizes, or
- $w = z_{\alpha/2} s_{\text{err}}$ for large samples.

The formula for s_{err} is

$$s_{\text{err}} = \sqrt{\frac{P_1(1 - P_1)}{N_1} + \frac{P_2(1 - P_2)}{N_2}}$$

We are all set, except that we also should ensure that our *family-wise* confidence level is as high as we wish. Again, Chapter 7's section on multiple confidence intervals has exactly what we need. In fact, everything in that section concerning multiple comparisons among means applies here to multiple comparisons among proportions (or percentages). We will not go through it all again, however. For illustrative purposes, we will simply construct 95% confidence intervals for the three **proportion differences** in our example. We may use $w = z_{\alpha/2} s_{\text{err}}$ as our half-width, since we have sufficiently large samples. From Table A.2, we get $z_{0.025} = 1.96$.

We number our samples from left to right in the original table (Urban Nonindigenes = 1, Urban Indigenes = 2, etc.). The first proportion difference, $P_2 - P_1$, is 5.64% divided by 100, or 0.0564. The standard error, s_{err}, is

$$s_{err} = \sqrt{\frac{P_1(1 - P_1)}{N_1} + \frac{P_2(1 - P_2)}{N_2}} = \sqrt{\frac{0.0353(0.9647)}{170} + \frac{0.0917(0.9083)}{109}}$$

$$= 0.0311$$

and $w = z_{\alpha/2} s_{err} = (1.96)(0.0311) = 0.0609$. The resulting confidence interval is $CI_{0.95} = [0.0564 - 0.0609, 0.0564 + 0.0609] = [-0.0044, 0.1173]$. In percentages, $CI_{0.95} = [-0.44\%, 11.73\%]$. The three 95% confidence intervals are shown in Table 9.19.

The confidence intervals tell us our proportion difference estimates are sufficiently imprecise that 0 is a plausible value for one out of the three comparisons, namely $P_2 - P_1$. There is, moreover, quite a bit of overlap among these intervals despite the increasing trend in the pairwise differences.

Percentages and percentage differences share an important limitation along with chi-square based measures of association. They are insensitive to what is called 'weak perfect' association. In order to understand why this limitation is important we need to find out what weak perfect association is. We will begin with an example in which that kind of association plays a crucial role.

Some years ago at James Cook University, a clinical psychologist, Dr. Georg Eifert, was conducting research into snake-phobia (herpetophobia, for those who enjoy terminology). He hypothesized that there are specific phobic reactions such as fear or disgust, but also general ones such as strong dislike. One subsidiary hypothesis was that anyone who is disgusted by a stimulus will also dislike it, but the converse may not hold. People who dislike the stimulus may not find it disgusting; they might dislike it for some other reason (e.g., fear). This is a weak perfect association because if we know someone is disgusted by a stimulus then they will dislike it, but if they are not disgusted by it then we do not know whether they will dislike it or not.

TABLE 9.19 Confidence intervals for arrest-rate comparisons

Comparison	Difference	s_{err}	w	$CI_{0.95}$
$P_2 - P_1$	0.0564	0.0311	0.0609	[−0.0044, 0.1173] or [−0.44%, 11.73%]
$P_3 - P_2$	0.0997	0.0432	0.0846	[0.0152, 0.1843] or [1.52%, 18.43%]
$P_4 - P_3$	0.2153	0.0720	0.1412	[0.0741, 0.3565] or [7.41%, 35.65%]

DEFINITION   More generally, an association is **strictly perfect** if every category of one variable uniquely predicts one category of the other. An association is **weakly perfect** if that is the case only for some of the categories on the predicting variable.

Eifert and his students collected self-reports on whether participants found snakes disgusting (yes or no) and whether they disliked snakes (yes or no). If the results agreed exactly with Eifert's hypothesis, then they would have a contingency table like Table 9.20. Everyone who is disgusted by snakes dislikes them. However, there are plenty of people (154) who dislike snakes but are not disgusted by them.

Despite the fact that we have a striking pattern in this table, $\chi^2 = 17.66$ and so $\phi^2 = 0.067$. The relevant percentage difference is only 25.96%. These statistics suggest that there is only a weak association between disgust and dislike. A number of researchers would balk at this interpretation. However, there is an alternative measure of association that is sensitive to weakly perfect associations and is widely used in health psychology, epidemiology, and other areas related to medicine and health. That measure is the odds ratio, and we will investigate it in the next section.

SUMMARY   Percentages and proportions are frequently used to interpret associations between categorical variables. *Column percentages* are used if the column variable is the predictor; and *row percentages* are used if the row variable is the predictor.

Percentage differences and **proportion differences** may be used to assess effects in much the same way as multiple comparisons are in ANOVA. They are easy to understand and to communicate to nonspecialists.

One of their main limitations is shared with chi-square-based measures of association, namely that they are not sensitive to weak perfect associations.

An association is **strictly perfect** if every category of one variable uniquely predicts one category of the other. An association is **weakly perfect** if that is the case only for some of the categories on the predicting variable.

TABLE 9.20 Hypothetical snake data

Disgusted by snakes	Dislike snakes		
	No	Yes	Total
Yes	0	54	54
No	54	154	208
Total	54	208	262

The odds ratio as a measure of association

The 'odds' often are familiar to horse-racing aficionados, but they are easy to understand even if you are not an habitual gambler. Suppose there are 54 people in a sample who are disgusted by snakes, and 208 who are not. Then the **odds** of randomly selecting someone in that sample who is disgusted by snakes are 54 to 208, or 54/208. Odds differ from probabilities because they involve the ratio of frequencies from two alternatives (in this case, disgusted versus not disgusted). The probability of randomly selecting someone who is disgusted by snakes would be $54/(54 + 208) = 54/262$. DEFINITION

In contingency tables, we work with **conditional odds** that are akin to conditional probabilities. Table 9.21 shows the real data from Eifert's study of disgust and dislike about snakes. To interpret the association between disgust and dislike, we compare the odds of disliking snakes given that a person is disgusted by them with the odds of disliking snakes when they are not disgusted by them. The odds of disliking snakes given that a person is disgusted are DEFINITION

$$\text{Odds}(\text{Dislike}|\text{Disgusted}) = 49/5 = 9.80.$$

The odds of disliking snakes given that a person is not disgusted are

$$\text{Odds}(\text{Dislike}|\text{Not disgusted}) = 159/49 = 3.24.$$

Clearly the odds of dislike are higher when people are disgusted than when they are not. We compare odds by taking the ratio of them, conventionally with the larger odds on top. Denoting the **odds ratio** by Ω, we have DEFINITION

$$\Omega = \frac{\text{Odds}(\text{Dislike}|\text{Disgusted})}{\text{Odds}(\text{Dislike}|\text{Not disgusted})} = \frac{9.80}{3.24} = 3.02$$

TABLE 9.21 Those dislikable and disgusting snakes

Disgusted by snakes	Dislike snakes?		
	No	Yes	Total
Yes	5	49	54
No	49	159	208
Total	54	208	262

The value of the odds ratio tells us that the odds of dislike are 3.02 times higher when people are disgusted than when they are not.

The main strengths of the odds ratio is that it overcomes two of the problems associated with the chi-square based measures and percentage differences. First, it is able to detect weak perfect associations. In fact, it doesn't differentiate between weak and strict perfect association. Consider again the table of hypothetical snake data in the previous section (Table 9.20). In that table, the odds of disliking snakes given that a person is disgusted is $54/0 = \infty$. The odds ratio then is infinity, which is as large as it can get.

The stronger the association between the two variables, the more extreme the odds ratio's value becomes. If there were no association between disgust and dislike (i.e., if they were statistically independent) then the odds ratio would equal 1. The reason for this is that the people who are disgusted by snakes would have no greater odds of disliking them than those who were not disgusted – disgust or lack of disgust would make no difference regarding the odds of dislike.

A second advantage of the odds ratio is that it does not change if you multiply a column or row of a contingency table by a constant. Returning to the table with the real data (Table 9.21), suppose we obtained 10 times as many people who were not disgusted by snakes, so that the second row frequencies were all multiplied by 10. There would be 490 people who neither disliked nor were disgusted by snakes, and 1590 who were not disgusted by them but disliked them nonetheless. Then the odds ratio would be exactly the same as before:

$$\Omega = \frac{\text{Odds}(\text{Dislike}|\text{Disgusted})}{\text{Odds}(\text{Dislike}|\text{Not disgusted})} = \frac{49/5}{1590/490} = \frac{9.80}{3.24} = 3.02$$

However, ϕ^2 would decrease from 0.0204 to 0.0028 and the relevant percentage difference would decline from 14.30% to 1.98%.

The fact that the odds ratio is invariant under column or row multiplication has endeared it to researchers in clinical, health, and medical areas. They often wish to compare clinical or patient samples with 'controls' from a corresponding nonclinical population, and the relative sizes of their samples usually are dictated by availability and resource constraints. Another related reason is that odds ratios highlight important differences between samples for risks whose magnitudes are low overall, whereas percentage-differences become tiny for rare events. We can see how this works by going back to Heubeck's data on parents' ratings of their children on the CBCL Aggressive Behavior subscale (this example was used in Chapters 7 and 8).

That scale has a 'Clinical Borderline' cutoff score of 20. In Chapter 7 we compared the proportions of clinically referred and nonreferred children who scored beyond this cutoff. In the clinically referred sample, 22 mothers out of 89 gave their children scores of 20 or more, whereas only two out of 89 mothers did in the nonreferred sample. Our sample proportions were

$$P_1 = 22/89 = 0.247$$

and

$$P_2 = 2/89 = 0.022.$$

The difference between these proportions is

$$P_1 - P_2 = 0.225.$$

We could re-express this as a 22.5% difference, which seems like a modest positive difference between the two samples.

What happens to this comparison when we use an odds ratio? In the clinically referred sample, 22 mothers gave their children scores of 20 or more, and $89 - 22 = 67$ did not. So,

$$\text{Odds}(\geq 20|\text{referred}) = 22/67 = 0.328.$$

On the other hand, two mothers rated their children at 20 or more in the nonreferred sample and $89 - 2 = 87$ did not, so

$$\text{Odds}(\geq 20|\text{nonreferred}) = 2/87 = 0.023.$$

The odds ratio is $\Omega = 0.328/0.023 = 14.26$, which means that the odds of a child from the referred sample getting a rating over the Clinical Borderline are *14.26 times higher* than the odds of a child from the nonreferred sample. This sounds rather more spectacular than a percentage difference of 22.5%.

The general formula for the odds ratio requires a bit of notation, mainly for the purpose of identifying which row and column of a contingency table is being referred to. So far, we have avoided this notation but it is quite frequently used in the research literature so it is worthwhile learning about it. The custom is to index the row and column of a cell with two subscripts, with the row first and column second. So N_{12} refers to the cell frequency in the first row and second column. Table 9.22 shows how this indexing works in a 2×2 table.

Now, suppose we are computing the **odds** that someone will be in category DEFINITIONS 1 on Y given that they are in category 1 on X. The formula for that odds is

$$\text{Odds}(Y = 1|X = 1) = N_{11}/N_{12}.$$

TABLE 9.22 A 2×2 contingency table

X	Υ		Total
	1	2	
1	$\mathcal{N}_{11}$	$\mathcal{N}_{12}$	
2	$\mathcal{N}_{21}$	$\mathcal{N}_{22}$	
Total			

The odds of being in category 1 on Υ if someone is in category 2 on X are

$$\mathrm{Odds}(\Upsilon = 1 | X = 2) = \mathcal{N}_{21}/\mathcal{N}_{22}.$$

The **odds ratio** (of the first odds to the second) is

$$\Omega = \frac{\mathrm{Odds}(\Upsilon = 1 | X = 1)}{\mathrm{Odds}(\Upsilon = 1 | X = 2)} = \frac{\mathcal{N}_{11}/\mathcal{N}_{12}}{\mathcal{N}_{21}/\mathcal{N}_{22}}$$

There are two drawbacks to odds ratios as a measure of association. One is that the odds ratio can achieve its maximum when there is either a weakly perfect *or* strictly perfect association between two variables. Whether this is a virtue or a vice depends on the researcher's goals and preferences. The second, more important, limitation is that the odds ratio does not provide a summary measure of association for tables larger than 2×2. It shares this disadvantage with percentage differences, but sets of odds ratios may be used to dissect the relationship between two variables in much the same way as percentage differences.

Using odds ratios for tables with more than two rows or columns involves similar decisions to those concerning percentage differences. None the less, odds ratios have a somewhat different interpretation. Since they are ratios, odds *ratios* are interpreted *multiplicatively*, whereas percentage *differences* are interpreted *additively*. To see how this works, we will revisit the arrest data one more time.

Table 9.23 shows the percentages of people in each sample who were arrested and the odds of arrest for each sample. For instance, the percentage of the Urban Nonindigenous sample who had been arrested was $100 \times (6/170) = 3.53\%$, whereas the odds of arrest for that sample was $6/164 = 0.0366$. Now, the percentage difference between the Urban Nonindigenous and Urban Indigenous arrest percentages is $9.17\% - 3.53\% = 5.64\%$, so we say that there are 5.64% *more* arrests in the latter sample. On the other hand, the odds of arrest in the Urban Indigenous sample is 0.1010, and the ratio of those odds to the odds of arrest in the Urban

TABLE 9.23 Percentage differences versus odds ratios

	Percentage arrests vs. odds of arrest			
	Urban NonInd.	Urban Indig.	Trust-A. Indig.	Trust-A. Attempt.
% of arrests	3.53%	9.17%	19.15%	40.68%
Odds of arrest	$6/164 = 0.0366$	$10/99 = 0.1010$	$27/114 = 0.2368$	$24/35 = 0.6857$

	Percentage differences vs. odds ratios			
	Urban NonInd.	Urban Indig.	Trust-A. Indig.	Trust-A. Attempt.
% diff.		5.64%	9.97%	21.53%
Odds ratio		2.760	2.345	2.896

NonIndigenous sample is $0.1010/0.0366 = 2.760$. So, we say that the odds of arrest in the Urban Indigenous sample is 2.76 *times higher* than in the Urban NonIndigenous sample.

To conclude this section, we will learn how to construct confidence intervals for odds ratios. The procedure is slightly more complicated than for percentage differences, but the underlying principles are very similar. It turns out that the *natural logarithm* (i.e., the logarithm to the base e, which is approximately 2.71828) *of the odds ratio* Ω has a normal sampling distribution for moderate to large sample sizes. The rule-of-thumb is that the sampling distribution of $\ln(\Omega)$ approximates a normal distribution quite well for samples of 25 or more.

If we denote the sample estimate of the odds ratio by W, then the **con-** DEFINITIONS **fidence interval around $\ln(\Omega)$** has the form

$$\Pr(\ln(W) - w < \ln(\Omega) < \ln(W) + w) = 1 - \alpha,$$

where $w = z_{\alpha/2}s_{err}$ just as it does for any confidence interval of this kind. Without going into mathematical detail, the formula for the **standard error of $\ln(W)$** is

$$s_{err} = \sqrt{1/N_{11} + 1/N_{12} + 1/N_{21} + 1/N_{22}}$$

where the N_{ij} denote the relevant cell frequencies. To convert our confidence interval around $\ln(\Omega)$ into one around Ω, we have to raise e to the power of $\ln(\Omega)$ and do the same for the lower and upper limits.

Let us try this on the snake phobia example. The sample odds ratio for the snake data was 3.02, which meant that the odds of disliking snakes was 3.02 times higher for those who were disgusted by them than for those who were not. We will construct a confidence interval around $\ln(\Omega)$ of the form

$$\Pr(\ln(3.02) - w < \ln(\Omega) < \ln(3.02) + w) = 1 - \alpha,$$

by following these steps.

1. Decide on a confidence level, say 95%.
2. Compute $\ln(W)$, which is $\ln(3.02) = 1.105$.
3. Compute the standard error, which is

$$s_{err} = \sqrt{1/N_{11} + 1/N_{12} + 1/N_{21} + 1/N_{22}}$$

$$= \sqrt{1/5 + 1/49 + 1/49 + 1/59} = 0.497$$

4. Compute the half-width of the interval,

$$w = z_{\alpha/2} s_{err} = (1.96)(0.497) = 0.974.$$

5. Substitute the appropriate numbers in the confidence interval statement, getting

$$\Pr(1.105 - 0.974 < \ln(\Omega) < 1.105 + 0.974) = 0.95,$$

so the resulting confidence interval for $\ln(\Omega)$ is $CI_{0.95} = [0.131, 2.080]$.
6. Raise e to the power of the lower and upper limits (0.131 and 2.080), to get a 95% confidence interval for Ω of $[1.140, 8.001]$.

The outcome of this exercise is that 1 is not a plausible value for this odds ratio, but the plausible values range from 1.14 to 8.001. The fact that 1 is not a plausible value of Ω indicates that if we had a null hypothesis that there was no difference between people who are disgusted by snakes and those who are not in terms of their odds of disliking snakes, we could reject that hypothesis.

SUMMARY

2×2 Table

X	Y	
	1	2
1	N_{11}	N_{12}
2	N_{21}	N_{22}

The odds (or more properly, **conditional odds**) that someone will be in category 1 on Y given that they are in category 1 on X are

$$\text{Odds}(Y = 1 | X = 1) = N_{11}/N_{12}.$$

The odds of being in category 1 on Y given that someone is in category 2 on X are

$\text{Odds}(Y = 1 | X = 2) = N_{21}/N_{22}.$

SUMMARY

The **odds ratio** (of the first odds to the second) is

$$\Omega = \frac{\text{Odds}(Y = 1 | X = 1)}{\text{Odds}(Y = 1 | X = 2)} = \frac{N_{11}/N_{12}}{N_{21}/N_{22}}$$

If X and Y are statistically *independent*, then $\Omega = 1$. Otherwise, the more strongly they are associated, the more extreme the value of the odds ratio. If the larger odds are put on top, an odds ratio can become infinitely large. If the larger odds are put on the bottom, then the odds ratio can go as low as 0.

For sufficiently large samples, we may construct a **confidence interval** for the odds ratio by working with the natural logarithm of it (i.e., $\ln(\Omega)$). If we denote the sample estimate of the odds ratio by W, then the confidence interval around $\ln(\Omega)$ has the form

$$\Pr(\ln(W) - w < \ln(\Omega) < \ln(W) + w) = 1 - \alpha,$$

where $w = z_{\alpha/2} s_{err}$ and the standard error of $\ln(W)$ is

$$s_{err} = \sqrt{1/N_{11} + 1/N_{12} + 1/N_{21} + 1/N_{22}}$$

To convert our confidence interval around $\ln(\Omega)$ into one around Ω, we raise e to the power of $\ln(\Omega)$ and do the same for the lower and upper limits.

Odds ratios are *invariant under row or column multiplication.*

They also are *sensitive to both weakly perfect and strictly perfect associations.*

Odds ratios are the basis for an entire family of modern statistical techniques for analyzing 'multi-way' contingency tables involving more than two variables.

Questions and exercises

Q.9.1. One feature of specific medical procedures is geographical variation in their adoption rates. The decision to elect a Caesarean section is a notable example, showing a great variability both internationally and regionally. The table below shows data from public hospitals for pregnancy outcomes during 1992–1993 in an Australian state. The data refer to the number of normal vaginal births versus Caesarean deliveries distributed by geographical location of the hospital – whether remote, metropolitan, or regional.

Delivery method	Hospital location			
	Remote	Metro	Regional	Total
Caesarean	385	3848	2079	6312
Vaginal	2373	14075	12408	28856
Total	2758	17923	14487	35168

(a) Compare the percentages of women who have Caesarian sections from the three hospital locations. Use the appropriate percentages and percentage differences to do this.

(b) What percentage of Caesarian sections occur in metropolitan hospitals? What percentage occur in remote ones?

Q.9.2. A health psychologist has found from large-sample studies over many years that in his country, 41.90% of the people rate their health as 'excellent,' 29.36% as 'good,' and 28.74% as 'poor to fair.' These figures have proved to be so stable over time that he is willing to treat them as population norms. He has recently surveyed a disadvantaged ethnic population who claim, among other things, substantially poorer health than the norm for the nation. Although there are physiological indicators of health that have been measured on this population, he wishes to ascertain whether their subjective wellbeing differs from the national norms. His data are tabulated below. Ascertain whether or not it is plausible that they are the same as his population norms. Use a 99% confidence level. Does this population seem to rate their health lower than the population at large?

Excellent	Good	Poor to Fair
104	106	68

Q.9.3. Use **AIDSPatch** to explore how the false-positive problem changes as a function of infection rates. Ascertain how accurate the HIV test would have to be to ensure that the probability of someone actually being infected given that their test is positive is high.

Q.9.4. A neuropsychologist wishes to determine whether preference for music as a hobby is related to hemispheric dominance. He randomly samples 1060 people from the community, tests them for hemispheric dominance, and asks whether music is one of their hobbies or not. He obtains the following data:

Music?	Dominant hemisphere	
	Right	Left
Yes	30	40
No	70	920

(a) Test whether these two variables are independent, using a 95% confidence level.

(b) What is the level of association between these two variables?

(c) Interpret the relationship, insofar as one exists.

Q.9.5.   Launch the **Chipatch** module. After you've got past the welcome message, choose the two-way chi-square option and work through the problem presented to you. After you've finished the problem, go on to the exploratory part of the module by answering 'yes' to the question that comes up after the completion of the problem. Once you're in the exploratory section, you may change the values in the table cells by clicking on them and entering new ones.

CROSSPATCH

PROVIDES

MORE

PRACTICE

PROBLEMS

INVOLVING

ODDS RATIOS

- Write down the current value of chi-square (to save yourself having to memorize it).
- Click on the cell with the smallest number and enter a value that is 7 less than it (or enter 0 if the original number is 7 or less). Write down the resulting chi-square value.
- Now re-enter the original number into that cell so the table is back to the way it was before.
- Click on the cell with the largest number and enter a value that is 7 less than that. Write down the resulting chi-square value.
- Which change altered the value of chi-square more? Why do you think this might be the case?

Q.9.6.   This question pertains to the data-file called **Doctor**. The data comprise two variables, one called 'Pracmode' and another called 'Sex.' These data are from a published study by Gerrity *et al.* (1992) of a sample of American physicians. Test whether gender is related to the tendency of these physicians to become specialists or general practitioners.

Q.9.7.   Use an odds ratio to interpret the relationship between gender and the tendency to become specialists or general practitioners. The contingency table is shown below. Construct a 95% confidence interval around the odds ratio. A researcher in this area has claimed that men have more than four times greater odds than women of becoming a specialist. Is this plausible, given your confidence interval?

DEM91

PROVIDES

MORE

PRACTICE

WITH CI'S

FOR ODDS

RATIOS

	Gender	
	Male	Female
G.P.	174	39
Specialist	164	12

More than Two Variables: A Peek at Multivariate Analysis

CONTENTS

Concepts for multivariate analysis

This chapter 'looks forward' into the domain of multivariate research and the statistical techniques on which it is based. We start with reasons for studying more than one thing at a time and then explore some of the issues and problems that await us when we do so. The most important issues concern how a relationship between two variables may change depending on a third variable, and how that may be interpreted in view of theoretical concepts or research questions.

At the beginning of the section in Chapter 8 on correlation, prediction, and causation, we encountered the slogan 'correlation is not causation.' One of the examples used to make this point demonstrated that an apparent relationship between two variables (number of fire engines and cost of damage to the building) might be 'explained away' by their relationship with a third (size of the fire). This example contains elements of multivariate analysis, because it examines a relationship between two variables while taking a third one into account.

What does it really mean to 'explain away' a relationship in this sense? Suppose we encountered a similar psychological example, in a study of depression, anxiety, and stress. Imagine that we have classified 100 people according to whether they are depressed or not, stressed or not, and anxious or not; and suppose it turns out that there is a strictly perfect relationship between anxiety and depression. The 50 people who are depressed also are anxious, and the 50 who are not depressed also are not anxious.

If our third variable, stress, accounts for the depression/anxiety relationship in the same way that size of fire did for the fire-engines/cost relationship, then we should find that all high-stressed people are both anxious and depressed whereas low-stressed people are neither anxious nor depressed. This is the situation displayed in Figure 10.1. We have taken the contingency table for depression and anxiety and decomposed it into two tables, one for the high-stress and another for the low-stress group. In these subtables there is no relationship between depression and anxiety because all of the people clump together in one cell in each table. Two things cannot covary if neither one of them varies.

The problem here is that all three variables are *simultaneously related* to one another. We could perform the same trick using these data to 'explain away' the stress–depression relationship via anxiety, or the anxiety–stress relationship via depression. Each pair of variables is perfectly related as long as we do not take the third one into account. Once we stratify on the third variable, the relationship disappears. In some traditions, researchers say that the relationship between two variables is **spurious** or **confounded** by the third variable. DEFINITIONS The statistician's phrase is that two variables are **conditionally independent** of one another if their relationship vanishes when a third variable is taken into account.

The concept of conditional independence is better than spuriousness or confounding in this example because there is no airtight way to give one of these variables causal priority over the others. In the fire-engine example, we could justifiably claim that size of fire causes the other two variables. Such a claim would be difficult to substantiate here. Does stress cause anxiety and depression? Or could anxiety be a stressor and depressor in itself? Might not depression make people anxious and cause them stress? Conditional independence gets around this quandary by addressing the conditional nature of the relationship itself, without having to refer to causal priority.

Another possibility is that a third variable may not make a relationship disappear. In fact, sometimes two variables may appear to be unrelated until a third variable is taken into account, in which case we say they are **conditionally dependent**. In these circumstances, the third variable is DEFINITION

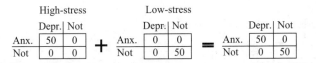

FIGURE 10.1 A relationship 'explained away' by a third variable

sometimes called a **masking variable** because it masks (or suppresses) the relationship between the other two variables. Figure 10.2 demonstrates conditional dependence, whereby anxiety and depression are completely unrelated until they are stratified on stress. It turns out that for high-stress people, anxiety and depression are positively related; but for low-stress people they are negatively related. The positive and negative relationships cancel one another out when we combine the high-stress and low-stress groups.

Masking and conditional dependence are crucial possibilities to bear in mind when you are doing research (or reading other people's research reports). All of us are tempted to lose interest if we find that there is no relationship between two variables. Faced with a table like the one on the right-hand side of the figure below, many researchers would conclude that anxiety and depression are unrelated and leave it at that. The importance of looking for masking variables cannot be overemphasized.

DEFINITION   The conditional dependence example highlights one more essential concept in multivariate analysis, namely the notion of an **interaction**. The relationship between one variable and another *interacts* with a third if the relationship is not the same on all levels of the third variable. Stress is a masking variable because of the type of interaction it has with the relationship between depression and anxiety, namely because that relationship is reversed when we go from the high-stress to the low-stress group. The idea of an interaction is a very general notion, and you will find it used widely in the research literature.

Although the concepts of an interaction or conditional dependence might seem complicated initially, you undoubtedly already understand them very well in real life. A cricket commentator, when asked if adding more spin-bowlers to the Pakistani side will increase their chances against the West Indies in their test-match next weekend, might reasonably say that it depends on the condition of the wicket. Does Jane sing better in front of an audience than in a recording studio? Her live performances are better than her studio recordings if the audience is friendly, but worse if they are hostile. These are examples of the statement that the effect of X on Y depends on Z, and that captures the essence of an interaction.

DATA
FILENAME
MENTAL   Now let's try a research example. In Chapter 5 we took a brief look at a study of public mental health literacy in Australia (Jorm *et al.*, 1997). Half the respondents in this study were presented with a vignette describing a person

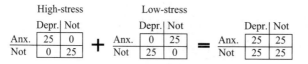

FIGURE 10.2 A relationship 'masked' by a third variable

suffering symptoms of depression, and the other half a vignette describing a person suffering symptoms of schizophrenia. Respondents were asked to 'diagnose' the target person in their own words. Their diagnoses were then coded into categories, two of which were 'depressed' and 'stressed.' If respondents made more than one diagnosis then that was coded accordingly, so it was possible for a respondent to diagnose the target as both depressed and stressed.

One plausible hypothesis is that those who diagnose the target as depressed will not think they are stressed and vice-versa. We will investigate this hypothesis by examining the relationship between these two diagnoses for the entire sample (i.e., regardless of the type of vignette). As you can see, the data in Table 10.1 provide very little support for this hypothesis. The chi-square value of 5.346 is rather low given the large sample, and this is reflected in the extremely low phi coefficient, $\phi^2 = 0.003$. The odds ratio is not far from 1, also indicating only a very weak relationship between the diagnoses of depression and stress. Should the researcher conclude that the relationship between these variables is, for all practical purposes, nonexistent?

If we stratify the relationship between these two variables on the type of vignette, then a different story emerges. The study randomly assigned participants to one of two vignettes: symptoms of depression and schizophrenic symptoms. Table 10.2 splits the depressed–stress contingency table into two tables, one for each kind of vignette. If we examine the relationship between diagnosis of depression and stress for the depression vignette then there is a discernible tendency for those who have not diagnosed the target as depressed to be more likely to diagnose them as stressed. The relevant odds ratio (Ω) is 2.309 and there is a substantial chi-square value of 25.781. In the schizophrenia vignette, on the other hand, there is virtually no relationship. The chi-square value is very small (0.778) and the odds ratio is close to 1.

The type of vignette has acted as a masking variable insofar as it has obscured a relationship between the stress and depression diagnoses. More importantly, our hypothesis appears to be true only for one vignette, namely

TABLE 10.1 Depression versus stress

Stress	Depression		Total
	No	Yes	
No	1158	584	1742
	84.5%	88.4%	85.8%
Yes	212	77	289
	15.5%	11.6%	14.2%
Total	1370	661	2031
	100%	100%	

$\chi^2 = 5.346$, $\phi^2 = 0.003$, $\Omega = 1.389$.

TABLE 10.2 Depression versus stress, by scenario

Depression scenario

Stress	Depression		Total
	No	Yes	
No	433	349	782
	71.9%	85.5%	77.4%
Yes	169	59	228
	28.1%	14.5%	22.6%
Total	602	408	1010
	100%	100%	

$\chi^2 = 25.781$, $\phi^2 = 0.026$, $\Omega = 2.309$.

Schizophrenia scenario

Stress	Depression		Total
	No	Yes	
No	725	235	960
	94.4%	92.9%	94.0%
Yes	43	18	61
	5.6%	7.1%	6.0%
Total	768	253	1021
	100%	100%	

$\chi^2 = 0.778$, $\phi^2 = 0.0008$, $\Omega = 1.291$.

the depressive one. The nature of the interaction here is that the relationship between diagnoses occurs in one vignette but not the other.

DATA
FILENAME
CONTRA-
CEP

The concepts of conditional independence, masking variables, and interactions extend to all other kinds of variables and measures of association. Here is another example, this one involving regression and correlation. In Chapter 8, we used a demographer's data set of 58 developing countries, and constructed a linear regression model predicting birthrate from the percentage of adults using contraception. The demographer (Keyfitz) also classified those countries into four groups on the basis of their family planning programs: strong, moderate, weak, and none. One of his objectives was to assess the impact of the type of family planning program on population increase. One potential confounding factor is the wealth of the country, since surplus wealth enables a government to afford family planning initiatives. There is also plenty of evidence that wealthier countries have lower birthrates.

Suppose we were to investigate the impact of national wealth as measured by GDP (Gross Domestic Product per capita) on birthrate. In Figure 10.3, you can see that GDP (actually, the logarithm of GDP per capita in this analysis) is

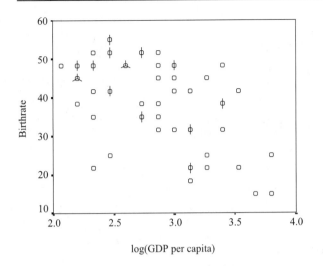

FIGURE 10.3 Relationship between log GDP and birthrate

negatively correlated with birthrate, just as other studies have found. The correlation is -0.571, so $R^2 = 0.326$ and therefore about 32.6% of the variance in birthrate is accounted for by GDP. So perhaps it is not family planning that produces low birthrates, but GDP instead. We would like to find out whether a family planning program has an impact on birthrate that is distinct from its relationship with GDP. Another pertinent question is whether the effect of family planning programs varies across different levels of GDP. Since GDP is a quantitative variable, it makes no sense to divide countries into groups based on GDP. How can we effectively address these questions?

One reasonable starting-point is to stratify the countries by the kind of family planning program they have, and examine the relationship between GDP and birthrate within each stratum. For this purpose, I have divided them into two groups: Those with no or weak programs, and those with moderately strong or strong ones. Figures 10.4 and 10.5 show the relationship between log (GDP) and birthrate in the group with moderate or strong programs, versus countries with either weak or no family planning programs. The squared correlation for the first scatterplot is $R^2 = 0.407$, so about 40.7% of the variance in birthrate is accounted for among these countries. The slope of the regression line is -10.142, steeper than the one shown in the scatterplot of Figure 10.5, for countries with either weak or no family planning programs. The slope of that regression line is only -7.135. The squared correlation for this scatterplot is $R^2 = 0.179$, so only about 17.9% of the variance in birthrate is accounted for among these countries, less than half of the percentage of variance for the other group. The relationship between GDP and birthrate appears to be weaker for countries that lack substantial family planning programs.

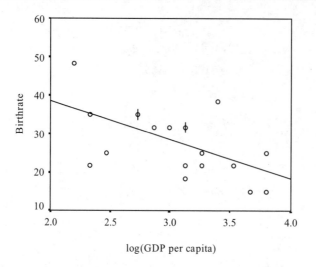

FIGURE 10.4 Countries with moderate or strong family planning

What does this tell us about the joint impact of GDP and family planning on birthrates? We have found evidence that GDP has a stronger negative correlation with birthrate when there are good family planning programs. One possible interpretation is that national wealth, on its own, does not help control birthrates nearly as well as it does when family planning programs are in place. Perhaps such programs provide an effective deployment of a portion of that wealth. While our analyses do not clear up this issue on their own, they do suggest further investigations.

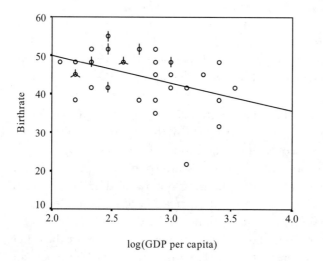

FIGURE 10.5 Countries with weak or no family planning

Multivariate statistical methods (i.e., multiple regression) would enable us to find out how strongly family planning and birthrate are related, *statistically controlling for the relationship between both of them and GDP*. We have only done a crude approximation of that here, but we may outline the remaining steps toward addressing the question we began with, namely whether family planning program has an impact on birthrate once GDP has been taken into account.

We would want to reinterpret the relationship between family planning program and birthrate in view of its interaction with GDP. We could begin by superimposing the two regression lines on one graph, like the one in Figure 10.6. This graph makes two things quite clear. First, countries with weak family planning programs have higher birthrates than those with strong programs at any level of GDP in the sample. Second, that difference increases with higher GDP, so greater national wealth enhances the impact of family planning programs.

The next step would be to construct a confidence interval around the difference between the slopes of these regression lines, to give us some idea of the range of plausible values for that difference. After all, slopes of -10.142 and -7.135 may seem different, but they are only sample estimates. Is 0 a plausible value for the difference between these slopes? In Chapter 8, we learned that the regression slope's sampling distribution is a t-distribution. We used that fact to construct confidence intervals around a slope, and we also observed at the time that we could use the statistical techniques from Chapter 7 (confidence intervals for the difference between two means and ANOVA) to compare two or more slopes.

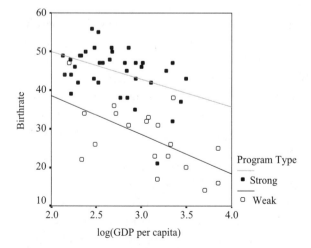

FIGURE 10.6 Two regression lines

I will briefly outline how we could construct a 95% confidence interval around the difference between our two slopes, $b_1 = -10.142$ and $b_2 = -7.135$. Their difference is $b_2 - b_1 = 3.007$. Since each of the b's sampling distribution is a t-distribution, so is the sampling distribution of $b_2 - b_1$. The half-width of a 95% confidence interval around them is $w = t_{0.025}s_{\text{err}}$. Rather than going into the details of how to obtain a standard error for $b_2 - b_1$, I will simply report that for these data that it is $s_{\text{err}} = 3.846$. The relevant degrees of freedom for comparing two regression slopes is $\text{df} = (N_1 - 2) + (N_2 - 2) = (20 - 2) + (38 - 2) = 54$. From Table A.3, we find that $t_{0.025}$ is about 2.005, so our half-width is

$$w = t_{0.025}s_{\text{err}} = (2.005)(3.846) = 7.711.$$

The resulting confidence interval is

$$\text{CI}_{0.95} = [b_2 - b_1 - w,\ b_2 - b_1 + w] = [3.007 - 7.711,\ 3.007 + 7.711]$$

$$= [-4.704, 10.718].$$

We can see that 0 is a plausible population value for this difference, so we cannot rule out the possibility that there actually is no interaction between GDP and family planning program.

Finally, if we were really going to pursue this exercise to the point where we could make policy-relevant predictions, we would want to construct confidence intervals around each of the regression lines so that we could tell any country the range of plausible values for the expected decline in birthrate, given their current GDP per capita, if they strengthened their family planning program from one of Keyfitz's levels to another. This step is beyond the scope of this book, but it would certainly be a reasonable request for a government to put to any demographic consultant.

Now that we have introduced several concepts for dealing with relationships among more than two variables, we are ready to take on an example of the statistical techniques for analyzing such relationships. We will do this shortly in the section on two-way ANOVA. First, however, we need to examine the concept of 'statistical control' and its connection with experimental control more closely. That will occupy the next section.

The relationship between two variables may change when a third variable is taken into consideration. If when we stratify on the third variable, the relationship disappears, then the relationship between two variables is said to be **spurious** or **confounded** by the third variable.

The statistician's phrase is that two variables are **conditionally independent** of one another if their relationship vanishes when a third variable is taken into account.

If two variables are unrelated until a third variable is taken into account, we say they are **conditionally dependent**. In these circumstances, the third variable is sometimes called a **masking variable**.

The relationship between one variable and another **interacts** with a third if the relationship is not the same on all levels of the third variable. This contingent relationship is referred to as an **interaction effect**. In other words, an interaction exists whenever the effect of one variable on another depends on a third.

SUMMARY

Statistical and experimental control

So far, we have investigated multivariate analysis in the context of nonexperimental studies. There, the nub of the matter has been *statistical control*. The primary motivating idea behind **statistical control** is that we may understand a relationship between two variables better by taking a third one into account. This third variable usually is referred to as a **covariate**, to distinguish it from the variables of primary interest (e.g., the dependent and independent variables).

DEFINITION

In the research literature, you may encounter any of several terms that refer to statistically controlling for a covariate, including 'adjusting for it,' 'holding it constant,' 'partialing it out,' and 'stratifying on it.' These all refer to much the same thing. Adjusting for a covariate, stratifying on it, or holding it constant all mean understanding the relationship between two variables *within* a level or category of the covariate. Thus, if we want to speak of the correlation between log(GDP) and birthrate in Keyfitz's data, adjusting for family planning program, we would say that for countries where programs are weak or nonexistent R^2 is about 0.179, whereas for moderately strong or strong programs R^2 is about 0.407.

The phrase 'partialing out,' on the other hand, is most often used in conjunction with an overall assessment of the relationship between two variables conditional on their relationships with the covariate. For instance, in the example of conditional independence between anxiety and depression when controlling for stress, we would say that when stress is partialed out, there is no relationship between anxiety and depression.

In psychological research, statistical control is often not the sole method of control available. In fact, many psychologists think of scientific research primarily in terms of *experimental control*. Whereas statistical control entails taking account of one or more covariates, along with random sampling, **experimental control** requires randomized assignment and independent manipulation of experimental variables; so that they are forced to be unrelated regardless of whether they are in the real world or not. Experimental and statistical control are not exclusive of one another, nor are they competitors. In fact, much of the best psychological research uses both. Nevertheless, as Darlington (1990: 93) points out, their relative strengths and weaknesses are most easily understood by pretending to pit one against the other.

DEFINITION

A primary reason for this is that some of the most powerful motivations for doing experiments arise from limitations of statistical control. Two of these are already familiar. First, no amount of statistical control will ever tell us whether one variable *causes* another. Second, the list of known potential covariates often is very large or, worse still, incomplete. A third, less obvious limitation is that we may easily *overcontrol* in a study by adding too many covariates for the number of observations. You can always perfectly 'explain' N people's different scores on a variable by finding $N - 1$ differences among the people on other variables. Bring in enough covariates and eventually you will attain this goal, even if by pure chance.

Fourth, statistical control assumes that we have measured our covariates without measurement error. In practice this is rarely the case, particularly when the covariate is an imperfect measure of some underlying construct such as self-esteem or degree of identification with a group. Fifth, statistical control still requires that we work with the relationships between the covariate and our variables of interest as we find them in the 'real world.' If a covariate is strongly related to the variable we want to use as a predictor, statistical control will not enable us to distinguish between the predictor's and covariate's ability to predict the dependent variable.

Randomized assignment offers a neat way of transcending these limitations and difficulties, which is the main reason for its popularity. By randomly assigning people to an experimental condition, three things are accomplished at the same time. First, and most obviously, the experimenter predetermines the possible conditions to which they may be assigned. Second, people's values or states on *all possible covariates* (including those unknown to the experimenter) are randomly distributed across the experimental conditions. This does not guarantee that the experimental groups will be exactly equivalent on all those covariates, but it does guarantee that differences between those groups on those covariates will be due to chance alone. Third, randomized assignment guarantees that all possible covariates will be statistically independent of (unrelated to) the independent variable(s) manipulated by the experimenter. This last point is crucial when it comes to disentangling the effect of an independent variable from a covariate, since they are forced to be unrelated to one another.

Because randomized assignment has such appeal to researchers, the term often is bandied about rather freely in research reports and sometimes people may be misled into treating all independent variables in an experiment as randomly assigned when they are not. Experimenters using gender as an independent variable, for instance, cannot treat gender as randomly assigned. Many experimental studies involve a mixture of randomly and nonrandomly assigned independent variables, so it is worthwhile ascertaining which is which.

Randomized assignment has its own limitations, aside from the risk of chance effects. First, unlike random sampling, it does not address questions of external validity (generalizability). Second, randomized assignment does not tell us whether we have ignored any variables that intervene between our independent and dependent variables. Third, it does not inform us of whether any covariates mask or otherwise mediate the effect of the independent variable. In particular, it tells us nothing about how covariates and independent variables are related in the real world (because the covariates have been forced to be unrelated to the independent variables, thanks to randomized assignment). Finally, for many important predictors and independent variables, randomized assignment may be immoral, illegal, impractical, or outright impossible.

Darlington (1990: 103–4) makes an excellent case for combining statistical control with randomized assignment. I will paraphrase his reasons and augment them slightly. Perhaps the most important reason is that whereas experimental control is best suited to establishing that an effect exists, statistical control is superior at teasing out exactly how it works. Statistical control enables researchers to identify intervening variables, masking variables, and the like. A second reason is that statistical control can be used to adjust for imperfect experimental designs, in which participants have dropped out or some data have gone missing. A third reason has more to do with random sampling than with statistical control per se, namely that random sampling combined with randomized assignment enables the researcher to handle questions of external validity (via random sampling) as well as internal validity (via randomized assignment). There is no reason, for instance, that random sample surveys could not have experimental designs built into them where appropriate, via randomized assignment of respondents to particular versions of the survey instrument. Conversely, random sampling from specified populations often is under-utilized by experimenters even when it is quite feasible.

SUMMARY

Statistical control involves understanding a relationship between two variables by taking a third one into account.

This third variable usually is referred to as a **covariate**, to distinguish it from the variables of primary interest (e.g., the dependent and independent variables). Adjusting for a covariate, stratifying on it, or holding it constant all refer to understanding the relationship between two variables *within* a level or category of the covariate.

Limitations of statistical control include:

1. It does not tell us whether one variable causes another;
2. The list of potential covariates may be endless or unknown;
3. We may easily overcontrol in a study by adding too many covariates for the number of observations;
4. It assumes that we have measured our covariates without measurement error;
5. It limits us to working with the relationships between the covariate and our variables of interest as we find them in the 'real world'.

Experimental control requires randomized assignment to experimental conditions and independent manipulation of experimental variables. It achieves three things:

1. The experimenter determines the possible states on the independent variable(s) to which participants may be assigned;
2. People's values or states on *all possible covariates* (including those unknown to the experimenter) are randomly distributed across the experimental conditions;
3. It ensures that all possible covariates will be statistically independent of (unrelated to) the independent variable(s) manipulated by the experimenter.

Limitations of experimental control include:

1. It involves the risk of chance effects;
2. It does not address questions of external validity (generalizability);
3. It does not tell us whether we have ignored any variables that intervene between our independent and dependent variables;
4. It tells us nothing about how covariates and independent variables are related in the real world;
5. It may not be feasible for ethical, legal, practical or theoretical reasons.

In summary, whenever feasible, it is best to use a combination of experimental and statistical controls.

Introduction to two-way ANOVA

Now that you have a grasp of the relative strengths and weaknesses of statistical and experimental control, you are well-equipped to learn how they are deployed in experiments that involve more than one independent variable. This section extends ANOVA to handle two independent variables (hence, two-way ANOVA), and we will find out how ANOVA can be used to disentangle the effect of each independent variable as well as helping researchers interpret the joint effect of both variables.

In many areas of psychology, the most popular experimental design is the **factorial experiment**, in which two or more categorical independent variables are cross-classified to form all possible combinations of conditions. Participants are then randomly assigned to conditions on each of those variables, and thence to a particular cell in the experimental design. Randomized assignment thereby makes it possible for researchers to assess both the independent and joint effects of the independent variables. DEFINITION

At the end of Chapter 7, when we ascertained that ANOVA is a special kind of regression, we used a fictitious small-scale experiment in which students were randomly assigned to two teaching methods (the 'Old' way and the 'New' way). These methods were compared via students' exam scores. Imagine a slightly more elaborate version of this experiment, in which the researcher decided to also randomly assign students to take either an open-book or closed-book exam.

How might teaching method and type of exam jointly affect students' exam scores? There are two distinct possibilities. One is that their effects might be **independent** and therefore combine **additively**. Suppose the students under DEFINITION the New method average 12.5 points higher on their exams than students under the Old method. If this effect is independent of whether the exam is open- or closed-book, then that 12.5-point difference should be found in both kinds of exam. Likewise, suppose the students taking the open-book exam average 5.5 points higher than those taking the closed-book exam. Then this difference should be found to be the same under both kinds of teaching method. Likewise, the average gain for the student who is taught by the New method *and* takes the open-book exam is just the sum of each of those effects: $12.5 + 5.5 = 18$ points. An example of this situation is shown in Table 10.3, which displays the mean scores for each combination of teaching method and exam type.

Why would the effects of teaching method and exam type combine additively if they are independent? The mean exam score for students studying under the New method is $70.625 - 58.125 = 12.5$ points higher than the mean for students under the Old method. Our table of means shows that this is true for both the open-book exam ($73.375 - 60.875 = 12.5$) and the closed-book

TABLE 10.3 Mean scores: independent effects

	Closed	Open	
Old	55.375	60.875	58.125
New	67.875	73.375	70.625
	61.625	67.125	64.375

exam $(67.875 - 55.375 = 12.5)$. Likewise, the mean for students taking the open-book exam is 5.5 points higher than that for the closed-book exam, regardless of which method of instruction they received. Finally, the average gain for the student who is taught by the New method *and* takes the open-book exam is the sum of those effects $(73.375 - 55.375 = 18)$.

A common (and useful) practice of researchers is to plot the cell means in a graph like the one in Figure 10.7. They select one of the independent variables' categories to be represented on the horizontal axis and the other to be represented by separate lines connecting the means. Here, I have chosen to represent type of exam on the horizontal axis and use separate lines for the New and Old teaching methods. The most important aspect of this graph is that the lines are parallel, indicating that the increase in mean score from closed- to open-book exam is the same under the New and Old methods. If the lines were not parallel, that would indicate that the effects of exam type and teaching method are not independent.

Earlier I said there were two ways that teaching method and exam type might jointly affect exam scores, and the first was that they are independent and therefore combined additively. The second possibility is that they are **DEFINITION** **dependent** and therefore combine **nonadditively**. In other words, the effect of one variable depends on the other. In that case, we say that there is an **interaction** involving the independent variables. The next table of means (Table 10.4) presents an example of this situation. The mean exam score for

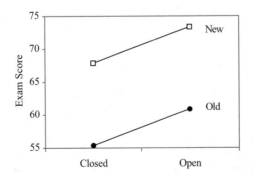

FIGURE 10.7 Plot of cell means for additive effects

TABLE 10.4 Mean scores: dependent effects

	Closed	Open	
Old	55.375	65.500	60.4375
New	67.875	70.750	69.3125
	61.625	68.125	64.875

students studying under the New method is $69.3125 - 60.4375 = 8.875$ points higher than the mean for students under the Old method. However, this difference does not hold constant across types of exam. For students taking the closed-book exam, the difference between means for the New and Old teaching methods is $67.875 - 55.375 = 12.5$ points, whereas the difference for students taking the open-book exam is only $70.75 - 65.5 = 5.25$ points. It appears that the effect of teaching method depends on the type of exam. Likewise, the effect of exam type depends on the teaching method. Under the Old method, students taking the open-book exam score 10.125 points higher, but under the New method, they score only 2.875 points higher.

A plot of the cell means (Figure 10.8) reveals that the lines for Old and New teaching methods are not parallel, reflecting the fact that the difference between exam type is much less under the New method than under the Old (i.e., an interaction). Although this graph may not seem necessary for such a simple experiment as this one, nonadditive effects in experiments with several conditions on each independent variable can be quite difficult to interpret without such graphs.

Two-way ANOVA provides a method of assessing whether or not each independent variable has an effect and whether those effects are independent or not. This is accomplished by what amounts to a series of comparisons between simple (no-effect or null) models and more complex models that include effects. First, we need to develop a way of expressing these models,

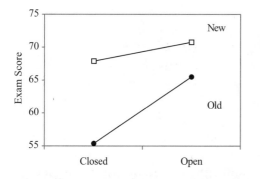

FIGURE 10.8 Plot of cell means for nonadditive effects

since they are a bit more elaborate than those we have employed so far. In Chapter 7, we saw that one-way ANOVA could be thought of as a predictive model in which an individual's score was predicted with the model

$$X = \mu_i + e,$$

where μ_i was the mean score on the ith experimental condition. The models in two-way ANOVA are an elaboration of this basic idea. We have two experimental variables, and so an individual's score is predicted by a model

$$X = \mu_{ij} + e,$$

where μ_{ij} is the mean score on the ith condition of one independent variable and the jth condition of the other.

The various models that are compared in two-way ANOVA all involve a particular way of thinking about experimental effects, namely in terms of deviations away from the mean of all the scores (the 'grand mean'). Denoting the grand mean by μ, the ith condition mean by $\mu_{i.}$, and the deviation for the ith condition by α_i, we put

$$\mu_{i.} = \mu + \alpha_i.$$

Since the mean of the $\mu_{i.}$'s is μ, the sum of the α_i's must be 0. In our independent-effects example, the grand mean is $\mu = 64.375$. The mean under the Old method is $\mu_{1.} = 58.125$ and the mean under the New method is $\mu_{2.} = 70.625$, so we have

$$\mu_{1.} = \mu + \alpha_1 = 64.375 - 6.25 = 58.125$$

and

$$\mu_2 = \mu + \alpha_2 = 64.375 + 6.25 = 70.625.$$

Note that $\alpha_1 = -\alpha_2$ so that they sum to 0.

Now, we may do the same thing by way of modeling the exam-type effect. To keep track of rows and columns, many researchers use a notation for subscripts that is analogous to the notation used in contingency tables. The first subscript indexes the row and the second indexes the column. For instance, μ_{21} refers to the mean in the second row and first column. An additional useful convention is the 'dot' notation for representing a row or column mean. A dot in the first subscript indicates a column mean and a dot in the second indicates a row mean. Thus, the corresponding model for the exam-type effect on the column means is conventionally written as

$$\mu_{.j} = \mu + \beta_j,$$

with β_j indicating the effect of being in the jth condition on the column variable. In our independent-effects example, the mean for the closed-book exam is $\mu_{.1} = 61.625$ and the mean for the open-book exam is $\mu_{.2} = 67.125$, so we have

$$\mu_{.1} = \mu + \beta_1 = 64.375 - 2.75 = 61.625$$

and

$$\mu_{.2} = \mu + \beta_2 = 64.375 + 2.75 = 67.125.$$

Again, $\beta_1 = -\beta_2$ so that they sum to 0.

An **independent effects model** would incorporate both the teaching DEFINITION method (row) and exam-type (column) effects to predict each cell mean:

$$\mu_{ij} = \mu + \alpha_i + \beta_j.$$

Table 10.5 displays how this model works in our independent effects example.

For a **dependent effects model**, we need one more term in the model that DEFINITION represents the joint effect of being in the ith condition on the row variable and the jth condition on the column variable (Table 10.6). Conventionally, this term is denoted by $\alpha\beta_{ij}$, so our model becomes

$$\mu_{ij} = \mu + \alpha_i + \beta_j + \alpha\beta_{ij}.$$

TABLE 10.5 Independent effects model (additive)

	Closed	Open	
Old	$\mu_{11} = \mu + \alpha_1 + \beta_1$	$\mu_{12} = \mu + \alpha_1 + \beta_2$	$\mu_{1.} = \mu + \alpha_1$
New	$\mu_{21} = \mu + \alpha_2 + \beta_1$	$\mu_{22} = \mu + \alpha_2 + \beta_2$	$\mu_{2.} = \mu + \alpha_2$
	$\mu_{.1} = \mu + \beta_1$	$\mu_{.2} = \mu + \beta_2$	μ

	Closed	Open	
Old	$55.375 = 64.375 - 6.25 - 2.75$	$60.875 = 64.375 - 6.25 + 2.75$	$58.125 = 64.375 - 6.25$
New	$67.875 = 64.375 + 6.25 - 2.75$	$73.375 = 64.375 + 6.25 + 2.75$	$70.625 = 64.375 + 6.25$
	$61.625 = 64.375 - 2.75$	$67.125 = 64.375 + 2.75$	64.375

TABLE 10.6 Dependent effects models (nonadditive)

	Closed	Open	
Old	$\mu_{11} = \mu + \alpha_1 + \beta_1 + \alpha\beta_{11}$	$\mu_{12} = \mu + \alpha_1 + \beta_2 + \alpha\beta_{12}$	$\mu_{1.} = \mu + \alpha_1$
New	$\mu_{21} = \mu + \alpha_2 + \beta_1 + \alpha\beta_{21}$	$\mu_{22} = \mu + \alpha_2 + \beta_2 + \alpha\beta_{22}$	$\mu_{2.} = \mu + \alpha_2$
	$\mu_{.1} = \mu + \beta_1$	$\mu_{.2} = \mu + \beta_2$	μ

	Closed	Open	
Old	$55.375 = 64.875$ $-4.4375 - 3.25 - 1.8125$	$65.500 = 64.875$ $-4.4375 + 3.25 + 1.8125$	$60.4375 = 64.875$ -4.4375
New	$67.875 = 64.875$ $+4.4375 - 3.25 + 1.8125$	$70.750 = 64.875$ $+4.4375 + 3.25 - 1.8125$	$69.3125 = 64.875$ $+4.4375$
	$61.625 = 64.875$ -3.25	$68.125 = 64.875$ $+3.25$	64.875

The easiest way to think of $\alpha\beta_{ij}$ is as the deviation away from the cell-mean value that an independent effects model would predict, so that

$$\alpha\beta_{ij} = \mu_{ij} - (\mu + \alpha_i + \beta_j).$$

In other words, $\alpha\beta_{ij}$ measures how far each mean departs from additive effects. The $\alpha\beta_{ij}$ always sum to 0 across each row and column. Table 10.6 above shows how this model works in our dependent effects example.

All logical combinations of effects are possible. In other words, we may find that we have no effects, an effect for only the row variable, an effect for only the column variable, an interaction effect only, both a row and column effect, a row and an interaction effect, column and interaction effect, or all three effects. The graphs in Figure 10.9 illustrate some of these possibilities. For this

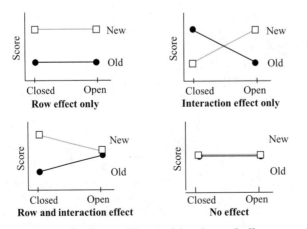

FIGURE 10.9 Some possible combinations of effects

reason, two-way ANOVA tests for every effect separately. In the next section we will examine how these tests work and how we may arrive at a final model that contains all pertinent effects.

The **factorial experiment** is an experimental design in which two or more categorical independent variables are cross-classified to form all possible combinations of conditions. Participants are then randomly assigned to one condition for each variable.

SUMMARY

The effects of the independent variables may be **independent** and therefore combine **additively**, or they may be **dependent** and combine **nonadditively**. In the latter case, we say that there is an **interaction** between the independent variables, meaning that the effect of one variable differs across levels of the other variable. Another way of thinking of this is that the effect of one variable depends on the other.

An **independent effects model** incorporates both the row and column variable effects to predict each cell mean:

$$\mu_{ij} = \mu + \alpha_i + \beta_j.$$

A **dependent effects model** adds a term representing the joint effect of being in the ith condition on the row variable and the jth condition on the column variable:

$$\mu_{ij} = \mu + \alpha_i + \beta_j + \alpha\beta_{ij}.$$

The row and column effects themselves are deviations of row and column means from the grand mean μ :

$$\alpha_i = \mu_{i.} - \mu$$

and

$$\beta_j = \mu_{.j} - \mu.$$

Likewise, the interaction effect is a deviation of the cell mean from the value that an independent effects model would predict:

$$\alpha\beta_{ij} = \mu_{ij} - (\mu + \alpha_i + \beta_j).$$

Model comparison and *F*-tests for two-way ANOVA

The statistical aspects of two-way ANOVA boil down to an adjudication among models with or without each of the various terms. Accordingly, there are separate *F*-tests for the row (α_i), column (β_j), and interaction ($\alpha\beta_{ij}$) effects. These tests operate in a very similar manner to the one-way ANOVA test we explored in Chapter 7. The data for this example are displayed in Table 10.7, along with the cell means and the sums of squares (SS) within each cell.

TABLE 10.7 Data for teaching example

	Old/Cl.	New/Cl.	Old/Op.	New/Op.
	68	50	79	53
	56	75	66	79
	59	65	68	67
	57	71	68	74
	50	62	60	66
	48	69	57	71
	50	74	61	78
	55	77	65	78
Mean	55.375	67.875	65.500	70.750
SS	287.875	544.875	318.000	535.500

DEFINITION   First, we should perform an **omnibus test** to find out whether there are any effects from the independent variables at all. To do that, we analyze these data using a one-way ANOVA approach, ignoring the structure of the experiment and simply treating it as if there were four experimental conditions. If we did that, following the steps outlined in Chapter 7, we would obtain the ANOVA results shown in Table 10.8. We might construct a 95% confidence interval around F under the null hypothesis (no effects) model. From Table A.4, using $df_b = 3$ and $df_w = 28$, we find $F_{0.05} = 2.9467$, so the confidence interval statement is

$$\Pr(F(3, 28) < 2.9467) = 0.95.$$

From our ANOVA table, $F(3, 28) = 5.940$, which is not inside the confidence interval and so we may reject the null hypothesis that there are no effects. This omnibus test does not tell us what the effects are, but it does enable us to calculate their combined effect size:

$$R^2 = SS_b/SS_t = 1073.250/2759.500 = 0.389,$$

which is a large effect by Cohen's (1988) standards and would be regarded as such in many (but not all) areas in psychology.

TABLE 10.8 One-way ANOVA table for teaching example

Source	SS	df	s^2	F
Between	1073.250	3	357.750	5.940
Within	1686.250	28	60.223	
Total	2759.500	31		

Having ascertained that there are effects of some kind, we may turn to the conventional two-way ANOVA which is designed to test whether there are detectable **row, column, or interaction effects**. It does this by **partitioning SS_b** into separate components for these effects. When the experiment has equal numbers of people in each cell, then

$$SS_b = SS_r + SS_c + SS_{rc}.$$

The row and column SS terms are exactly like the SS_b terms in one-way ANOVA. For instance, SS_r is the sum of the squared differences between each row mean and the grand mean, each multiplied by the number of people in its row (which is 16 for both rows). Since those differences are just the α_i's, we may use the α_i terms from the dependent effects model table, getting

$$SS_r = \Sigma N_{i.} \alpha_i^2 = 16(4.4375)^2 + 16(-4.4375)^2 = 630.125.$$

The same argument may be made for the column SS, so that

$$SS_c = \Sigma N_{.j} \beta_j^2 = 16(3.25)^2 + 16(-3.25)^2 = 338.000.$$

Finally, the interaction SS term uses the $\alpha\beta_{ij}$'s and number of people in each cell, N_{ij}, to get

$$SS_{rc} = \Sigma N_{ij} \alpha\beta_{ij}^2 = 8(-1.8125)^2 + 8(-1.8125)^2 + 8(1.8125)^2$$
$$+ 8(-1.8125)^2 = 105.125.$$

Now we can verify that

$$SS_b = 630.125 + 338.000 + 105.125 = 1073.250.$$

Table 10.9 includes the two-way ANOVA results along with the one-way (total between) results.

The remainder of the routine for the two-way ANOVA involves working out degrees of freedom and s^2-terms for each of the effects. It turns out that **degrees of freedom** for factorial experiments operate in much the same way as for a contingency table. For a row effect

$$df_r = r - 1,$$

where r is the number of rows; for a column effect

$$df_c = c - 1,$$

TABLE 10.9 Two-way ANOVA table for teaching example

Source	SS	df	s^2	F	R^2
Method	630.125	1	630.125	10.463	0.228
Exam	338.000	1	338.000	5.612	0.122
Meth. × Exam	105.125	1	105.125	1.746	0.038
Total between	1073.250	3	357.750	5.940	0.389
Within	1686.250	28	60.223		
Total	2759.500	31			

and for an interaction effect

$$df_{rc} = (r - 1)(c - 1).$$

Degrees of freedom add up in the same way that SS-terms do, so for an $r \times c$ factorial experiment,

$$df_b = df_r + df_c + df_{rc} = r - 1 + c - 1 + (r - 1)(c - 1) = rc - 1.$$

The **variance estimates** associated with each effect are the SS-terms divided by their corresponding df's:

$$s_r^2 = SS_r/df_r = 630.125/1 = 630.125;$$

$$s_c^2 = SS_c/df_c = 338.000/1 = 338.000;$$

$$s_{rc}^2 = SS_{rc}/df_{rc} = 105.125/1 = 105.125.$$

Then, the **F-statistics** for each effect compare their respective variance estimates against s_w^2:

$$F_r = s_r^2/s_w^2 = 630.125/60.223 = 10.463;$$

$$F_c = s_c^2/s_w^2 = 338.000/60.223 = 5.612;$$

$$F_{rc} = s_{rc}^2/s_w^2 = 105.125/60.223 = 1.746.$$

Each of these F's may be assessed for whether it lies inside its corresponding null-hypothesis confidence interval. In this example, since the df's for these F-statistics are all the same, the confidence interval is the same for all of them as well. If we use a 95% confidence level, then, given a numerator df of 1 and $df_w = 28$, we find $F_{0.05} = 4.1960$, so the confidence interval statement is

$$\Pr(F(1, 28) < 4.1960) = 0.95.$$

Both the row and column F-values lie outside this interval but the interaction F does not. So we may reject the null hypothesis of no effect for the row and column effects, but we cannot rule it out for the interaction effect. Thus, even though the plot of the cell means had lines that were not parallel, we would have to be 'agnostic' about whether there really is an interaction effect or not.

Finally, the **effect sizes**, R^2, simply divide the appropriate SS term by SS_t. Moreover, since $SS_b = SS_r + SS_c + SS_{rc}$, the R^2's 'add up' too:

$$R^2 = R_r^2 + R_c^2 + R_{rc}^2.$$

In Table 10.9, we can see that teaching method accounts for about 22.8% of the variance in exam scores, exam accounts for 12.2%, and the interaction between the two accounts for only about 3.8%. These sum to the total percentage of 38.9%, allowing for roundoff error.

Because there is an F-test for each of the three effects and because they form a partitioning of SS_b and R^2, two-way ANOVA can be used to compare models that range from the simplest (no effects at all) to the most complex (all effects). This **model comparison** procedure is common to most multivariate techniques, and knowing its rationale and logic will enable you to interpret many research reports and design sophisticated studies.

The basic approach is to begin with simple models and then add effects only if those effects contribute sufficiently to predicting the dependent variable. When we run out of effects that make substantial contributions, we stop adding them. Our final model is thereby as parsimonious as it can be while incorporating all of the contributive influences from the independent variables. The criterion for a 'sufficient' contribution conventionally is whether we can reject the null hypothesis that a potential effect makes no contribution. Other criteria may be stipulated, however, especially in studies with large samples and/or high statistical power. In those circumstances, usually some minimum effect size is used as a criterion instead.

Our example is a small experiment and not very statistically powerful, so we will use the F-tests as our criterion. The simplest models other than the null model are those that include just one effect. They are tabulated below, along with their R^2-values. The F-test for each of these simple models compares them against the no-effects (null) model and assesses whether the amount of variance each explains is large enough to be statistically significant. In this example, the row and column effect models both yield significant F-values (and therefore R^2), but the interaction effect model does not.

Model	Form	R^2 contribution
No effects	$X_{ij} = \mu + e$	0
Row effect only	$X_{ij} = \mu + \alpha_i + e$	0.228
Column effect only	$X_{ij} = \mu + \beta_j + e$	0.122
Interaction effect only	$X_{ij} = \mu + \alpha\beta_{ij} + e$	0.038

Since the row and column effects are independent, when they are combined in a model their R^2-values are simply added together. If we compare a row effects model against one that includes both row and column effects, then the amount of change in R^2 is 0.122, the amount contributed by the column effect. Since we already know from the column effect F-test that this contribution is significant, we are willing to complicate our model by incorporating both row and column effects. On the other hand, although adding the interaction effect increases R^2 by 0.038, we already know that this is not a significant contribution. So our final model is the row and column effects model.

Model	Form	R^2	R^2 contribution
Row effect only	$X_{ij} = \mu + \alpha_i + e$	0.228	
Row and column effects	$X_{ij} = \mu + \alpha_i + \beta_j + e$	0.351	0.122
Row, column, and interactions effects	$X_{ij} = \mu + \alpha_i + \beta_j + \alpha\beta_{ij} + e$	0.389	0.038

Let us work through another example, this one with a slightly more elaborate experimental design. Dr. Alex Haslam and his student Erin Parker, both at the Australian National University, were studying the antecedents of achievement motivation in organizations (Haslam & Parker, 1998). They decided to use a Need for Achievement scale (McClelland *et al.*, 1953) as their measure of achievement motivation. Contrary to the usual view of need for achievement as a stable personality trait, Haslam & Parker proposed that this motivation would vary as a function of two organizational structural factors: the individual's *status* in the organization and the perceived *permeability* of the various status levels (i.e., the ease of mobility from one status level to a higher level).

They hypothesized that these two factors would influence achievement motivation in the following way. If permeability is high, then achievement motivation should be high regardless of status level. Organizational members will want to increase their status via achievement because they believe it is possible. If permeability is very low, on the other hand, then achievement motivation will be lower across all status levels *and* will decline with status level. What is the point of achieving if rewards for achievement are unattainable? This hypothesis really refers to two main effects and an interaction effect. One main effect is due to mobility; i.e., we would predict lower achievement motivation with lower permeability. The interaction effect arises from the fact that under low permeability we would predict lower achievement motivation with lower status, but we would not predict an effect for status under high permeability. The second main effect falls out as a consequence of the hypothesized interaction, since the net effect of status on achievement motivation should be a positive association between them.

To test their hypothesis, Haslam & Parker set up an experiment in which secondary school students were randomly assigned to either a low, middle, or high status position in a fictitious organization. Likewise, the students were randomly assigned to one of two conditions regarding information about mobility among status levels. In the 'Permeable' condition they were led to believe that status levels were readily permeable and in the 'Impermeable' condition they were told that permeability was very low. The students all completed the Need for Achievement scale questionnaire.

Our example slightly modifies their study's results, to make it a clearer illustration. Suppose the mean Need for Achievement scores for each of the six conditions turned out as in Figure 10.10. We can see that the mean scores under the Permeable condition are all higher than their counterparts in the Impermeable condition (this is the main effect for permeability). Moreover, while the means for the Permeable condition are all fairly similar to one another, those in the Impermeable condition show a marked decline from High to Low status (this is the interaction effect). Circumstantial evidence, then, appears to support the hypothesis on both counts: a main effect for permeability and an interaction effect.

We may quantify the possible effects here by computing the terms for the dependent effects model

$$X_{ij} = \mu + \alpha_i + \beta_j + \alpha\beta_{ij} + e.$$

The mean Need for Achievement scores are crosstabulated in the first part of Table 10.10, with Status taking the role of the row variable and Permeability the column variable. The row (α_i), Column (β_j), and interaction $(\alpha\beta_{ij})$ effects are tabulated in the lower part of the table.

If we wish to use a model-comparison approach to assess these effects, then we would begin by comparing a model for each such effect against a null (no effects) model. The two-way ANOVA table (Table 10.11) contains the

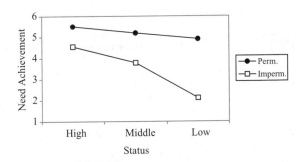

FIGURE 10.10 Plot of mean need for achievement scores

TABLE 10.10 Mean need for achievement scores

Means

	Perm.	Imperm.	Row
High	5.511	4.556	5.034
Middle	5.200	3.790	4.495
Low	4.911	2.111	3.511
Column	5.207	3.486	4.347

Effects

	Perm.	Imperm.	Row
High	$\alpha\beta_{11} = -0.383$	$\alpha\beta_{12} = 0.383$	$\alpha_1 = 0.687$
Middle	$\alpha\beta_{21} = -0.156$	$\alpha\beta_{22} = 0.156$	$\alpha_2 = 0.148$
Low	$\alpha\beta_{31} = 0.539$	$\alpha\beta_{32} = -0.539$	$\alpha_3 = -0.836$
Column	$\beta_1 = 0.861$	$\beta_2 = -0.861$	Grand mean = 4.347

required information to carry out those comparisons. All we need to do is rearrange this information and perform the relevant F-tests.

As in the earlier example, the omnibus F-test serves the purpose of telling us whether there are any effects. If we use a 99% confidence level, then, given a numerator df of 5 and $df_w = 84$, we would like to find $F_{.01}$ from Table A.4. The difficulty here is that there is no entry for $df_w = 84$. However, we can see that for $df_w = 80$, $F_{0.01} = 3.2551$, and for $df_w = 90$, $F_{0.01} = 3.2276$. Interpolating between these two values gives us $F_{0.01} = 3.2441$ for $df_w = 84$. Our confidence interval statement is

$$\Pr(F(5, 84) < 3.2441) = 0.99.$$

Since the F-value for the total between entry in the table above, which is 18.164, lies outside that interval we may reject the null hypothesis that there are no effects.

TABLE 10.11 Two-way ANOVA table for achievement example

Source	SS	df	s^2	F	R^2
Status	35.749	2	17.875	13.957	0.160
Permeability	66.713	1	66.713	52.093	0.298
Perm. × Status	13.850	2	6.925	5.408	0.062
Total between	116.313	5	23.263	18.164	0.520
Within	107.575	84	1.281		
Total	223.888	89			

Now we may examine the F-tests for each of the one-effect models, which compares them against the no-effects (null) model. Again, we will use interpolated F-values based on those in Table A.4 for df_w of 80 vs. 90. It turns out that the row, column, and interaction effect models all yield significant F-values (and therefore R^2). The relevant confidence intervals are tabulated below along with the R^2 values.

Model	Form	R^2	99% CI for F
No effects	$X_{ij} = \mu + e$	0	
Row (Status) effect	$X_{ij} = \mu + \alpha_i + e$	0.160	$\Pr(F(2, 84) < 4.8390) = 0.99$
Column (Perm) effect	$X_{ij} = \mu + \beta_j + e$	0.298	$\Pr(F(1, 84) < 6.9132) = 0.99$
Interaction effect	$X_{ij} = \mu + \alpha\beta_{ij} + e$	0.062	$\Pr(F(2, 84) < 4.8390) = 0.99$

Our final model therefore is the most complex available to us, including row, column, and interaction effects:

$$X_{ij} = \mu + \alpha_i + \beta_j + \alpha\beta_{ij} + e.$$

The total proportion of variance in Need for Achievement scores explained by this model is $R^2 = 0.160 + 0.298 + 0.062 = 0.520$, which is a very large effect by Cohen's standards (remember, Cohen thinks any R^2 above 0.25 is large).

SUMMARY

In two-way ANOVA, we perform an **omnibus test** to find out whether there are any effects from the independent variables at all. This test is a one-way ANOVA that ignores the structure of the experiment. Given r row-variable conditions and c column-variable conditions, the F-test uses the confidence interval

$$\Pr(F(df_b, df_w) < F_\alpha) = 1 - \alpha,$$

where $df_b = rc - 1$ and $df_w = \mathcal{N} - df_b - 1$.

The two-way ANOVA is designed to test whether there are detectable **row**, **column**, or **interaction** effects. It does this by **partitioning SS$_b$** into separate components for these effects. When the experiment has equal numbers of people in each cell, $SS_b = SS_r + SS_c + SS_{rc}$.

The formulas for the three tests and effect sizes are tabulated below.

SS	df	s^2	F	R^2
$SS_r = \Sigma \mathcal{N}_{i\cdot}\alpha_i^2$	$df_r + r - 1$	$s_r^2 = S_r / df_r$	$F_r = s_r^2 / s_w^2$	$R_r^2 = SS_r / SS_w$
$SS_c = \Sigma \mathcal{N}_{\cdot j}\beta_j^2$	$df_c = c - 1$	$s_c^2 = SS_c / df_c$	$F_c = s_c^2 / s_w^2$	$R_c^2 = SS_c / SS_w$
$SS_{rc} = \Sigma \mathcal{N}_{ij}\alpha\beta_{ij}^2$	$df_{rc} = (r-1)(c-1)$	$s_{rc}^2 = SS_{rc} / df_{rc}$	$F_{rc} = s_{rc}^2 / s_w^2$	$R_{rc}^2 = SS_{rc} / SS_w$

SUMMARY

The **model comparison** approach to multivariate analysis begins with simple models and then adds effects only if they contribute 'sufficiently' to predicting the dependent variable. The criterion for a 'sufficient' contribution conventionally is whether we can reject the null hypothesis that a potential effect makes no contribution. Other criteria may be stipulated, however, such as some minimum effect size.

Questions and exercises

Q.10.1. A community psychological researcher has conducted a survey in which respondents are classified as Depressed or Not Depressed, High Stress or Low Stress, and as having at least one confidant or having no confidant. The survey data have been crosstabulated on these three variables, as shown in the table below. The psychologist is primarily interested in the relationship between having or lacking a confidant and depression. Describe the effect of stress-level on that relationship, using whatever statistics are helpful.

	High Stress		Low Stress	
	Depr.	Not D.	Depr.	Not D.
Confidant	20	94	12	108
No confidant	12	31	18	23

Q.10.2. Suppose you have examined a large number of studies of gender differences in willingness to respond to requests for help, and have found that they present a bewilderingly conflicting picture. Some studies find that women help more than men; others have found that men help more than women; and still others have found no difference. Provide a plausible candidate for an explanation.

Q.10.3. Think of at least one predictor or independent variable for which randomized assignment fulfills one of each of these conditions:

(a) Unethical according to your own or another code of ethics;
(b) Illegal in your country;
(c) Impossible or impractical for other reasons.

Q.10.4. Which of the following is (or are) true?

(a) Experimental control requires random sampling.
(b) Statistical control assumes that we have measured covariates without error.

(c) Randomized assignment guarantees that all possible covariates (whether known to the experimenter or not) are randomly distributed across conditions.

(d) Under randomized assignment, no variable could have an effect by chance alone.

(e) Experimental control prevents researchers from identifying any potential masking variables.

Q.10.5. The educational psychologist back in Chapter 7 has spent her time while you were reading up to this point conducting a second study on Hanzi recognition. This time, not only has she randomly assigned five students to one of the three methods of teaching Chinese characters, but she has also assigned them randomly to either go on a month-long trip to China or to stay at home studying Chinese. Her Hanzi recognition test is the same as before, with a scale ranging from 0 to 15. The data are displayed in the next table.

	Trip			No Trip	
Method 1	Method 2	Method 3	Method 1	Method 2	Method 3
4	4	15	3	4	7
3	8	10	1	2	12
9	10	12	3	8	9
9	10	15	7	5	13
8	6	13	6	6	11

Conduct a two-way ANOVA on these data to find out the joint effect of teaching method and trip on student performance. Do the Trip and Method factors' effects combine additively or nonadditively? What model best describes these effects?

You may elect to do this by hand, or via a statistical package (the data-file is **Hanzi2**). The computational details and answers are laid out in **dem101**. Be sure to compute effect sizes and interpret the effects.

Demos

Q.10.6. Using the statistical package of your choice, open up the Aggro2 data-set. This is a rearrangement of Heubeck's data on mothers' and fathers' ratings of their children's aggressive and anxiety-depressive tendencies. There you will find two categorical independent variables:

- MOFA, whether the respondent is a mother or a father;
- CLIN, whether the child was referred for treatment or not.

There are two dependent variables: AGGRO, the aggressiveness rating, and ANXDEP, the anxiety-depressiveness rating. Perform a two-way ANOVA on at least one of these dependent variables to assess the joint effect of the parent and the referral status of the child on the ratings they received. Find the best model for these data. Do mothers or fathers give their children higher aggressiveness ratings, for instance, and is there any interaction involving parent and referral status?

Q.10.7.   Besides asking respondents to 'diagnose' the problem facing the person in a randomly selected scenario, Jorm *et al.* (1997) also asked them to rate how helpful various therapeutic options would be. Each option was rated on the following three-point scale: 1 = helpful, 2 = neither helpful nor harmful, and 3 = harmful.

For this question, I have added the responses together from five options that all refer to psychological and/or psychotherapeutic alternatives. The scale therefore is a 'harm' scale ranging from $1 \times 5 = 5$ to $3 \times 5 = 15$, with values below 10 indicating benefit and values above 10 indicating harm. The mean harmfulness ratings are shown below, for each scenario, and for the gender of the respondent. This makes a 4×2 design.

Scenario	Gender		Row
	Male	Female	
John/Depression	7.493	7.429	7.461
Mary/Depression	7.366	7.622	7.494
John/Schizophrenia	7.111	6.317	6.714
Mary/Schizophrenia	6.586	6.492	6.539
Column	7.131	6.926	7.029

The next table shows the results of a two-way ANOVA on these data. Establish whether and how gender and scenario affected respondents' ratings of the benefit/harmfulness of psychological interventions. Interpret your findings, including estimates of the effect sizes.

Source	SS	df	s^2	F	Sig.
Gender	9.643	1	9.643	2.326	0.127
Scenario	236.198	3	78.733	18.994	0.000
Gender × Scenario	47.370	3	15.790	3.809	0.010
Total between	304.406	7	43.387	10.491	0.000
Error	5310.029	1281	4.145		
Corrected Total	5614.434	1288			

Q.10.8.   Launch **dem102**, and change the means in the relevant table to reproduce the combinations of effects in Figure 10.9. Try creating a column-only effect, a column-and-interaction effect, and a column–row–interaction effect.

Demos

Putting Statistics into Perspective

11

CONTENTS

Measurement, data, and statistics

The chapter 'looks backward' (and perhaps sideways as well) over what we have covered and how it fits into the research enterprise and the accumulation of psychological knowledge. It is an attempt to provide materials out of which you can construct your own overview about what we do when we manipulate data, summarize it, and test various models against our findings and each other's interpretations. Whether you end up doing research or utilizing its findings, you will need an overview to avoid getting lost in technicalities or being led astray by rhetoric, statistically powered or otherwise.

In short, this chapter is essentially a summing-up. It should do more than just that, and in particular the rest of this chapter should tie up some loose ends, take up important but neglected topics, and give an overview of what we have covered. Finally, while we can never tie up *all* the loose ends in research, we can point many of them out and this will be attempted in the closing paragraphs.

One of the most important topics in data analysis that tends to be neglected when we are involved in learning the intricate details of a specific technique is when that technique should be used or when another technique should be preferred instead. A closely linked issue is how all these techniques are related to or distinct from one another. In this section, we are going to start practically where we began, namely with measurement and types of variables. The reason for starting there is that measurement and variable type partially direct our choice of data analytic techniques. To begin with, consider the constraints placed on researchers' choices when they are working with discrete variables.

Discrete variables can only take particular states or values and no others. They are categorical variables. Therefore, most of the time researchers focus on understanding the distribution of frequencies, proportions, or percentages across categories. All of the statistical techniques that are appropriate for discrete variables share this focus.

There are two kinds of discrete variables: nominal and ordinal. The statistical techniques we have covered that are designed for nominal variables include estimating proportions, comparing two proportions, and the chi-square statistic for comparing theoretical with observed frequency distributions. Of course, these techniques are suited to ordinal variables as well, but with ordinal variables we have a wider range of choices. Since they have ordered categories, researchers analyzing ordinal data may use cumulative frequency-based techniques, such as estimating or comparing quantiles (or percentiles).

Continuous variables, on the other hand, are quantified variables which (theoretically, at least) could take any value, or score, in their scale range. Researchers working with continuous variables usually focus on the distribution of scores. They have two broad classes of techniques from which to choose: the mean and standard deviation package, and the quantile package. The statistical techniques we have covered that are designed for continuous variables include estimating means, estimating quantiles or percentiles, comparing two means, comparing two quantiles, comparing two variances, chi-square for comparing more than two quantiles, ANOVA for comparing more than two means, and linear regression. It is also important to bear in mind that any of the techniques designed for nominal variables may be used on continuous variables, as long as the researcher is able to justify 'chunking' the variable's scale into ordered categories.

In conjunction with the distinction between discrete versus continuous variables, the **level of measurement** also influences our choice of techniques for displaying and summarizing data, as well as analyzing it. In Chapter 2 we covered the main kinds of data-displays for single variables, and then dealt with bivariate displays in later chapters. Table 11.1 surveys tabular and graphical ways of representing frequency distributions, and displays the conventional prescriptions concerning which kinds of displays and representations are appropriate for the four levels of measurement.

Much the same claims may be made about the impact of measurement level on the use of summary statistics and, therefore, the techniques for estimating them. Table 11.2 shows the conventional prescriptions regarding which summary statistics are sensible to use for different levels of measurement. These

TABLE 11.1 Representations of frequency distributions

Representation	Nominal	Ordinal	Interval/Ratio
Tabulation	Yes	Yes	Yes, if discrete or grouped
Contingency table	Yes	Yes	Yes, if discrete or grouped
Pie chart	Yes	Yes	Yes, if discrete or grouped
Bar chart	Yes	—	—
Histogram	—	Yes	Yes
Boxplot	No	Yes	Yes
Cumulative frequency plot	No	Yes	Yes
Stem-and-leaf plot	No	Yes	Yes
Frequency polygon	No	Yes	Yes
Scatterplot	No	Yes	Yes

prescriptions are, in some cases, hotly debated because they perform a 'gate-keeper' function regarding the use of statistical techniques. ANOVA and regression, for instance, are clearly restricted to interval/ratio data according to this table because they use both means and standard deviations. Many psychologists employ these techniques on data that are arguably ordinal.

Finally, the techniques for prediction and measures of association that have been dealt with in this book also may be classified according to the kinds of variable and measurement level involved. Table 11.3 does this, with the independent variables indexing the columns and dependent variables indexing the rows. The text in grey denotes statistical techniques or measures of association that are widely used but have not been covered in this book.

If there is one clear message that emerges from all these tables, it is that there is no unique prescription for which statistical technique is best to use. At best, we can provide rather loose guides to the range of options that we have, given the kinds of data we are trying to analyze. Although many research articles are written as if the data were analyzed in only one way, that often is not the case behind the scenes. Alternative analyses provide multiple viewpoints on the same data, and that is a boon to researchers who want to do

TABLE 11.2 Summary statistics

Statistic	Nominal	Ordinal	Interval/ratio
Mode	Yes	Yes	Yes, if discrete or grouped
Proportion	Yes	Yes	Yes, if discrete or grouped
Median	No	Yes	Yes
Quantile or percentile	No	Yes	Yes
Interquantile range	No	Yes	Yes
Mean	No	Debatable	Yes
Standard deviation	No	Debatable	Yes

TABLE 11.3 Bivariate techniques

Dependent variables	Independent variables		
	Nominal	Ordinal	Interval/ratio

Nominal	Chi-square
	Difference between
	  two proportions
	Odds ratios
		All nominal–nominal
		  techniques
		Quantile comparisons
		Logistic regression
			All nominal–nominal;
			  techniques
			Quantile comparisons
			Logistic regression

Ordinal	All nominal–nominal
	  techniques
	Mann–Whitney test
	Kruskal–Wallis test
		All nominal–nominal
		  and Nominal–ordinal
		  techniques
		Kendall's tau
		Spearman's rho
			All nominal and ordinal
			  techniques
			Regression/correlation (?)

Interval/
ratio
	All nominal and
	  nominal–ordinal
	  techniques
	ANOVA
		All nominal and ordinal
		  techniques
		ANOVA (?)
		Regression/correlation(?)
			All nominal and ordinal
			  techniques
			Regression/correlation

more than test preconceived hypotheses. Researchers who use several different techniques for analyzing the same data are more likely to make discoveries and come to a deep understanding of the data.

Researchers may select or highlight particular techniques for justifiable reasons that have little to do with statistical inference. For instance, they may want to compare their results with published studies, and therefore will need to use comparable statistical procedures. In some domains, researchers traditionally concentrate on a particular parameter, which in turn dictates the kinds of analyses they will conduct. Likewise, theories or hypotheses may specify parameters or statistical techniques. In short, the choice of statistics will always engage the researcher's acumen, judgment, and expertise in their research domain; it is never reducible to a recipe.

Review of statistical inference

Measurement and statistical inference are two sides of the same coin, namely the management of uncertainties in data analysis in their entirety (cf. Haslam & McGarty, 1998, Ch. 11). These may produce systematic error, i.e., extraneous influences that contain regularities and therefore bias the measurement outcomes. Alternatively they may produce random error, which does not bias measurement outcomes but nevertheless renders them less precise. Put bluntly, descriptive statistics are only as good as the craft of measurement that has gone into producing the data on which those statistics are based. Measurement error occurs whenever measurements are influenced by extraneous factors.

We have not dealt much with measurement error in this book, other than to alert you to it. It has a very extensive literature, particularly in areas such as psychological testing and psychometrics, and would require an entire course of its own. It cannot be said too often (and too often this is forgotten in published research) that managing statistical uncertainty does not mean that measurement uncertainty is automatically taken care of. It is all too easy to conduct research with valid statistics and invalid measurements.

Perhaps the most important relationship between measurement and statistical uncertainty is the tradeoff between the *sensitivity* of a measure and *statistical power*. A measure that is crude, coarse-grained, or otherwise insensitive to varying conditions will often seem highly reliable simply because a sufficiently crude or insensitive measure yields the same outcome every time. However, the less sensitive a measure is, the less able any statistical test will be to detect effects. In short, achieving reliability by resorting to crude or insensitive measures sacrifices statistical power. Conversely, sensitive and fine-grained measures will show up real effects, but they will also reveal unreliability.

Statistical inference, which has been emphasized in this book, is designed for two purposes:

- To infer some characteristic (usually a parameter) of a population or phenomenon on the basis of an estimate based on a random sample from that population;
- To describe and estimate the degree of confidence with which that inference may be made.

Statistical inference therefore is concerned primarily with sampling error, which refers to the variability of a sample estimate around the population parameter's true value.

The heart of statistical inference is a specification of the sampling distribution of a sample statistic, i.e., the probability of getting each possible value that the sample statistic can take. For example, once we know that the sampling distribution of a proportion is the binomial distribution, we are able to make precise estimates of the likelihood that a sample proportion will take on different possible values. A sample statistic should ideally be an unbiased estimator in the sense that its expected value is always the same as the corresponding population statistic's value.

The **Law of Large Numbers** tells us that an unbiased sample statistic will tend to be closer to its true population value as we take larger samples. In other words, the standard error (the standard deviation of a sample statistic) decreases as sample size increases. Many inferential techniques make use of this law by specifying a limiting distribution of a sample statistic, which is the distribution that its sampling distribution converges to as sample size increases. The most widely used limiting distribution is embodied in the **Central Limit Theorem**, which states that the limiting distribution of certain sample statistics (e.g., proportions and means) is a normal distribution.

We also made use of the *F*-distribution and the chi-square distribution as limiting distributions.

These inferential tools are combined to build a statistical model of a sample statistic with the following components:

- A true **population value** (whether known or not) for the statistic;
- A **sampling distribution** that describes how the sample statistic varies around the true population value;
- A way of measuring **sampling error**, such as the standard error of the sampling statistic;
- A **limiting distribution** that can be used to approximate the sampling distribution as N becomes large.

This model may be expressed in the following general form:

Sample statistic value = population statistic value + sampling error.

It is the sampling error term that has the sampling distribution, whether it be binomial, normal, *F*, or whatever. When we are dealing with an experiment that uses randomized assignment, the sampling error is essentially generated by the randomized assignment process.

Statistical inference without random sampling or randomized assignment?

Throughout this book, we have emphasized random sampling and randomized assignment. The briefest acquaintance with psychological research literature will reveal, however, that many published studies do not have either random samples or randomized assignment. Yet, the authors of those studies almost all use statistical inference. Are they all mistaken? When can we justifiably use statistical inference without a random sample or true experimental design?

A short answer is that we are justified in adopting this strategy whenever we are satisfied that we can model a phenomenon via a statistical model, and are sufficiently careful in specifying what inferences can and cannot be made. Imagine that we are running a small penal institution and we have a new twist on rehabilitation that we think might make inmates less likely to return to prison within the first 2 years of their release. Accordingly, we implement the new program and record the number of prisoners who return to prison within 2 years after release and the number who do not, until we have done so for a total of 20 prisoners. Moreover, we extract the same information from earlier prison records for, as it turns out, the 20 ex-prisoners who were incarcerated prior to our program.

Now, we want to compare the proportions of recidivists for these two groups. There is no random sample here and no randomized assignment, so in what sense are we justified in using statistical inference? If there really were no difference between the two groups, then a no-effects (null) model of the difference between their proportions of recidivists would hold true. That means the expected difference would be 0, and any difference that happened to crop up would be *solely due to chance*.

We may put a confidence interval around the difference and see whether 0 is contained in it. We may do this, given that we have neither a random sample nor randomized assignment, for the same reason that we may put a confidence interval around the observed proportion of heads in a series of coin-tosses. In both situations, we are using a model based on the sampling distribution of a proportion, assuming a sequence of independent events (i.e., recidivism or coin-tosses). There are even methods, although we have not covered them in this book, to evaluate whether the assumption of independent events seems tenable according to the data.

Once we decide to test the no-effects model for the difference between the two proportions, what inferences may we make? We *can* make inferences about whether or not randomness could account for the observed difference between those two groups. We *cannot* infer anything about any population or sample other than those two groups. For example, we are in no position to say anything about what would happen if we implemented the same program in another penal institution. Likewise, we cannot say anything about the impact of our program on lawbreakers in the same population from which our prisoners came.

As Darlington (1990: 373) puts it, we can say whether there is a 'meaningful' difference in recidivism rates, but we cannot use statistical inference here to say anything about the replicability or generality of our results without introducing some qualifications. We certainly can make inferences about *hypothetical populations* of prisoners under identical conditions to our groups, but we would need to provide extra arguments about whether any real populations are similar to our hypothetical ones. This is really no different from the situation in which we want to make inferences about populations other than the one from which we have sampled, or the same population in the past or future.

In this kind of situation we also need to carefully distinguish *statistical* from *predictive* or *causal* inferences. If our confidence interval contains 0 then we may not rule out the possibility that recidivism rates remained unchanged during both periods. Does that mean our program had no effect? Not necessarily, since some other unobserved factor might have changed between those two periods and offset the program's effect on recidivism. Conversely, statistical evidence that a change has occurred does not entitle us to award the credit for that to the program. Again, something else may have produced the change instead.

What about experiments that involve randomized assignment but no random sample? They permit us to use statistical inference to make assertions about causation, but not about replicability or generality without further qualifications and arguments of the kind mentioned above. There is one exception to this rule, namely when the experimental effect is known to go in one direction if it exists at all. For instance, some task-learning experiments have this property because the participant begins by knowing nothing about what is to be learned. Therefore, in a comparison with a baseline control condition where no instruction is provided, any effect will involve improvement in the participant's performative competence.

Statistical confidence and models

How do we realize the two goals of statistical inference? We use **confidence intervals** to reflect the imprecision of sample estimates and models incorporating the effects of both random and nonrandom influences on the variable concerned. The central approach in this book has been based on the confidence interval, a range of values containing a specified percentage of the sampling distribution of a statistic. That percentage establishes the confidence level, since it is the expected percentage of times that the interval would contain the population value of the statistic being estimated, under repeated identical random samples.

A **one-sided confidence interval** has only one limit (either the upper or lower one) that is free to vary, with the other limit fixed at one extreme of the distribution. A **two-sided confidence interval** has a lower and an upper limit that are free to vary. We have seen that in many situations its form is

$$\text{CI}_{1-\alpha} = [\text{estimate} - w, \ \text{estimate} + w],$$

or somewhat more formally,

$$\Pr(\text{estimate} - w < \text{population parameter} < \text{estimate} + w) = 1 - \alpha.$$

Throughout this book, this kind of interval has been represented by the delta-and-bar diagram shown here.

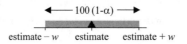

The half-width w is the product of two components. The first one is the score of the relevant statistic beyond which the area of the sampling distribution curve is $\alpha/2$. The second is the standard error of the sample estimate. For example, suppose we are estimating the population proportion, Π. For a large enough sample we may use the normal distribution to approximate the sampling distribution for the sample proportion P. We would therefore make a confidence interval statement about the population proportion as follows:

$$\text{CI}_{1-\alpha} = P \pm w, \text{ where } w = z_{\alpha/2}s_P.$$

The next three tables summarize most of the confidence intervals we have explored and used. Table 11.4 shows two-sided intervals, Table 11.5 has

TABLE 11.4 Two-sided confidence intervals

Interval around	Sampling distribution	df	$\text{CI}_{1-\alpha}$	
Proportion: Π	Binominal	N	$[P - a, \ P + b]$	
	Normal	—	$P \pm w$	$w = z_{\alpha/2}s_P$
				$s_P = \sqrt{\dfrac{P(1-P)}{N}}$
Mean: μ	t	$N - 1$	$\bar{X} \pm w,$	$w = t_{\alpha/2}s_{\bar{x}}$
	Normal	—		$w = z_{\alpha/2}s_{\bar{x}}$
				$s_{\bar{x}} = s/\sqrt{N}$
Difference of proportions: $\Pi_1 - \Pi_2$	t	$N_1 + N_2 - 2$	$P_1 - P_2 \pm w,$	$w = t_{\alpha/2}s_{\text{err}}$
	Normal	—		$w = z_{\alpha/2}s_{\text{err}}$
				$s_{\text{err}} = \sqrt{\dfrac{P_1(1-P_1)}{N_1} + \dfrac{P_2(1-P_2)}{N_2}}$
Difference of means: $\mu_1 - \mu_2$	t	$N_1 + N_2 - 2$	$\bar{X}_1 - \bar{X}_2 \pm w$	$w = t_{\alpha/2}s_{\text{err}}$
	Normal	—		$w = z_{\alpha/2}s_{\text{err}}$
				$s_{\text{err}} = \sqrt{s^2_{\text{pooled}}\left(\dfrac{1}{N_1} + \dfrac{1}{N_2}\right)}$
Regression coeff.	t	$N - 2$	$b \pm w,$	$w = t_{\alpha/2}s_{\text{errb}}$
	Normal	—	where	$w = z_{\alpha/2}s_{\text{errb}}$
				$s_{\text{errb}} = \sqrt{\dfrac{s^2_{Y\mid X}}{\text{SS}_X}}$

TABLE 11.5 Confidence intervals with transformations

Interval around	Sampling distribution	$CI_{1-\alpha}$	
Correlation: ρ Fisher's z transform: $R' = \frac{1}{2}\ln\left(\frac{1+R}{1-R}\right)$	Normal	$R' \pm w,$	$w = z_{\alpha/2}s_{R'}$ $s_{R'} = \sqrt{\dfrac{1}{N-3}}$
Odds-ratio: Ω Logarithm transform: $\ln(W)$	Normal	$\ln(W) \pm w,$	$w = z_{\alpha/2}s_{err}$ $s_{err} = \sqrt{1/N_{11} + 1/N_{12} + 1/N_{21} + 1/N_{22}}$

intervals requiring transformations, and Table 11.6 displays one-sided intervals.

A **confidence interval** enables us to assess whether any model that predicts a value of the statistic concerned is plausible or not. **Model error** is the difference between a hypothetical value of a population statistic and the true value of that statistic. A *plausible hypothetical value* of a population statistic is one that lies inside the confidence interval that has been constructed around a sample estimate. It is implausible if it lies outside the interval. Since a plausible model predicts plausible values, a plausible model is one for which 0 is a plausible value for model error.

Confidence intervals also contain all the hypothetical values that we cannot rule out. In this sense, they are a generalization of the traditional significance test, the procedure by which a researcher decides whether to reject a hypothesis or not on the basis of whether its predicted values of a statistic are plausible. A hypothesis is rejected if all of its predicted values of a statistic are implausible.

The **null hypothesis** (H_0) is the hypothesis tested in a significance test. Usually it is constructed in such a way that the alternative to it is the state of affairs that the researcher hopes is true. If the null hypothesis is rejected then its alternative (the alternative hypothesis, or H_1) must be plausible. Otherwise,

TABLE 11.6 One-sided confidence intervals

Interval around	Sampling distribution	df	$CI_{1-\alpha}$
F-statistic: $F(df_b, df_w)$	F	df_b, df_w	$[0, F_\alpha]$
Chi-square: $\chi^2(df)$	χ^2	$(r-1)(c-1)$	$[0, \chi^2_\alpha]$

we fail to reject it, and are left with two possibilities. One is that our study lacked sufficient statistical power to render our null hypothesis implausible. The other is that the null hypothesis is valid.

Type I error is rejecting a null hypothesis when it really is true. Type II error is failing to reject a null hypothesis when it really is false. The probability of making a Type I Error (α) is determined by specifying a confidence level of $100(1 - \alpha)\%$ for constructing confidence intervals.

Power is the probability of correctly rejecting the null hypothesis. **Type II error** probability (β) and power $(1 - \beta)$ are influenced by how far an alternative hypothesis value for a statistic is from the null hypothesis value, and the width of the confidence interval (which in turn depends on the confidence level and the sample size). Briefly:

- The further the alternative hypothesis value for a statistic is from the null hypothesis value, the higher power will be.
- The narrower the confidence intervals, the higher power will be. Confidence intervals may be made narrower either by lowering the confidence level or increasing sample size.

The Table 11.7 locates the two types of error and their probabilities in terms of whether the null hypothesis is true or not and what decision has been taken.

The determination of how much confidence we should have (or how small α should be) and how much power we should settle for is largely a matter of pragmatic judgment and scientific convention. Most researchers try to assess the tradeoff between power and Type I error probability, either in designing studies or when they have failed to reject a null hypothesis. Also, it is generally acknowledged that when computing sets of related confidence intervals or performing related significance tests, researchers should be concerned with the family-wise confidence level, the probability of one or more intervals excluding its population parameter. A Bonferroni correction is one way of dealing with this concern.

Probably the single most important realization about confidence intervals and significance tests is that whereas a significance test pits only one null

TABLE 11.7 Hypothesis-testing decision

Decision	State of reality	
	Null hypothesis H_0 is true	Null hypothesis H_0 is false
Do not reject H_0	Correct decision	**Type II error** β
Reject H_0	**Type I error** α	Correct decision **Power** $= 1 - \beta$

hypothesis against a (usually much broader) alternative, a confidence interval provides *a range of plausible values, centered on the observed sample value*. It is crucial that all of those values be taken seriously. For example, even if a confidence interval for a difference between a treatment and control mean contains 0, that does not imply that there is no difference between the means. It merely implies that 0 is a value that cannot be ruled out, along with all the other values in the interval.

Hunter & Schmidt (1990: 32) point out that the confidence interval not only is correctly centered on the sample value, but provides a better view than the significance test does of the extent of uncertainty due to sampling error. The upper limit of the interval tells us what the largest plausible difference could be, and the lower limit tells us what the smallest difference could be. A confidence interval lends itself to graphical (visual) representation. Moreover, any confidence interval that contains 0 (even if 0 is the observed value!) will also always contain some other nonzero values, which has prompted a number of commentators to draw attention to the illogicality of focusing on the null hypothesis of a significance test when there are other plausible values as well.

Effect sizes and effects models

For the most part, **effect sizes** are associated with models of the effects that an independent variable has on a dependent variable. An **independent variable** is a variable that is considered to be a predictor or sometimes a cause of another variable. A **dependent variable** is the variable predicted or caused by independent variable(s).

The simplest situation involves a comparison between a sample statistic and a (usually no-effects) null hypothesis value. The size of the difference between a sample statistic and a hypothetical value may be evaluated in two ways. One is relative to the range of the scale itself (*scale-based evaluation*) and another is relative to the dispersion of scores (*distribution-based evaluation*). Scale-based evaluation takes into account the scale range, coarseness, and position on the scale.

Distribution-based evaluation of effects usually employs standard deviation units, or other 'scale-free' units that are also unaffected by sample size. **Cohen's d** is a prominent example, namely the difference between the sample mean and the population mean in standard deviation units:

$$d = \frac{\bar{X} - \mu}{s}$$

The *t*-statistic may be rewritten in terms of Cohen's *d* multiplied by $\sqrt{N}$:

$$t(\mathrm{df}) = \frac{\bar{X} - \mu}{s/\sqrt{N}} = d\sqrt{N}$$

which implies that unlike the *t*-statistic, Cohen's *d* does not increase with N.

Like any distribution-based effect size measure, Cohen's *d* may be used for benchmarking power. We saw in Chapter 6 that we could determine the statistical power of a study to detect an effect size of *d*, given its sample estimate of *t*. Cohen's *d* also may be used in planning a study, to address the question of how large the sample should be. In Chapter 6 we found out how to ascertain the required sample size for a study to detect *d* with power of $1 - \beta$ when given a confidence level of $1 - \alpha$, and the smallest effect size that a study could detect with power of $1 - \beta$ when given a confidence level of $1 - \alpha$ and sample size N.

Most of the techniques that we have covered for prediction purposes compare a null or no-effects model against an effects model, where the effects are due to the independent variable(s). The null model has the form

Dependent variable = expected value + sampling error.

The effects model, on the other hand, has the form

Dependent variable = expected value + effects + residual sampling error.

The significance test associated with this comparison is used to decide whether the more elaborate effects model makes significantly less predictive error overall than the simpler null model does.

One very popular class of such model-comparison techniques is the **General Linear Model** which includes regression, ANOVA, and the *t*-test for comparing two independent means or proportions. ANOVA and regression share a number of crucial features. ANOVA may be translated into regression by converting binary variables into dummy variables that take a value of 0 for one category and 1 for the other. The regression analysis produces the same R^2-value and *F*-test results as the ANOVA does.

The amount of predictive error is measured by the squared difference between the observed value of the dependent variable Y and the value, Y', predicted by a model. For the null model in both regression and ANOVA, Y' is just the mean of Y, so

$$Y' = \mu_Y + e,$$

and the sum of the squared error is

$$SS_Y = \Sigma(Y - \bar{Y})^2.$$

For the effects model, the sum of the squared error is

$$SS_e = \Sigma(Y - Y')^2.$$

These are compared via the squared correlation coefficient R^2, a proportional reduction of error measure:

$$R^2 = \frac{SS_Y - SS_e}{SS_Y}$$

It measures the proportion of the error, SS_Y, in the null model that has been reduced by taking effects into account. R^2 does not increase with larger sample sizes, whereas F does. Thus, R^2 is to F as Cohen's d is to the t-statistic.

Finally, in Chapter 9 we investigated an effect-size measure for association between two categorical variables that goes with the chi-square statistic, namely $\phi^2 = \chi^2/N$ for 2×2 contingency tables and Cramer's extension of it which is corrected for larger tables. ϕ^2 is to χ^2 as Cohen's d is to the t-statistic. The general relationship between the 'test statistic' associated with a significance test, the degrees of freedom associated with it, and the corresponding effect-size measure may be summarized as follows:

$$\text{Test statistic} = \text{effect size} \times \text{size of study},$$

where 'Size of Study' is a function of the degrees of freedom. In one-sample tests such as the t-test the size of the study is simply a function of sample size, whereas in multivariate procedures such as ANOVA the size of the study reflects both sample size and additional relevant complexities such as the number of experimental conditions. Three examples of this relationship are shown in Table 11.8.

TABLE 11.8 Relationship of test statistic to effect size and size of study

	Test statistic =	Effect size	×	Size of study
One-sample t-test	$t =$	d	×	$\sqrt{N}$
One-way ANOVA	$F =$	$R^2/(1 - R^2)$	×	df_w/df_b
2×2 Contingency table	$\chi^2 =$	ϕ^2	×	N

Hypothesis testing and accumulating knowledge

There is a natural tension between two perfectly reasonable scientific goals. One is *hypothesis testing* based on the findings of one study, and the other is *accumulating knowledge* over more than one study. We have encountered this tension earlier in Chapter 5, where we saw that deciding whether or not a finding was statistically 'significant' was not an adequate way to summarize the findings of a study for comparison with other studies. For many reasons, researchers find themselves pressured to declare whether or not their study supports one model or hypothesis over another. Some of those reasons amount to academic convention, but others are justifiable in scientific or practical terms. It seems quite likely that we will have to live with both goals for the foreseeable future, and therefore we will need to be equipped with methods for managing the uncertainties entailed by each without doing damage to the other.

The past 40 years or so of statistics in psychological research has been dominated by significance testing. A number of psychologists have argued that this dominance has amounted to a 'stranglehold' (Rozeboom, 1960) at the expense of properly assessing the accumulation of knowledge. Replication and the development of sophisticated methods for comparing and combining results from studies were neglected until quite recently. Researchers may be unable to reject a null model for no other reason than low statistical power, and they will be able to find this out only if more studies are conducted and their results are effectively compared or combined. No replication means that 'nonsignificant' findings arising from Type II error are doomed to remain undetected, and real effects will be mistaken for chance effects.

We have already learned that one of the best ways of increasing power is to increase sample size, but the main limitation of this prescription is that it still focuses only on one study at a time. For many effects of interest, researchers may not be able to obtain sufficient resources to conduct the large-sample studies required to detect them. Hunter & Schmidt (1990: 33) make this point very effectively with sobering illustrations. Suppose, for instance, that we would like a 95% confidence interval for the correlation coefficient to have a width of 0.1. Then for a midrange correlation (0.44 to 0.66), the sample size needs to exceed 1000. For more extreme correlations the sample will have to be even larger.

If psychologists do not have the resources to run studies with samples of 1000 or more, then the only remaining alternative is to run replicated smaller-sample studies and then compare and combine their results. The methods for comparing and combining the results of studies are collectively called 'meta-analysis,' and they make extensive usage of effect-size measures and confidence intervals (for an introductory treatment see Rosenthal &

Rosnow, 1991; for more advanced texts see Glass, McGraw & Smith, 1980 or Hunter & Schmidt, 1990).

Despite demonstrations like the one in Chapter 5 that confidence intervals give us a better way of comparing studies than counting up the number of significant and nonsignificant findings, you will find (if you don't already know) that the traditional psychological research article seldom presents anything other than a significance test. This practice has largely been due to a widespread insistence by editors of major psychological journals on significance testing. It has also been reinforced for many years by textbooks that presented statistics mainly in terms of significance testing without much, if any, attention to confidence intervals.

If you haven't already read the Preface and my remarks to instructors, you may be interested to know that you are studying statistics in psychology at a time when all of this finally may be changing. A task-force of prominent psychologists in the American Psychological Association (APA) published its report on the APA website in 1996, recommending substantial reforms in statistical analysis and reporting:

> 'With respect to this topic the task force has identified three issues that are particularly germane to current practice.
>
> (a) We recommend that more extensive descriptions of the data be provided to reviewers and readers. This should include means, standard deviations, sample sizes, five-point summaries, box-and-whisker plots, other graphics, and descriptions related to missing data as appropriate.
> (b) Enhanced characterization of the results of analyses (beyond simple p value statements) to include both direction and size of effect (e.g., mean difference, regression and correlation coefficients, odds-ratios, more complex effect size indicators) and their confidence intervals should be provided routinely as part of the presentation. These characterizations should be reported in the most interpretable metric (e.g., the expected unit change in the criterion for a unit change in the predictor, Cohen's d).
> (c) The use of techniques to assure that the reported results are not produced by anomalies in the data (e.g., outliers, points of high influence, non-random missing data, selection, attrition problems) should be a standard component of all analyses.'

Modern statistical practices in many other fields already embody most of these recommendations, along with an emphasis on comparing models instead of significance testing as such.

Some researchers (e.g., Hunter, 1997) have called for a ban on significance testing altogether. Rather than banning significance tests, a healthier approach is probably to use confidence intervals and model comparisons, and to bear in mind that significance testing is a special case of each of them. That way, you can still read and understand the traditional psychological literature while not being condemned to use statistics in the same manner. A few years earlier, Gigerenzer (1993), who has written extensively on research methods and uncertainty, sounded a similar call for reform in both editorial policies and educational practices. This book has been my response to that call and to the prospect of revising our teaching of statistical methods so that you, the coming generation, need not repeat and perpetuate our errors.

On a more upbeat note, the concepts and skills that you have mastered in working through the material in this book will equip you to understand research and evidential arguments at a fairly sophisticated level. You now understand the fundamental ideas behind almost all statistical techniques that are widely used in psychology, the social sciences, and other areas as well. You are less likely to be fooled by popular misuses of statistics, and more likely to use them properly yourself.

You also possess knowledge and an orientation that those who have been trained in the more traditional way may not have. You are less likely than they to be fooled into thinking that a 'significant' result is an important result or a large effect. Researchers will have to do more than simply report significance tests to convince you that their findings are important. You are more likely to assess the actual effect size, and in reviewing collections of studies you are more likely to accurately assess where the weight of evidence lies by using confidence intervals instead of merely labeling findings 'significant' or 'nonsignificant.' You will be aware of the full range of alternative values, interpretations, and models that research findings encompass. In other words, your view of statistical uncertainty will probably be more realistic than traditionally educated psychologists. And that can only be good, both for you and the state of the art in psychology.

References

Achenbach, T.M. (1991). *Manual for the child behavior checklist 4–18 and 1991 Profile.* Burlington: University of Vermont Department of Psychiatry.

Agresti, A. (1990). *Categorical data analysis.* New York: Wiley.

Aiken, L.S., West, S.G., Sechrest, L. & Reno, R.R. (1990). Graduate training in statistics, methodology, and measurement in psychology: A survey of PhD programs in North America. *American Psychologist, 45,* 721–734.

Barrow, J.D. (1992). *Pi in the sky: Counting, thinking, and being.* Boston: Little, Brown, and Co.

Bryman, A. (1988). *Quality and quantity in social research.* London: Unwin.

Campbell, D.T. & Stanley, J.C. (1963). *Experimental and quasi-experimental designs for research.* Chicago: Rand-McNally.

Christensen-Szalanski, J.J.J. & Bushyhead, J.B. (1981). Physicians' use of probabilistic information in a real clinical setting. *Journal of Experimental Psychology: Human Perception and Performance, 7:* 928–935.

Cleveland, W.S. (1985). *The elements of graphing data.* Pacific Grove, California: Brooks Cole.

Cleveland, W.S. (1993). *Visualizing data.* Summit, New Jersey: Hobart Press.

Cohen, J. (1962). The statistical power of abnormal-social psychological research: A review. *Journal of Abnormal and Social Psychology, 65,* 145–153.

Cohen, J. (1988). *Statistical power analysis for behavioral sciences,* 2nd edition. Hillsdale, N.J.: Erlbaum.

Cook, T.D. & Campbell, D.T. (1979). *Quasi-experimentation: Design and analysis issues for field settings.* Boston: Houghton Mifflin.

Darlington, R.B. (1990). *Regression and linear models.* New York: McGraw-Hill.

Dennett, D. (1994). *Darwin's dangerous idea.* London: Penguin.

Downs, A. (1966). *Inside bureaucracy.* Boston: Little, Brown and Co.

Einhorn, H.J. & Hogarth, R.M. (1985). Ambiguity and uncertainty in probabilistic inference. *Psychological Review, 92,* 433–461.

Ellsberg, D. (1961). Risk, ambiguity and the Savage axioms. *Quarterly Journal of Economics, 75,* 643–669.

Fajak, A. & Haslam, S.A. (1998). Gender solidarity in hierarchical organizations. *British Journal of Social Psychology, 37,* 73–94.

Feynman, R.P. (1988). *What do you care what other people think?* London: Unwin.

Fischhoff, B. Slovic, P., & Lichtenstein, S. (1977). Knowing with certainty: The appropriateness of extreme confidence. *Journal of Experimental Psychology: Human Perception and Performance, 3,* 552–564.

Fischhoff, B., Slovic, P. & Lichtenstein, S. (1978). Fault trees: Sensibility of estimated failure probabilities to problem representation. *Journal of Experimental Psychology: Human Perception and Performance, 4*, 330–344.

Fischhoff, B. & Slovic, P. (1980). A little learning...: Confidence in multi-cue judgment. In R. Nickerson (Ed.), *Attention and Performance VIII.* Hillsdale, N.J.: Erlbaum.

Fleck, L. (1935/1979). *Genesis and development of a scientific fact* (Trans. F. Bradley & T. J. Trenn). Chicago: University Chicago Press.

Foddy, W. (1993). *Constructing questions for interviews and questionnaires.* Cambridge, U.K.: Cambridge University Press.

Funtowicz, S.O. & Ravetz, J.R. (1990). *Uncertainty and quality in science for policy.* Dordrecht: Kluwer.

Gerrity, M.S., Earp, J.A.L., & DeVellis, R.F. (1992). Uncertainty and professional work: Perceptions of physicians in clinical practice. *American Journal of Sociology, 97,* 1022–1051.

Gigerenzer, G. (1993). The superego, the ego and the id in statistical reasoning. In Kern, G. & Lewis, C. (Eds.) *A handbook for data analysis in the behavioral sciences: Methodological issues.* Hillsdale, N.J.: Erlbaum.

Glass, G.V., McGaw, B., & Smith, M.L. (1981). *Meta-analysis in social research.* Beverly Hills, CA: Sage.

Grinnell, F. (1987). *The scientific attitude.* Boulder, Colorado: Westview.

Hacking, I. (1975). *The emergence of probability.* Cambridge: Cambridge University Press.

Haslam, S.A. & McGarty, C. (1998). *Doing psychology: An introduction to research methodology and statistics.* London: Sage.

Haslam, S.A. & Parker, E. (1998). The role of group status and boundary permeability in motivation to achieve at work. Unpublished manuscript: The Australian National University.

Hovland, C.L. (1959). Reconciling conflicting results derived from experimental and survey studies of attitude change. *American Psychologist, 14,* 8–17.

Howell, W.C. (1972). Compounding uncertainty from internal sources. *Journal of Experimental Psychology, 95*: 6–13.

Hume, D. (1739/1945). *A treatise of human nature, Book 1, Of the understanding, Section 2.* LaSalle, Illinois: Open Court Publishing Co.

Hunter, J.E. (1997). Needed: A ban on the significance test. *Psychological Science, 8,* 3–7.

Hunter, J.E. & Schmidt, F.L. (1990). *Methods of meta-analysis: Correcting error and bias in research findings.* Newbury Park, CA: Sage.

Huston, T.L., Ruggerio, M., Conner, R., & Geis, G. (1981). Bystander intervention into crime: A study based on naturally-occurring episodes. *Social Psychological Quarterly, 44,* 14–23.

Jorm, A.F. Korten, A.E., Jacomb, P.A., Christensen, H., Rodgers, B., & Pollitt, P. (1997). Mental health literacy: A survey of the public's ability to recognize mental disorders and their beliefs about the effectiveness of treatment. *Medical Journal of Australia, 166,* 182–186.

Kaplan, R.M. & Saccuzzo, D.P. (1989). *Psychological testing: principles, applications, and issues,* 2nd edition. Pacific Grove, California: Brooks Cole.

Kerwin, A. (1993). None too solid: Medical ignorance. *Knowledge: Creation, Diffusion, Utilization, 15,* 166–185.

Keyfitz, N. (1989). The growing human population. *Scientific American, 261,* 74–81.

Liang, J., Boraswski, C.E., Liu, X., & Sugisawa, H. (1996). Transitions in cognitive status among the aged in Japan. *Social Science Medicine, 43,* 325–337.

Lichtenstein, S. & Fischhoff, B. (1980). Training for calibration. *Organizational Behavior and Human Performance, 26*: 149–171.

Lichtenstein, S., Fischhoff, B., & Phillips, L.D. (1982). Calibration of probabilities: The state of the art to 1980. In D. Kahneman, P. Slovic, and A. Tversky (Eds.), *Judgment under uncertainty: Heuristics and biases.* New York: Cambridge University Press.

Linnerooth, J. (1984). The political processing of uncertainty. *Acta Psychologica, 56,* 219–231.

Lockhart, R.S. (1998). *Introduction to statistics and data analysis for the behavioral sciences.* New York: W.H. Freeman.

Luce, R.D. (1997). Several unresolved conceptual problems of mathematical psychology. *Journal of Mathematical Psychology, 41,* 79–87.

Marsh, C. (1988). *Exploring data: An introduction to data analysis for social scientists.* Cambridge: Polity Press.

McClelland, D.C., Atkinson, J.W., Clark, R.A., & Lowell, E.L. (1953). *The achievement motive.* New York: Appleton-Century-Crofts.

Meehl, P.E. (1967). Theory testing in psychology and physics: A methodological paradox. *Philosophy of Science, 34,* 103–115.

Merton, R.K. (1973). *The sociology of science.* Chicago: University of Chicago Press.

Neuman, W.L. (1997). *Social research methods: Qualitative and quantitative approaches,* 3rd edition. Boston: Allyn and Bacon.

Oakes, M.L. (1986). *Statistical inference: A commentary for the social and behavioral sciences.* New York: Wiley.

Orne, M.T. (1962). On the social psychology of the psychological experiment: with particular reference to demand characteristics and their implications. *American Psychologist, 17,* 776–783.

Oskamp, S. (1965). The relationship of clinical experience and training methods to several criteria of clinical prediction. *Psychological Monographs, 76.*

Otway, H.J. & von Winterfeldt, D. (1982). Beyond acceptable risk: on the social acceptability of technologies. *Policy Sciences, 14,* 247–256.

Paulos, J.A. (1988). *Innumeracy: Mathematical illiteracy and its consequences.* London: Penguin.

Pinker, S. (1997). *How the mind works.* New York: W.W. Norton.

Plous, S. (1993). *The psychology of judgment and decision making.* New York: McGraw-Hill.

Ragin, C.L. (1994). *Constructing social research.* Thousand Oaks, California: Pine Forge Press.

Rosenthal, R. (1990). How are we doing in soft psychology? *American Psychologist, 45,* 775–777.

Rosenthal, R. & Rosnow, R.L. (1991). *Essentials of behavioral research: methods and data analysis,* 2nd edition. New York: McGraw-Hill.

Rozeboom, W.W. (1960). The fallacy of the null hypothesis significant test. *Psychological Bulletin, 57,* 416–428.

Schmidt, F.L. (1996). Statistical significance testing and cumulative knowledge in psychology: implications for training of researchers. *Psychological Methods, 1,* 115–129.

Sedlmeier, P. & Gigerenzer, G. (1989). Do studies of statistical power have any effect on the power of studies? *Psychological Bulletin, 105,* 309–316.

Sjoberg, L. (1997). Explaining risk perception: An empirical evaluation of cultural theory. *Risk Decision and Policy, 2,* 113–130.

Slovic, P. & Peters, E. (1998). The importance of worldviews in risk perception. *Risk Decision and Policy, 3,* 171–174.

Smithson, M.J. (1989). *Ignorance and uncertainty: Emerging paradigms.* New York: Springer-Verlag.

Smithson, M.J. (1990). Ignorance and disasters. *International Journal of Mass Emergencies and Disasters, 8,* 207–235.

Smithson, M., Amato, P.R., & Pearce, P.L. (1983). *Dimensions of helping behaviour.* Oxford: Pergamon Press.

Smithson, M., Reser, J.P., Taylor, J.C., & Reser, P. (1991). *The James Cook University Aboriginal suicide project: Interim report to the ACC.* Unpublished manuscript, Townsville, Australia.

Sommers, C.H. (1994). *Who stole feminism?* New York: Simon and Schuster.

Spears, M.L. (1952). *Charting statistics.* New York.

Stael von Holstein, C.-A.S. (1971). An experiment in probabilistic weather forecasting. *Journal of Applied Meteorology, 10,* 635–645.

Tufte, E.R. (1983). *The visual display of quantitative information.* Cheshire, Connecticut: Graphics Press.

Tversky, A. & Kahneman, D. (1971). Belief in the law of small numbers. *Psychological Bulletin, 76,* 105–110.

Tversky, A. & Koehler, D. J. (1994). Support theory: a nonextensional representation of subjective probability. *Psychological Review, 101,* 547–567.

Wallsten, T., Budescu, D. Rappoport, A., Zwick, R., & Forsyth, B. (1986). Measuring the vague meanings of probability terms. *Journal of Experimental Psychology: General, 115,* 348–365.

Wason, P.C. & Johnson-Laird, P.N. (1972). *Psychology of reasoning: structure and content.* London: Batsford.

Weinstein, R.M. (1979). Patient attitudes toward mental hospitalization: A review of quantitative research. *Journal of Health and Behavior, 21,* 397–401.

Answers to Selected Questions and Exercises

Chapter 1

Q.1.1 (a) Scientific, for the most part. Some might argue that the voltmeter is being used as the embodiment of an 'authority' on the measurement of voltage.

(b) Authoritative.

(c) Rationalistic, since it uses a logical deduction from a premise.

(d) Intuitive.

(e) Authoritative, for the most part. Some might argue that the *OED* is being used as a database, so there is also an element of scientific approach here.

(f) Scientific, mainly, with a bit of rationality included because of the implicit theory about the effect Madras powder on heat.

Q.1.4. This is an example of topical uncertainty, because the psychologists disagree over what should be included in the topic of 'categorization'.

Q.1.5. An argument (not the only one) favoring a single scale for happiness: People generally talk about being happy in greater or lesser degree, and do not seem to distinguish between more than one kind of happiness. An argument (not the only one) favoring two scales for happiness: People may be happy because of having enjoyed good outcomes or because of having avoided bad outcomes. These may be distinguishable emotional states.

Chapter 2

Q.2.1. Motivation.

Q.2.3. A demand characteristic, namely social desirability. Many people will be reluctant to report that they donated nothing to charity.

Q.2.5. The number of hairs on a goat can take on only integer values (i.e., $0, 1, 2, \ldots$) and therefore is not a continuous variable.

Q.2.6. (a) It is continuous.

Q.2.8. (c) It has interval-level measurement.

Q.2.9. (a) Discrete
(b) Continuous
(c) Continuous
(d) Discrete
(e) Continuous

Q.2.10. It lacks a *reference frame*, since it does not specify whether this is income before or after tax.

Chapter 3

Q.3.1. There is no figure to tell us what the previous year's volume was, so we have no benchmark against which to assess how large the 350% increase is. Also, the statement doesn't tell us how sales volume is being measured.

Q.3.3. (a) The mean will shift from 20 to $20 + 5 = 25$ if we add 5 to each score.
(b) The mean will become $20/5 = 4$ if we divide each score by 5.
(c) The standard deviation will remain unchanged if we add 5 to each score, since the squared difference between each score and the mean remains unaffected by adding 5 to each score.

Q.3.4. The cumulative frequency and percentage distributions are tabulated below. They are also contained in the Excel file called Ch3Q4, in the Dataset folder. To start the cumulative frequency distribution for the males, since we are accumulating downward from the oldest to the youngest, the cell entry for the 80+ age group is just its frequency, namely 95.
Since the total number of males is 5727, the cumulative percentage for this age group is $100(95/5727) = 1.66\%$.
For the 70 to 79 age group, the cumulative frequency is the number of males in the 80+ age group plus the 294 in the 70 to 79 age group, which gives a cumulative frequency of 389. The corresponding cumulative percentage is therefore $100(389/5727) = 6.79\%$.
And so on, until we accumulate to 100% when we reach the 0 to 9 age group. The table over displays the results of this procedure.

Age	Males	Cum. f.	Cum. %	Age	Females	Cum. f.	Cum. %
80+	95	95	1.66	80+	203	203	3.28
70 to 79	294	389	6.79	70 to 79	426	629	10.16
60 to 69	462	851	14.86	60 to 69	514	1143	18.47
50 to 59	522	1373	23.97	50 to 59	591	1734	28.02
40 to 49	715	2088	36.46	40 to 49	714	2448	39.56
30 to 39	831	2919	50.97	30 to 39	825	3273	52.89
20 to 29	1110	4029	70.35	20 to 29	1032	4305	69.57
10 to 19	899	4928	86.05	10 to 19	1073	5378	86.91
0 to 9	799	5727	100.00	0 to 9	810	6188	100.00
Total	5727			Total	6188		

Q.3.5. The female median is likely to be higher because down to age 30 we have already accumulated 52.89% of the females whereas down to that age we have accumulated only 50.97% of the males.

Q.3.6. The distribution is positively skewed, so we should expect the mean to be higher than the median.

Q.3.8. There probably is no conventional graph that would be well-suited for representing these data, because the numbers vary from 25 to 1,200,000 which is difficult to represent visually. You may want to try a bar chart for yourself, to verify that a bar whose height is 25 is so small compared to one whose height is 1,200,000 that a graph with all bars visible is very difficult to fit onto a single sheet of A4 or letter-size paper.

Q.3.9. As also remarked in Chapter 3, the upper half of the cholesterol distributions increased while the lower half stayed much the same, thereby making the distributions more skewed over the four-year period. Since outliers affect the mean more than the median, this would explain why the median did not increase but the mean did.

Q.3.10 (a) Any symmetric distribution around 2. One with nothing but 2's would do, but so would one with an equal number of 1's and 3's.

(b) There are two distributions that would maximize the difference between the mean and median, and they are mirror-images of one another. One would have 110 1's and 109 10's; the other would have 109 1's and 110 10's.

(c) A bimodal distribution with one 1 and one 10 would give a standard deviation of 6.36. The mean is 5.5, so the sum of the squared differences is $(1 - 5.5)^2 + (10 - 5.5)^2 = 40.5$. We have just two observations, so $N - 1 = 1$. The standard deviation is therefore just the square-root of 40.5, which is about 6.36.

Any other bimodal distribution with all scores at 1 or 10 will produce quite large standard deviations but none as big as this one.

Chapter 4

Q.4.1. (a) The complete list of households provided by the City Council.

(b) Once she has randomly selected a household, she then randomly selects one adult there to test, so she is taking a multistage cluster sample (with two stages).

(c) No, since some households may contain more adults than others. Each *household* has an equal chance of being selected.

(d) The mean reading-age of the adult population in that community.

(e) She can statistically generalize to the population of adults in the community around the time she conducted her tests.

Q.4.2. (a) He selects every 10th client file on the list, so he is taking a systematic sample.

(b) He is sampling without replacement, since no client can be selected more than once.

(c) He should expect that the proportion will be $1500/10,000 = 0.15$.

Q.4.4. First, she has not established whether pride or motivation comes first. One could plausibly argue that motivation results in pride or vice versa. Second, she has not produced arguments for ruling out other influences on both motivation and pride that might account for the apparent relationship between them.

Q.4.5. The pool of applicants for the positions at Cynosure Ltd. could be labeled {F1, F2, F3, M1, M2}. The possible pairings in the two positions are:

$$\{F1, F2\} \quad \{F1, F3\} \quad \underline{\{F1, M1\}} \quad \underline{\{F1, M2\}}$$
$$\{F2, F3\} \quad \underline{\{F2, M1\}} \quad \underline{\{F2, M2\}}$$
$$\underline{\{F3, M1\}} \quad \underline{\{F3, M2\}}$$
$$\{M1, M2\}$$

There are 10 pairings in all, of which six (the underlined ones) have a man and woman in them. So the probability that one man and one woman would be chosen to fill those positions is 6/10. The probability that either two men or two women would be chosen is 4/10.

Q.4.6. (a) $P(\text{Smoker}) = 135/442 = 0.305$.

(b) $P(\text{Under } 30) = 185/442 = 0.419$.

(c) If smoking and being under 30 are independent, then

$$P(\text{Smoker \& Under 30}) = P(\text{Smoker})P(\text{Under 30})$$
$$= (0.305)(0.419) = 0.128.$$

Q.4.7. We know also that 40 people are both smokers and under 30. Denote Smoker by 'S' and Under 30 by 'U.'

(a) Since 40 people are both S and U, $P(\text{S \& U}) = 40/442 = 0.090$. So, $P(\text{S or U}) = P(\text{S}) + P(\text{U}) - P(\text{S \& U}) = 0.305 + 0.419 - 0.090 = 0.634$.

(b) $P(\text{S}|\text{U}) = P(\text{S \& U})/P(\text{U}) = 0.090/0.419 = 0.215$.

(c) $P(\text{U}|\text{S}) = P(\text{S \& U})/P(\text{S}) = 0.090/0.305 = 0.295$.

Q.4.8. (a) The exercise levels are mutually exclusive, so $P(\text{None or Light}) = P(\text{None}) + P(\text{Light}) = 0.21 + 0.29 = 0.50$.

(b) The largest possible value for $P(\text{None and } 60+)$ is the smaller of $P(\text{None})$ and $P(60+)$, which is 0.21.

(c) Yes, because $P(\text{None}) = 0.21$ which is smaller than $P(60+) = 0.22$, so at least someone in the 60+ group must be doing some exercise.

YOU CAN PRACTICE SIMILAR PROBLEMS TO Q.4.7 AND 4.8 WITH PROBPATCH

Q.4.10. If the drug improves 60% of cases, then the probability of improvement is 0.60. Either the client improves or not, so this problem involves the binomial distribution. For $N = 5$, the probability of fewer than three improvements is obtainable from the part of Table A.1 shown below:

0.60	0.55	0.50	No.	N
0.07776	0.05033	0.03125	5	5
0.25920	0.20589	0.15625	4	
0.34560	0.33691	0.31250	3	
0.23040	0.27565	0.31250	2	
0.07680	0.11277	0.15625	1	
0.01024	0.01845	0.03125	0	
...	...	...	...	...

The probability of fewer than three improvements is therefore

$$P(0 \text{ or } 1 \text{ or } 2) = 0.01024 + 0.07680 + 0.23040 = 0.31744.$$

Q.4.11. In a population with IQ normally distributed whose mean IQ is 100 and standard deviation 15, an IQ of 115 is one standard deviation above the mean. From Table A.2, we can see that the area beyond z is 0.1587. So, the probability of randomly selecting *one* person with an IQ of 115 or more is 0.1587. The probability of randomly selecting *two* such people, on the other hand, is $(0.1587)(0.1587) = 0.07556$, since these are two independent events and the probability of both events occurring is the product of their individual probabilities.

Q.4.12. The fact that the first person sampled has an IQ of 80 has no bearing on the IQs of the remaining nine people. Remember gambler's fallacy! So we should expect those nine to have an average IQ of 100. The average IQ of all 10 people, therefore, we would expect to be

$$\frac{9(100) + 80}{10} = 980/10 = 98.$$

Chapter 5

Q.5.1. Since $N < 20$, we shall have to construct our confidence interval using the binomial distribution, following the five steps outlined in Chapter 5. Step 1 has been done. Step 2 requires us to find the sample estimate of the population proportion, and that is $7/10 = 0.7$. The relevant column from Table A may be found by using the *bottom-row* values for P, which is where $P = 0.7$. Find the part of the table where $N = 10$, and select the column where $P = 0.7$. For Step 3, we note that since 5% of the sampling distribution must be excluded, we want to exclude no more than 2.5% (or 0.025) from each tail of the distribution.

For Step 4, starting at the top, we find that we cannot exclude 10 out of 10 events because the probability of that happening is 0.02825, which is larger than 0.025. So our upper limit is 10/10 or 1.

For Step 5, we can exclude 0, 1, 2, and 3 events out of 10 because their probabilities sum to $0.00001 + 0.00014 + 0.00145 + 0.009 = 0.01016$, but going any further excludes more than 0.025. So our lower limit is $4/10 = 0.4$. Our confidence interval is therefore from 0.4 to 1.0.

Q.5.2. First, calculate the standard error of the mean by dividing the standard deviation by the square-root of the sample size ($18\sqrt{15} = 4.648$). Then, ascertain the total proportion of the sampling distribution that will be excluded from the confidence interval. Convert the confidence level (90%) to a proportion (0.90) and subtract it from 1 to get this proportion ($1 - 0.90 = 0.10$).

Using Table A.3, find the cell entry in the row corresponding to d.f. = $N - 1 = 14$ and the column corresponding to a two-tail area of 0.10. The cell entry is $t_{0.05} = 1.7613$.

Compute the half-width of the confidence interval by multiplying the standard error by $t_{0.05}$ to get $w = (1.7613)(4.648) = 8.186$. The resulting confidence interval statement is

$$\Pr(104 - 8.186 < \mu < 104 + 8.186) = 0.90,$$

or just

$$Pr(95.814 < \mu < 112.186) = 0.90.$$

Q.5.3. (a) *False*, since greater confidence means less precision, all else being equal.
   (b) *True*. Intervals based on sample proportions of either 0 to 1 have widths of 0.
   (c) *False*, since the width of such confidence intervals varies inversely with the square-roof of sample size rather than with sample size itself. A sample size of 25 would produce a confidence interval twice as wide as one based on a sample size of 100.
   (d) *False*, since the Central Limit Theorem states that he sampling distribution of the mean approaches a normal distribution as N gets large regardless of how the scores are distributed.
   (e) *True*, since greater confidence is purchased by less precision and vice versa.
   (f) *False*. Both width and location vary because of sampling error.
   (g) *True*. The standard error is the square root of $P(1-P)/N$, and the $P(1-P)$ part is largest when $P = 0.5$. So the confidence interval for a sample proportion is widest when $P = 0.5$ if we are using the normal approximation.

Q.5.4. For this problem, we need to find out what the range of plausible values for the hypothetical population mean is. We therefore need to construct a 95% confidence interval around our sample mean and ascertain whether that interval contains 125. First, calculate the standard error of the mean by dividing the standard deviation by the square-root of the sample size ($9.2/\sqrt{13} = 2.552$). Since $N < 20$ we will use the t distribution as the sampling distribution for the mean. Using Table A.3, find the cell entry in the row corresponding to df $= N - 1 = 12$ and the column corresponding to a 2-tail area of 0.05. The cell entry is $t_{0.025} = 2.1788$. Compute the half-width of the confidence interval by multiplying the standard error by $t_{0.025}$ to get $w = (2.1788)(2.552) = 5.560$. The resulting confidence interval statement is

$$Pr(117 - 5.560 < \mu < 117 + 5.560) = 0.95$$

or just

$$Pr(111.440 < \mu < 122.560) = 0.95.$$

The results are tabulated below in the output from **Dem51**.

Sample size N	Sample mean	Std dev.	Std error	Confid. level
13	117	9.2	2.552	0.95
$t_{\alpha/2}$	w	CI limits		
2.1788	5.560	111.440	Lower	
		122.560	Upper	

Clearly, 125 is not contained in this confidence interval and therefore it is not a plausible value for the population mean blood-pressure. That should strike the psychologist as very interesting, since it indicates that his program might very well lower the average blood pressure of the managers. We will deal much more with this kind of issue in the next chapter.

Q.5.5. This is a slightly tricky problem, but it gives a taste of what some real-world pollsters do. Without knowing anything about the proportion of people who might vote 'Yes,' ensuring that a 99% confidence interval around the sample proportion will have a half-width of less than 0.025 boils down to ensuring that when $P = 0.5$ the half-width is less than 0.025.

$$w = z_{\alpha/2}s_P = (2.5758)s_P = 0.025.$$

So

$$s_P = 0.025/2.5758 = 0.00971.$$

Now, if $P = 0.5$, then

$$s_P = \sqrt{0.5(1 - 0.5)/N} = \sqrt{0.25/N}$$

and if we square both sides of this formula we have

$$s_P^2 = 0.25/N = (0.00971)^2$$

which may be rearranged to solve for N:

$$N = 0.25/(0.00971)^2 = 2653.97, \text{ or about } 2654.$$

You can find out required sample sizes to fulfill confidence interval width requirements for proportions via either **ConfiPatch** or **Dem55**.

Chapter 6

Q.6.1. A random sample of 100 technicians yields a mean income before tax of $44,000 and a standard deviation of $3400. The standard error is $s/\sqrt{N} = 3400/\sqrt{100} = 340$. We could use a normal approximation here, in which case we need $z_{0.025} = 1.96$. Our interval half-width is therefore

$$w = z_{\alpha/2}s_{\bar{X}} = (1.96)(340) = 666.40.$$

The resulting interval is

$$\text{CI}_{0.95} = [43{,}333.6, 44{,}666.4],$$

and since the Government's figure is not contained in this interval it is not plausible. However, the Government could easily make their figure plausible by demanding a higher confidence level, thereby widening the confidence interval. Nevertheless, they would have to demand a confidence level of 99.7% in order to have their figure included in the interval, which would strike many people as a ridiculously high level. You may wish to explore this issue by using **Dem52**, which has both the *t*-distribution and normal distribution versions of a confidence interval around the mean.

Demos

Q.6.2. The conclusions depend partly on what confidence level you decide to use for constructing an interval around the sample proportion. The sample proportion is

$$P = 104/169 = 0.615$$

the standard deviation is

$$\sqrt{0.615(1 - 0.616)} = 0.4865,$$

and the standard error is

$$s_P = 0.4865/\sqrt{169} = 0.0374.$$

If you used a 95% confidence level, then you would need $z_{0.025} = 1.96$. The interval half-width would therefore be

$$w = z_{0.025}s_P = (1.96)(0.0374) = 0.0733,$$

and the confidence interval would be $\text{CI}_{0.95} = [0.542, 0.698]$.

This CI includes values from hypothesis B but neither of the other two, so B appears to provide the only plausible model among the three. Making the interval wider by using a higher confidence level (e.g., 99%) would enable it to include some values from hypothesis C, and extremely high levels would even include values from A. That said, you would be quite reasonable in concluding that B is the most plausible hypothesis because its values are included in *all* CIs around *P*, regardless of confidence level. You can explore this issue further by using **Dem54**, which provides the normal approximation for a confidence interval around Π.

Demos

Q.6.3.   (a)   Power would be greater if Π really was 0.2 than if Π really was 0.1.
    False, since 0.1 is further away from the null hypothesis value of 1/2 than 0.2 is.

   (b)   Power would be greater if $N = 15$ than if $N = 10$.
    True, since 15 is a larger sample than 10, thereby increasing power by narrowing the confidence interval.

   (c)   Power would be greater if $\alpha = 0.01$ instead of 0.05.
    False, since $\alpha = 0.01$ entails a confidence level of 99%, which is higher than the confidence level of 95% associated with $\alpha = 0.05$. Higher confidence means wider confidence intervals, which means lower power.

   (d)   We would be more likely to reject the null hypothesis if $\alpha = 0.01$ instead of 0.05.
    False, since $\alpha = 0.01$ entails a higher confidence level and therefore a wider confidence interval, which is more likely to include the null hypothesis value than a narrower one.

Q.6.6.   In Q.6.5, you should have found that you could reject the null hypothesis of no change in mean cholesterol levels, both for the year 1–year 2 and year 2–year 3 comparisons. However, that does not mean these two changes are equal. The change in mean cholesterol level from the end of year 1 to year 2 (Chol2yr vs. Chol1yr) is 5.300, with a standard deviation of 8.5147. Since our null hypothesis mean change is 0, Cohen's *d* is

$$d_{\mathrm{h}} = (5.300 - 0)/8.5147 = 0.6225.$$

The mean change from year 2 to year 3 (Chol3yr vs. Chol2yr) is 4.720 with a standard deviation of 11.7213, so Cohen's *d* is

$$d_{\mathrm{h}} = (4.720 - 0)/11.7213 = 0.4027.$$

The first *d* value is rather larger than the second, indicating a relatively bigger change in mean levels relative to the spread of the cholesterol scores.

Q.6.8. The first program produces a mean increase of 6.2 months, with a standard deviation of 4.5. Given a null hypothesis increase of 4 months and a sample size of $N = 24$, the effect size as measured by Cohen's d is

$$d_h = (6.2 - 4)/4.5 = 0.4889.$$

The second program produces a mean increase of 6.2 months, with a standard deviation of 3.2. Given a null hypothesis increase of 4 months and a sample size of $N = 24$, the effect size is

$$d_h = (6.2 - 4)/3.2 = 0.6875.$$

The reason why the second program's effect size is larger is because of the smaller standard deviation, which indicates that a larger portion of the children's increases in reading age are above four months. You may wish to work with **dem62** to explore the impact of sample size and standard deviation on Cohen's d.

Q.6.9. The developmental psychologists want to be able to detect an effect size of at least 0.3 with power = 0.90. They also want to use a confidence level of 99% (0.99) for their confidence interval when they estimate the increase in reading age. The sample size they will need is determined by the formula

$$N = [(z_{\alpha/2} + z_\beta)/d]^2.$$

From Table A.2, we get $z_{\alpha/2} = z_{0.995} = 2.576$ and $z_\beta = z_{0.90} = 1.282$. Plugging these and the required Cohen's $d = 0.3$ into the formula, we get

$$N = [(2.576 + 1.282)/0.3]^2 = (12.86)^2 = 165.38,$$

or about $N = 165$.

To gain more familiarity with the tradeoffs involving confidence level, power, sample size, and effect size, try exploring them by using **dem63**.

Chapter 7

Q.7.1. The best way to advise the clinician is by reframing her question in terms of a difference between sample proportions. The proportion of her clients successfully completing therapeutic programs the year before last is $P_1 = 0.629$, with $N = 89$. The proportion of her clients successfully completing therapeutic programs last year is $P_2 = 0.566$, with $N = 83$. The difference is $P_1 - P_2 = 0.629 - 0.566 = 0.063$.

The standard error is

$$s_{err}\sqrt{\frac{P_1(1-P_1)}{N_1} + \frac{P_2(1-P_2)}{N_2}} = \sqrt{\frac{0.629(0.371)}{89} + \frac{0.566(0.434)}{83}} = 0.073$$

She wants to know whether it is possible that this apparent decline in completion rate could be a 'chance fluctuation.' The statistical equivalent to this would be asking whether a difference of 0 is a plausible value, given the data. The answer to this depends on what level of confidence the clinician wishes to use for a confidence interval for the difference in proportions. If we use a 95% confidence level, since both years' client samples are large enough for the normal approximation to be appropriate, from Table A.2 we get $z_{0.025} = 1.96$. So, the half-width of the confidence interval is

$$w = z_{\alpha/2}s_{err} = (1.96)(0.073) = 0.144.$$

The result is $CI_{0.95} = 0.063 \pm 0.144$, or $CI_{0.95} = [-0.081, 0.207]$.

```
        ◄──── 95% ────►
  ▬▬▬▬▬▬▬▬▬▬▬▬▬▬▬▬▬▬▬▬▬▬
 ─────────────────────────────
 -0.081  ▲  0.063    0.207
         |
         0
```

This interval contains 0, so it is plausible that the apparent decline in proportions is just a chance fluctuation (i.e., that the two sample proportions were generated by processes that have identical population proportions).

You may wish to use **dem71** to gain familiarity with between-subjects t-tests for differences between means and proportions.

Demos

Q.7.2.   Using SPSS or any other accurate statistics package to analyze the data file called **Skull**, you should find that the means and standard deviations for the skull-lengths of the two species are as follows.

Species	N	Mean	Std. dev.
Homo erectus	8	195.38	8.65
Neanderthal	8	202.50	6.91

The difference between these means is 7.13 mm and the pooled standard deviation is 3.91. The resulting t-statistic has the value $t(14) = 1.820$. The 95% confidence interval around the difference of the means yields

$$CI_{0.95} = [-1.27, 15.52].$$

The physical anthropologist's hypothesis that the difference is between 5 and 10 mm certainly is plausible, since her interval is entirely contained in the confidence interval. However, other hypotheses are plausible too, such as the hypothesis that the species do not differ at all in skull length.

Q.7.5. If you want to construct confidence intervals for all possible mean differences in an experiment that has four experimental conditions, then there are six confidence intervals involved. Given that you would like a family-wise confidence level of 99%, your family-wise $\alpha = 0.01$, and a Bonferroni correction would dictate that each confidence interval must have a confidence level of $1 - \alpha/6 = 1 - 0.01/6 = 0.998$. Since this is very high, you could expect your confidence intervals to be so wide as to be relatively uninformative unless you have very large samples.

Q.7.6. If you used a standard statistics package that runs ANOVA, you probably obtained an ANOVA table similar to the one shown below.

Source	SS	df	s^2	F	Sig.
Between	487.750	2	243.875	4.205	0.029
Within	1217.875	21	57.994		
Total	1705.625	23			

(a) This table contains all of the information needed to test the hypothesis that there is a difference in the mean consumption levels of the three groups. The 'Sig.' column displays the portion of the F-distribution lying beyond $F = 4.205$. Since that is less than 0.05, we may reject the null hypothesis that there is no difference among the means. Another way to do this (which we would use if the 'Sig.' figure was not reported) is to construct our 95% confidence interval for F. Consulting Table A.4 and finding the column with $df_b = 2$ and the row with $df_w = 21$, we find that $F_{0.05} = 3.47$. Our confidence interval statement therefore is $\Pr(F(2, 21) < 3.47) = 0.95$, and the F-value we have obtained from the data is 4.205, which lies outside that interval. We may therefore reject the null hypothesis.

(b) The next table shows the mean number of drinks consumed by each group of participants. The means for the No Therapy and Drug Treatment groups are very similar, while the Behavior Modification group mean is much lower (which is a good thing). Clearly the Behavior Modification method has succeeded in reducing the consumption of alcoholic drinks, whereas the Drug Treatment hardly differs from No Therapy at all.

	N	Mean	Std. dev.	Std. error
No Therapy	8	27.50	9.55	3.38
Drug Treatment	8	27.63	6.84	2.42
Behavior Mod.	8	18.00	6.00	2.12
Total	24	24.38	8.61	1.76

(c) Finally, the size of the effect may be computed from the ANOVA table, by using the formula $R^2 = SS_b/SS_t = 487.750/1705.625 = 0.286$. Thus, about 28.6% of the variance in drinks consumed has been acounted for by experimental effects.

Q.7.7. You can use the formula for converting the information from the report that '$F(3, 213) = 4.32$, $p < 0.05$' to R^2:

$$R^2 = \frac{3(4.32)}{213 + 3(4.32)} = 0.057.$$

This is a rather small effect, although not trivial by Cohen's (1988) and most psychologists' standards. The fairly large sample size indicated by $df_2 = 213$ has given the study enough power to detect small effects.

Chapter 8

Q.8.1. The two variables are indeed positively linearly related, and apparently strongly so. A scatterplot shows that the points lie in a nearly straight line with no outliers.

(a) The regression coefficient measures how much X causes Y.
False, since we cannot infer causation from correlation or regression.
(b) A correlation of 0 means there is no relationship between X and Y.
False. It merely means there is no linear relationship (there might be some other kind).
(c) A correlation coefficient of -0.9 indicates a strong positive relationship between X and Y.
False, since the minus-sign indicates a negative relationship.
(d) The regression line always passes through the point located at 0 for X and 0 for Y.
False. The regression line always passes through the means for X and Y.
(e) Regression minimizes the average squared deviation of the data from the regression line.
True. This is why it is often referred to as "least squares" regression.

Q.8.4. The regression model's prediction that when given $X = \$0$ by the experimenter the amount that a person is predicted to donate is $Y = \$41.4$ is meaningless, since it means they are donating more money than they were given in the first place. It is also problematic because it is based on $X = \$0$, which was not a condition of the experiment and is therefore beyond the range of the data.

Q.8.5. (a) Let $X =$ caseload and $Y =$ days absent. The regression equation for these two variables is $Y' = -5.741 + 0.256X$.
If $X = 38$, then the model predicts that

$$Y' = -5.741 + 0.256(38) = -5.741 + 9.728 = 3.987$$

or close to 4 days absent.

(b) It does make implausible predictions beyond the range of its data. For instance, someone with a sufficiently light caseload (e.g., 10) is predicted to have a negative number of days absent (-3.181).

(c) The slope of the regression line is $b = 0.256$, so an increase of 5 in caseload would yield a predicted increase of $0.256(5) = 1.28$ days' absence.

(d) According to the ANOVA table below, we can reject the no-effects model because the F-value of 19.989 lies outside the 99% confidence interval for F under the null hypothesis.

Source	SS	df	s^2	F	Sig.
Regression	10.970	1	10.970	19.989	0.007
Residual	2.744	5	0.549		
Total	13.714	6			

(e) $R^2 = SS_r/SS_t = 10.970/13.714 = 0.800$. So caseload accounts for 80% of the variance in the number of days absent. This is a very large effect by Cohen's standards.

(f) To construct a 95% confidence interval around b, we need SS_e and SS_X. From the ANOVA table above, we get $SS_e = 2.744$. We may plug this value into our formula for the squared standard error of the estimate, $s^2_{Y|X}$:

$$s^2_{Y|X} = SS_e/(N-2) = 2.744/5 = 0.5488.$$

The variance for X is $s^2_X = 27.905 = SS_X/(N-1)$. So, we get
$SS_X = (6)(27.905) = 167.43$.
Now we can obtain the standard error for b:

$$s_{\text{err}b} = \sqrt{\frac{S_{Y|X}^2}{\text{SS}_X}} = \sqrt{\frac{0.5488}{167.43}} = 0.0573$$

Our df $= N - 2 = 5$. From Table A.3, we obtain $t_{0.025} = 2.5706$, so our half-width is

$$w = t_{0.025}s_{\text{err}b} = (2.5706)(0.0573) = 0.147$$

The resulting confidence interval is

$$\text{CI}_{0.95} = b \pm w = 0.256 \pm 0.147, \text{ or } \text{CI}_{0.95} = [0.109, 0.403].$$

Q.8.8. All four studies have nearly identical means and standard deviations for X and Y, as well as nearly identical linear regression equations and correlations. Based on those figures, we could be lulled into believing that the four data-sets are very similar. However, scatterplots reveal them to be quite different! The moral of this example is to always display your data in different ways to yourself to avoid being misled through reliance on one statistic.

Q.8.9. We need to first obtain the Fisher's z transformation of R. Since $R = 0.546$, we get

$$R' = \frac{1}{2}\ln\left(\frac{1+R}{1-R}\right) = 0.5\ln\left(\frac{1.546}{0.454}\right) = 0.5\ln(3.405) = 0.6127.$$

The standard error of R' is

$$s_{R'} = \frac{1}{\sqrt{N-3}} = 1/\sqrt{175} = 0.0756.$$

From Table A.2, $z_{0.025} = 1.96$, and the half-width is

$$w = z_{a/2}s_{R'} = (1.96)(0.0756) = 0.1482.$$

Our confidence interval around ρ' is

$$\text{Pr}(R' - w < \rho' < R' + w) = \text{Pr}(0.4645 < \rho' < 0.7608) = 0.95$$

If we apply our inverse transformation formula to convert this interval back to an interval around ρ, we get

$$\text{Pr}(0.4337 < \rho < 0.6416) = 0.95.$$

The hypothesis that the correlation between parental ratings will not fall below 0.5 might be mistaken, since our confidence interval includes values below 0.5. Only a more statistically powerful study would enlighten us any further on this issue.

Chapter 9

Q.9.1. (a) The appropriate percentages are *column percentages*, since we are interested in the percentage of Caesarian deliveries out of each type of hospital.

	Remote	Metro	Regional	Total
Caesarian	13.96%	21.47%	14.35%	17.95%
Vaginal	86.04%	78.53%	85.65%	82.05%
Total	100.00%	100.00%	100.00%	100.00%

From the column percentage table here, you can see that the metropolitan hospitals have the highest percentage of Caesarian deliveries, $21.47\% - 13.96\% = 7.51\%$ higher than the remote hospitals, for instance.

(b) Row percentages are needed here, since we are dealing with percentage of Caesarian deliveries. While 60.96% of the Caesarian deliveries occur in metropolitan hospitals, only 6.10% of them take place in the remote hospitals. This is due, of course, not only to the lower rate of Caesarian deliveries in remote hospitals but also to their smaller numbers of deliveries altogether.

	Remote	Metro	Regional	Total
Caesarian	6.10%	60.96%	32.94%	100.00%
Vaginal	8.22%	48.78%	43.00%	100.00%
Total	7.84%	50.96%	41.19%	100.00%

Q.9.2. The health psychologist's data are tabulated below, along with the expected frequencies according to his population figures. The expected frequencies are found by taking the population percentages, converting them to proportions by dividing them by 100, and then multiplying them by the total number of people in his sample (278).

$$\text{Excellent } f_e = (41.90/100)(278) = 116.48$$

$$\text{Good } f_e = (29.36/100)(278) = 81.62$$

$$\text{Poor/Fair } f_e = (28.74/100)(278) = 79.90$$

Excellent	Good	Poor to fair	
104	106	68	f_o
116.48	81.62	79.90	f_e
1.337	7.282	1.772	$(f_o - f_e)^2/f_e$ $\quad \chi^2 = 10.391$

The expected frequencies (f_e) and observed frequencies (f_o) are compared with each other by computing the squared standardized residuals and then summing them to obtain $\chi^2 = 10.391$. A 99% confidence interval statement for χ^2 if there is no difference between this ethnic population and the population at large is $\Pr(\chi^2(2) < 9.210) = 0.99$. The χ^2 value we have obtained lies outside this interval, so the hypothesis of no difference is implausible.

However, we cannot leap immediately to the conclusion that this population rates its health lower. The reason for this is that while f_o is lower than f_e for the Excellent category, the same is true for the Poor to Fair category. There are more people rating their health as Good than would be expected if their ratings had the same distribution as the population at large.

For more practice with one-way chi-square problems similar to this one, use **ChiPatch**.

StatPatch

Q.9.4. The neuropsychologist's data are shown below.

Music?	Dominant Hemisphere		Total
	Right	Left	
Yes	30	40	70
No	70	920	990
Total	100	960	1060

(a) To test whether the two variables are independent, we need to perform a two-way chi-square test. The expected frequencies are computed as follows:

$$\text{Yes} - \text{Right } f_e = (70)(100)/(1060) = 6.6$$
$$\text{Yes} - \text{Left } f_e = (70)(960)/(1060) = 63.4$$
$$\text{No} - \text{Right } f_e = (990)(100)/(1060) = 93.4$$
$$\text{No} - \text{Left } f_e = (990)(960)/(1060) = 896.6$$

Music?	Dominant Hemisphere		Total
	Right	Left	
Yes	6.6	63.4	70
No	93.4	896.6	990
Total	100	960	1060

$$\chi^2 = (30 - 6.6)^2/6.6 + (40 - 63.4)^2/63.4 + (70 - 93.4)^2/93.4$$
$$+ (920 - 896.6)^2/896.6$$
$$= 82.96 + 8.64 + 5.86 + 0.611 = 98.07$$

The df for this is $(2 - 1)(2 - 1) = 1$. For a 95% confidence level, $\alpha = 0.05$, and from Table A.5 we find $\chi^2_{0.05} = 3.841$. The confidence interval statement is $\Pr(\chi^2(1) < 3.841) = 0.95$. The χ^2 value we have obtained lies well outside this interval, so the hypothesis of independence is implausible.

(b) The level of association may be measured by

$$\phi^2 = \chi^2/N = 98.07/1060 = 0.0925,$$

which is a moderate level of association by Cohen's standards.

(c) As for interpreting the relationship, one approach is using column percentages to compare the percentages of right-dominant and left-dominant people who take up music as a hobby. The table below reveals that 30% of the right-dominant people take up music whereas only 4.2% of the left-dominant people do.

	Dominant Hemisphere	
Music?	Right	Left
Yes	30.0%	4.2%
No	70.0%	95.8%
Total	100.0%	100.0%

Another way to interpret the relationship would be via the odds ratio:

$$\Omega = \frac{\text{Odds(Yes|Right)}}{\text{Odds(Yes|Left)}} = \frac{30/70}{40/920} = \frac{0.428}{0.043} = 9.857.$$

Right-dominant people have 9.857 times greater odds of taking up music than left-dominant people.

Q.9.7. The odds ratio for Gerrity's data is

$$\Omega = \frac{\text{Odds(Spec.|Male)}}{\text{Odds(Spec.|Female)}} = \frac{164/174}{12/39} = \frac{0.9425}{0.3077} = 3.063$$

The rule-of-thumb is that the sampling distribution of $\ln(\Omega)$ approximates a normal distribution well enough for samples of 25 or more, so we are able to construct a confidence interval here. Our confidence interval around $\ln(\Omega)$ has the form

$$\Pr(\ln(W) - w < \ln(\Omega) < \ln(W) + w) = 1 - \alpha,$$

or

$$\Pr(\ln(3.063) - w < \ln(\Omega) < \ln(3.063) + w) = 0.95.$$

$$w = z_{\alpha/2} s_{\text{err}} = (1.96) s_{\text{err}}$$

and

$$s_{\text{err}} \sqrt{1/N_{11} + 1/N_{12} + 1/N_{21} + 1/N_{22}}$$
$$= \sqrt{1/174 + 1/164 + 1/12 + 1/39} = 0.3476$$

so $w = (1.96)(0.3476) = 0.6813$.

Since $\ln(3.063) = 1.1195$, our confidence interval statement is

$$\Pr(1.1195 - 0.6813 < \ln(\Omega) < 1.1195 + 0.6813) = 0.95,$$

or

$$\text{CI}_{0.95} = [0.4382, 1.8008].$$

Finally, we raise e to the power of the lower and upper limits, to get a 95% confidence interval for Ω of $\text{CI}_{0.95} = [1.550, 6.054]$. The researcher's claim that that men have more than four times greater odds than women of becoming a specialist cannot be ruled out as implausible, given these results.

You may wish to explore odds-ratio confidence intervals via **dem91**.

Chapter 10

Q.10.1. An odds ratio for each subtable would be one way of describing the effect that stress has on the relationship. For the low-stress subtable, the odds ratio is

$$\Omega = \frac{\text{Odds(Dep.|No confid.)}}{\text{Odds(Dep.|Confidant)}} = \frac{12/31}{20/94} = 1.819,$$

and for the high-stress subtable it is

$$\Omega = \frac{\text{Odds(Dep.|No confid.)}}{\text{Odds(Dep.|Confidant)}} = \frac{18/23}{12/108} = 7.043$$

The odds of depression are higher for those with no confidant in both the low- and high-stress groups, but substantially higher for the high-stress group. There is an interaction there.

Q.10.2. One possibility (which turned out to have some validity, according to Smithson *et al.*'s (1983) overview) is that it depends on the type of help required. In Western societies, for instance, even these days men still are socialized to help out in 'masculine' matters such as rescuing people, while women are socialized to help in 'feminine' matters such as caring for the ill. Type of helping, in this situation, is acting as a masking variable.

Q.10.4. The only true options are (b) and (c).

(a) Experimental control requires random sampling.
   False, since experimental control requires randomized assignment.
(b) Statistical control assumes that we have measured covariates without error. *True*, and this is one of its limitations if used carelessly.
(c) Randomized assignment guarantees that all possible covariates (whether known to the experimenter or not) are randomly distributed across conditions. *True*, and that is the main basis for using statistical inference in experiments with randomized assignment.
(d) Under randomized assignment, no variable could have an effect by chance alone. *False*. Under randomized assignment, a chance effect could occur.
(e) Experimental control prevents researchers from identifying any potential masking variables. *False*. If a masking variable is either a covariate or an experimental variable, it is possible to detect that it has a masking effect.

Q.10.7. The means are all below 10, so at least the average rating for psychological interventions was not one that indicated harm-doing! The ANOVA table's Total between (omnibus) test indicates that we may reject the no-effects hypothesis. The rest of the table suggests that we may reject no-effect hypotheses for the scenario main effect and the interaction effect, but not for the gender main effect. Our final model therefore is:

$$X_{ij} = \mu + \alpha_i + \alpha\beta_{ij} + e,$$

where α_i refers to the scenario (row) effect.
The effect sizes are not large. R^2 for the scenario main effect is 0.043 and for the interaction is only 0.009. The study has a large sample and that gives it the statistical power to detect small effects.

Source	SS	df	s^2	F	Sig.	R^2
Gender	9.643	1	9.643	2.326	0.127	0.002
Scenario	236.198	3	78.733	18.994	0.000	0.043
Gender × Scenario	47.370	3	15.790	3.809	0.010	0.009
Total between	304.406	7	43.487	10.491	0.000	0.054
Error	5310.029	1281	4.145			
Corrected total	5614.434	1288				

The graph below shows the means for the four scenarios, for male and female respondents. Both male and female respondents rated psychological interventions as more beneficial (less harmful) for the Schizophrenic scenarios, particularly the Mary/Schizophrenic one.

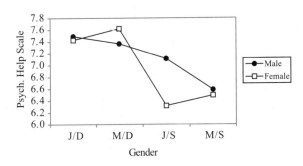

The row, column, and interaction effects are shown in the next table. It is clear that the main departures from additivity are the the M/D and J/S scenarios, which in the graph are the ones for which the male and female respondents differ most markedly. Female respondents rate psychological interventions as less beneficial in the M/D scenario and more so in the J/S scenario than male respondents do.

	Male	Female	Row
J/D	−0.071	0.071	0.432
M/D	−0.230	0.230	0.465
J/S	0.295	−0.295	−0.315
M/S	−0.055	0.055	−0.490
Column	0.102	−0.102	

Appendix
Statistical Tables

TABLE A.1 **Binomial distribution**

		P ≤ 0.5											
							P ≤ 0.5						
N	No. of events	0.05	0.10	0.15	0.20	0.25	0.30	0.35	0.40	0.45	0.50	No. of events	*N*
1	0	0.95000	0.90000	0.85000	0.80000	0.75000	0.70000	0.65000	0.60000	0.55000	0.50000	1	1
	1	0.05000	0.10000	0.15000	0.20000	0.25000	0.30000	0.35000	0.40000	0.45000	0.50000	0	
2	0	0.90250	0.81000	0.72250	0.64000	0.56250	0.49000	0.42250	0.36000	0.30250	0.25000	2	2
	1	0.09500	0.18000	0.25500	0.32000	0.37500	0.42000	0.45500	0.48000	0.49500	0.50000	1	
	2	0.00250	0.01000	0.02250	0.04000	0.06250	0.09000	0.12250	0.16000	0.20250	0.25000	0	
3	0	0.85738	0.72900	0.61413	0.51200	0.42188	0.34300	0.27463	0.21600	0.16638	0.12500	3	3
	1	0.13538	0.24300	0.32513	0.38400	0.42188	0.44100	0.44363	0.43200	0.40838	0.37500	2	
	2	0.00713	0.02700	0.05738	0.09600	0.14063	0.18900	0.23888	0.28800	0.33413	0.37500	1	
	3	0.00013	0.00100	0.00338	0.00800	0.01563	0.02700	0.04288	0.06400	0.09113	0.12500	0	
4	0	0.81451	0.65610	0.52201	0.40960	0.31641	0.24010	0.17851	0.12960	0.09151	0.06250	4	4
	1	0.17148	0.29160	0.36848	0.40960	0.42188	0.41160	0.38488	0.34560	0.29948	0.25000	3	
	2	0.01354	0.04860	0.09754	0.15360	0.21094	0.26460	0.31054	0.34560	0.36754	0.37500	2	
	3	0.00048	0.00360	0.01148	0.02560	0.04688	0.07560	0.11148	0.15360	0.20048	0.25000	1	
	4	0.00001	0.00010	0.00051	0.00160	0.00391	0.00810	0.01501	0.02560	0.04101	0.06250	0	
5	0	0.77378	0.59049	0.44371	0.32768	0.23730	0.16807	0.11603	0.07776	0.05033	0.03125	5	5
	1	0.20363	0.32805	0.39150	0.40960	0.39551	0.36015	0.31239	0.25920	0.20589	0.15625	4	
	2	0.02143	0.07290	0.13818	0.20480	0.26367	0.30870	0.33642	0.34560	0.33691	0.31250	3	
	3	0.00113	0.00810	0.02438	0.05120	0.08789	0.13230	0.18115	0.23040	0.27565	0.31250	2	
	4	0.00003	0.00045	0.00215	0.00640	0.01465	0.02835	0.04877	0.07680	0.11277	0.15625	1	
	5	0.00000	0.00001	0.00008	0.00032	0.00098	0.00243	0.00525	0.01024	0.01845	0.03125	0	
6	0	0.73509	0.53144	0.37715	0.26214	0.17798	0.11765	0.07542	0.04666	0.02768	0.01563	6	6
	1	0.23213	0.35429	0.39933	0.39322	0.35596	0.30253	0.24366	0.18662	0.13589	0.09375	5	
	2	0.03054	0.09842	0.17618	0.24576	0.29663	0.32414	0.32801	0.31104	0.27795	0.23438	4	

N	No of events	0.50	0.55	0.60	0.65	0.70	0.75	0.80	0.85	0.90	0.95	No of events	N
	3	0.31250	0.30322	0.27648	0.23549	0.18522	0.13184	0.08192	0.04145	0.01458	0.00214	3	
	4	0.23438	0.18607	0.13824	0.09510	0.05954	0.03296	0.01536	0.00549	0.00122	0.00008	2	
	5	0.09375	0.06089	0.03686	0.02048	0.01021	0.00439	0.00154	0.00039	0.00005	0.00000	1	
	6	0.01563	0.00830	0.00410	0.00184	0.00073	0.00024	0.00006	0.00001	0.00000	0.00000	0	
7	0	0.00781	0.01522	0.02799	0.04902	0.08235	0.13348	0.20972	0.32058	0.47830	0.69834	7	7
	1	0.05469	0.08719	0.13064	0.18478	0.24706	0.31146	0.36700	0.39601	0.37201	0.25728	6	
	2	0.16406	0.21402	0.26127	0.29848	0.31765	0.31146	0.27525	0.20965	0.12400	0.04062	5	
	3	0.27344	0.29185	0.29030	0.26787	0.22689	0.17303	0.11469	0.06166	0.02296	0.00356	4	
	4	0.27344	0.23878	0.19354	0.14424	0.09724	0.05768	0.02867	0.01088	0.00255	0.00019	3	
	5	0.16406	0.11722	0.07741	0.04660	0.02500	0.01154	0.00430	0.00115	0.00017	0.00001	2	
	6	0.05469	0.03197	0.01720	0.00836	0.00357	0.00128	0.00036	0.00007	0.00001	0.00000	1	
	7	0.00781	0.00374	0.00164	0.00064	0.00022	0.00006	0.00001	0.00000	0.00000	0.00000	0	
8	0	0.00391	0.00837	0.01680	0.03186	0.05765	0.10011	0.16777	0.27249	0.43047	0.66342	8	8
	1	0.03125	0.05481	0.08958	0.13726	0.19765	0.26697	0.33554	0.38469	0.38264	0.27933	7	
	2	0.10938	0.15695	0.20902	0.25869	0.29648	0.31146	0.29360	0.23760	0.14880	0.05146	6	
	3	0.21875	0.25683	0.27869	0.27859	0.25412	0.20764	0.14680	0.08386	0.03307	0.00542	5	
	4	0.27344	0.26266	0.23224	0.18751	0.13614	0.08652	0.04588	0.01850	0.00459	0.00036	4	
	5	0.21875	0.17192	0.12386	0.08077	0.04668	0.02307	0.00918	0.00261	0.00041	0.00002	3	
	6	0.10938	0.07033	0.04129	0.02175	0.01000	0.00385	0.00115	0.00023	0.00002	0.00000	2	
	7	0.03125	0.01644	0.00786	0.00335	0.00122	0.00037	0.00008	0.00001	0.00000	0.00000	1	
	8	0.00391	0.00168	0.00066	0.00023	0.00007	0.00002	0.00000	0.00000	0.00000	0.00000	0	
		0.95	0.90	0.85	0.80	0.75	0.70	0.65	0.60	0.55	$P \geqslant 0.5$	No of events	N

$P \geqslant 0.5$

(continued)

TABLE A.1 (*continued*)

N	No. of events	0.05	0.10	0.15	0.20	0.25	0.30	0.35	0.40	0.45	0.50		
9	0	0.63025	0.38742	0.23162	0.13422	0.07508	0.04035	0.02071	0.01008	0.00461	0.00195	9	9
	1	0.29854	0.38742	0.36786	0.30199	0.22525	0.15565	0.10037	0.06047	0.03391	0.01758	8	
	2	0.06285	0.17219	0.25967	0.30199	0.30034	0.26683	0.21619	0.16124	0.11099	0.07031	7	
	3	0.00772	0.04464	0.10692	0.17616	0.23360	0.26683	0.27162	0.25082	0.21188	0.16406	6	
	4	0.00061	0.00744	0.02830	0.06606	0.11680	0.17153	0.21939	0.25082	0.26004	0.24609	5	
	5	0.00003	0.00083	0.00499	0.01652	0.03893	0.07351	0.11813	0.16722	0.21276	0.24609	4	
	6	0.00000	0.00006	0.00059	0.00275	0.00865	0.02100	0.04241	0.07432	0.11605	0.16406	3	
	7	0.00000	0.00000	0.00004	0.00029	0.00124	0.00386	0.00979	0.02123	0.04069	0.07031	2	
	8	0.00000	0.00000	0.00000	0.00002	0.00010	0.00041	0.00132	0.00354	0.00832	0.01758	1	
	9	0.00000	0.00000	0.00000	0.00000	0.00000	0.00002	0.00008	0.00026	0.00076	0.00195	0	
10	0	0.59874	0.34868	0.19687	0.10737	0.05631	0.02825	0.01346	0.00605	0.00253	0.00098	10	10
	1	0.31512	0.38742	0.34743	0.26844	0.18771	0.12106	0.07249	0.04031	0.02072	0.00977	9	
	2	0.07463	0.19371	0.27590	0.30199	0.28157	0.23347	0.17565	0.12093	0.07630	0.04395	8	
	3	0.01048	0.05740	0.12983	0.20133	0.25028	0.26683	0.25222	0.21499	0.16648	0.11719	7	
	4	0.00096	0.01116	0.04010	0.08808	0.14600	0.20012	0.23767	0.25082	0.23837	0.20508	6	
	5	0.00006	0.00149	0.00849	0.02642	0.05840	0.10292	0.15357	0.20066	0.23403	0.24609	5	
	6	0.00000	0.00014	0.00125	0.00551	0.01622	0.03676	0.06891	0.11148	0.15957	0.20508	4	
	7	0.00000	0.00001	0.00013	0.00079	0.00309	0.00900	0.02120	0.04247	0.07460	0.11719	3	
	8	0.00000	0.00000	0.00001	0.00007	0.00039	0.00145	0.00428	0.01062	0.02289	0.04395	2	
	9	0.00000	0.00000	0.00000	0.00000	0.00003	0.00014	0.00051	0.00157	0.00416	0.00977	1	
	10	0.00000	0.00000	0.00000	0.00000	0.00000	0.00001	0.00003	0.00010	0.00034	0.00098	0	
11	0	0.56880	0.31381	0.16734	0.08590	0.04224	0.01977	0.00875	0.00363	0.00139	0.00049	11	11
	1	0.32931	0.38355	0.32484	0.23622	0.15486	0.09322	0.05183	0.02661	0.01254	0.00537	10	
	2	0.08666	0.21308	0.28663	0.29528	0.25810	0.19975	0.13955	0.08868	0.05129	0.02686	9	
	3	0.01368	0.07103	0.15174	0.22146	0.25810	0.25682	0.22542	0.17737	0.12590	0.08057	8	
	4	0.00144	0.01578	0.05356	0.11073	0.17207	0.22013	0.24276	0.23649	0.20602	0.16113	7	
	5	0.00011	0.00246	0.01323	0.03876	0.08030	0.13208	0.18300	0.22072	0.23598	0.22559	6	
	6	0.00001	0.00027	0.00233	0.00969	0.02677	0.05661	0.09854	0.14715	0.19308	0.22559	5	

$P \leqslant 0.5$

$P \leqslant 0.5$

No of events	0.50	0.55	0.60	0.65	0.70	0.75	0.80	0.85	0.90	0.95	No of events	N
7	0.16113	0.11284	0.07007	0.03790	0.01733	0.00637	0.00173	0.00029	0.00002	0.00000	4	
8	0.08057	0.04616	0.02336	0.01020	0.00371	0.00106	0.00022	0.00003	0.00000	0.00000	3	
9	0.02686	0.01259	0.00519	0.00183	0.00053	0.00012	0.00002	0.00000	0.00000	0.00000	2	
10	0.00537	0.00206	0.00069	0.00020	0.00005	0.00001	0.00000	0.00000	0.00000	0.00000	1	12
11	0.00049	0.00015	0.00004	0.00001	0.00000	0.00000	0.00000	0.00000	0.00000	0.00000	0	
0	0.00024	0.00077	0.00218	0.00569	0.01384	0.03168	0.06872	0.14224	0.28243	0.54036	12	12
1	0.00293	0.00752	0.01741	0.03675	0.07118	0.1267	0.20616	0.30122	0.37657	0.34128	11	
2	0.01611	0.03385	0.06385	0.10885	0.16779	0.23229	0.28347	0.29236	0.23013	0.09879	10	
3	0.05371	0.09233	0.14189	0.19537	0.23970	0.25810	0.23622	0.17198	0.08523	0.01733	9	
4	0.12085	0.16996	0.21284	0.23669	0.23114	0.19358	0.13288	0.06828	0.02131	0.00205	8	
5	0.19336	0.22250	0.22703	0.20392	0.15850	0.10324	0.05315	0.01928	0.00379	0.00017	7	
6	0.22559	0.21238	0.17658	0.12810	0.07925	0.04015	0.01550	0.00397	0.00049	0.00001	6	
7	0.19336	0.14895	0.10090	0.05912	0.02911	0.01147	0.00332	0.00060	0.00005	0.00000	5	
8	0.12085	0.07617	0.04204	0.01990	0.00780	0.00239	0.00052	0.00007	0.00000	0.00000	4	
9	0.05371	0.02770	0.01246	0.00476	0.00149	0.00035	0.00006	0.00001	0.00000	0.00000	3	
10	0.01611	0.00680	0.00249	0.00077	0.00019	0.00004	0.00000	0.00000	0.00000	0.00000	2	
11	0.00293	0.00101	0.00030	0.00008	0.00001	0.00000	0.00000	0.00000	0.00000	0.00000	1	
12	0.00024	0.00007	0.00002	0.00000	0.00000	0.00000	0.00000	0.00000	0.00000	0.00000	0	
					$P \geqslant 0.5$					0.95	$P \geqslant 0.5$	

(continued)

TABLE A.1 (*continued*)

P ≤ 0.5

N	No. of events	0.05	0.10	0.15	0.20	0.25	0.30	0.35	0.40	0.45	0.50	No. of events	
13	0	0.51334	0.25419	0.12091	0.05498	0.02376	0.00969	0.00370	0.00131	0.00042	0.00012	13	13
	1	0.35123	0.36716	0.27737	0.17867	0.10295	0.05398	0.02588	0.01132	0.00448	0.00159	12	
	2	0.11092	0.24477	0.29369	0.26801	0.20590	0.13881	0.08361	0.04528	0.02200	0.00952	11	
	3	0.02140	0.09972	0.19003	0.24567	0.25165	0.21813	0.16508	0.11068	0.06601	0.03491	10	
	4	0.00282	0.02770	0.08384	0.15355	0.20971	0.23371	0.22223	0.18446	0.13503	0.08728	9	
	5	0.00027	0.00554	0.02663	0.06910	0.12583	0.18029	0.21539	0.22135	0.19886	0.15710	8	
	6	0.00002	0.00082	0.00627	0.02303	0.05592	0.10302	0.15464	0.19676	0.21694	0.20947	7	
	7	0.00000	0.00009	0.00111	0.00576	0.01864	0.04415	0.08327	0.13117	0.17749	0.20947	6	
	8	0.00000	0.00001	0.00015	0.00108	0.00466	0.01419	0.03363	0.06559	0.10892	0.15710	5	
	9	0.00000	0.00000	0.00001	0.00015	0.00086	0.00338	0.01006	0.02429	0.04951	0.08728	4	
	10	0.00000	0.00000	0.00000	0.00001	0.00012	0.00058	0.00217	0.00648	0.01620	0.03491	3	
	11	0.00000	0.00000	0.00000	0.00000	0.00001	0.00007	0.00032	0.00118	0.00362	0.00952	2	
	12	0.00000	0.00000	0.00000	0.00000	0.00000	0.00000	0.00003	0.00013	0.00049	0.00159	1	
	13	0.00000	0.00000	0.00000	0.00000	0.00000	0.00000	0.00000	0.00001	0.00003	0.00012	0	
14	0	0.48767	0.22877	0.10277	0.04398	0.01782	0.00678	0.00240	0.00078	0.00023	0.00006	14	14
	1	0.35934	0.35586	0.25390	0.15393	0.08315	0.04069	0.01812	0.00731	0.00265	0.00085	13	
	2	0.12293	0.25701	0.29124	0.25014	0.18016	0.11336	0.06341	0.03169	0.01412	0.00555	12	
	3	0.02588	0.11423	0.20558	0.25014	0.24021	0.19433	0.13657	0.08452	0.04621	0.02222	11	
	4	0.00375	0.03490	0.09977	0.17197	0.22019	0.22903	0.20223	0.15495	0.10397	0.06110	10	
	5	0.00039	0.00776	0.03521	0.08599	0.14680	0.19631	0.21778	0.20660	0.17013	0.12219	9	
	6	0.00003	0.00129	0.00932	0.03224	0.07340	0.12620	0.17590	0.20660	0.20880	0.18329	8	
	7	0.00000	0.00016	0.00188	0.00921	0.02796	0.06181	0.10825	0.15741	0.19524	0.20947	7	
	8	0.00000	0.00002	0.00029	0.00202	0.00816	0.02318	0.05100	0.09182	0.13978	0.18329	6	
	9	0.00000	0.00000	0.00003	0.00034	0.00181	0.00662	0.01831	0.04081	0.07624	0.12219	5	
	10	0.00000	0.00000	0.00000	0.00004	0.00030	0.00142	0.00493	0.01360	0.03119	0.06110	4	
	11	0.00000	0.00000	0.00000	0.00000	0.00004	0.00022	0.00097	0.00330	0.00928	0.02222	3	
	12	0.00000	0.00000	0.00000	0.00000	0.00000	0.00002	0.00013	0.00055	0.00190	0.00555	2	
	13	0.00000	0.00000	0.00000	0.00000	0.00000	0.00000	0.00001	0.00006	0.00024	0.00085	1	
	14	0.00000	0.00000	0.00000	0.00000	0.00000	0.00000	0.00000	0.00000	0.00001	0.00006	0	

$N = 15$

No. of events	0.50	0.55	0.60	0.65	0.70	0.75	0.80	0.85	0.90	0.95	No. of events
0	0.00003	0.00013	0.00047	0.00156	0.00475	0.01336	0.03518	0.08735	0.20589	0.46329	15
1	0.00046	0.00156	0.00470	0.01262	0.03052	0.06682	0.13194	0.23123	0.34315	0.36576	14
2	0.00320	0.00896	0.02194	0.04756	0.09156	0.15591	0.23090	0.28564	0.26690	0.13475	13
3	0.01389	0.03177	0.06339	0.11096	0.17004	0.22520	0.25014	0.21843	0.12851	0.03073	12
4	0.04166	0.07798	0.12678	0.17925	0.21862	0.22520	0.18760	0.11564	0.04284	0.00485	11
5	0.09164	0.14036	0.18594	0.21234	0.20613	0.16515	0.10318	0.04490	0.01047	0.00056	10
6	0.15274	0.19140	0.20660	0.19056	0.14724	0.09175	0.04299	0.01320	0.00194	0.00005	9
7	0.19638	0.20134	0.17708	0.13193	0.08113	0.03932	0.01382	0.00300	0.00028	0.00000	8
8	0.19638	0.16474	0.11806	0.07104	0.03477	0.01311	0.00345	0.00053	0.00003	0.00000	7
9	0.15274	0.10483	0.06121	0.02975	0.01159	0.00340	0.00067	0.00007	0.00000	0.00000	6
10	0.09164	0.05146	0.02449	0.00961	0.00298	0.00068	0.00010	0.00001	0.00000	0.00000	5
11	0.04166	0.01914	0.00742	0.00235	0.00058	0.00010	0.00001	0.00000	0.00000	0.00000	4
12	0.01389	0.00522	0.00165	0.00042	0.00008	0.00001	0.00000	0.00000	0.00000	0.00000	3
13	0.00320	0.00099	0.00025	0.00005	0.00001	0.00000	0.00000	0.00000	0.00000	0.00000	2
14	0.00046	0.00012	0.00002	0.00000	0.00000	0.00000	0.00000	0.00000	0.00000	0.00000	1
15	0.00003	0.00001	0.00000	0.00000	0.00000	0.00000	0.00000	0.00000	0.00000	0.00000	0

$P \geqslant 0.5$ $P \geqslant 0.5$

(continued)

TABLE A.1 (*continued*)

$P \leqslant 0.5$							$P \leqslant 0.5$						
N	No. of events	0.05	0.10	0.15	0.20	0.25	0.30	0.35	0.40	0.45	0.50		
16	0	0.44013	0.18530	0.07425	0.02815	0.01002	0.00332	0.00102	0.00028	0.00007	0.00002	16	16
	1	0.37063	0.32943	0.20965	0.11259	0.05345	0.02279	0.00875	0.00301	0.00092	0.00024	15	
	2	0.14630	0.27452	0.27748	0.21111	0.13363	0.07325	0.03533	0.01505	0.00563	0.00183	14	
	3	0.03593	0.14234	0.22851	0.24629	0.20788	0.14650	0.08877	0.04681	0.02151	0.00854	13	
	4	0.00615	0.05140	0.13106	0.20011	0.22520	0.20405	0.15535	0.10142	0.05718	0.02777	12	
	5	0.00078	0.01371	0.05551	0.12007	0.18016	0.20988	0.20076	0.16227	0.11229	0.06665	11	
	6	0.00007	0.00279	0.01796	0.05503	0.11010	0.16490	0.19818	0.19833	0.16843	0.12219	10	
	7	0.00001	0.00044	0.00453	0.01965	0.05243	0.10096	0.15245	0.18889	0.19687	0.17456	9	
	8	0.00000	0.00006	0.00090	0.00553	0.01966	0.04868	0.09235	0.14167	0.18121	0.19638	8	
	9	0.00000	0.00001	0.00014	0.00123	0.00583	0.01854	0.04420	0.08395	0.13179	0.17456	7	
	10	0.00000	0.00000	0.00002	0.00021	0.00136	0.00556	0.01666	0.03918	0.07548	0.12219	6	
	11	0.00000	0.00000	0.00000	0.00003	0.00025	0.00130	0.00489	0.01425	0.03368	0.06665	5	
	12	0.00000	0.00000	0.00000	0.00000	0.00003	0.00023	0.00110	0.00396	0.01148	0.02777	4	
	13	0.00000	0.00000	0.00000	0.00000	0.00000	0.00003	0.00018	0.00081	0.00289	0.00854	3	
	14	0.00000	0.00000	0.00000	0.00000	0.00000	0.00000	0.00002	0.00012	0.00051	0.00183	2	
	15	0.00000	0.00000	0.00000	0.00000	0.00000	0.00000	0.00000	0.00001	0.00006	0.00024	1	
	16	0.00000	0.00000	0.00000	0.00000	0.00000	0.00000	0.00000	0.00000	0.00000	0.00002	0	
17	0	0.41812	0.16677	0.06311	0.02252	0.00752	0.00233	0.00066	0.00017	0.00004	0.00001	17	17
	1	0.37411	0.31501	0.18934	0.09570	0.04260	0.01695	0.00604	0.00192	0.00054	0.00013	16	
	2	0.15752	0.28001	0.26730	0.19140	0.11359	0.05811	0.02602	0.01023	0.00351	0.00104	15	
	3	0.04145	0.15556	0.23586	0.23925	0.18932	0.12452	0.07006	0.03410	0.01436	0.00519	14	
	4	0.00764	0.06050	0.14568	0.20935	0.22087	0.18678	0.13205	0.07958	0.04113	0.01816	13	
	5	0.00104	0.01748	0.06684	0.13608	0.19142	0.20813	0.18486	0.13793	0.08749	0.04721	12	
	6	0.00011	0.00388	0.02359	0.06804	0.12761	0.17840	0.19908	0.18391	0.14317	0.09442	11	
	7	0.00001	0.00068	0.00654	0.02673	0.06684	0.12014	0.16846	0.19267	0.18407	0.14838	10	
	8	0.00000	0.00009	0.00144	0.00835	0.02785	0.06436	0.11338	0.16056	0.18826	0.18547	9	
	9	0.00000	0.00001	0.00025	0.00209	0.00928	0.02578	0.06105	0.10704	0.15403	0.18547	8	
	10	0.00000	0.00000	0.00004	0.00042	0.00248	0.00946	0.02630	0.05709	0.10082	0.14838	7	
	11	0.00000	0.00000	0.00000	0.00007	0.00053	0.00258	0.00901	0.02422	0.05249	0.09442	6	

No of events (left)	0.50	0.55	0.60	0.65	0.70	0.75	0.80	0.85	0.90	0.95	No of events (right)	N
12	0.04721	0.02147	0.00807	0.00243	0.00055	0.00009	0.00001	0.00000	0.00000	0.00000	5	
13	0.01816	0.00676	0.00207	0.00050	0.00009	0.00001	0.00000	0.00000	0.00000	0.00000	4	
14	0.00519	0.00158	0.00039	0.00008	0.00001	0.00000	0.00000	0.00000	0.00000	0.00000	3	
15	0.00104	0.00026	0.00005	0.00001	0.00000	0.00000	0.00000	0.00000	0.00000	0.00000	2	
16	0.00013	0.00003	0.00000	0.00000	0.00000	0.00000	0.00000	0.00000	0.00000	0.00000	1	
17	0.00001	0.00000	0.00000	0.00000	0.00000	0.00000	0.00000	0.00000	0.00000	0.00000	0	
0	0.00000	0.00002	0.00010	0.00043	0.00163	0.00564	0.01801	0.05365	0.15009	0.39721	18	18
1	0.00007	0.00031	0.00122	0.00416	0.01256	0.03383	0.08106	0.17041	0.30019	0.37631	17	
2	0.00058	0.00217	0.00691	0.01903	0.04576	0.09584	0.17226	0.25561	0.28351	0.16835	16	
3	0.00311	0.00948	0.02455	0.05465	0.10460	0.17038	0.22968	0.24057	0.16801	0.04726	15	
4	0.01167	0.02908	0.06139	0.11035	0.16810	0.21298	0.21533	0.15920	0.07000	0.00933	14	
5	0.03268	0.06663	0.11459	0.16638	0.20173	0.19878	0.15073	0.07867	0.02178	0.00137	13	
6	0.07082	0.11811	0.16552	0.19411	0.18732	0.14356	0.08165	0.03008	0.00524	0.00016	12	
7	0.12140	0.16567	0.18916	0.17918	0.13762	0.08204	0.03499	0.00910	0.00100	0.00001	11	
8	0.16692	0.18637	0.17340	0.13266	0.08110	0.03760	0.01203	0.00221	0.00015	0.00000	10	
9	0.18547	0.16943	0.12844	0.07937	0.03862	0.01393	0.00334	0.00043	0.00002	0.00000	9	
10	0.16692	0.12476	0.07707	0.03846	0.01490	0.00418	0.00075	0.00007	0.00000	0.00000	8	
11	0.12140	0.07424	0.03737	0.01506	0.00464	0.00101	0.00014	0.00001	0.00000	0.00000	7	
12	0.07082	0.03543	0.01453	0.00473	0.00116	0.00020	0.00002	0.00000	0.00000	0.00000	6	
13	0.03268	0.01338	0.00447	0.00118	0.00023	0.00003	0.00000	0.00000	0.00000	0.00000	5	
14	0.01167	0.00391	0.00106	0.00023	0.00004	0.00000	0.00000	0.00000	0.00000	0.00000	4	
15	0.00311	0.00085	0.00019	0.00003	0.00000	0.00000	0.00000	0.00000	0.00000	0.00000	3	
16	0.00058	0.00013	0.00002	0.00000	0.00000	0.00000	0.00000	0.00000	0.00000	0.00000	2	
17	0.00007	0.00001	0.00000	0.00000	0.00000	0.00000	0.00000	0.00000	0.00000	0.00000	1	
18	0.00000	0.00000	0.00000	0.00000	0.00000	0.00000	0.00000	0.00000	0.00000	0.00000	0	

$P \geqslant 0.5$

$P \geqslant 0.5$

(continued)

TABLE A.1 (*continued*)

P ≤ 0.5

P ≤ 0.5

N	No. of events	0.05	0.10	0.15	0.20	0.25	0.30	0.35	0.40	0.45	0.50		
19	0	0.37735	0.13509	0.04560	0.01441	0.00423	0.00114	0.00028	0.00006	0.00001	0.00000	19	19
	1	0.37735	0.28518	0.15289	0.06845	0.02678	0.00928	0.00285	0.00077	0.00018	0.00004	18	
	2	0.17875	0.28518	0.24283	0.15402	0.08034	0.03580	0.01382	0.00463	0.00134	0.00033	17	
	3	0.05331	0.17956	0.24283	0.21820	0.15175	0.08695	0.04218	0.01750	0.00619	0.00185	16	
	4	0.01122	0.07980	0.17141	0.21820	0.20233	0.14905	0.09086	0.04665	0.02026	0.00739	15	
	5	0.00177	0.02660	0.09075	0.16365	0.20233	0.19164	0.14677	0.09331	0.04973	0.02218	14	
	6	0.00022	0.00690	0.03737	0.09546	0.15737	0.19164	0.18440	0.14515	0.09494	0.05175	13	
	7	0.00002	0.00142	0.01225	0.04432	0.09742	0.15253	0.18440	0.17971	0.14427	0.09611	12	
	8	0.00000	0.00024	0.00324	0.01662	0.04871	0.09805	0.14894	0.17971	0.17705	0.14416	11	
	9	0.00000	0.00003	0.00070	0.00508	0.01984	0.05136	0.09802	0.14643	0.17705	0.17620	10	
	10	0.00000	0.00000	0.00012	0.00127	0.00661	0.02201	0.05278	0.09762	0.14486	0.17620	9	
	11	0.00000	0.00000	0.00002	0.00026	0.00180	0.00772	0.02325	0.05325	0.09697	0.14416	8	
	12	0.00000	0.00000	0.00000	0.00004	0.00040	0.00221	0.00835	0.02366	0.05290	0.09611	7	
	13	0.00000	0.00000	0.00000	0.00001	0.00007	0.00051	0.00242	0.00850	0.02330	0.05175	6	
	14	0.00000	0.00000	0.00000	0.00000	0.00001	0.00009	0.00056	0.00243	0.00817	0.02218	5	
	15	0.00000	0.00000	0.00000	0.00000	0.00000	0.00001	0.00010	0.00054	0.00223	0.00739	4	
	16	0.00000	0.00000	0.00000	0.00000	0.00000	0.00000	0.00001	0.00009	0.00046	0.00185	3	
	17	0.00000	0.00000	0.00000	0.00000	0.00000	0.00000	0.00000	0.00001	0.00007	0.00033	2	
	18	0.00000	0.00000	0.00000	0.00000	0.00000	0.00000	0.00000	0.00000	0.00001	0.00004	1	
	19	0.00000	0.00000	0.00000	0.00000	0.00000	0.00000	0.00000	0.00000	0.00000	0.00000	0	
20	0	0.35849	0.12158	0.03876	0.01153	0.00317	0.00080	0.00018	0.00004	0.00001	0.00000	20	20
	1	0.37735	0.27017	0.13680	0.05765	0.02114	0.00684	0.00195	0.00049	0.00010	0.00002	19	
	2	0.18868	0.28518	0.22934	0.13691	0.06695	0.02785	0.00998	0.00309	0.00082	0.00018	18	
	3	0.05958	0.19012	0.24283	0.20536	0.13390	0.07160	0.03226	0.01235	0.00401	0.00109	17	
	4	0.01333	0.08978	0.18212	0.21820	0.18969	0.13042	0.07382	0.03499	0.01393	0.00462	16	
	5	0.00224	0.03192	0.10285	0.17456	0.20233	0.17886	0.12720	0.07465	0.03647	0.01479	15	
	6	0.00030	0.00887	0.04537	0.10910	0.16861	0.19164	0.17123	0.12441	0.07460	0.03696	14	
	7	0.00003	0.00197	0.01601	0.05455	0.11241	0.16426	0.18440	0.16588	0.12207	0.07393	13	
	8	0.00000	0.00036	0.00459	0.02216	0.06089	0.11440	0.16135	0.17971	0.16230	0.12013	12	

N	0.50	0.55	0.60	0.65	0.70	0.75	0.80	0.85	0.90	0.95	No of events
9	0.16018	0.17705	0.15974	0.11584	0.06537	0.02706	0.00739	0.00108	0.00005	0.00000	11
10	0.17620	0.15935	0.11714	0.06861	0.03082	0.00992	0.00203	0.00021	0.00001	0.00000	10
11	0.16018	0.11852	0.07099	0.03359	0.01201	0.00301	0.00046	0.00003	0.00000	0.00000	9
12	0.12013	0.07273	0.03550	0.01356	0.00386	0.00075	0.00009	0.00000	0.00000	0.00000	8
13	0.07393	0.03662	0.01456	0.00449	0.00102	0.00015	0.00001	0.00000	0.00000	0.00000	7
14	0.03696	0.01498	0.00485	0.00121	0.00022	0.00003	0.00000	0.00000	0.00000	0.00000	6
15	0.01479	0.00490	0.00129	0.00026	0.00004	0.00000	0.00000	0.00000	0.00000	0.00000	5
16	0.00462	0.00125	0.00027	0.00004	0.00001	0.00000	0.00000	0.00000	0.00000	0.00000	4
17	0.00109	0.00024	0.00004	0.00001	0.00000	0.00000	0.00000	0.00000	0.00000	0.00000	3
18	0.00018	0.00003	0.00000	0.00000	0.00000	0.00000	0.00000	0.00000	0.00000	0.00000	2
19	0.00002	0.00000	0.00000	0.00000	0.00000	0.00000	0.00000	0.00000	0.00000	0.00000	1
20	0.00000	0.00000	0.00000	0.00000	0.00000	0.00000	0.00000	0.00000	0.00000	0.00000	0
					$P \geqslant 0.5$						$P \geqslant 0.5$

TABLE A.2 Normal Distribution

z	Area below z	Area beyond z	z	Area below z	Area beyond z
0.00	0.5000	0.5000	0.50	0.6915	0.3085
0.01	0.5040	0.4960	0.51	0.6950	0.3050
0.02	0.5080	0.4920	0.52	0.6985	0.3015
0.03	0.5120	0.4880	0.53	0.7019	0.2981
0.04	0.5160	0.4840	0.54	0.7054	0.2946
0.05	0.5199	0.4801	0.55	0.7088	0.2912
0.06	0.5239	0.4761	0.56	0.7123	0.2877
0.07	0.5279	0.4721	0.57	0.7157	0.2843
0.08	0.5319	0.4681	0.58	0.7190	0.2810
0.09	0.5359	0.4641	0.59	0.7224	0.2776
0.10	0.5398	0.4602	0.60	0.7257	0.2743
0.11	0.5438	0.4562	0.61	0.7291	0.2709
0.12	0.5478	0.4522	0.62	0.7324	0.2676
0.13	0.5517	0.4483	0.63	0.7357	0.2643
0.14	0.5557	0.4443	0.64	0.7389	0.2611
0.15	0.5596	0.4404	0.65	0.7422	0.2578
0.16	0.5636	0.4364	0.66	0.7454	0.2546
0.17	0.5675	0.4325	0.67	0.7486	0.2514
0.18	0.5714	0.4286	0.68	0.7517	0.2483
0.19	0.5753	0.4247	0.69	0.7549	0.2451
0.20	0.5793	0.4207	0.70	0.7580	0.2420
0.21	0.5832	0.4168	0.71	0.7611	0.2389
0.22	0.5871	0.4129	0.72	0.7642	0.2358
0.23	0.5910	0.4090	0.73	0.7673	0.2327
0.24	0.5948	0.4052	0.74	0.7704	0.2296
0.25	0.5987	0.4013	0.75	0.7734	0.2266
0.26	0.6026	0.3974	0.76	0.7764	0.2236
0.27	0.6064	0.3936	0.77	0.7794	0.2206
0.28	0.6103	0.3897	0.78	0.7823	0.2177
0.29	0.6141	0.3859	0.79	0.7852	0.2148
0.30	0.6179	0.3821	0.80	0.7881	0.2119
0.31	0.6217	0.3783	0.81	0.7910	0.2090
0.32	0.6255	0.3745	0.82	0.7939	0.2061
0.33	0.6293	0.3707	0.83	0.7967	0.2033
0.34	0.6331	0.3669	0.84	0.7995	0.2005
0.35	0.6368	0.3632	0.85	0.8023	0.1977
0.36	0.6406	0.3594	0.86	0.8051	0.1949
0.37	0.6443	0.3557	0.87	0.8078	0.1922
0.38	0.6480	0.3520	0.88	0.8106	0.1894
0.39	0.6517	0.3483	0.89	0.8133	0.1867
0.40	0.6554	0.3446	0.90	0.8159	0.1841
0.41	0.6591	0.3409	0.91	0.8186	0.1814
0.42	0.6628	0.3372	0.92	0.8212	0.1788
0.43	0.6664	0.3336	0.93	0.8238	0.1762
0.44	0.6700	0.3300	0.94	0.8264	0.1736
0.45	0.6736	0.3264	0.95	0.8289	0.1711
0.46	0.6772	0.3228	0.96	0.8315	0.1685
0.47	0.6808	0.3192	0.97	0.8340	0.1660
0.48	0.6844	0.3156	0.98	0.8365	0.1635
0.49	0.6879	0.3121	0.99	0.8389	0.1611

TABLE A.2 *(continued)*

z	Area below z	Area beyond z	z	Area below z	Area beyond z
1.00	0.8413	0.1587	1.50	0.9332	0.0668
1.01	0.8438	0.1562	1.51	0.9345	0.0655
1.02	0.8461	0.1539	1.52	0.9357	0.0643
1.03	0.8485	0.1515	1.53	0.9370	0.0630
1.04	0.8508	0.1492	1.54	0.9382	0.0618
1.05	0.8531	0.1469	1.55	0.9394	0.0606
1.06	0.8554	0.1446	1.56	0.9406	0.0594
1.07	0.8577	0.1423	1.57	0.9418	0.0582
1.08	0.8599	0.1401	1.58	0.9429	0.0571
1.09	0.8621	0.1379	1.59	0.9441	0.0559
1.10	0.8643	0.1357	1.60	0.9452	0.0548
1.11	0.8665	0.1335	1.61	0.9463	0.0537
1.12	0.8686	0.1314	1.62	0.9474	0.0526
1.13	0.8708	0.1292	1.63	0.9484	0.0516
1.14	0.8729	0.1271	1.64	0.9495	0.0505
1.15	0.8749	0.1251	1.65	0.9505	0.0495
1.16	0.8770	0.1230	1.66	0.9515	0.0485
1.17	0.8790	0.1210	1.67	0.9525	0.0475
1.18	0.8810	0.1190	1.68	0.9535	0.0465
1.19	0.8830	0.1170	1.69	0.9545	0.0455
1.20	0.8849	0.1151	1.70	0.9554	0.0446
1.21	0.8869	0.1131	1.71	0.9564	0.0436
1.22	0.8888	0.1112	1.72	0.9573	0.0427
1.23	0.8907	0.1093	1.73	0.9582	0.0418
1.24	0.8925	0.1075	1.74	0.9591	0.0409
1.25	0.8944	0.1056	1.75	0.9599	0.0401
1.26	0.8962	0.1038	1.76	0.9608	0.0392
1.27	0.8980	0.1020	1.77	0.9616	0.0384
1.28	0.8997	0.1003	1.78	0.9625	0.0375
1.29	0.9015	0.0985	1.79	0.9633	0.0367
1.30	0.9032	0.0968	1.80	0.9641	0.0359
1.31	0.9049	0.0951	1.81	0.9649	0.0351
1.32	0.9066	0.0934	1.82	0.9656	0.0344
1.33	0.9082	0.0918	1.83	0.9664	0.0336
1.34	0.9099	0.0901	1.84	0.9671	0.0329
1.35	0.9115	0.0885	1.85	0.9678	0.0322
1.36	0.9131	0.0869	1.86	0.9686	0.0314
1.37	0.9147	0.0853	1.87	0.9693	0.0307
1.38	0.9162	0.0838	1.88	0.9699	0.0301
1.39	0.9177	0.0823	1.89	0.9706	0.0294
1.40	0.9192	0.0808	1.90	0.9713	0.0287
1.41	0.9207	0.0793	1.91	0.9719	0.0281
1.42	0.9222	0.0778	1.92	0.9726	0.0274
1.43	0.9236	0.0764	1.93	0.9732	0.0268
1.44	0.9251	0.0749	1.94	0.9738	0.0262
1.45	0.9265	0.0735	1.95	0.9744	0.0256
1.46	0.9279	0.0721	1.96	0.9750	0.0250
1.47	0.9292	0.0708	1.97	0.9756	0.0244
1.48	0.9306	0.0694	1.98	0.9761	0.0239
1.49	0.9319	0.0681	1.99	0.9767	0.0233

(continued)

TABLE A.2 (*continued*)

z	Area below z	Area beyond z	z	Area below z	Area beyond z
2.00	0.9772	0.0228	2.50	0.9938	0.0062
2.01	0.9778	0.0222	2.51	0.9940	0.0060
2.02	0.9783	0.0217	2.52	0.9941	0.0059
2.03	0.9788	0.0212	2.53	0.9943	0.0057
2.04	0.9793	0.0207	2.54	0.9945	0.0055
2.05	0.9798	0.0202	2.55	0.9946	0.0054
2.06	0.9803	0.0197	2.56	0.9948	0.0052
2.07	0.9808	0.0192	2.57	0.9949	0.0051
2.08	0.9812	0.0188	2.58	0.9951	0.0049
2.09	0.9817	0.0183	2.59	0.9952	0.0048
2.10	0.9821	0.0179	2.60	0.9953	0.0047
2.11	0.9826	0.0174	2.61	0.9955	0.0045
2.12	0.9830	0.0170	2.62	0.9956	0.0044
2.13	0.9834	0.0166	2.63	0.9957	0.0043
2.14	0.9838	0.0162	2.64	0.9959	0.0041
2.15	0.9842	0.0158	2.65	0.9960	0.0040
2.16	0.9846	0.0154	2.66	0.9961	0.0039
2.17	0.9850	0.0150	2.67	0.9962	0.0038
2.18	0.9854	0.0146	2.68	0.9963	0.0037
2.19	0.9857	0.0143	2.69	0.9964	0.0036
2.20	0.9861	0.0139	2.70	0.9965	0.0035
2.21	0.9864	0.0136	2.71	0.9966	0.0034
2.22	0.9868	0.0132	2.72	0.9967	0.0033
2.23	0.9871	0.0129	2.73	0.9968	0.0032
2.24	0.9875	0.0125	2.74	0.9969	0.0031
2.25	0.9878	0.0122	2.75	0.9970	0.0030
2.26	0.9881	0.0119	2.76	0.9971	0.0029
2.27	0.9884	0.0116	2.77	0.9972	0.0028
2.28	0.9887	0.0113	2.78	0.9973	0.0027
2.29	0.9890	0.0110	2.79	0.9974	0.0026
2.30	0.9893	0.0107	2.80	0.9974	0.0026
2.31	0.9896	0.0104	2.81	0.9975	0.0025
2.32	0.9898	0.0102	2.82	0.9976	0.0024
2.33	0.9901	0.0099	2.83	0.9977	0.0023
2.34	0.9904	0.0096	2.84	0.9977	0.0023
2.35	0.9906	0.0094	2.85	0.9978	0.0022
2.36	0.9909	0.0091	2.86	0.9979	0.0021
2.37	0.9911	0.0089	2.87	0.9979	0.0021
2.38	0.9913	0.0087	2.88	0.9980	0.0020
2.39	0.9916	0.0084	2.89	0.9981	0.0019
2.40	0.9918	0.0082	2.90	0.9981	0.0019
2.41	0.9920	0.0080	2.91	0.9982	0.0018
2.42	0.9922	0.0078	2.92	0.9982	0.0018
2.43	0.9925	0.0075	2.93	0.9983	0.0017
2.44	0.9927	0.0073	2.94	0.9984	0.0016
2.45	0.9929	0.0071	2.96	0.9985	0.0015
2.46	0.9931	0.0069	2.98	0.9986	0.0014
2.47	0.9932	0.0068	3.00	0.9987	0.0013
2.48	0.9934	0.0066	3.03	0.9988	0.0012
2.49	0.9936	0.0064	3.06	0.9989	0.0011

TABLE A.2 (*continued*)

z	Area below z	Area beyond z	z	Area below z	Area beyond z
3.09	0.9990	0.0010	3.27	0.9995	0.0005
3.12	0.9991	0.0009	3.33	0.9996	0.0004
3.15	0.9992	0.0008	3.39	0.9997	0.0003
3.18	0.9993	0.0007	3.49	0.9998	0.0002
3.22	0.9994	0.0006	3.62	0.9999	0.0001
			3.90	1.0000	0.0000

TABLE A.3 *t*-Distribution

df	0.3	0.2	Two-tailed test 0.1	0.05	0.01	0.001
	0.15	0.1	One-tailed test 0.05	0.025	0.005	0.0005
1	1.9626	3.0777	6.3137	12.7062	63.6559	636.5776
2	1.3862	1.8856	2.9200	4.3027	9.9250	31.5998
3	1.2498	1.6377	2.3534	3.1824	5.8408	12.9244
4	1.1896	1.5332	2.1318	2.7765	4.6041	8.6101
5	1.1558	1.4759	2.0150	2.5706	4.0321	6.8685
6	1.1342	1.4398	1.9432	2.4469	3.7074	5.9587
7	1.1192	1.4149	1.8946	2.3646	3.4995	5.4081
8	1.1081	1.3968	1.8595	2.3060	3.3554	5.0414
9	1.0997	1.3830	1.8331	2.2622	3.2498	4.7809
10	1.0931	1.3722	1.8125	2.2281	3.1693	4.5868
11	1.0877	1.3634	1.7959	2.2010	3.1058	4.4369
12	1.0832	1.3562	1.7823	2.1788	3.0545	4.3178
13	1.0795	1.3502	1.7709	2.1604	3.0123	4.2209
14	1.0763	1.3450	1.7613	2.1448	2.9768	4.1403
15	1.0735	1.3406	1.7531	2.1315	2.9467	4.0728
16	1.0711	1.3368	1.7459	2.1199	2.9208	4.0149
17	1.0690	1.3334	1.7396	2.1098	2.8982	3.9651
18	1.0672	1.3304	1.7341	2.1009	2.8784	3.9217
19	1.0655	1.3277	1.7291	2.0930	2.8609	3.8833
20	1.0640	1.3253	1.7247	2.0860	2.8453	3.8496
21	1.0627	1.3232	1.7207	2.0796	2.8314	3.8193
22	1.0614	1.3212	1.7171	2.0739	2.3188	3.7922
23	1.0603	1.3195	1.7139	2.0687	2.8073	3.7676
24	1.0593	1.3178	1.7109	2.0639	2.7970	3.7454
25	1.0584	1.3163	1.7081	2.0595	2.7874	3.7251
26	1.0575	1.3150	1.7056	2.0555	2.7787	3.7067
27	1.0567	1.3137	1.7033	2.0518	2.7707	3.6895
28	1.0560	1.3125	1.7011	2.0484	2.7633	3.6739
29	1.0553	1.3114	1.6991	2.0452	2.7564	3.6595
30	1.0547	1.3104	1.6973	2.0423	2.7500	3.6460
35	1.0520	1.3062	1.6896	2.0301	2.7238	3.5911
40	1.0500	1.3031	1.6839	2.0211	2.7045	3.5510
45	1.0485	1.3007	1.6794	2.0141	2.6896	3.5203
50	1.0473	1.2987	1.6759	2.0086	2.6778	3.4960
60	1.0455	1.2958	1.6706	2.0003	2.6603	3.4602
80	1.0432	1.2922	1.6641	1.9901	2.6387	3.4164
100	1.0418	1.2901	1.6602	1.9840	2.6259	3.3905
120	1.0409	1.2886	1.6576	1.9799	2.6174	3.3734
∞	1.0364	1.2815	1.6448	1.9600	2.5758	3.2905

TABLE A.4 *F*-Distribution

	α	1	2	3	4	5	6	7	8	9	10	11	12	13	14	15	20	25	30	40	50	60	80	100
1	0.05	161.45	199.50	215.71	224.58	230.16	233.99	236.77	238.88	240.54	241.88	242.98	243.90	244.69	245.36	245.95	248.02	249.26	250.10	251.14	251.77	252.20	252.72	253.04
	0.01	4052	4999	5404	5624	5764	5859	5928	5981	6022	6056	6083	6107	6126	6143	6157	6209	6240	6260	6286	6302	6313	6326	6334
	0.005	16212	19997	21614	22501	23056	23440	23715	23924	24091	24222	24334	24427	24505	24572	24632	24837	24959	25041	25146	25213	25254	25306	25339
2	0.05	18.51	19.00	19.16	19.25	19.30	19.33	19.35	19.37	19.38	19.40	19.40	19.41	19.42	19.42	19.43	19.45	19.46	19.46	19.47	19.48	19.48	19.48	19.49
	0.01	98.50	99.00	99.16	99.25	99.30	99.33	99.36	99.38	99.39	99.40	99.41	99.42	99.42	99.43	99.43	99.45	99.46	99.47	99.48	99.48	99.48	99.48	99.49
	0.005	198.50	199.01	199.16	199.24	199.30	199.33	199.36	199.38	199.39	199.39	199.42	199.42	199.42	199.42	199.43	199.45	199.45	199.48	199.48	199.48	199.48	199.48	199.48
3	0.05	10.13	9.55	9.28	9.12	9.01	8.94	8.89	8.85	8.81	8.79	8.76	8.74	8.73	8.71	8.70	8.66	8.63	8.62	8.59	8.58	8.57	8.56	8.55
	0.01	34.12	30.82	29.46	28.71	28.24	27.91	27.67	27.49	27.34	27.23	27.13	27.05	26.98	26.92	26.87	26.69	26.58	26.50	26.41	26.35	26.32	26.27	26.24
	0.005	55.55	49.80	47.47	46.20	45.39	44.84	44.43	44.13	43.88	43.68	43.52	43.39	43.27	43.17	43.08	42.78	42.59	42.47	42.31	42.21	42.15	42.07	42.02
4	0.05	7.71	6.94	6.59	6.39	6.26	6.16	6.09	6.04	6.00	5.96	5.94	5.91	5.89	5.87	5.86	5.80	5.77	5.75	5.72	5.70	5.69	5.67	5.66
	0.01	21.20	18.00	16.69	15.98	15.52	15.21	14.98	14.80	14.66	14.55	14.45	14.37	14.31	14.25	14.20	14.02	13.91	13.84	13.75	13.69	13.65	13.61	13.58
	0.005	31.33	26.28	24.26	23.15	22.46	21.98	21.62	21.35	21.14	20.97	20.82	20.70	20.60	20.51	20.44	20.17	20.00	19.89	19.75	19.67	19.61	19.54	19.50
5	0.05	6.61	5.79	5.41	5.19	5.05	4.95	4.88	4.82	4.77	4.74	4.70	4.68	4.66	4.64	4.62	4.56	4.52	4.50	4.46	4.44	4.43	4.41	4.41
	0.01	16.26	13.27	12.06	11.39	10.97	10.67	10.46	10.29	10.16	10.05	9.96	9.89	9.82	9.77	9.72	9.55	9.45	9.38	9.29	9.24	9.20	9.16	9.13
	0.005	22.78	18.31	16.53	15.56	14.94	14.51	14.20	13.96	13.77	13.62	13.49	13.38	13.29	13.21	13.15	12.90	12.76	12.66	12.53	12.45	12.40	12.34	12.30
6	0.05	5.99	5.14	4.76	4.53	4.39	4.28	4.21	4.15	4.10	4.06	4.03	4.00	3.98	3.96	3.94	3.87	3.83	3.81	3.77	3.75	3.74	3.72	3.71
	0.01	13.75	10.92	9.78	9.15	8.75	8.47	8.26	8.10	7.98	7.87	7.79	7.72	7.66	7.60	7.56	7.40	7.30	7.23	7.14	7.09	7.06	7.01	6.99
	0.005	18.63	14.54	12.92	12.03	11.46	11.07	10.79	10.57	10.39	10.25	10.13	10.03	9.95	9.88	9.81	9.59	9.45	9.36	9.24	9.17	9.12	9.06	9.03
7	0.05	5.59	4.74	4.35	4.12	3.97	3.87	3.79	3.73	3.68	3.64	3.60	3.57	3.55	3.53	3.51	3.44	3.40	3.38	3.34	3.32	3.30	3.29	3.27
	0.01	12.25	9.55	8.45	7.85	7.46	7.19	6.99	6.84	6.72	6.62	6.54	6.47	6.41	6.36	6.31	6.16	6.06	5.99	5.91	5.86	5.82	5.78	5.75
	0.005	16.24	12.40	10.88	10.05	9.52	9.16	8.89	8.68	8.51	8.38	8.27	8.18	8.10	8.03	7.97	7.75	7.62	7.53	7.42	7.35	7.31	7.25	7.22
8	0.05	5.32	4.46	4.07	3.84	3.69	3.58	3.50	3.44	3.39	3.35	3.31	3.28	3.26	3.24	3.22	3.15	3.11	3.08	3.04	3.02	3.01	2.99	2.97
	0.01	11.26	8.65	7.59	7.01	6.63	6.37	6.18	6.03	5.91	5.81	5.73	5.67	5.61	5.56	5.52	5.36	5.26	5.20	5.12	5.07	5.03	4.99	4.96
	0.005	14.69	11.04	9.60	8.81	8.30	7.95	7.69	7.50	7.34	7.21	7.10	7.01	6.94	6.87	6.81	6.61	6.48	6.40	6.29	6.22	6.18	6.12	6.09
9	0.05	5.12	4.26	3.86	3.63	3.48	3.37	3.29	3.23	3.18	3.14	3.10	3.07	3.05	3.03	3.01	2.94	2.89	2.86	2.83	2.80	2.79	2.77	2.76
	0.01	10.56	8.02	6.99	6.42	6.06	5.80	5.61	5.47	5.35	5.26	5.18	5.11	5.05	5.01	4.96	4.81	4.71	4.65	4.57	4.52	4.48	4.44	4.41
	0.005	13.61	10.11	8.72	7.96	7.47	7.13	6.88	6.69	6.54	6.42	6.31	6.23	6.15	6.09	6.03	5.83	5.71	5.62	5.52	5.45	5.41	5.36	5.32
10	0.05	4.96	4.10	3.71	3.48	3.33	3.22	3.14	3.07	3.02	2.98	2.94	2.91	2.89	2.86	2.85	2.77	2.73	2.70	2.66	2.64	2.62	2.60	2.59
	0.01	10.04	7.56	6.55	5.99	5.64	5.39	5.20	5.06	4.94	4.85	4.77	4.71	4.65	4.60	4.56	4.41	4.31	4.25	4.17	4.12	4.08	4.04	4.01
	0.005	12.83	9.43	8.08	7.34	6.87	6.54	6.30	6.12	5.97	5.85	5.75	5.66	5.59	5.53	5.47	5.27	5.15	5.07	4.97	4.90	4.86	4.80	4.77
11	0.05	4.84	3.98	3.59	3.36	3.20	3.09	3.01	2.95	2.90	2.85	2.82	2.79	2.76	2.74	2.72	2.65	2.60	2.57	2.53	2.51	2.49	2.47	2.46
	0.01	9.65	7.21	6.22	5.67	5.32	5.07	4.89	4.74	4.63	4.54	4.46	4.40	4.34	4.29	4.25	4.10	4.01	3.94	3.86	3.81	3.78	3.73	3.71
	0.005	12.23	8.91	7.60	6.88	6.42	6.10	5.86	5.68	5.54	5.42	5.32	5.24	5.16	5.10	5.05	4.86	4.74	4.65	4.55	4.49	4.45	4.39	4.36
12	0.05	4.75	3.89	3.49	3.26	3.11	3.00	2.91	2.85	2.80	2.75	2.72	2.69	2.66	2.64	2.62	2.54	2.50	2.47	2.43	2.40	2.38	2.36	2.35
	0.01	9.33	6.93	5.95	5.41	5.06	4.82	4.64	4.50	4.39	4.30	4.22	4.16	4.10	4.05	4.01	3.86	3.76	3.70	3.62	3.57	3.54	3.49	3.47
	0.005	11.75	8.51	7.23	6.52	6.07	5.76	5.52	5.35	5.20	5.09	4.99	4.91	4.84	4.77	4.72	4.53	4.41	4.33	4.23	4.17	4.12	4.07	4.04
13	0.05	4.67	3.81	3.41	3.18	3.03	2.92	2.83	2.77	2.71	2.67	2.63	2.60	2.58	2.55	2.53	2.46	2.41	2.38	2.34	2.31	2.30	2.27	2.26
	0.01	9.07	6.70	5.74	5.21	4.86	4.62	4.44	4.30	4.19	4.10	4.02	3.96	3.91	3.86	3.82	3.66	3.57	3.51	3.43	3.38	3.34	3.30	3.27
	0.005	11.37	8.19	6.93	6.23	5.79	5.48	5.25	5.08	4.94	4.82	4.72	4.64	4.57	4.51	4.46	4.27	4.15	4.07	3.97	3.91	3.87	3.81	3.78
14	0.05	4.60	3.74	3.34	3.11	2.96	2.85	2.76	2.70	2.65	2.60	2.57	2.53	2.51	2.48	2.46	2.39	2.34	2.31	2.27	2.24	2.22	2.20	2.19
	0.01	8.86	6.51	5.56	5.04	4.69	4.46	4.28	4.14	4.03	3.94	3.86	3.80	3.75	3.70	3.66	3.51	3.41	3.35	3.27	3.22	3.18	3.14	3.11
	0.005	11.06	7.92	6.68	6.00	5.56	5.26	5.03	4.86	4.72	4.60	4.51	4.43	4.36	4.30	4.25	4.06	3.94	3.86	3.76	3.70	3.66	3.60	3.57

Degrees of freedom of numerator

df	α																							
15	0.05	2.12	2.14	2.16	2.18	2.20	2.25	2.28	2.33	2.40	2.42	2.45	2.48	2.51	2.54	2.59	2.64	2.71	2.79	2.90	3.06	3.29	3.68	4.54
	0.01	2.98	3.00	3.05	3.08	3.13	3.21	3.28	3.37	3.52	3.56	3.61	3.67	3.73	3.80	3.89	4.00	4.14	4.32	4.56	4.89	5.42	6.36	8.68
	0.005	3.39	3.43	3.48	3.52	3.59	3.69	3.77	3.88	4.07	4.12	4.18	4.25	4.33	4.42	4.54	4.67	4.85	5.07	5.37	5.80	6.48	7.70	10.80
16	0.05	2.07	2.08	2.11	2.12	2.15	2.19	2.23	2.28	2.35	2.37	2.40	2.42	2.46	2.49	2.54	2.59	2.66	2.74	2.85	3.01	3.24	3.63	4.49
	0.01	2.86	2.89	2.93	2.97	3.02	3.10	3.16	3.26	3.41	3.45	3.50	3.55	3.62	3.69	3.78	3.89	4.03	4.20	4.44	4.77	5.29	6.23	8.53
	0.005	3.25	3.28	3.33	3.37	3.44	3.54	3.62	3.73	3.92	3.97	4.03	4.10	4.18	4.27	4.38	4.52	4.69	4.91	5.21	5.64	6.30	7.51	10.58
17	0.05	2.02	2.03	2.06	2.08	2.10	2.15	2.18	2.23	2.31	2.33	2.35	2.38	2.41	2.45	2.49	2.55	2.61	2.70	2.81	2.96	3.20	3.59	4.45
	0.01	2.76	2.79	2.83	2.87	2.92	3.00	3.07	3.16	3.31	3.35	3.40	3.46	3.52	3.59	3.68	3.79	3.93	4.10	4.34	4.67	5.19	6.11	8.40
	0.005	3.12	3.15	3.21	3.25	3.31	3.41	3.49	3.61	3.79	3.84	3.90	3.97	4.05	4.14	4.25	4.39	4.56	4.78	5.07	5.50	6.16	7.35	10.38
18	0.05	1.98	1.99	2.02	2.04	2.06	2.11	2.14	2.19	2.27	2.29	2.31	2.34	2.37	2.41	2.46	2.51	2.58	2.66	2.77	2.93	3.16	3.55	4.41
	0.01	2.68	2.70	2.75	2.78	2.84	2.92	2.98	3.08	3.23	3.27	3.32	3.37	3.43	3.51	3.60	3.71	3.84	4.01	4.25	4.58	5.09	6.01	8.29
	0.005	3.01	3.04	3.10	3.14	3.20	3.30	3.38	3.50	3.68	3.73	3.79	3.86	3.94	4.03	4.14	4.28	4.44	4.66	4.96	5.37	6.03	7.21	10.22
19	0.05	1.94	1.96	1.98	2.00	2.03	2.07	2.11	2.16	2.23	2.26	2.28	2.31	2.34	2.38	2.42	2.48	2.54	2.63	2.74	2.90	3.13	3.52	4.38
	0.01	2.60	2.63	2.67	2.71	2.76	2.84	2.91	3.00	3.15	3.19	3.24	3.30	3.36	3.43	3.52	3.63	3.77	3.94	4.17	4.50	5.01	5.93	8.18
	0.005	2.91	2.95	3.00	3.04	3.11	3.21	3.29	3.40	3.59	3.64	3.70	3.76	3.84	3.93	4.04	4.18	4.34	4.56	4.85	5.27	5.92	7.09	10.07
20	0.05	1.91	1.92	1.95	1.97	1.99	2.04	2.07	2.12	2.20	2.22	2.25	2.28	2.31	2.35	2.39	2.45	2.51	2.60	2.71	2.87	3.10	3.49	4.35
	0.01	2.54	2.56	2.61	2.64	2.69	2.78	2.84	2.94	3.09	3.13	3.18	3.23	3.29	3.37	3.46	3.56	3.70	3.87	4.10	4.43	4.94	5.85	8.10
	0.005	2.83	2.86	2.92	2.96	3.02	3.12	3.20	3.32	3.50	3.55	3.61	3.68	3.76	3.85	3.96	4.09	4.26	4.47	4.76	5.17	5.82	6.99	9.94
21	0.05	1.88	1.89	1.92	1.94	1.96	2.01	2.05	2.10	2.18	2.20	2.22	2.25	2.28	2.32	2.37	2.42	2.49	2.57	2.68	2.84	3.07	3.47	4.32
	0.01	2.48	2.50	2.55	2.58	2.64	2.72	2.79	2.88	3.03	3.07	3.12	3.17	3.24	3.31	3.40	3.51	3.64	3.81	4.04	4.37	4.87	5.78	8.02
	0.005	2.75	2.79	2.84	2.88	2.95	3.05	3.13	3.24	3.43	3.48	3.54	3.60	3.68	3.77	3.88	4.01	4.18	4.39	4.68	5.09	5.73	6.89	9.83
22	0.05	1.85	1.86	1.89	1.91	1.94	1.98	2.02	2.07	2.15	2.17	2.20	2.23	2.26	2.30	2.34	2.40	2.46	2.55	2.66	2.82	3.05	3.44	4.30
	0.01	2.42	2.45	2.50	2.53	2.58	2.67	2.73	2.83	2.98	3.02	3.07	3.12	3.18	3.26	3.35	3.45	3.59	3.76	3.99	4.31	4.82	5.72	7.95
	0.005	2.69	2.72	2.77	2.82	2.88	2.98	3.06	3.18	3.36	3.41	3.47	3.54	3.61	3.70	3.81	3.94	4.11	4.32	4.61	5.02	5.65	6.81	9.73
23	0.05	1.82	1.84	1.86	1.88	1.91	1.96	2.00	2.05	2.13	2.15	2.18	2.20	2.24	2.27	2.32	2.37	2.44	2.53	2.64	2.80	3.03	3.42	4.28
	0.01	2.37	2.40	2.45	2.48	2.54	2.62	2.69	2.78	2.93	2.97	3.02	3.07	3.14	3.21	3.30	3.41	3.54	3.71	3.94	4.26	4.76	5.66	7.88
	0.005	2.62	2.66	2.71	2.76	2.82	2.92	3.00	3.12	3.30	3.35	3.41	3.47	3.55	3.64	3.75	3.88	4.05	4.26	4.54	4.95	5.58	6.73	9.63
24	0.05	1.80	1.82	1.84	1.86	1.89	1.94	1.97	2.03	2.11	2.13	2.15	2.18	2.22	2.25	2.30	2.36	2.42	2.51	2.62	2.78	3.01	3.40	4.26
	0.01	2.33	2.36	2.40	2.44	2.49	2.58	2.64	2.74	2.89	2.93	2.98	3.03	3.09	3.17	3.26	3.36	3.50	3.67	3.90	4.22	4.72	5.61	7.82
	0.005	2.57	2.60	2.66	2.70	2.77	2.87	2.95	3.06	3.25	3.30	3.35	3.42	3.50	3.59	3.69	3.83	3.99	4.20	4.49	4.89	5.52	6.66	9.55
25	0.05	1.78	1.80	1.82	1.84	1.87	1.92	1.96	2.01	2.09	2.11	2.14	2.16	2.20	2.24	2.28	2.34	2.40	2.49	2.60	2.76	2.99	3.39	4.24
	0.01	2.29	2.32	2.36	2.40	2.45	2.54	2.60	2.70	2.85	2.89	2.94	2.99	3.06	3.13	3.22	3.32	3.46	3.63	3.85	4.18	4.68	5.57	7.77
	0.005	2.52	2.55	2.61	2.65	2.72	2.82	2.90	3.01	3.20	3.25	3.30	3.37	3.45	3.54	3.64	3.78	3.94	4.15	4.43	4.84	5.46	6.60	9.48
26	0.05	1.76	1.79	1.80	1.81	1.85	1.90	1.94	1.99	2.07	2.09	2.12	2.15	2.18	2.22	2.27	2.32	2.39	2.47	2.59	2.74	2.98	3.37	4.23
	0.01	2.25	2.28	2.33	2.36	2.42	2.50	2.57	2.66	2.81	2.86	2.90	2.96	3.02	3.09	3.18	3.29	3.42	3.59	3.82	4.14	4.64	5.53	7.72
	0.005	2.47	2.51	2.56	2.61	2.67	2.77	2.85	2.97	3.15	3.20	3.26	3.33	3.40	3.49	3.60	3.73	3.89	4.10	4.38	4.79	5.41	6.54	9.41
27	0.05	1.74	1.76	1.79	1.81	1.84	1.88	1.92	1.97	2.06	2.08	2.10	2.13	2.17	2.20	2.25	2.31	2.37	2.46	2.57	2.73	2.96	3.35	4.21
	0.01	2.22	2.25	2.29	2.33	2.38	2.47	2.54	2.63	2.78	2.82	2.87	2.93	2.99	3.06	3.15	3.26	3.39	3.56	3.78	4.11	4.60	5.49	7.68
	0.005	2.43	2.47	2.52	2.57	2.63	2.73	2.81	2.93	3.11	3.16	3.22	3.28	3.36	3.45	3.56	3.69	3.85	4.06	4.34	4.74	5.36	6.49	9.34
28	0.05	1.73	1.74	1.77	1.79	1.82	1.87	1.91	1.96	2.04	2.06	2.09	2.12	2.15	2.19	2.24	2.29	2.36	2.45	2.56	2.71	2.95	3.34	4.20
	0.01	2.19	2.22	2.26	2.30	2.35	2.44	2.51	2.60	2.75	2.79	2.84	2.90	2.96	3.03	3.12	3.23	3.36	3.53	3.75	4.07	4.57	5.45	7.64
	0.005	2.39	2.43	2.48	2.53	2.59	2.69	2.77	2.89	3.07	3.12	3.18	3.25	3.32	3.41	3.52	3.65	3.81	4.02	4.30	4.70	5.32	6.44	9.28
29	0.05	1.71	1.73	1.75	1.77	1.81	1.85	1.89	1.94	2.03	2.05	2.08	2.10	2.14	2.18	2.22	2.28	2.35	2.43	2.55	2.70	2.93	3.33	4.18
	0.01	2.16	2.19	2.23	2.27	2.33	2.41	2.48	2.57	2.73	2.77	2.81	2.87	2.93	3.00	3.09	3.20	3.33	3.50	3.73	4.04	4.54	5.42	7.60
	0.005	2.36	2.39	2.45	2.49	2.56	2.66	2.74	2.86	3.04	3.09	3.15	3.21	3.29	3.38	3.48	3.61	3.77	3.98	4.26	4.66	5.28	6.40	9.23
30	0.05	1.70	1.71	1.74	1.76	1.79	1.84	1.88	1.93	2.01	2.04	2.06	2.09	2.13	2.16	2.21	2.27	2.33	2.42	2.53	2.69	2.92	3.32	4.17
	0.01	2.13	2.16	2.21	2.25	2.30	2.39	2.45	2.55	2.70	2.74	2.79	2.84	2.91	2.98	3.07	3.17	3.30	3.47	3.70	4.02	4.51	5.39	7.56
	0.005	2.32	2.36	2.42	2.46	2.52	2.63	2.71	2.82	3.01	3.06	3.11	3.18	3.25	3.34	3.45	3.58	3.74	3.95	4.23	4.62	5.24	6.35	9.18

TABLE A.4 *(continued)*

Degrees of freedom of numerator

	α	1	2	3	4	5	6	7	8	9	10	11	12	13	14	15	20	25	30	40	50	60	80	100
32	0.05	4.15	3.29	2.90	2.67	2.51	2.40	2.31	2.24	2.19	2.14	2.10	2.07	2.04	2.01	1.99	1.91	1.85	1.82	1.77	1.74	1.71	1.69	1.67
	0.01	7.50	5.34	4.46	3.97	3.65	3.43	3.26	3.13	3.02	2.93	2.86	2.80	2.74	2.70	2.65	2.50	2.41	2.34	2.25	2.20	2.16	2.11	2.08
	0.005	9.09	6.28	5.17	4.56	4.17	3.89	3.68	3.52	3.39	3.29	3.20	3.12	3.06	3.00	2.95	2.77	2.65	2.57	2.47	2.40	2.36	2.30	2.26
34	0.05	4.13	3.28	2.88	2.65	2.49	2.38	2.29	2.23	2.17	2.12	2.08	2.05	2.02	1.99	1.97	1.89	1.83	1.80	1.75	1.71	1.69	1.66	1.65
	0.01	7.44	5.29	4.42	3.93	3.61	3.39	3.22	3.09	2.98	2.89	2.82	2.76	2.70	2.66	2.61	2.46	2.37	2.30	2.21	2.16	2.12	2.07	2.04
	0.005	9.01	6.22	5.11	4.50	4.11	3.84	3.63	3.47	3.34	3.24	3.15	3.07	3.01	2.95	2.90	2.72	2.60	2.52	2.42	2.35	2.30	2.25	2.21
36	0.05	4.11	3.26	2.87	2.63	2.48	2.36	2.28	2.21	2.15	2.11	2.07	2.03	2.00	1.98	1.95	1.87	1.81	1.78	1.73	1.69	1.67	1.64	1.62
	0.01	7.40	5.25	4.38	3.89	3.57	3.35	3.18	3.05	2.95	2.86	2.79	2.72	2.67	2.62	2.58	2.43	2.33	2.26	2.18	2.12	2.08	2.03	2.00
	0.005	8.94	6.16	5.06	4.46	4.06	3.79	3.58	3.42	3.30	3.19	3.10	3.03	2.96	2.90	2.85	2.67	2.56	2.48	2.37	2.30	2.26	2.20	2.17
38	0.05	4.10	3.24	2.85	2.62	2.46	2.35	2.26	2.19	2.14	2.09	2.05	2.02	1.99	1.96	1.94	1.85	1.80	1.76	1.71	1.68	1.65	1.62	1.61
	0.01	7.35	5.21	4.34	3.86	3.54	3.32	3.15	3.02	2.92	2.83	2.75	2.69	2.64	2.59	2.55	2.40	2.30	2.23	2.14	2.09	2.05	2.00	1.97
	0.005	8.88	6.11	5.02	4.41	4.02	3.75	3.54	3.39	3.26	3.15	3.06	2.99	2.92	2.87	2.82	2.63	2.52	2.44	2.33	2.27	2.22	2.16	2.12
40	0.05	4.08	3.23	2.84	2.61	2.45	2.34	2.25	2.18	2.12	2.08	2.04	2.00	1.97	1.95	1.92	1.84	1.78	1.74	1.69	1.66	1.64	1.61	1.59
	0.01	7.31	5.18	4.31	3.83	3.51	3.29	3.12	2.99	2.89	2.80	2.73	2.66	2.61	2.56	2.52	2.37	2.27	2.20	2.11	2.06	2.02	1.97	1.94
	0.005	8.83	6.07	4.98	4.37	3.99	3.71	3.51	3.35	3.22	3.12	3.03	2.95	2.89	2.83	2.78	2.60	2.48	2.40	2.30	2.23	2.18	2.12	2.09
42	0.05	4.07	3.22	2.83	2.59	2.44	2.32	2.24	2.17	2.11	2.06	2.03	1.99	1.96	1.94	1.91	1.83	1.77	1.73	1.68	1.65	1.62	1.59	1.57
	0.01	7.28	5.15	4.29	3.80	3.49	3.27	3.10	2.97	2.86	2.78	2.70	2.64	2.59	2.54	2.50	2.34	2.25	2.18	2.09	2.03	1.99	1.94	1.91
	0.005	8.78	6.03	4.94	4.34	3.95	3.68	3.48	3.32	3.19	3.09	3.00	2.92	2.86	2.80	2.75	2.57	2.45	2.37	2.26	2.20	2.15	2.09	2.06
44	0.05	4.06	3.21	2.82	2.58	2.43	2.31	2.23	2.16	2.10	2.05	2.01	1.98	1.95	1.92	1.90	1.81	1.75	1.72	1.67	1.63	1.61	1.58	1.56
	0.01	7.25	5.12	4.26	3.78	3.47	3.24	3.08	2.95	2.84	2.75	2.68	2.62	2.56	2.52	2.47	2.32	2.22	2.15	2.07	2.01	1.97	1.92	1.89
	0.005	8.74	5.99	4.91	4.31	3.92	3.65	3.45	3.29	3.16	3.06	2.97	2.89	2.83	2.77	2.72	2.54	2.42	2.34	2.24	2.17	2.12	2.06	2.03
46	0.05	4.05	3.20	2.81	2.57	2.42	2.30	2.22	2.15	2.09	2.04	2.00	1.97	1.94	1.91	1.89	1.80	1.75	1.71	1.65	1.62	1.60	1.57	1.55
	0.01	7.22	5.10	4.24	3.76	3.44	3.22	3.06	2.93	2.82	2.73	2.66	2.60	2.54	2.50	2.45	2.30	2.20	2.13	2.04	1.99	1.95	1.90	1.86
	0.005	8.70	5.96	4.88	4.28	3.90	3.62	3.42	3.26	3.14	3.03	2.94	2.87	2.80	2.75	2.70	2.51	2.40	2.32	2.21	2.14	2.10	2.04	2.00
48	0.05	4.04	3.19	2.80	2.57	2.41	2.29	2.21	2.14	2.08	2.03	1.99	1.96	1.93	1.90	1.88	1.79	1.74	1.70	1.64	1.61	1.59	1.56	1.54
	0.01	7.19	5.08	4.22	3.74	3.43	3.20	3.04	2.91	2.80	2.71	2.64	2.58	2.53	2.48	2.44	2.28	2.18	2.12	2.02	1.97	1.93	1.88	1.84
	0.005	8.66	5.93	4.85	4.25	3.87	3.60	3.40	3.24	3.11	3.01	2.92	2.85	2.78	2.72	2.67	2.49	2.37	2.29	2.19	2.12	2.07	2.01	1.97
50	0.05	4.03	3.18	2.79	2.56	2.40	2.29	2.20	2.13	2.07	2.03	1.99	1.95	1.92	1.89	1.87	1.78	1.73	1.69	1.63	1.60	1.58	1.54	1.52
	0.01	7.17	5.06	4.20	3.72	3.41	3.19	3.02	2.89	2.78	2.70	2.63	2.56	2.51	2.46	2.42	2.27	2.17	2.10	2.01	1.95	1.91	1.86	1.82
	0.005	8.63	5.90	4.83	4.23	3.85	3.58	3.38	3.22	3.09	2.99	2.90	2.82	2.76	2.70	2.65	2.47	2.35	2.27	2.16	2.10	2.05	1.99	1.95
55	0.05	4.02	3.16	2.77	2.54	2.38	2.27	2.18	2.11	2.06	2.01	1.97	1.93	1.90	1.88	1.85	1.76	1.71	1.67	1.61	1.58	1.55	1.52	1.50
	0.01	7.12	5.01	4.16	3.68	3.37	3.15	2.98	2.85	2.75	2.66	2.59	2.53	2.47	2.42	2.38	2.23	2.13	2.06	1.97	1.91	1.87	1.82	1.78
	0.005	8.55	5.84	4.77	4.18	3.80	3.53	3.33	3.17	3.05	2.94	2.85	2.78	2.71	2.66	2.61	2.42	2.31	2.23	2.12	2.05	2.00	1.94	1.90

df	α																							
60	0.05	4.00	3.15	2.76	2.53	2.37	2.25	2.17	2.10	2.04	1.99	1.95	1.92	1.89	1.86	1.84	1.75	1.69	1.65	1.59	1.56	1.53	1.50	1.48
	0.01	7.08	4.98	4.13	3.65	3.34	3.12	2.95	2.82	2.72	2.63	2.56	2.50	2.44	2.39	2.35	2.20	2.10	2.03	1.94	1.88	1.84	1.78	1.75
	0.005	8.49	5.79	4.73	4.14	3.76	3.49	3.29	3.13	3.01	2.90	2.82	2.74	2.68	2.62	2.57	2.39	2.27	2.19	2.08	2.01	1.96	1.90	1.86
65	0.05	3.99	3.14	2.75	2.51	2.36	2.24	2.15	2.08	2.03	1.98	1.94	1.90	1.87	1.85	1.82	1.73	1.68	1.63	1.58	1.54	1.52	1.49	1.46
	0.01	7.04	4.95	4.10	3.62	3.31	3.09	2.93	2.80	2.69	2.61	2.53	2.47	2.42	2.37	2.33	2.17	2.07	2.00	1.91	1.85	1.81	1.75	1.72
	0.005	8.44	5.75	4.69	4.11	3.73	3.46	3.26	3.10	2.98	2.87	2.79	2.71	2.65	2.59	2.54	2.36	2.24	2.16	2.05	1.98	1.93	1.87	1.83
70	0.05	3.98	3.13	2.74	2.50	2.35	2.23	2.14	2.07	2.02	1.97	1.93	1.89	1.86	1.84	1.81	1.72	1.66	1.62	1.57	1.53	1.50	1.47	1.45
	0.01	7.01	4.92	4.07	3.60	3.29	3.07	2.91	2.78	2.67	2.59	2.51	2.45	2.40	2.35	2.31	2.15	2.05	1.98	1.89	1.83	1.78	1.73	1.70
	0.005	8.40	5.72	4.66	4.08	3.70	3.43	3.23	3.08	2.95	2.85	2.76	2.68	2.62	2.56	2.51	2.33	2.21	2.13	2.02	1.95	1.90	1.84	1.80
80	0.05	3.96	3.11	2.72	2.49	2.33	2.21	2.13	2.06	2.00	1.95	1.91	1.88	1.84	1.82	1.79	1.70	1.64	1.60	1.54	1.51	1.48	1.45	1.43
	0.01	6.96	4.88	4.04	3.56	3.26	3.04	2.87	2.74	2.64	2.55	2.48	2.42	2.36	2.31	2.27	2.12	2.01	1.94	1.85	1.79	1.75	1.69	1.65
	0.005	8.33	5.67	4.61	4.03	3.65	3.39	3.19	3.03	2.91	2.80	2.72	2.64	2.58	2.52	2.47	2.29	2.17	2.08	1.97	1.90	1.85	1.79	1.75
90	0.05	3.95	3.10	2.71	2.47	2.32	2.20	2.11	2.04	1.99	1.94	1.90	1.86	1.83	1.80	1.78	1.69	1.63	1.59	1.53	1.49	1.46	1.43	1.41
	0.01	6.93	4.85	4.01	3.53	3.23	3.01	2.84	2.72	2.61	2.52	2.45	2.39	2.33	2.29	2.24	2.09	1.99	1.92	1.82	1.76	1.72	1.66	1.62
	0.005	8.28	5.62	4.57	3.99	3.62	3.35	3.15	3.00	2.87	2.77	2.68	2.61	2.54	2.49	2.44	2.25	2.13	2.05	1.94	1.87	1.82	1.75	1.71
100	0.05	3.94	3.09	2.70	2.46	2.31	2.19	2.10	2.03	1.97	1.93	1.89	1.85	1.82	1.79	1.77	1.68	1.62	1.57	1.52	1.48	1.45	1.41	1.39
	0.01	6.90	4.82	3.98	3.51	3.21	2.99	2.82	2.69	2.59	2.50	2.43	2.37	2.31	2.27	2.22	2.07	1.97	1.89	1.80	1.74	1.69	1.63	1.60
	0.005	8.24	5.59	4.54	3.96	3.59	3.33	3.13	2.97	2.85	2.74	2.66	2.58	2.52	2.46	2.41	2.23	2.11	2.02	1.91	1.84	1.79	1.72	1.68
120	0.05	3.92	3.07	2.68	2.45	2.29	2.18	2.09	2.02	1.96	1.91	1.87	1.83	1.80	1.78	1.75	1.66	1.60	1.55	1.50	1.46	1.43	1.39	1.37
	0.01	6.85	4.79	3.95	3.48	3.17	2.96	2.79	2.66	2.56	2.47	2.40	2.34	2.28	2.23	2.19	2.03	1.93	1.86	1.76	1.70	1.66	1.60	1.56
	0.005	8.18	5.54	4.50	3.92	3.55	3.28	3.09	2.93	2.81	2.71	2.62	2.54	2.48	2.42	2.37	2.19	2.07	1.98	1.87	1.80	1.75	1.68	1.64
160	0.05	3.90	3.05	2.66	2.43	2.27	2.16	2.07	2.00	1.94	1.89	1.85	1.81	1.78	1.75	1.73	1.64	1.57	1.53	1.47	1.43	1.40	1.36	1.34
	0.01	6.80	4.74	3.91	3.44	3.13	2.92	2.75	2.62	2.52	2.43	2.36	2.30	2.24	2.20	2.15	1.99	1.89	1.82	1.72	1.66	1.61	1.55	1.51
	0.005	8.10	5.48	4.44	3.87	3.50	3.24	3.04	2.88	2.76	2.66	2.57	2.50	2.43	2.38	2.33	2.14	2.02	1.93	1.82	1.75	1.69	1.62	1.58
200	0.05	3.89	3.04	2.65	2.42	2.26	2.14	2.06	1.98	1.93	1.88	1.84	1.80	1.77	1.74	1.72	1.62	1.56	1.52	1.46	1.41	1.39	1.35	1.32
	0.01	6.76	4.71	3.88	3.41	3.11	2.89	2.73	2.60	2.50	2.41	2.34	2.27	2.22	2.17	2.13	1.97	1.87	1.79	1.69	1.63	1.58	1.52	1.48
	0.005	8.06	5.44	4.41	3.84	3.47	3.21	3.01	2.86	2.73	2.63	2.54	2.47	2.40	2.35	2.30	2.11	1.99	1.91	1.79	1.71	1.66	1.59	1.54
400	0.05	3.86	3.02	2.63	2.39	2.24	2.12	2.03	1.96	1.90	1.85	1.81	1.78	1.74	1.72	1.69	1.60	1.53	1.49	1.42	1.38	1.35	1.31	1.28
	0.01	6.70	4.66	3.83	3.37	3.06	2.85	2.68	2.56	2.45	2.37	2.29	2.23	2.17	2.13	2.08	1.92	1.82	1.75	1.64	1.58	1.53	1.46	1.42
	0.005	7.97	5.37	4.34	3.78	3.41	3.15	2.95	2.80	2.68	2.57	2.49	2.41	2.35	2.29	2.24	2.06	1.93	1.85	1.73	1.65	1.60	1.52	1.47
∞	0.05	3.84	3.00	2.60	2.37	2.21	2.10	2.01	1.94	1.88	1.83	1.79	1.75	1.72	1.69	1.67	1.57	1.51	1.46	1.39	1.35	1.32	1.27	1.24
	0.01	6.63	4.61	3.78	3.32	3.02	2.80	2.64	2.51	2.41	2.32	2.25	2.18	2.13	2.08	2.04	1.88	1.77	1.70	1.59	1.52	1.47	1.40	1.36
	0.005	7.88	5.30	4.28	3.72	3.35	3.09	2.90	2.74	2.62	2.52	2.43	2.36	2.29	2.24	2.19	2.00	1.88	1.79	1.67	1.59	1.53	1.45	1.40

TABLE A.5 Chi-square distribution

| df | \multicolumn{10}{c}{Area beyond χ^2} |
	0.99	0.95	0.9	0.8	0.2	0.1	0.05	0.01	0.005	0.001
1	0.0002	0.0039	0.0158	0.0642	1.6424	2.7055	3.8415	6.6349	7.8794	10.8274
2	0.0201	0.1026	0.2107	0.4463	3.2189	4.6052	5.9915	9.2104	10.5965	13.8150
3	0.1148	0.3518	0.5844	1.0052	4.6416	6.2514	7.8147	11.3449	12.8381	16.2260
4	0.2971	0.7107	1.0636	1.6488	5.9886	7.7794	9.4877	13.2767	14.8602	18.4662
5	0.5543	1.1455	1.6103	2.3425	7.2893	9.2363	11.0705	15.0863	16.7496	20.5147
6	0.8721	1.6354	2.2041	3.0701	8.5581	10.6446	12.5916	16.8119	18.5475	22.4575
7	1.2390	2.1673	2.8331	3.8223	9.8032	12.0170	14.0671	18.4753	20.2777	24.3213
8	1.6465	2.7326	3.4895	4.5936	11.0301	13.3616	15.5073	20.0902	21.9549	26.1239
9	2.0879	3.3251	4.1682	5.3801	12.2421	14.6837	16.9190	21.6660	23.5893	27.8767
10	2.5582	3.9403	4.8652	6.1791	13.4420	15.9872	18.3070	23.2093	25.1881	29.5879
11	3.0535	4.5748	5.5778	6.9887	14.6314	17.2750	19.6752	24.7250	26.7569	31.2635
12	3.5706	5.2260	6.3038	7.8073	15.8120	18.5493	21.0261	26.2170	28.2997	32.9092
13	4.1069	5.8919	7.0415	8.6339	16.9848	19.8119	22.3620	27.6882	29.8193	34.5274
14	4.6604	6.5706	7.7895	9.4673	18.1508	21.0641	23.6848	29.1412	31.3194	36.1239
15	5.2294	7.2609	8.5468	10.3070	19.3107	22.3071	24.9958	30.5780	32.8015	37.6978
16	5.8122	7.9616	9.3122	11.1521	20.4651	23.5418	26.2962	31.9999	34.2671	39.2518
17	6.4077	8.6718	10.0852	12.0023	21.6146	24.7690	27.5871	33.4087	35.7184	40.7911
18	7.0149	9.3904	10.8649	12.8570	22.7595	25.9894	28.8693	34.8052	37.1564	42.3119
19	7.6327	10.1170	11.6509	13.7158	23.9004	27.2036	30.1435	36.1908	38.5821	43.8194
20	8.2604	10.8508	12.4426	14.5784	25.0375	28.4120	31.4104	37.5663	39.9969	45.3142
21	8.8972	11.5913	13.2396	15.4446	26.1711	29.6151	32.6706	38.9322	41.4009	46.7963
22	9.5425	12.3380	14.0415	16.3140	27.3015	30.8133	33.9245	40.2894	42.7957	48.2676
23	10.1957	13.0905	14.8480	17.1865	28.4288	32.0069	35.1725	41.6383	44.1814	49.7276
24	10.8563	13.8484	15.6587	18.0618	29.5533	33.1962	36.4150	42.9798	45.5584	51.1790
25	11.5240	14.6114	16.4734	18.9397	30.6752	34.3816	37.6525	44.3140	46.9280	52.6187
26	12.1982	15.3792	17.2919	19.8202	31.7946	35.5632	38.8851	45.6416	48.2898	54.0511

(continued)

Area beyond χ^2

df	0.99	0.95	0.9	0.8	0.2	0.1	0.05	0.01	0.005	0.001
27	12.8785	16.1514	18.1139	20.7030	32.9117	36.7412	40.1133	46.9628	49.6450	55.4751
28	13.5647	16.9279	18.9392	21.5880	34.0266	37.9159	41.3372	48.2782	50.9936	56.8918
29	14.2564	17.7084	19.7677	22.4751	35.1394	39.0875	42.5569	49.5878	52.3355	58.3006
30	14.9535	18.4927	20.5992	23.3641	36.2502	40.2560	43.7730	50.8922	53.6719	59.7022
31	15.6555	19.2806	21.4336	24.2551	37.3591	41.4217	44.9853	52.1914	55.0025	61.0980
32	16.3622	20.0719	22.2706	25.1478	38.4663	42.5847	46.1942	53.4857	56.3280	62.4873
33	17.0735	20.8665	23.1102	26.0422	39.5718	43.7452	47.3999	54.7754	57.6483	63.8694
34	17.7891	21.6643	23.9522	26.9383	40.6756	44.9032	48.6024	56.0609	58.9637	65.2471
35	18.5089	22.4650	24.7966	27.8359	41.7780	46.0588	49.8018	57.3420	60.2746	66.6192
36	19.2326	23.2686	25.6433	28.7350	42.8788	47.2122	50.9985	58.6192	61.5811	67.9850
37	19.9603	24.0749	26.4921	29.6355	43.9782	48.3634	52.1923	59.8926	62.8832	69.3476
38	20.6914	24.8839	27.3430	30.5373	45.0763	49.5126	53.3835	61.1620	64.1812	70.7039
39	21.4261	25.6954	28.1958	31.4405	46.1730	50.6598	54.5722	62.4281	65.4753	72.0550
40	22.1642	26.5093	29.0505	32.3449	47.2685	51.8050	55.7585	63.6908	66.7660	73.4029
41	22.9056	27.3256	29.9071	33.2506	48.3628	52.9485	56.9424	64.9500	68.0526	74.7441
42	23.6501	28.1440	30.7654	34.1574	49.4560	54.0902	58.1240	66.2063	69.3360	76.0842
43	24.3976	28.9647	31.6255	35.0653	50.5480	55.2302	59.3035	67.4593	70.6157	77.4184
44	25.1480	29.7875	32.4871	35.9744	51.6389	56.3685	60.4809	68.7096	71.8923	78.7487
45	25.9012	30.6123	33.3504	36.8844	52.7288	57.5053	61.6562	69.9569	73.1660	80.0776
46	26.6572	31.4390	34.2152	37.7955	53.8177	58.6405	62.8296	71.2015	74.4367	81.3998
47	27.4158	32.2676	35.0814	38.7075	54.9056	59.7743	64.0011	72.4432	75.7039	82.7198
48	28.1770	33.0981	35.9491	39.6205	55.9926	60.9066	65.1708	73.6826	76.9689	84.0368
49	28.9406	33.9303	36.8182	40.5344	57.0786	62.0375	66.3387	74.9194	78.2306	85.3499
50	29.7067	34.7642	37.6886	41.4492	58.1638	63.1671	67.5048	76.1538	79.4898	86.6603

Index

433